Comparison ✓ **W9-BVI-364**

Process

Design

Clarity

Grammar

Punctuation

Mechanics

Argument

Research

Basics

RULES FOR WRITERS

FIFTH EDITION

Diana Hacker

Prince George's Community College

Bedford/St. Martin's
Boston ◆ New York

For Bedford/St. Martin's

Senior Developmental Editor: Michelle M. Clark
Associate Editor: Caroline Thompson
Senior Production Editor: Anne Noonan
Senior Production Supervisor: Joe Ford
Marketing Manager: Richard Cadman
Editorial Assistant: Amy Hurd
Production Assistant: Kristen Merrill
Copyeditor: Barbara G. Flanagan
Text Design: Claire Seng-Niemoeller
Cover Design: Hannus Design Associates
Composition: Monotype Composition Company, Inc.
Printing and Binding: R.R. Donnelley & Sons, Inc.

President: Joan E. Feinberg
Editorial Director: Denise B. Wydra
Editor in Chief: Karen S. Henry
Director of Marketing: Karen Melton
Director of Editing, Design, and Production: Marcia Cohen
Managing Editor: Elizabeth M. Schaaf

Library of Congress Control Number: 2003101699

Manufactured in the United States of America.

8 7 6 5 4 3
f e d c b

For information, write: Bedford/St. Martin's, 75 Arlington Street, Boston, MA 02116 (617-399-4000)

ISBN: 0–312–40685–1

Acknowledgments

Nelson W. Aldrich Jr. Excerpt from *Old Money: The Mythology of America's Upper Class.* Copyright © 1988 by Nelson W. Aldrich Jr. Reprinted by permission of Alfred A. Knopf, a division of Random House, Inc.

Preface for Instructors

This book is grounded in my many years of teaching first- and second-year composition to a wide range of students: young and mature, mainstream and multiethnic, talented and under-prepared. As I've drafted and revised *Rules for Writers,* my goal has never been to sell students on my own views about language and politics — or to endorse popular trends in the teaching of English. Instead, I've tried to look squarely at the problems students face and come up with practical solutions. Many of this book's charts and some of its text and exercises began as handouts I prepared for my own students or for the writing center at Prince George's Community College.

To keep *Rules for Writers* brief, I have limited myself within each section to the essentials: straightforward rules backed up by concise explanations, realistic examples, and short comments on examples. In its coverage, however, the book is complete. It is a guide to the full range of conventions of grammar, punctuation, mechanics, and usage as well as to the writing process, paragraphs, document design, style, argument, and the research process.

What's new to this edition

Most of my revisions respond to technological change. In addition to updating the book for the digital age, I have improved the sections on critical thinking and made the book more useful for students writing MLA and APA papers. Here, briefly, are some highlights.

Integration of the book with its companion Web site. Because most students are now working online, I've extended my book beyond its paper covers by linking it explicitly to its Web site. Throughout the book, On the Web boxes take students to locations on the Web site, where they will find a variety of supplements to the book: electronic grammar exercises, exercises on avoiding plagiarism and integrating sources, a links library, essays called Language Debates, and so on. Because the Web site is an extension of the book, I have written nearly all of its content myself. For more about these Web features, see pages ix–xii.

Updated advice on finding and evaluating sources.   With the help of reference librarian Barbara Fister, I have revised the sections on finding and evaluating sources with the awareness that the library and the Web now depend on one another. I encourage students to enter the Web through a library's portal or another "juried" venue that assures some sort of quality control. Also, I emphasize the need for evaluation throughout the research process — from choosing a search engine or database to selecting reliable sources to reading those sources.

Discipline-specific rhetorical advice for MLA and APA styles. Handbook advice on drafting a thesis, avoiding plagiarism, and integrating sources has traditionally been illustrated only with MLA examples. To make the fifth edition of *Rules for Writers* more useful for students writing APA papers, I now present discipline-specific examples on these important matters in separate color-coded sections. Students in social science classes no longer need to "translate" the examples, mentally replacing MLA's in-text citations with APA's quite different style of in-text citations. In both sections, examples are tied to topics appropriate to the discipline.

Expanded MLA and APA guidelines, especially for Web sources. Because many Web sources have corporate or unknown authors and because most lack stable page numbers, I now pay special attention to authorship and pagination in my presentation of MLA and APA in-text citations. It is easier for students to document both print and Web sources if they focus on a clear first step: identifying the author of a source. Once students grasp that the author's name links an in-text citation to an entry in the works cited or reference list, they can better understand the intricacies of MLA and APA styles: how to handle multiple authors, for example, or corporate authors or unknown authors. As for the issue of page numbers, I explain the MLA and APA guidelines, along with their implications, in more detail than before.

To help students better grasp the concept of MLA and APA in-text citations, I now highlight the parts of the citation in color (see pp. 414 and 466 for examples).

The works cited and reference list models now cover a wider range of multimedia and Web sources because students are relying more heavily on such sources in their papers. In addition, more models are given for sources retrieved from online databases such as *InfoTrac* and *ProQuest.*

New sample papers. A new MLA paper that advocates regulating the use of cell phones while driving is paired with a paper opposing such regulation; the second paper appears on the book's companion Web site. Each paper draws on both print and electronic sources.

New to Part I, The Writing Process, is a model paper titled "Hooked on Credit Cards." The paper's rough draft is annotated with comments from peer reviewers working online. In Part VII, Argument, a new paper takes a stand against allowing snowmobile access to Yellowstone National Park. Another paper, which argues in favor of continued snowmobile access, appears on the *Rules for Writers* companion Web site.

Thoroughly revised sections on critical thinking and argument. The section on argument devotes more attention to audience and the need to build credibility. A new section on evaluating arguments shows students how argumentative tactics, such as generalizing and appealing to emotions, can work either to build or to undermine a writer's credibility.

What's the same

Although technology has led to a number of changes in the book, many of the book's features will be familiar to users of the previous edition. The features that have most contributed to the book's success are detailed in this section.

A brief menu and a user-friendly index. Designed for student use, a brief menu inside the front cover displays icons representing the book's nine parts and lists only the numbered sections. The traditional, more detailed handbook menu, which is useful for instructors but too daunting for many students, appears on the back endpapers.

The handbook's index (which I write myself) helps students find what they are looking for even if they don't know grammatical terminology. When facing a choice between *I* and *me,* for example, students may not know to look up "Case" or even

"Pronoun, case of." They are more likely to look up "*I*" or "*me,*" so I have included index entries for "*I* vs. *me*" and "*me* vs. *I.*" Similar user-friendly entries appear throughout the index.

Clear, uncluttered page design. Because grammar rules and hand-edited examples are highlighted in a second color (teal), students can easily skim the book's central sections for quick answers to questions. The book's second color also highlights charts and boxes; these charts and boxes are easy to find and, just as important, they are easy to skip.

Quick reference charts. Many of the handbook's charts help students review for common problems in their own writing, such as fragments and subject-verb agreement. Other charts summarize important material: a checklist for global revision, strategies for avoiding sexist language, guidelines for evaluating Web sites, and so on.

Grammar checker boxes. Throughout the book, I show students what grammar and spell checkers can do — and what they can't do. As you have no doubt discovered, students sometimes produce strange errors because they have taken the advice of a grammar checker without thinking first. And many students believe that once they have run a grammar checker, their problems are over.

To discover the capabilities and limits of current grammar checkers, I have run a large bank of exercise sentences (many containing errors), along with some student drafts, through two commonly used programs. The results, summarized in boxes throughout the book, show that grammar checkers help with some but by no means all of the typical problems in a draft.

Help for culturally diverse students. More than ten years ago, I was the first handbook author to write a special section for students who speak English as a second (or third or fourth) language. Over the years, I have expanded the section and added a number of ESL boxes throughout the book. ESL students are of course my primary audience, but many instructors and tutors who work with culturally diverse students have also found this material helpful.

Extensive exercises, some with answers. At least one exercise set accompanies nearly every section of the book. Most sets begin with five lettered sentences with answers in the back of the book so students can test their understanding independently. The sets then continue with numbered sentences. The answers to the numbered exercises appear only in the Instructor's Edition. Students who need more practice can go to the book's companion Web site (see below for details).

To help students learn to use the handbook independently as a reference, I have included five tutorials in "How to Use This Book."

What's on the companion Web site

The features described here are intended for students. Instructor resources, both print and electronic, are listed on page xi.

Language Debates. The companion Web site's Language Debates are brief essays in which I explore controversial issues of grammar and usage, such as split infinitives, by citing experts and weighing their arguments. The inspiration for these essays came from e-mails I've received from student users of my books: queries about passive verbs, *that* versus *which,* and so on. My goal in the Language Debates is to encourage students to think about the rationales for a rule and then make their own rhetorical decisions.

Electronic grammar exercises. Nearly one thousand exercise items covering grammar, punctuation, and style appear on the *Rules for Writers* companion Web site. Over the past two years, I have played an active role in creating the exercises and revising them in light of suggestions from student focus groups and faculty reviewers. In addition, I've written nearly all of the feedback for correct and incorrect responses. Students receive this feedback after each exercise item (not just at the end of a set), so they are learning as they go along (not simply being tested).

Instructors who would like to track their students' progress can do so with built-in reports accessible online.

Electronic research and writing exercises. Using material from pencil-and-paper research exercises that I put together for my own students, I have created scorable electronic exercises on matters such as avoiding plagiarism, integrating sources, and using MLA and APA documentation. Many students have a hard time understanding these matters just by reading the book; when they work through a couple of exercises, I've found, they begin to grasp the issues. At the very least, they can't tell me later that they had no idea copying was wrong!

To accompany Part I, The Writing Process, I've written a few electronic exercises on thesis statements, peer review, point of view, transitions, and the like. These too are scorable.

Links library.   From the companion site students can link to resources such as online writing centers, tutorials on creating Web sites, and online libraries.

Model papers.   Model papers on the Web site include a paper-in-progress; two argument papers; two MLA research papers; and research papers in APA, *Chicago,* and CBE styles. Annotations highlight important points about each paper's style, content, and method of documentation.

Research and Documentation Online.   As its title suggests, this online resource helps students conduct research and document their sources. Reference librarian Barbara Fister has updated her advice on finding sources and provided new links to resources in a variety of disciplines, and she continues to maintain the research portion of the site. My role has been to update guidelines for documenting print and online sources in MLA, APA, *Chicago,* and CBE styles.

Ancillaries for students

Both print and electronic ancillaries are available for students.

PRINT RESOURCES

Developmental Exercises to Accompany RULES FOR WRITERS

Answers to Exercises in RULES FOR WRITERS

Research and Documentation in the Electronic Age, Third Edition

ELECTRONIC RESOURCES

Rules for Writers companion Web site (see the On the Web box on p. xviii)

Ancillaries for instructors

Practical and professional resources for instructors are available in print form. Other resources appear on the instructor portion of the book's companion Web site. The publisher is making available most of the resources accompanying *The Bedford Handbook*, Sixth Edition. These supplements can easily be used with the fifth edition of *Rules for Writers* because most of its section numbers (1–45 and 61–64) correspond with those in *The Bedford Handbook*.

PRACTICAL RESOURCES FOR INSTRUCTORS

Instructor's Edition

Quizzes and Diagnostic Tests to Accompany THE BEDFORD HANDBOOK

Transparency Masters to Accompany THE BEDFORD HANDBOOK

PROFESSIONAL RESOURCES FOR INSTRUCTORS

Background Readings for Instructors Using THE BEDFORD HANDBOOK

The Bedford Guide for Writing Tutors, Third Edition

The Bedford Bibliography for Teachers of Writing, Fifth Edition

WEB RESOURCES FOR INSTRUCTORS

Rules for Writers instructor site at dianahacker.com/rules/instructor, which includes:

— *Exercise Masters,* print-format versions of all of the exercises in the book

— *Quiz Masters,* print format quizzes on key topics in the book

— *Electronic Diagnostic Tests,* a test bank for instructors to use

— *Preparing for the CLAST*

— *Preparing for the TASP*

Acknowledgments

No author can possibly anticipate the many ways in which a variety of students might respond to a text: Where might students be confused? How much explanation is enough? What is too intimidating? Do the examples appeal to a range of students? Are they free of stereotypes? To help me answer such questions, dozens of instructors contributed useful insights based on their varied experiences in the classroom.

For their many helpful suggestions, I would like to thank a perceptive group of reviewers:

Rebecca Albright, University of Maine
Sharon Anthony, Portland Community College
Janet Bean, University of Akron
James Beasley, Valparaiso University
Diane Boehm, Saginaw Valley State University
Patricia Brennecke, Massachusetts Institute of Technology
Joyce D. Brotton, Northern Virginia Community College at
   Annandale
Suzanne W. Churchill, Davidson College
Holly Davis, Smith College
Debra Deroian, Bristol Community College
Debra Dew, University of Colorado at Colorado Springs
Crystal Q. Edmonds, Robeson Community College
Janet Carey Eldred, University of Kentucky
Daylanne K. English, Bowie State University
Sondra Fishinger, Union County College
Terrance Flaherty, Minnesota State University
Simone M. Gers, Pima College
Barbara J. Grossman, Essex County College
Tracie Church Guzzio, SUNY Plattsburgh
Andrew J. Haggerty, Broome Community College
Pamela S. Hardman, Cuyahoga Community College
Joan Husley, Columbia State Community College
Ejner J. Jensen, University of Michigan
Nancy Joseph, Oakland University
George Kanieski, Cuyahoga Community College
Craig Kleinman, SUNY Ulster
Mary S. Koncel, Smith College
Jeff Kosse, Iowa Western Community College
Kimmarie Lewis, Lord Fairfax Community College
Maurice L'Heureux, Northern Virginia Community College
P. Berniece Longmore, Essex County College
William Major, Hillyer College, University of Hartford
William J. Martin, Niagara University
Theodore Matula, University of Illinois at Springfield
David McDowell, Anne Arundel Community College
Linn Cary Mehta, Barnard College

Robert D. Murray, St. Thomas Aquinas College
Dianne Perkins, Community College of Philadelphia
Priscilla Perkins, Roosevelt University
D. R. Ransdell, University of Arizona
John Raymer, Holy Cross College
Bethany Reid, Everett Community College
Jay Rubin, College of Alameda
Kathryn L. Schmitz, National Technical Institute of the Deaf
Janet L. Smith, Robeson Community College
Leslie E. St. Martin, College of the Canyons
Howard Tinberg, Bristol Community College
Pauline Uchmanowicz, SUNY New Paltz
Bill Walker, University of Oregon
L. Ray Wheeler, Dickinson State University
Gayle Williamson, Cuyahoga Community College
Lynn Wright, Pasadena City College

Writing a handbook is truly a collaborative effort. Librarian Barbara Fister helped me reorganize the research sections and bring them up-to-date (no small feat). William Peirce assisted with the sections on argument, and Lloyd Shaw helped me improve the research sections. For the book's companion Web site, Carolyn Lengel has created several well-written exercises on a variety of interesting topics.

I am indebted to the students whose essays appear in this edition or on its companion Web site — Angela Daly, Paul Levi, Aaron Lund, Rekha Sanghvi, Karen Shaw, Matt Watson, and Tom Weitzel — not only for permission to use their work but for allowing me to adapt it for pedagogical purposes as well. My thanks also go to the students who granted me permission to use their paragraphs: Diana Crawford, Connie Hailey, Kathleen Lewis, Chris Mileski, Margaret Smith, Margaret Stadt, John Clyde Thatcher, and David Warren.

Thanks are also due to senior editor Michelle Clark, associate editor Caroline Thompson, and editorial assistant Amy Hurd. Michelle directed the project — both the book and its Web site — with spirit and good humor. The book is improved because of her attention to language and her fresh eye. Caroline coordinated the creation of the book's companion Web site, orchestrated reviews, and helped me field e-mail queries in a timely and professional manner. Amy Hurd assisted Caroline with reviews and the Web site and handled other matters too numerous to mention. This team — Michelle, Caroline, and Amy — worked under the adroit leadership of editor in chief Karen Henry, who stepped in occasionally to help us solve especially thorny problems.

Book editor Anne Noonan expertly steered the manuscript through production, with the help of Kristen Merrill. In addition, Anne offered helpful insights on matters of both style and design. Copyeditor Barbara Flanagan has once again brought grace and consistency to the final manuscript. Her knowledge of MLA and APA styles proved especially valuable as we worked to clarify guidelines for documenting electronic sources.

I would also like to thank marketing manager Richard Cadman and director of marketing Karen Melton for promoting my book so enthusiastically and for helping to guide its revision in light of the needs of instructors and their students.

Special thanks are due to Joan Feinberg, president of Bedford/ St. Martin's, and Chuck Christensen, recently retired. Years ago, I had the good fortune to work with Chuck and Joan shortly after they launched Bedford Books as a small imprint of St. Martin's Press. It is no exaggeration to say that Joan taught me how to write a handbook. In her roles as publisher, editor, and teacher, Joan has consistently set a standard of excellence and nudged me toward it, always with intelligence, grace, and good humor. It would be impossible to overstate my gratitude to Joan and Chuck.

Finally, for their support and encouragement, a note of thanks goes to my husband, Robert Hacker; to the families of Greg and Joyce Tarvin, Jeff and Eileen Hacker, Jack and Chris Dougherty, and Steve and Peggy Shearer; to Robbie Wallin, Austin Nichols, Elaine Pirozzi, Kate Miller, Jessica and Aaron Hansen, Rima Koyler, Steve Zate, Greg Krakower, Betty Renshaw, Bill Fry, John Bodnar, Sandra Kurtinitis, Joanne Amberson, Margaret Van de Ree, Joyce Neff, Christine McMahon, and Joan Naake; to the English department at Prince George's Community College; and to the many students over the years who have taught me that errors, a natural by-product of the writing process, are simply problems waiting to be solved.

Diana Hacker
Prince George's Community College

How to Use This Book and Its Web Site

Though it is small enough to hold in your hand, *Rules for Writers* will answer most of the questions you are likely to ask as you plan, draft, and revise a piece of writing: How do I choose and narrow a topic? What can I do if I get stuck? How do I know when to begin a new paragraph? Should I write *each was* or *each were*? When does a comma belong before *and*? What is the difference between *accept* and *except*? How do I cite a source from the Web?

This book's companion Web site extends this book beyond its covers. See page xviii for details.

How to find information with an instructor's help

When you are revising an essay that has been marked by your instructor, tracking down information is simple. If your instructor marks problems with a number such as *16* or a number and letter such as *12e*, you can turn directly to the appropriate section of the handbook. Just flip through the colored tabs on the upper right-hand corners of the pages until you find the number in question. The number *16*, for example, leads you to the rule "Tighten wordy sentences," and *12e* takes you to the subrule "Repair dangling modifiers." If your instructor uses an abbreviation such as *w* or *dm* instead of a number, consult the list of abbreviations and symbols on the page right before the back endpapers. There you will find the name of the problem (*wordy; dangling modifier*) and the number of the section to consult.

How to find information on your own

With a little practice, you will be able to find information in this book without an instructor's help — usually by tracking the icons that appear on the cover and inside the front cover. At times, you may want to consult the detailed menu inside the back cover, the index, the Glossary of Usage, or one of the directories to the documentation models.

The icons and brief menu.   Because the icons are right on the cover, it won't take you long to become familiar with the organization of *Rules for Writers*. These icons also appear on a brief menu inside the front cover. Usually this menu is the fastest way into the book.

Let's say that you are having problems with run-on sentences. Your first step is to find the appropriate icon on the menu inside the front cover — in this case the check mark for "Grammar." Next, find the appropriate numbered topic: "20. Run-on sentences." Finally, use the tabs on the corners of the right-hand pages to find section 20. The running head next to the tab ("Run-on sentences") will tell you that you are just where you want to be.

At times you can work straight from the icons on the cover. These icons appear on every left-hand page of the book and on the part openers. To look up correct uses of the semicolon, for example, you can find the traffic light icon (for "Punctuation") on the left-hand pages, and then, just by flipping, you can locate the appropriate running head ("The semicolon") on the right-hand pages.

The detailed menu.   The detailed menu appears inside the back cover. When the numbered section you're looking for is broken up into quite a few lettered subsections, try consulting this menu. For instance, if you have a question about the proper use of commas for items in a series, this menu will lead you quickly to section 32c.

The index.   If you aren't sure which topic to choose from one of the menus, consult the index at the back of the book. For example, you may not realize that the issue of whether to use *have* or *has* is a matter of subject-verb agreement (section 21). In that case, simply look up "*has* vs. *have*" in the index and you will be directed to specific pages in two sections covering the topic of subject-verb agreement.

The Glossary of Usage. When in doubt about the correct use of a particular word (such as *affect* and *effect, among* and *between,* or *hopefully*), consult the Glossary of Usage at the back of the book. This glossary explains the difference between commonly confused words; it also lists colloquialisms and jargon that are inappropriate in formal written English.

Directories to documentation models. When you are documenting a research paper with either MLA or APA style, you can find appropriate documentation models by consulting the MLA or APA directories. The MLA directories to in-text citation and works cited models appear in the pages marked with a vertical band of teal; the APA directories to in-text citation and references models appear in the pages marked with a vertical band of black.

How to use this book and its Web site for self-study

In a composition class, most of your time should be spent writing. Therefore, it is unlikely that you will want to study all of the chapters in this book in detail. Instead you should focus on the problems that tend to crop up in your own writing. Your instructor (or a tutor in your college's writing center) will be glad to help you design an individual program of self-study.

Rules for Writers has been designed so that you can learn from it on your own. By providing answers to some exercise sentences, it allows you to test your understanding of the material. Most exercise sets begin with five sentences lettered a–e and conclude with five or ten numbered sentences. Answers to the lettered sentences appear in an appendix at the end of the book.

The chart on page xviii describes the features on the book's companion Web site (dianahacker.com/rules). Each feature — whether an electronic exercise or a Language Debate — has been developed for you to use on your own whenever you need it.

Diana Hacker

ON THE WEB

Throughout *Rules for Writers,* Fifth Edition, On the Web boxes direct you to relevant resources on the book's companion Web site.

Simply go to **dianahacker.com/rules** and click on

▶ **Electronic Writing Exercises**
Interactive exercises on topics such as choosing a thesis statement and conducting a peer review

▶ **Electronic Grammar Exercises**
Interactive exercises on grammar, style, and punctuation skills

▶ **Electronic Research Exercises**
Interactive exercises on topics such as integrating quotations and documenting sources in MLA and APA styles

▶ **Language Debates**
Mini-essays exploring controversial issues of grammar and usage, such as split infinitives

▶ **Links Library**
Carefully selected and annotated links to additional online resources for every part of the book

▶ **Model Papers**
Annotated sample papers in MLA, APA, *Chicago,* and CBE styles; a paper-in-progress; and two argument papers.

▶ **Research and Documentation Online**
Advice on finding sources and up-to-date guidelines for documenting print and online sources in MLA, APA, *Chicago,* and CBE styles

▶ **Additional Resources**
Print-format versions of the exercises in the book

Tutorials

> The following tutorials will give you practice using the book's menus, index, Glossary of Usage, and MLA directory. Answers to the tutorials begin on page 545.

TUTORIAL 1
Using the menus

Each of the following "rules" violates the principle it expresses. Using the brief menu inside the front cover or the more detailed menu inside the back cover, find the section in *Rules for Writers* that explains the principle. Then fix the problem. Examples:

Tutors in

~~In~~ the writing center, ~~they~~ say that vague pronoun reference
  ^

is unacceptable.   *23*

                                    come
Be alert for irregular verbs that have ~~came~~ to you in the
                                       ^

wrong form.   *27a*

1. A verb have to agree with its subject.
2. Each pronoun should agree with their antecedent.
3. About sentence fragments. You should avoid them.
4. Its important to use apostrophe's correctly.
5. Check for *-ed* verb endings that have been drop.
6. Discriminate careful between adjectives and adverbs.
7. If your sentence begins with a long introductory word group use a comma to separate the word group from the rest of the sentence.
8. Don't write a run-on sentence, you must connect independent clauses with a comma and a coordinating conjunction or with a semicolon.
9. For clarity, a writer must be careful not to shift your point of view.
10. When dangling, watch your modifiers.

TUTORIAL 2
Using the index

Assume that you have written the following sentences and want to know the answers to the questions in brackets. Use the index at the back of the book to locate the information you need, and edit the sentences if necessary.

1. Each of the candidates have agreed to participate in tonight's debate. [Does the subject *Each* agree with *has* or *have*?]
2. We had intended to go surfing but spent most of our vacation lying on the beach. [Should I use *lying* or *laying*?]
3. We only looked at two houses before buying the house of our dreams. [Is *only* in the right place?]
4. In Saudi Arabia it is considered ill mannered for you to accept a gift. [Is it okay to use *you* to mean "anyone in general"?]
5. In Canada, Joanne picked up several bottles of maple syrup for her sister and me. [Should I write *for her sister and I*?]

TUTORIAL 3
Using the menus or the index

Imagine that you are in the following situations. Using either the menus or the index, find the information you need.

1. You are Ray Farley, a community college student who has been out of high school for ten years. You recall learning to punctuate items in a series by putting a comma between all items except the last two. In your college readings, however, you have noticed that most writers use a comma between all items. You're curious about the current rule. Which section of *Rules for Writers* will you consult?
2. You are Maria Sanchez, an honors student working in your university's writing center. Mike Lee, a nonnative speaker of English, has come to you for help. He is working on a rough draft that contains a number of problems involving the use of articles (*a, an,* and *the*). You know how to use articles, but you aren't able to explain the rather complicated rules on their correct use. Which section of *Rules for Writers* will you and Mike Lee consult?

3. You are John Pell, engaged to marry Jane Dalton. In a note to Jane's parents, you have written "Thank you for giving Jane and myself such a generous contribution toward our honeymoon trip to Hawaii." You wonder if you should write "Jane and I" or "Jane and me" instead. Upon consulting *Rules for Writers,* what do you learn?

4. You are Selena Young, an intern supervisor at a housing agency. Two of your interns, Jake Gilliam and Susan Green, have writing problems involving *-s* endings on verbs. Jake tends to drop *-s* endings; Susan tends to add them where they don't belong. You suspect that both problems stem from nonstandard dialects spoken at home.

   Susan and Jake are in danger of losing their jobs because your boss thinks that anyone who writes "the tenant refuse" or "the landlords agrees" is beyond hope. You disagree. Susan and Jake are more intelligent than your boss supposes, and they have asked for your help. Where in *Rules for Writers* can they find the rules they need?

5. You are Joe Thompson, a first-year college student. Your friend Samantha, who has completed two years of college, seems to enjoy correcting your English. Just yesterday she corrected your sentence "I felt badly about her death" to "I felt bad about her death." You're sure you've heard many educated people, including professors, say "I felt badly." Upon consulting *Rules for Writers,* what do you discover?

TUTORIAL 4
Using the Glossary of Usage

Consult the Glossary of Usage to see if the italicized words are used correctly. Then edit any sentences containing incorrect usage. Example:

> Glossary of Usage
>
> This glossary includes words commonly confused (such as *accept* and *except*), words commonly misused (such as *aggravate*), and words that are nonstandard (such as *hisself*). It also lists colloquialisms and jargon. Colloquialisms are expressions that may be appropriate in informal speech but are inappropriate in formal writing. Jargon is needlessly technical or pretentious language that is inappropriate in most contexts. If an item is not listed here, consult the index. For irregular verbs (such as *sing, sang, sung*), see 27a. For idiomatic use of prepositions, see 18d.

an
The pediatrician gave my daughter ~~a~~ injection for her allergy.

1. Changing attitudes *toward* alcohol have *effected* the beer industry.
2. It is *mankind's* nature to think wisely and act foolishly.
3. This afternoon I plan to *lie* out in the sun and work on my tan.
4. Our goal this year is to *grow* our profits by 9 percent.
5. Most sleds are pulled by no *less* than two dogs and no more than ten.

TUTORIAL 5
Using the directory to MLA works cited models

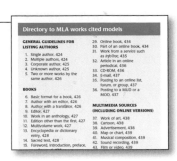

Assume that you have written a short research paper on the growth of gambling operations on Indian reservations. You have cited the following sources in your paper, using MLA documentation, and you are ready to type your list of works cited. Turn to page 423 and use the MLA directory to locate the appropriate models. Then write a correct entry for each source and arrange the entries in a properly formatted list of works cited. *Note:* Do not number the entries in a list of works cited.

A book by Jeff Benedict entitled *Without Reservation: The Making of America's Most Powerful Indian Tribe and the World's Largest Casino.* The book was published in New York by Harper in 2000.

An article by Jerry Useem entitled "The Big Game: Have American Indians Found Their New Buffalo?" from the biweekly magazine *Fortune.* The article appears on nonconsecutive pages beginning with page 22 of the October 2, 2000, issue of the magazine.

An e-mail with the subject line "Casinos on Reservations in the Northeast," sent to you by Helen Codoga on April 10, 2001.

A journal article by Susan Johnson entitled "From Wounded Knee to Capitol Hill." The article appears in *State Legislatures,* which is paginated by issue. The volume number is 24, the issue number is 9, and the year is 1998. You found this article using the *InfoTrac* database *Expanded Academic ASAP* at the University of Pittsburgh library on April 6, 2001.

A short Web document entitled "Tribal Gaming Myths and Facts" written by the National Indian Gaming Association and published in 2000 on the group's Web site at http://www.indiangaming.org/info/pr/myths.shtml. The title of the site is *National Indian Gaming Association.* You found the document on April 4, 2001.

A radio segment entitled "Indian Gaming" from the program *All Things Considered* hosted by Robert Siegel. The program was produced by National Public Radio on March 5, 2001. You listened to the program on WDUQ in Pittsburgh.

Contents

Grammar 155

Argument   343

Research Guide 369

The Basics 495

Process

Process

Design

Clarity

Grammar

Punctuation

Mechanics

Argument

Research

Basics

Since it's not possible to think about everything all at once, most experienced writers handle a piece of writing in stages. Roughly speaking, those stages are planning, drafting, and revising. You should generally move from planning to drafting to revising, but be prepared to circle back to earlier stages whenever the need arises.

1

Generate ideas and sketch a plan.

Before attempting a first draft, spend some time generating ideas. Mull over your subject while listening to music or driving to work, jot down inspirations on scratch paper, and explore your insights with anyone willing to listen. At this stage you should be collecting information and experimenting with ways of focusing and organizing it to best reach your readers.

1a Assess the writing situation.

Begin by taking a look at the writing situation in which you find yourself. The key elements of the writing situation include your subject, the sources of information available to you, your purpose, your audience, and constraints such as length, document design, review sessions, and deadlines.

It is unlikely that you will make final decisions about all of these matters until later in the writing process — after a first draft, for example. Nevertheless, you can save yourself time by thinking about as many of them as possible in advance. For a quick checklist, see page 3.

ESL What counts as good writing varies from culture to culture and even among groups within cultures. In some situations, you will need to become familiar with the writing styles — such as direct or indirect, personal or impersonal, plain or embellished — that are valued by the culture or discourse community for which you are writing.

Checklist for assessing the writing situation

SUBJECT

- Has a subject (or a range of possible subjects) been given to you, or are you free to choose your own?
- Why is your subject worth writing about?
- How broadly should you cover the subject? Do you need to narrow it to a more specific topic (because of length restrictions, for instance)?
- How detailed should your coverage be?

SOURCES OF INFORMATION

- Where will your information come from: Personal experience? Direct observation? Interviews? Questionnaires? Reading?
- If your information comes from reading, what sort of documentation is required?

PURPOSE

- Why are you writing: To inform readers? To persuade them? To entertain them? To call them to action? Some combination of these?

AUDIENCE

- Who are your readers? How well informed are they about your subject?
- How interested and attentive are they likely to be? Will they resist any of your ideas?
- What is your relationship to them: Employee to supervisor? Citizen to citizen? Expert to novice? Scholar to scholar?
- How much time are they willing to spend reading?

LENGTH AND DOCUMENT DESIGN

- Do you have any length specifications? If not, what length seems appropriate, given your purpose and audience?
- Must you use a particular design for your document? If so, do you have guidelines or examples that you can consult?

REVIEWERS AND DEADLINES

- Who will be reviewing your draft in progress: Your instructor? A writing center tutor? Your classmates? A friend? Someone in your family?
- What are your deadlines? How much time will you need to allow for the various stages of writing, including typing and proofreading the final draft?

Subject

Frequently your subject will be given to you. In a psychology class, for example, you might be asked to explain Bruno Bettelheim's Freudian analysis of fairy tales. Or in a course on the history of filmmaking, you might be assigned to write an essay on the political impact of D. W. Griffith's silent film *The Birth of a Nation.* In the business world, your assignment might be to draft a quarterly sales report or craft a diplomatic e-mail to a customer who has complained about your firm's computer software.

In a composition class, assignments often ask you to respond to readings. At times, though, you will be free to choose your own subject. Then you will be wise to select a subject that you already know something about or one that you can reasonably investigate in the time you have.

Sources of information

Where will your facts, details, and examples come from? Can your topic be illustrated by personal experience, or will you need to search for relevant information through direct observation, interviews, questionnaires, or reading?

PERSONAL EXPERIENCE   You can develop many topics wholly through personal experience, depending of course on your own life experiences. For example, students have written with the voice of experience about lifeguarding, learning disabilities, weight loss through hypnotism, company-sponsored day care, and free-fall parachuting. When narrowing their subjects, those students chose to limit themselves to information they had at hand. Instead of writing about company-sponsored day care in general — a subject that would have required a great deal of research — one student limited her discussion to the successful day care center at the company for which she worked.

DIRECT OBSERVATION   Direct observation is an excellent means of collecting information about a wide range of subjects, such as male-female relationships on the television program *Will and Grace,* the clichéd language of sports announcers, or the appeal of a local art museum. For such subjects, do not rely on your memory alone; your information will be fresher and

Ways to narrow a subject to a topic

SUBDIVIDING YOUR SUBJECT

Many subjects can be subdivided. Instead of writing about censorship of popular songs, for example, you might select a subdivision of this general subject: government labeling of CDs for content. Or instead of writing about homelessness in general, you might focus on the homeless in a particular city.

RESTRICTING YOUR PURPOSE

Often you can restrict your purpose. For example, if your subject is drug testing in the workplace, you might at first hope to persuade readers that it should be banned in all situations. Upon further reflection, however, you might realize that this goal is more than you could hope to accomplish, given your word limit. By adopting a more limited purpose — to show that drug testing is unreliable, to argue that its use by private employers should be banned, or to demonstrate that it violates an innocent person's right to privacy — you would have a better chance of success.

RESTRICTING YOUR AUDIENCE

Consider writing for a particular audience. For example, instead of writing to a general audience on a subject such as teenage pregnancy, you might address persons with a special interest in the subject: young people, parents, or counselors working for Planned Parenthood.

CONSIDERING THE INFORMATION AVAILABLE TO YOU

Look at the information you have collected. If you have gathered a great deal of information on one aspect of your subject (for example, discrimination against persons with AIDS) and less information on other aspects (such as the causes of AIDS or promising treatments for AIDS), you may have found your topic.

ON THE WEB

For lists of subjects you might choose to write about, go to
dianahacker.com/rules

and click on ▶ Additional Resources
              ▶ **Subjects for writing**

more detailed if you actively collect it, with a notebook or tape recorder in hand. As writer Stuart Chase advises young journalists assigned to report on their city's water system, "You will write a better article if you heave yourself out of a comfortable chair and go down in tunnel 3 and get soaked."

INTERVIEWS AND QUESTIONNAIRES   Interviews and questionnaires can supply you with detailed and interesting information on a variety of subjects. A nursing student interested in the care of premature infants might interview a neonatal nurse; a political science major might speak with a local judge to learn about alternative sentencing for first offenders; a future teacher might conduct a survey on the classroom use of computers in local elementary schools.

It is a good idea to tape interviews to preserve any lively quotations that you might want to weave into your essay. Keep questionnaires simple and specify a deadline to ensure that you get a reasonable number of responses.

READING   Reading will be your primary source of information for many college assignments, which will generally be of two kinds: (1) analytical assignments that call for a close reading of one book, essay, or literary work and (2) research assignments that ask you to find and consult a variety of sources on a particular topic.

For analytical essays, you can usually assume that your reader is familiar with the work and has a copy of it at hand. You select details from the work not to inform readers but to support an interpretation. When you quote from the work, page references are often sufficient. For research papers, however, you cannot assume that your reader is familiar with your sources or has them close at hand. This means that you must formally document all quoted and summarized or paraphrased material (see 52 and 57). When in doubt about the need for documentation, consult your instructor.

Purpose

Your purpose will often be dictated by your specific writing situation. Perhaps you have been asked to take minutes for a club meeting, to draft a letter requesting payment from a client, or to describe the results of a biology experiment. Even though your overall purpose is fairly obvious in such situations, a close look at that purpose can help you make a variety of necessary decisions. How detailed should the minutes be? Is your purpose to summarize the meeting or to establish a careful record of discussion in case future controversies arise? How firmly should your letter request payment? Do you need the money at all costs, or do you hope to get it without risking loss of the client's business? How technical does your biology professor want your report to be?

In many writing situations, part of your challenge will be discovering a purpose. Consider, for example, the topic of magnet schools — schools that draw students from different neighborhoods because of features such as advanced science classes or late-afternoon day care. Your purpose could be to inform parents of the options available in your county. Or you might argue that the county's magnet schools are not promoting racial integration as had been planned. Or you might propose that the board of education create a magnet high school for the arts on your college campus.

Although no precise guidelines will lead you to a purpose, you can begin by asking yourself which one or more of the following aims you hope to accomplish.

PURPOSES FOR WRITING

to inform	to evaluate
to persuade	to recommend
to call readers to action	to request
to change attitudes	to propose
to analyze	to provoke thought
to argue	to express feelings
to theorize	to entertain
to summarize	to give aesthetic pleasure

It is surprising how often writers misjudge their own purposes: informing, for example, when they should be recommending; summarizing when they should be analyzing; or expressing feelings about problems instead of proposing solutions. Before beginning any writing task, therefore, pause to ask, "Why am I communicating with my readers?" And this question will lead you to another important question: "Just who are those readers?"

Audience

Audience analysis can often suggest an effective strategy for reaching your readers. One writer, whose purpose was to persuade teenagers not to smoke, jotted down the following observations about her audience:

> dislike lectures, especially from older people
>
> have little sense of their own mortality
>
> are concerned about physical appearance and image
>
> want to be socially accepted
>
> have limited budgets

This analysis led the writer to focus more on the social aspects of smoking (she pointed out, for instance, that kissing a smoker is like licking an ashtray) than on the health risks. Her audience analysis also warned her against adopting a preachy tone that her readers might find offensive. Instead of lecturing to her audience, she decided to draw examples from her own experience as a hooked smoker: burning holes in her best sweater, driving in zero-degree weather late at night in search of a twenty-four-hour convenience store to buy cigarettes, rummaging through ashtrays for stale butts, and so on. The result was an essay that reached its readers instead of alienating them.

Of course, in some writing situations the audience will not be neatly defined for you. Nevertheless, many of the choices that you make as you write will tell readers who you think they are (novices or experts, for example), so it is best to be consistent — even if this means creating an audience that is in some sense a fiction.

For an audience checklist, see the chart on page 3.

BUSINESS AUDIENCES   Writers in the business world often find themselves writing for multiple audiences. A letter to a client, for instance, might be distributed to sales representatives as well. Readers of a report may include persons with and without technical expertise or readers who want details and those who prefer a quick overview.

To satisfy the demands of multiple audiences, business writers have developed a variety of strategies: attaching cover letters to detailed reports, adding boldface headings, placing summaries in the left margin, and so on.

ACADEMIC AUDIENCES In the academic world, considerations of audience can be more complex than they seem at first. Your professor will read your essay, of course, but most professors play multiple roles while reading. Their first and most obvious roles are as coach and judge; less obvious is their role as an intelligent and objective reader, the kind of person who might reasonably be informed, convinced, entertained, or called to action by what you have to say.

Some professors create writing assignments that specify an audience, such as a hypothetical supervisor, readers of a local newspaper, or fellow academics in a particular field of study. Other professors expect you to imagine an audience appropriate to your purpose and your subject. Still others prefer that you write for a general audience of educated readers — nonspecialists who can be expected to read with an intelligent, critical eye. When in doubt about an appropriate audience for a particular assignment, check with your professor.

Length and document design

Writers seldom have complete control over length and document design. Journalists usually write within strict word limits set by their editors, businesspeople routinely aim for conciseness, and most college assignments specify an approximate length.

Certain document designs may also be required by your writing situation. Specific formats are used in the business world for documents such as letters, memos, reports, budget analyses, and personnel records. In the academic world, you may need to learn precise conventions for lab reports, critiques, research papers, and so on. For undergraduate essays in most academic disciplines, a standard manuscript format is acceptable (see 6a).

In some writing situations, you will be free to create your own document design, complete with headings, displayed lists, and perhaps even visuals, such as charts and graphs. Quite sophisticated results are now possible with software, and both writers and readers are becoming increasingly interested in designs that improve readability. For a discussion of the principles of document design, see 5.

Reviewers and deadlines

Professional and business writers rarely work alone. Many work with reviewers, often called editors, who offer advice throughout the writing process. In college classes, too, the use of reviewers is increasingly common. Some instructors will play the role of reviewer for you; others may ask you to visit your college's writing center. Still others schedule peer review sessions in class (sometimes conducted online). Such sessions give you a chance to hear what other students think about your draft in progress — and to play the role of reviewer yourself.

Deadlines are a key element of any writing situation. They tell you what is possible and help you plan your time. For complex writing projects, such as research papers, you'll need to plan your time quite carefully. By working backward from the final deadline, you can create a schedule of target dates for completing various parts of the process. (See p. 376 for a sample schedule.)

ON THE WEB

For an electronic exercise on considering purpose and audience, go to **dianahacker.com/rules**

and click on ▶ **Electronic Writing Exercises**
▶ **E-ex 1–1**

1b Experiment with ways to explore your subject.

Instead of just plunging into a first draft, experiment with one or more techniques for exploring your subject, perhaps one of these:

listing	annotating texts
clustering	freewriting
asking questions	talking and listening

You can use most of these techniques whether you are working with pencil and paper or entering ideas into a computer.

Whatever technique you turn to, the goal is the same: to generate a wealth of ideas. At this early stage of the writing process, you should aim for quantity, not necessarily quality, of ideas. If an idea proves to be off the point, trivial, or too far-fetched, you can always throw it out later.

Listing

You might begin by simply listing ideas, putting them down in the order in which they occur to you — a technique sometimes known as *brainstorming*. Here, for example, is a list one student writer jotted down:

> The Phillips Collection
>
> Washington, D.C.
>
> 1612 21st Street, close to Mass. Ave.
>
> near Dupont Circle, in an interesting neighborhood
>
> hard to find a parking space; better to take subway
>
> elegant red brick townhouse, once home of Duncan and Marjorie Phillips (art collectors)
>
> turned into a museum in 1918
>
> facade reminds me of a bygone era   teas and debutante balls
>
> free concerts on Sundays
>
> mostly Impressionists, Postimpressionists, and modern masters
>
> Renoir's *Luncheon of the Boating Party* — warm and joyful — you can almost smell the breeze off the Seine and hear the hum of conversation
>
> you can wander through small rooms filled with paintings by van Gogh, Degas, Cézanne, Bonnard, and Klee
>
> the Rothko room, with huge color paintings — pulsating, sensuous reds, yellows, blues, greens
>
> the new wing — no more bygone era — clean and uncluttered lines appropriate for modern masters like Picasso, Pollock, Dalí, Braque
>
> a walled garden

The ideas appear here in the order in which they first occurred to the writer. Later she felt free to rearrange them, to cluster them under general categories, to delete some, and to add others. In other words, she treated her initial list as a source of ideas and a springboard to new ideas, not as an outline.

Clustering

Unlike listing, the technique of clustering highlights relationships among ideas. To cluster ideas, write your topic in the center of a sheet of paper, draw a circle around it, and surround that with related ideas connected to it with lines. If some of the satellite ideas lead to more specific clusters, write them down as well. The writer of the following diagram was exploring ideas for an essay on home uses for computers.

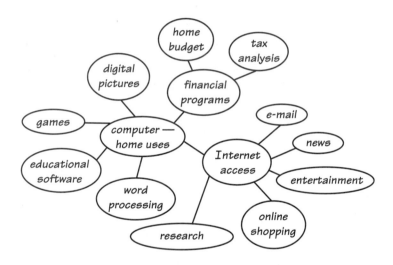

Asking questions

By asking relevant questions, you can generate many ideas — and you can make sure that you have adequately surveyed your subject. When gathering material for a story, journalists routinely ask themselves Who? What? When? Where? Why? and How? In addition to helping journalists get started, these questions ensure that they will not overlook an important fact: the date of a prospective summit meeting, for example, or the exact location of a neighborhood burglary.

Whenever you are writing about events, whether current or historical, the journalist's questions are one way to get started. One student, whose subject was the negative reaction in 1915 to D. W. Griffith's silent film *The Birth of a Nation*, began exploring her topic with this set of questions:

Who objected to the film?

What were the objections?

When were protests first voiced?

Where were protests most strongly expressed?

Why did protesters object to the film?

How did protesters make their views known?

In the academic world, scholars often generate ideas with questions related to a specific discipline: one set of questions for analyzing short stories, another for evaluating experiments in social psychology, still another for reporting field experiences in anthropology. If you are writing in a particular discipline, try to discover the questions that its scholars typically explore.

Annotating texts

When you write about reading, one of the best ways to explore ideas is to mark up the text — on the pages themselves if you own the work, on photocopies if you don't. Here, for example, are two paragraphs from an essay by philosopher Michael Tooley as one student annotated them.

Why is the American policy debate not focused more intensely on the relative merits or demerits of our current approach to drugs and of possible alternatives to it? The lack of discussion of this issue is rather striking, given that America has the most serious drug problem in the world, that alternatives to a prohibitionist approach are under serious consideration in other countries, and that the grounds for reconsidering our current approach are, I shall argue, so weighty. . . .

But the subject has been discussed.

I mean he's for legalizing drugs. Why doesn't he say so?

True? How is he defining "drug problem"?

I want to turn in detail to perhaps the two most important reasons for reconsidering our current drug policy: first, the difficulty of providing any adequate justification for the restrictions that prohibitive laws place on people's liberty; and second, the enormous social and personal costs associated with a prohibitionist approach.

This first reason seems off the point. Is it really worth half of our attention?

Biased language?

Aren't there important aspects of the subject that he's ignoring?

Freewriting

In its purest form, freewriting is simply nonstop writing. You set aside ten minutes or so and write whatever comes to mind, without pausing to think about word choice, spelling, or even meaning. If you get stuck, you can write about being stuck, but you should keep your pencil moving or your fingers tapping the keys. The point is to loosen up, relax, and see what happens. Even if nothing much happens, you have lost only ten minutes. It's more likely, though, that something interesting will emerge on paper or on the screen — perhaps an eloquent sentence, an honest expression of feeling, or a line of thought worth exploring.

To explore ideas on a particular topic, consider using a technique known as *focused freewriting.* Again, you write quickly and freely — without regard for word choice, spelling, punctuation, or even paragraphing — but this time you focus on a subject and pay some attention to meaning.

Talking and listening

The early stages of the writing process need not be lonely. Many writers begin a writing project by brainstorming ideas in a group, debating a point with friends, or engaging in conversation with a professor. Others turn to themselves for company — by talking nonstop into a tape recorder.

Some writers "virtually converse" by exchanging ideas through e-mail, by joining an Internet chat group, or by following a mailing list discussion. If you are part of a networked classroom, you may be encouraged to exchange ideas with your classmates and instructor online. One advantage of engaging in such discussions is that while you are "talking" you are actually writing. That writing might prove useful later. For example, a student who participated in the chat shown on next page was able to cut and paste some of her own words into an essay.

Talking can be a good way to get to know your audience. If you're planning to write a narrative, for instance, you can test its dramatic effect on a group of friends. Or if you hope to advance a certain argument, you can try it out on listeners who hold a different view.

As you have no doubt discovered, conversation can deepen and refine your ideas before you even begin to set them down

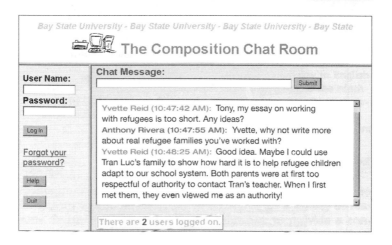

Bay State University - Bay State University - Bay State University - Bay State

on paper. Our first thoughts are not necessarily our wisest thoughts; by talking and listening to others we can all stretch our potential as thinkers and as writers.

1c Settle on a tentative focus.

As you explore your subject, you will begin to see possible ways to focus your material. At this point, try to settle on a tentative central idea. The more complex your subject, the more your initial central idea will change as your drafts evolve.

For many types of writing, your central idea can be asserted in one sentence, a generalization preparing readers for the supporting details that will follow. Such a sentence, which will ordinarily appear in the opening paragraph of your finished essay, is called a *thesis*. A successful thesis —like the following, all taken from articles in *Smithsonian* — points both the writer and the reader in a definite direction.

> Much maligned and the subject of unwarranted fears, most bats are harmless and highly beneficial.

> Geometric forms known as fractals may have a profound effect on how we view the world, not only in art and film but in many

branches of science and technology, from astronomy to economics to predicting the weather.

Aside from his more famous identities as colonel of the Rough Riders and president of the United States, Theodore Roosevelt was a lifelong professional man of letters.

The thesis sentence usually contains a key word or controlling idea that limits its focus. The preceding sentences, for example, prepare for essays that focus on the *beneficial* aspects of bats, the *effect* of fractals on how we view the world, and Roosevelt's identity as a writer, or *man of letters.*

It's a good idea to formulate a thesis early in the writing process, perhaps by jotting it on scratch paper, by putting it at the head of a rough outline, or by attempting to write an introductory paragraph that includes the thesis. Your tentative thesis will probably be less graceful than the thesis you include in the final version of your essay. Here, for example, is one student's early effort:

> Although they both play percussion instruments, drummers and percussionists are very different.

The thesis that appeared in the final draft of the student's paper was more polished:

> Two types of musicians play percussion instruments—drummers and percussionists—and they are as different as Quiet Riot and the New York Philharmonic.

Don't worry too soon about the exact wording of your thesis, however, because your main point may change as you refine your ideas.

For a more detailed discussion of the thesis, see 2a.

1d Sketch a tentative plan.

Once you have generated some ideas and formulated a tentative thesis, you may want to sketch an informal outline. Informal outlines can take many forms. Perhaps the most common is simply the thesis followed by a list of major supporting ideas.

> Hawaii is losing its cultural identity.
> — pure-blooded Hawaiians increasingly rare

— native language diluted
— natives forced off ancestral lands
— little emphasis on native culture in schools
— customs exaggerated and distorted by tourism

Clustering diagrams, often used to generate ideas, can also serve as rough outlines (see p. 12). And if you began by jotting down a list of ideas (see p. 11), you may be able to turn the list into a rough outline by crossing out some ideas, adding others, and numbering the ideas to create a logical order.

When to use a formal outline

Early in the writing process, rough outlines have certain advantages over their more formal counterparts: They can be produced more quickly, they are more obviously tentative, and they can be revised more easily should the need arise. However, a formal outline may be useful later in the writing process, after you have written a rough draft, especially if your subject is complex.

The following formal outline brought order to the research paper that appears in section 55b. Notice that the student's thesis is an important part of the outline. Everything else in the outline supports it, directly or indirectly.

Thesis: States must regulate use of cell phones on the road because drivers using phones are seriously impaired and because laws on negligent and reckless driving are not sufficient to punish offenders.

    I. Drivers distracted by cell phones are seriously impaired.
       A. Cell phones have been a factor in traffic deaths.
       B. Expert testimony, public opinion, and even cartoons suggest that driving while phoning is dangerous.
       C. Scientific research confirms the dangers of using phones while driving.
    II. Laws on negligent and reckless driving are not adequate.
       A. Under state laws, drivers distracted by phones can receive light punishment even when they have caused fatal accidents.
       B. When certain kinds of driver behavior are especially dangerous, we draft special laws making them illegal; phoning in a moving vehicle should be no exception.

III. In the United States, state legislatures must take the responsibility for passing laws regulating use of cell phones in moving vehicles.
   A. Many other countries have passed legislation regulating use of car phones, but the U.S. government leaves such matters to the states.
   B. Although some counties and towns in the United States have restricted use of cell phones on the road, local laws are not likely to have the impact of state laws.
   C. Because of mounting public awareness of the dangers of driving while phoning, state legislators must begin to take the problem seriously; the time for legislation has arrived.

Guidelines for constructing an outline

1. Put the thesis at the top.

2. Make items at the same level of generality as parallel as possible (see 9).

3. Use sentences unless phrases are clear.

4. Use the conventional system of numbers and letters for the levels of generality.

   I.
      A.
      B.
         1.
         2.
            a.
            b.
   II.

5. Always use at least two subdivisions for a category, since nothing can be divided into fewer than two parts.

6. Limit the number of major sections in the outline; if the list of roman numerals begins to look like a laundry list, find some way of clustering the items into a few major categories with more subcategories.

7. Be flexible; in other words, be prepared to change your outline as your drafts evolve.

2

Rough out an initial draft.

As long as you treat an initital draft as a rough draft, you can focus your attention on ideas and organization, knowing that problems with sentence structure and word choice can always be dealt with later.

Overcoming writer's block

Before beginning a first draft, gather your prewriting materials — lists, diagrams, outlines, freewriting, and so on. In addition to helping you get started, such notes and blueprints will encourage you to keep moving. With your earlier thoughts close by, you won't need to pause so frequently, staring at a blank page or screen in search of ideas. Writing tends to flow better when it is drafted relatively quickly, without many stops and starts. The trick, of course, is to relax — to overcome the fear that grips many of us as we face that blank page.

At one time or another, we all experience writer's block. But if writer's block is a chronic problem for you, consider whether you're being too hard on yourself. Do you demand that your sentences all be stylish and perfectly grammatical right from the start? Do you expect your ideas to emerge full-blown, like Athena from the head of Zeus?

Professional writers are not so tough on themselves. Jacques Barzun, for example, lets his rough-draft sentences be "as stupid" as they wish. Joan Didion acknowledges that she discovers ideas *as she writes*; for her, writing is a way of learning, not just a means of revealing already known truths. As Didion puts it, "I write entirely to find out what I'm thinking, what I'm looking at, what I see and what it means."

ON THE WEB

For links to online writing labs and other resources that will help you with the writing process, go to **dianahacker.com/rules**

and click on ▶ **Links Library**
▶ **The Writing Process**

2a For most types of writing, draft an introduction that includes a thesis.

The introduction announces the main point; the body develops it, usually in several paragraphs; the conclusion drives it home. You can begin drafting, however, at any point. If you find it difficult to introduce a paper that you have not yet written, you can write the body first and save the introduction for later.

For most writing tasks, your introduction will be a paragraph of 50 to 150 words. Perhaps the most common strategy is to open the paragraph with a few sentences that engage the reader and to conclude it with a statement of the essay's main point. The sentence stating the main point is called a *thesis*. (See also 1c.) In each of the following examples, the thesis has been italicized.

> To the Australian aborigines, the Dreamtime was the time of creation. It was then that the creatures of the earth, including man, came into being. There are many legends about that mystical period, but unfortunately, the koala does not fare too well in any of them. *Slow-witted though it is in life, the koala is generally depicted in myth and folklore as a trickster and a thief.*
> — Roger Caras, "What's a Koala?"

> Credit card companies love to extend credit to college students, especially those just out of high school. Ads for credit cards line campus bulletin boards, flash across commercial Web sites for students, and get stuffed into shopping bags at college bookstores. Why do the companies market their product so vigorously to a population that lacks a substantial credit history and often has no steady source of income? The answer is that significant profits can be earned through high interest rates and assorted penalties and fees. *By granting college students liberal lending arrangements, credit card companies often hook them on a cycle of spending that can ultimately lead to financial ruin.*
> — Matt Watson, student

Ideally, the sentences leading to the thesis should hook the reader, perhaps with one of the following:

a startling statistic or unusual fact

a vivid example

a description

a paradoxical statement

a quotation or bit of dialogue

a question

an analogy

a joke or an anecdote

Such hooks are particularly important when you cannot assume your reader's interest in the subject. Hooks are less necessary in scholarly essays and other writing aimed at readers with a professional interest in the subject.

Although the thesis frequently appears at the end of the introduction, it can just as easily appear at the beginning. Much work-related writing, in which a straightforward approach is most effective, commonly begins with the thesis.

> *Flextime scheduling, which has proved its effectiveness at the Library of Congress, should be introduced on a trial basis at the main branch of the Montgomery County Public Library.* By offering flexible work hours, the library can boost employee morale, cut down on absenteeism, and expand its hours of operation.
> — David Warren, student

For some types of writing, it may be difficult or impossible to express the central idea in a thesis sentence; or it may be unwise or unnecessary to put a thesis sentence in the essay itself. A personal narrative, for example, may have a focus too subtle to be distilled in a single sentence, and such a sentence might ruin the story. Strictly informative writing, like that found in many business memos, may be difficult to summarize in a thesis. In such instances, do not try to force the central idea into a thesis sentence. Instead, think in terms of an overriding purpose, which may or may not be stated directly.

Characteristics of an effective thesis

An effective thesis should be a generalization, not a fact; it should be limited, not too broad; and it should be sharply focused, not too vague.

Because a thesis must prepare readers for facts and details, it cannot itself be a fact. It must always be a generalization demanding proof or further development.

TOO FACTUAL   The first polygraph was developed by Dr. John A. Larson in 1921.

REVISED   Because the polygraph has not been proved reliable, even under the most controlled conditions, its use by private employers should be banned.

Although a thesis must be a generalization, it must not be *too* general. You will need to narrow the focus of any thesis that you cannot adequately develop in the space allowed. Unless you were writing a book or a very long research paper, the following thesis would be too broad.

TOO BROAD   Many drugs are now being used successfully to treat mental illnesses.

You would need to restrict the thesis, perhaps like this:

REVISED   Despite its risks and side effects, Prozac is an effective treatment for depression.

Finally, a thesis should be sharply focused, not too vague. Beware of any thesis containing a fuzzy, hard-to-define word such as *interesting, good,* or *disgusting.*

TOO VAGUE   Many of the songs played on station WXQP are disgusting.

The word *disgusting* is needlessly vague. To sharpen the focus of this thesis, the writer should be more specific.

REVISED   Of the songs played on station WXQP, too many depict sex crudely, sanction the beating or rape of women, or foster gang violence.

In the process of making a vague thesis more precise, you may find yourself outlining the major sections of your paper, as in the preceding example. This technique, known as *blueprinting,* helps readers know exactly what to expect as they read on. It also helps you, the writer, control the shape of your essay.

ESL

If you come from a culture that prefers an indirect approach in writing, you may feel that asserting a thesis early in an essay sounds unrefined or even rude. In the United States, however, a direct approach is usually appreciated; when you state your point as directly as possible, you show that you value your reader's time.

EXERCISE 2-1

In each of the following pairs, which sentence might work well as a thesis for a two-to-five-page college paper? What is the problem with the other one? Is it too factual? Too broad? Too vague?

1a. By networking with friends, a single parent can manage to strike a balance among work, school, a social life, and family.

 b. Single parents face many challenges as they try to juggle all of their responsibilities.

2a. At the Special Olympics, disabled athletes are taught that with hard work and support from others they can accomplish anything: that they can indeed be winners.

 b. Working with the Special Olympics program is rewarding.

3a. History 201, taught by Professor Brown, is offered at 10 A.M. on Tuesdays and Thursdays.

 b. Whoever said that history is nothing but polishing tombstones must have missed History 201, because in Professor Brown's class history is very much alive.

4a. So far, research suggests that zero-emissions vehicles are not a sensible solution to the problem of steadily increasing air pollution.

 b. Because air pollution is of serious concern to many people in the world today, several government agencies in the United States have implemented plans to begin solving the problem.

5a. Anorexia nervosa is a dangerous, sometimes deadly eating disorder found mainly in young, upper-middle-class teenagers.

 b. The eating disorder anorexia nervosa is rarely cured by one treatment alone; only by combining drug therapy with psychotherapy and family therapy can the patient begin the long, torturous journey to wellness.

ON THE WEB

For electronic exercises on thesis statements and introductions, go to **dianahacker.com/rules**

and click on   ▶ **Electronic Writing Exercises**
                    ▶ **E-ex 2-1 and E-ex 2-2**

2b   Fill out the body.

Before drafting the body of an essay, take a careful look at your introduction, focusing especially on your thesis sentence. What does the thesis promise readers? Try to keep this focus in mind.

It's a good idea to have a plan in mind as well. If your thesis sentence outlines a plan (see 2a) or if you have sketched a preliminary outline, try to block out your paragraphs accordingly. If you do not have a plan, you would be wise to pause for a moment and sketch one (see 1d). Of course it is also possible to begin without a plan—assuming you are prepared to treat your first attempt as a "discovery draft" that will almost certainly be tossed (or radically rewritten) once you discover what you really want to say.

For more detailed advice about paragraphs in the body of an essay, see section 4.

2c   Attempt a conclusion.

The conclusion should echo the main idea, without dully repeating it. Often the concluding paragraph can be relatively short. By the end of the essay, readers should already understand your main point; your conclusion simply drives it home and perhaps suggests its significance.

In addition to echoing your main idea, a conclusion might summarize the essay's key points, pose a question for future study, offer advice, or propose a course of action. To end an essay detailing the social skills required of a bartender, one writer concludes with some advice:

> If someone were to approach me one day looking for the secret to running a good bar, I suppose I would offer the follow-

ing advice: Get your customers to pour out their ideas at a greater rate than you pour out the liquor. You will both win in the end.

—Kathleen Lewis, student

To make the conclusion memorable, you might include a detail, example, or image from the introduction to bring readers full circle; a quotation or bit of dialogue; an anecdote; or a humorous, witty, or ironic comment. To end a narrative describing a cash register holdup, one student uses an anecdote that includes some dialogue:

It took me a long time to get over that incident. Countless times I found myself gasping as someone "pointed" a dollar bill at me. On one such occasion, a jovial little man buying a toy gun for his son came up to me and said in a Humphrey Bogart impression, "Give me all your money, Sweetheart." I didn't laugh. Instead, my heart skipped a beat, for I had heard those words before.   —Diana Crawford, student

Whatever concluding strategy you choose, avoid introducing wholly new ideas at the end of an essay. Also avoid apologies and other limp, indeterminate endings. The essay should end crisply, preferably on a positive note.

Do not become discouraged if the perfect conclusion eludes you at the rough-draft stage of the writing process. Because the conclusion is so closely tied to the rest of the essay in both content and tone, you may well decide to rework it (or even replace it) as your drafts evolve.

3

Make global revisions; then revise sentences.

For experienced writers, revising is rarely a one-step process. Global matters generally receive attention first — the focus, organization, content, and overall strategy. Improvements in sentence structure, word choice, grammar, punctuation, and mechanics come later.

3a Make global revisions: Think big.

Global revisions address the larger elements of writing. Usually they affect chunks of text longer than a sentence, and frequently they can be quite dramatic. Whole paragraphs might be dropped, others added. Material once stretched over two or three paragraphs might be condensed into one. Entire sections might be rearranged. Even the content may change dramatically, for the process of revising stimulates thought.

Many of us resist global revisions because we find it difficult to distance ourselves from a draft. We tend to review our work from our own, not from our audience's, perspective.

To distance yourself from a draft, put it aside for a while, preferably overnight or even longer. When you return to it, try to play the role of your audience as you read. If possible, enlist the help of reviewers — persons willing to play the role of audience for you. Ask your reviewers to focus on the larger issues of writing, not on the fine points. The following checklist for global revision may help them get started.

Checklist for global revision

PURPOSE AND AUDIENCE

- Does the draft accomplish its purpose — to inform readers, to persuade them, to entertain them, to call them to action (or some combination of these)?
- Is the draft appropriate for its audience? Does it take into consideration the audience's knowledge of the subject, level of interest in the subject, and possible attitudes toward the subject?

FOCUS

- Do the introduction and conclusion focus clearly on the main point? Is the thesis clear enough and is it placed where readers will notice it? (If there is no thesis, is there a good reason for omitting one?)
- Are any ideas obviously off the point?

(continued)

Checklist for global revision (*continued*)

ORGANIZATION AND PARAGRAPHING

- Are there enough organizational cues for readers (such as topic sentences, transitions, or headings)?
- Are ideas ordered effectively?
- Does the paragraphing make sense?
- Are any paragraphs too long or too short for easy reading?

CONTENT

- Is the supporting material persuasive?
- Which ideas need further development?
- Are the parts proportioned sensibly? Do major ideas receive enough attention?
- Where might material be deleted?

POINT OF VIEW

- Is the draft free of distracting shifts in point of view (from *I* to *you*, for example, or from *it* to *they*)?
- Is the dominant point of view — first person (*I* or *we*), second person (*you*), or third person (*he, she, it, one,* or *they*) — appropriate, given the paper's purpose and audience? (See 13a.)

ON THE WEB

For tips on being a good peer reviewer, go to **dianahacker.com/rules**

and click on ▶ Additional Resources
　　　　　　　　▶ **Guidelines for Peer Reviewers**

ON THE WEB

For an electronic exercise on responding to another student's writing, go to **dianahacker.com/rules**

and click on ▶ Electronic Writing Exercise
　　　　　　　　▶ **E-ex 3-1**

The Writing Process

ON THE WEB

For an electronic exercise on choosing an appropriate point of view, go to **dianahacker.com/rules**

and click on ▶ **Electronic Writing Exercises**
▶ **E-ex 3-2**

3b Revise and edit sentences; proofread the final draft.

When you revise sentences, you focus on effectiveness; when you edit, you check for correctness. Proofreading is a slow and careful reading in search of typos and other obvious mistakes.

Revising and editing sentences

Most of the rest of this book offers advice on revising sentences for clarity and on editing them for grammar, punctuation, and mechanics.

Some writers handle most sentence-level revisions directly at the computer, experimenting on-screen with a variety of possible improvements. Other writers prefer to print out a hard copy of the draft, mark it up, and then return to the computer. Here, for example, is a rough-draft paragraph as one student edited it for a variety of sentence-level problems:

> Finally ~~we decided~~ *deciding* that perhaps our dream needed ~~some~~
>
> prompting, ~~and~~ we visited a fertility doctor and began the
>
> expensive, time-consuming round of procedures that held out
> ~~some~~ *our dream's fulfillment. Our efforts, however, were*
> ~~the~~ promise of ~~fulfilling our dream. All this was~~ to no avail, /
> *As* *could no longer*
> ~~and as~~ we approached the sixth year of our marriage, we ~~had~~
>
> ~~reached the point where we couldn't~~ even discuss our childless-
>
> ness without becoming very depressed. We questioned why this
> *such a*
> had happened to us. Why had we been singled out for ~~this~~
>
> major disappointment?

The original paragraph was flawed by wordiness and an excessive reliance on structures connected with *and*. Such problems can be addressed through any number of acceptable revisions. The first sentence, for example, could have been changed like this:

> Finally we decided that perhaps our dream needed ~~some~~
> *After visiting*   *we*
> prompting,/. ~~and we visited~~ a fertility doctor, ~~and~~ began the
>   ^   ^   *promised hope*
> expensive, time-consuming round of procedures that ~~held out~~
>   ^   ^
> ~~the promise~~ of fulfilling our dream.

Though some writers might argue about the effectiveness of these improvements compared with the previous revision, most would agree that both versions are better than the original.

Some of the paragraph's improvements involve less choice and are not so open to debate. The hyphen in *time-consuming* is necessary; a noun must be substituted for the pronoun *this* in the second sentence, which was being used more loosely than grammar allows; and the question mark in the next to last sentence must be changed to a period.

> GRAMMAR CHECKERS on your computer can help with some but not all of the sentence-level problems in a typical draft. Because so many problems — such as faulty parallelism, mixed constructions, and misplaced modifiers — lack mathematical precision, they slip right past the grammar checker. Even when the grammar checker has the capability of flagging a potential problem, such as the passive voice, you must still decide whether your sentence is effective.

Proofreading

After revising and editing, you are ready to prepare the final manuscript. (See 6a for guidelines.) At this point, make sure to allow yourself enough time for proofreading — the final and most important step in manuscript preparation.

Proofreading is a special kind of reading: a slow and methodical search for misspellings, typographical mistakes, and omitted words or word endings. Such errors can be difficult to spot in your own work because you may read what you intended to write, not what is actually on the page. To fight this tendency, try proofreading out loud, articulating each word as it is actually written.

Although proofreading may be dull, it is crucial. Errors strewn throughout an essay are distracting and annoying. If the writer doesn't care about this piece of writing, thinks the reader, why should I? A carefully proofread essay, however, sends a positive message: It shows that you value your writing and respect your readers.

> SPELL CHECKERS are more reliable than grammar checkers, but they too must be used with caution. Many typographical errors (such as *quiet* for *quite*) and misused words (such as *effect* for *affect*) slip past the spell checker because the checker flags only words not found in its dictionary.

STUDENT ESSAY

Matt Watson, who wrote "Hooked on Credit Cards" (pp. 34–38), was responding to the following assignment:

> In an essay of 500–1,000 words, alert readers to a significant problem facing today's college students. Assume that your audience consists of general readers, not simply college students.
>
> If you use any sources, document them with MLA in-text citations and a list of works cited (see section 51 in *Rules for Writers*).

When he received the assignment, Watson considered several possibilities before settling on the topic of credit cards. He already knew something about the topic because his older sister had run up large credit card bills while in college and was working hard to pay them off.

To get started on his paper, Watson interviewed his sister over the phone and then typed the following list of ideas into his computer.

> easy to get hooked on credit cards and run up huge debts
>
> Why do credit card companies try to sign up students? Aren't we

a bad risk? But they must be profiting, or they'd stop. High interest rates.

advertisements for credit cards appear all over campus and on the Web

using plastic--doesn't seem like spending money

tactics used by the companies--offering low interest rates at first, setting high credit limits, allowing a revolving balance

What happens to students who get in debt but don't have parents who can bail them out?

With this list of ideas, Watson began writing a first draft. He wrote it quickly, focusing more on ideas than on grammar, style, and mechanics. Then he made some additions and deletions and fixed a few typos before submitting the draft for peer review in a networked classroom. Here is the draft he submitted, together with the most helpful comments he received from classmates. The peer reviewers were asked to comment on global issues — focus, organization, content, point of view, and audience appeal — and to ignore any problems with grammar and punctuation.

ROUGH DRAFT

Hooked on Credit Cards

Some students do have jobs. (Sara)

Good question. What's the answer? (Mark)

The assignment asks for a general audience; your thesis shouldn't be about "us." (Sara)

Shouldn't your thesis focus more on how card companies hook students? (Tim)

Credit card companies love to extend credit to college students. You see ads for these cards on campus bulletin boards and also on the Web. Why do companies market their product to a population that has no job and lacks a substantial credit history? They seem to be trying to hook us on their cards; unfortunately many of us do get hooked on a cycle of spending that leads to financial ruin.

Banks require applicants for a loan to demonstrate a good credit history and some evidence

ood point. The card
companies are going
too easy on sudents.
(Sara)

Maybe you could also
mention the solicitors
who show up during
orientation. (Mark)

This sentence sounds
too informal. (Tim)

I like this example.
(Mark)

Why not give us some
numbers here? Just
how low and how
high? (Sara)

The shifts to "you"
seems odd. (Sara)

Maybe you could get
some statistics from
the Internet. (Mark)

This paragraph seems
sort of skimpy. (Tim)

Maybe you could find
some facts to back up
your points. (Mark)

of a source of income, but credit card companies
don't. On campus, students are bombarded with
offers of pre-approved credit cards. Then there are
the Web sites. Sites with lots of student traffic are
plastered with banner ads like this one: "To get a
credit card, you need to establish credit. To establish credit, you need a credit card. Stop the
vicious cycle! Apply for our student MasterCard."

Credit card companies often entice students
with low interest rates, then they jack up the
rates later. A student may not think about the
cost of interest. That new stereo or back-to-school
wardrobe can get pretty expensive at 17.9%
interest if it's compounded over several months.
Would you have bought that $600 item if you
knew it would end up costing you $900?

Most cards allow the holder to keep a revolving balance, which means that they don't have to
pay the whole bill, they just pay a minimum
amount. The minimum is usually not too much,
but a young person may be tempted to keep running up debt. The companies also give students an
unrealistically high credit limit. I've heard of
undergraduates who had a limit as high as $4,000.

Card companies make money not just from
high interest rates. Often they charge fees for late
payments. I've heard of penalties for going over
the credit limit too.

Often students discover too late that they
are thoroughly trapped. Some drop out of school,
others graduate and then can't find a good job

because they have a poor credit rating. There are

psychological problems too. Your parents may bail

you out of debt, but you'll probably feel guilty. On

a Web site, I read that two students felt so bad

they committed suicide.

Credit cards are a part of life these days,

and everyone is probably wise to have a charge

account for emergencies. But every college student

must take a hard look at their financial picture.

The very things that make those cards so conve-

nient and easy to use can lead to a mountain of

debt that will take years to pay off.

> Professor Mills won't like your shifts to "you" and "I" here.
>
> Also, he wants us to cite our sources. (Sara)

> Your paper focuses on the tactics that the companies use, but your conclusion doesn't mention them. (Tim)

After rereading his draft and considering the feedback from his classmates, Watson decided that his paper needed more facts. He located several Web sites and rejected those that were obviously promotional. He decided to rely on sites sponsored by two reputable organizations, Nellie Mae and the Consumer Federation of America.

In his next draft, Watson reworked his introduction and then strengthened his content by supplying more facts. While adding facts, he discovered ways of improving the organization. Then, when he was more or less satisfied with the paper as a whole, he worked to polish his sentences. Watson's final draft begins on the next page.

Matt Watson

Professor Mills

English 101

12 March 2001

Hooked on Credit Cards

Introduction orients readers and ends with a thesis.

Credit card companies love to extend credit to college students, especially those just out of high school. Ads for credit cards line campus bulletin boards, flash across commercial Web sites for students, and get stuffed into shopping bags at college bookstores. Why do the companies market their product so vigorously to a population that lacks a substantial credit history and often has no steady source of income? The answer is that significant profits can be earned through high interest rates and assorted penal-

Thesis announces the writer's main point.

ties and fees. By granting college students liberal lending arrangements, credit card companies often hook them on a cycle of spending that can ultimately lead to financial ruin.

Clear topic sentences guide readers through the body of the paper.

Whereas banks require applicants for a loan to demonstrate a good credit history and some evidence of an income flow, credit card companies make no such demands on students. On campus, students find themselves bombarded with offers of pre-approved cards--and not just on flyers pinned to bulletin boards. Many campuses allow credit card vendors to solicit applications during orientation week. In addition to offering pre-approved cards, these vendors often give away T-shirts or CDs to entice students to apply. Students are bombarded on the Web as

Watson 2

well. Sites with heavy student traffic are emblazoned
with banner ads like this one: "To get a credit card, you
need to establish credit. To establish credit, you need a
credit card. Stop the vicious cycle! Apply for our student
MasterCard."

Credit card companies often entice students with low
"teaser" interest rates of 13% and later raise those rates
to 18% or even higher. Others charge high rates up front,
trusting that students won't read the fine print. Some
young people don't think about the cost of interest, let
alone the cost of interest compounding month after month.
That back-to-school wardrobe can get pretty expensive at
17.9% interest compounded over several months. A $600
trip to Fort Lauderdale is not such a bargain when in the
long run it costs $900 or more.

In addition to charging high interest rates, credit
card companies try to maximize the amount of interest
generated. One tactic is to extend an unreasonably high
credit limit to students. According to Nellie Mae statistics,
in 1998 undergraduates were granted an average credit
limit of $3,683; for graduate students, the figure jumped
to $15,721. Nearly 10% of the students in the Nellie Mae
study carried balances near or exceeding these credit
limits (Blair).

Another tactic is to allow students to maintain a revolving balance. A revolving balance permits the debtor
to pay only part of a current bill, often an amount just a

Body para-
graphs are
developed with
details and
examples.

Transition
serves as a
bridge between
paragraphs.

Summary of
source is in
the student's
own words.

Source is docu-
mented with
an MLA in-text
citation.

little larger than the accumulated interest. The indebted student is tempted to keep on charging, paying a minimum amount every month, because there aren't any immediate consequences to doing so.

Once a student is hooked on a cycle of debt, the companies profit even further by assessing a variety of fees and penalties. According to a press release issued by Consumer Action and the Consumer Federation of America, many credit card companies charge late fees and "over the limit" penalties as high as $29 per month. In addition, grace periods are often shortened to ensure that late fees kick in earlier. Many companies also raise interest rates for those who fail to pay on time or exceed the credit limit. Those "penalty" rates can climb as high as 25% (1-2).

The writer cites a Web article from a reputable source.

Often students discover too late that they are thoroughly hooked. The results can be catastrophic. Some students are forced to drop out of school and take low-paying full-time jobs. Others, once they graduate, have difficulty landing good jobs because of their poor credit rating. Many students suffer psychologically as well. Even those who have parents willing to bail them out of debt often experience a great deal of anxiety and guilt. Two students recently grew so stressed by their accumulating debt that they committed suicide (Consumer Federation of Amer. 3).

Conclusion echoes the writer's main idea.

Credit cards are a part of life these days, and there is nothing wrong with having one or two of them. Before signing up for a particular card, however, college students

Watson 4

should take the time to read the fine print and do some comparison shopping. Students also need to learn to resist the many seductive offers that credit card companies extend to them once they have signed up. Students who can't "just say no" to temptations such as high credit limits and revolving balances could well become hooked on a cycle of debt from which there is no easy escape.

The Writing Process

Works Cited

Works cited
page follows
MLA format.

Blair, Alan D. "A High Wire Act: Balancing Student Loan and

Credit Card Debt." Nellie Mae. 1999. 6 Nov. 2000

<http://www.nelliemae.com/shared/bal.htm>.

Consumer Action and Consumer Federation of America.

"Card Issuers Hike Fees and Rates to Bolster Profits."

Consumer Federation of America. 5 Nov. 1998. 5 pp.

6 Nov. 2000 <http://www.consumerfed.org/

cardissuerspr.pdf>.

Consumer Federation of America. "Credit Card Debt Imposes

Huge Costs on Many College Students." Consumer

Federation of America. 8 June 1999. 7 pp. 6 Nov. 2000

<http://www.consumerfed.org/ccstudent.pdf>.

4

Build effective paragraphs.

Except for special-purpose paragraphs, such as introductions and conclusions (see 2a and 2c), paragraphs are clusters of information supporting an essay's main point (or advancing a story's action). Aim for paragraphs that are clearly focused, well developed, organized, coherent, and neither too long nor too short for easy reading.

● **4a** Focus on a main point.

A paragraph should be unified around a main point. The point should be clear to readers, and all sentences in the paragraph must relate to it.

Stating the main point in a topic sentence

As readers move into a paragraph, they need to know where they are — in relation to the whole essay — and what to expect in the sentences to come. A good topic sentence, a one-sentence summary of the paragraph's main point, acts as a signpost pointing in two directions: backward toward the thesis of the essay and forward toward the body of the paragraph.

Like a thesis statement (see 1c and 2a), a topic sentence is more general than the material supporting it. Usually the topic sentence comes first.

> *Nearly all living creatures manage some form of communication.* The dance patterns of bees in their hive help to point the way to distant flower fields or announce successful foraging. Male stickleback fish regularly swim upside-down to indicate outrage in a courtship contest. Male deer and lemurs mark territorial ownership by rubbing their own body secretions on boundary stones or trees. Everyone has seen a frightened dog put his tail between his legs and run in panic. We, too, use gestures, expressions, postures, and movement to give our words point. [Italics added.]
> — Olivia Vlahos, *Human Beginnings*

Sometimes the topic sentence is introduced by a transitional sentence linking it to earlier material. In the following paragraph, the topic sentence (italicized) has been delayed to allow for a transition.

> But flowers are not the only source of spectacle in the wilderness. *An opportunity for late color is provided by the berries of wildflowers, shrubs, and trees.* Baneberry presents its tiny white flowers in spring but in late summer bursts forth with clusters of red berries. Bunchberry, a ground-cover plant, puts out red berries in the fall, and the red berries of wintergreen last from autumn well into winter. In California, the bright red, fist-sized clusters of Christmas berries can be seen growing beside highways for up to six months of the year. [Italics added.]
> —James Crockett et al., *Wildflower Gardening*

Occasionally the topic sentence may be withheld until the end of the paragraph — but only if the earlier sentences hang together so well that the reader perceives their direction, if not their exact point. The opening sentences of the following paragraph state facts, so they are supporting material rather than topic sentences, but they strongly suggest a central idea. The topic sentence at the end is hardly a surprise.

> Tobacco chewing starts as soon as people begin stirring. Those who have fresh supplies soak the new leaves in water and add ashes from the hearth to the wad. Men, women, and children chew tobacco and all are addicted to it. Once there was a shortage of tobacco in Kaobawa's village and I was plagued for a week by early morning visitors who requested permission to collect my cigarette butts in order to make a wad of chewing tobacco. Normally, if anyone is short of tobacco, he can request a share of someone else's already chewed wad, or simply borrow the entire wad when its owner puts it down somewhere. *Tobacco is so important to them that their word for "poverty" translates as "being without tobacco."* [Italics added.]
> —Napoleon A. Chagnon, *Yanomamo: The Fierce People*

Although it is generally wise to use topic sentences, at times they are unnecessary. A topic sentence may not be needed if a paragraph continues developing an idea clearly introduced in a previous paragraph, if the details of the paragraph unmistakably suggest its main point, or if the paragraph appears in a narrative of events where generalizations might interrupt the flow of the story.

Sticking to the point

Sentences that do not support the topic sentence destroy the unity of a paragraph. If the paragraph is otherwise well focused, such offending sentences can simply be deleted or perhaps moved elsewhere. In the following paragraph describing the inadequate facilities in a high school, the information about the word processing instructor (in italics) is clearly off the point.

> As the result of tax cuts, the educational facilities of Lincoln High School have reached an all-time low. Some of the books date back to 1985 and have long since shed their covers. The lack of lab equipment makes it necessary for four to five students to work at one table, with most watching rather than performing experiments. The few computers in working order must share one dot matrix printer. *Also, the word processing instructor left to have a baby at the beginning of the semester, and most of the students don't like the substitute.* As for the furniture, many of the upright chairs have become recliners, and the desk legs are so unbalanced that they play seesaw on the floor.

Sometimes the cure for a disunified paragraph is not as simple as deleting or moving material. Writers often wander into uncharted territory because they cannot think of enough evidence to support a topic sentence. Feeling that it is too soon to break into a new paragraph, they move on to new ideas for which they have not prepared the reader. When this happens, the writer is faced with a choice: Either find more evidence to support the topic sentence or adjust the topic sentence to mesh with the evidence that is available.

EXERCISE 4–1

Underline the topic sentence in the following paragraph and cross out any material that does not clarify or develop the central idea.

> Historically, quilt making has served as an important means of social, political, and artistic expression for women. In the nineteenth century, especially, quilting circles provided one of the few opportunities for the women of a community to forge social bonds outside of their families. Once a week or more, they came together to sew as well as trade small talk, advice, and news. They used dyed cotton fabrics much like the fabrics quilters use today; surprisingly, quilters' basic materials haven't changed that much over the years. Sometimes the women joined their efforts in the support of a political cause, making

quilts that would be raffled to raise money for temperance societies, hospitals for sick and wounded soldiers, and the fight against slavery. The abolitionist movement, in particular, led one activist, Sarah Grimké, to memorably express her hopes for herself and fellow quilters: "May the points of our needles prick the slave owner's conscience." Quilt making also afforded women a means of artistic expression at a time when they had few other creative outlets. Within their socially acceptable roles as homemakers, many quilters subtly — and perhaps subconsciously — pushed back at the restrictions placed on them by experimenting with color, design, and technique.

ON THE WEB

For an electronic exercise on topic sentences, go to
dianahacker.com/rules

and click on ▶ **Electronic Writing Exercises**
▶ **E-ex 4-1**

4b Develop the main point.

Though an occasional short paragraph is fine, particularly if it functions as a transition or emphasizes a point, a series of brief paragraphs suggests inadequate development. How much development is enough? That varies, depending on the writer's purpose and audience.

For example, when she wrote a paragraph attempting to convince readers that it is impossible to lose fat quickly, health columnist Jane Brody knew that she would have to present a great deal of evidence because many dieters want to believe the opposite. She did *not* write:

> When you think about it, it's impossible to lose — as many diets suggest — 10 pounds of *fat* in ten days, even on a total fast. Even a moderately active person cannot lose so much weight so fast. A less active person hasn't a prayer.

This three-sentence paragraph is too skimpy to be convincing. But the paragraph that Brody wrote contains enough evidence to convince even skeptical readers.

When you think about it, it's impossible to lose — as many diets suggest — 10 pounds of *fat* in ten days, even on a total fast. A pound of body fat represents 3,500 calories. To lose 1 pound of fat, you must expend 3,500 more calories than you consume. Let's say you weigh 170 pounds and, as a moderately active person, you burn 2,500 calories a day. If your diet contains only 1,500 calories, you'd have an energy deficit of 1,000 calories a day. In a week's time that would add up to a 7,000-calorie deficit, or 2 pounds of real fat. In ten days, the accumulated deficit would represent nearly 3 pounds of lost body fat. Even if you ate nothing at all for ten days and maintained your usual level of activity, your caloric deficit would add up to 25,000 calories. . . . At 3,500 calories per pound of fat, that's still only 7 pounds of lost fat.   — Jane Brody, *Jane Brody's Nutrition Book*

4c   Choose a suitable pattern of organization.

Although paragraphs (and indeed whole essays) may be patterned in any number of ways, certain patterns of organization occur frequently, either alone or in combination: examples and illustrations, narration, description, process, comparison and contrast, analogy, cause and effect, classification and division, and definition. There is nothing particularly magical about these patterns (sometimes called *methods of development*). They simply reflect some of the ways in which we think.

Examples and illustrations

Examples, perhaps the most common pattern of development, are appropriate whenever the reader might be tempted to ask, "For example?" Though examples are just selected instances, not a complete catalog, they are enough to suggest the truth of many topic sentences, as in the following paragraph.

Normally my parents abided scrupulously by "The Budget," but several times a year Dad would dip into his battered black strongbox and splurge on some irrational, totally satisfying luxury. Once he bought over a hundred comic books at a flea market, doled out to us thereafter at the tantalizing rate of two a week. He always got a whole flat of pansies, Mom's favorite flower, for us to give her on Mother's Day. One day a boy stopped at our house selling fifty-cent raffle tickets on a sailboat and Dad bought every ticket the boy had left — three books' worth.   — Connie Hailey, student

Illustrations are extended examples, frequently presented in story form. Because they require several sentences apiece, they are used more sparingly than examples. When well selected, however, they can be a vivid and effective means of developing a point. The writer of the following paragraph uses illustrations to demonstrate that Harriet Tubman, famous conductor on the underground railroad for escaping slaves, was a genius at knowing how and when to retreat.

> Part of Harriet Tubman's strategy of conducting was, as in all battle-field operations, the knowledge of how and when to retreat. Numerous allusions have been made to her moves when she suspected that she was in danger. When she feared the party was closely pursued, she would take it for a time on a train southward bound. No one seeing Negroes going in this direction would for an instant suppose them to be fugitives. Once on her return she was at a railway station. She saw some men reading a poster and she heard one of them reading it aloud. It was a description of her, offering a reward for her capture. She took a southbound train to avert suspicion. At another time when Harriet heard men talking about her, she pretended to read a book which she carried. One man remarked, "This cannot be the woman. The one we want can't read or write." Harriet devoutly hoped the book was right side up.   — Earl Conrad, *Harriet Tubman*

Narration

A paragraph of narration tells a story or part of a story. Narrative paragraphs are usually arranged in chronological order, but they may also contain flashbacks, interruptions that take the story back to an earlier time. The following paragraph, from Jane Goodall's *In the Shadow of Man,* recounts one of the author's experiences in the African wild.

> One evening when I was wading in the shallows of the lake to pass a rocky outcrop, I suddenly stopped dead as I saw the sinuous black body of a snake in the water. It was all of six feet long, and from the slight hood and the dark stripes at the back of the neck I knew it to be a Storm's water cobra — a deadly reptile for the bite of which there was, at that time, no serum. As I stared at it an incoming wave gently deposited part of its body on one of my feet. I remained motionless, not even breathing, until the wave rolled back into the lake, drawing the snake with it. Then I leaped out of the water as fast as I could, my heart hammering.   — Jane Goodall, *In the Shadow of Man*

Description

A descriptive paragraph sketches a portrait of a person, place, or thing by using concrete and specific details that appeal to one or more of our senses—sight, sound, smell, taste, and touch. Consider, for example, the following description of the grasshopper invasions that devastated the midwestern landscape in the late 1860s.

> They came like dive bombers out of the west. They came by the millions with the rustle of their wings roaring overhead. They came in waves, like the rolls of the sea, descending with a terrifying speed, breaking now and again like a mighty surf. They came with the force of a williwaw and they formed a huge, ominous, dark brown cloud that eclipsed the sun. They dipped and touched earth, hitting objects and people like hailstones. But they were not hail. These were live demons. They popped, snapped, crackled, and roared. They were dark brown, an inch or longer in length, plump in the middle and tapered at the ends. They had transparent wings, slender legs, and two black eyes that flashed with a fierce intelligence.
>
> — Eugene Boe, "Pioneers to Eternity"

Process

A process paragraph is patterned in time order, usually chronologically. A writer may choose this pattern either to describe a process or to show readers how to perform a process. The following paragraph describes what happens when water freezes.

> In school we learned that with few exceptions the solid phase of matter is more dense than the liquid phase. Water, alone among common substances, violates this rule. As water begins to cool, it contracts and becomes more dense, in a perfectly typical way. But about four degrees above the freezing point, something remarkable happens. It ceases to contract and begins expanding, becoming less dense. At the freezing point the expansion is abrupt and drastic. As water turns to ice, it adds about one-eleventh to its liquid volume.
>
> — Chet Raymo, "Curious Stuff, Water and Ice"

Here is a paragraph explaining how to perform a "roll cast," a popular fly fishing technique:

> Begin by taking up a suitable stance, with one foot slightly in front of the other and the rod pointing down the line. Then

begin a smooth, steady draw, raising your rod hand to just above shoulder height and lifting the rod to the 10:30 or 11:00 position. This steady draw allows a loop of line to form between the rod top and the water. While the line is still moving, raise the rod slightly, then punch it rapidly forward and down. The rod is now flexed and under maximum compression, and the line follows its path, bellying out slightly behind you and coming off the water close to your feet. As you power the rod down through the 3:00 position, the belly of the line will roll forward. Follow through smoothly so that the line unfolds and straightens above the water.

— *The Dorling Kindersley Encyclopedia of Fishing*

Comparison or contrast

To compare two subjects is to draw attention to their similarities, although the word *compare* also has a broader meaning that includes a consideration of differences. To contrast is to focus only on differences.

Whether a paragraph stresses similarities or differences, it may be patterned in one of two ways. The two subjects may be presented one at a time, block style, as in the following paragraph of contrast.

So Grant and Lee were in complete contrast, representing two diametrically opposed elements in American life. Grant was the modern man emerging; beyond him, ready to come on the stage, was the great age of steel and machinery, of crowded cities and a restless burgeoning vitality. Lee might have ridden down from the old age of chivalry, lance in hand, silken banner fluttering over his head. Each man was the perfect champion of his cause, drawing both his strengths and weaknesses from the people he led.

— Bruce Catton, "Grant and Lee: A Study in Contrasts"

Or a paragraph may proceed point by point, treating the two subjects together, one aspect at a time. The following paragraph uses the point-by-point method to contrast the writer's academic experiences in an American high school with those in an Irish convent.

Strangely enough, instead of being academically inferior to my American high school, the Irish convent was superior. In my class at home, *Love Story* was considered pretty heavy reading, so imagine my surprise at finding Irish students who could recite passages from *War and Peace.* In high school we complained about having to study *Romeo and Juliet* in one semester, whereas in Ireland we simultaneously studied *Macbeth* and Dickens's *Hard Times,* in addition to writing a composition a day in English class. In high school, I didn't even begin algebra until the ninth grade, while at the convent seventh graders (or their Irish equivalent) were doing calculus and trigonometry.

— Margaret Stack, student

Analogy

Analogies draw comparisons between items that appear to have little in common. Writers turn to analogies for a variety of reasons: to make the unfamiliar seem familiar, to provide a concrete understanding of an abstract topic, to argue a point, or to provoke fresh thoughts or changed feelings about a subject. In the following paragraph, physician Lewis Thomas draws an analogy between the behavior of ants and that of humans. Thomas's analogy helps us understand the social behavior of ants and forces us to question the superiority of our own human societies.

Ants are so much like human beings as to be an embarrassment. They farm fungi, raise aphids as livestock, launch armies into wars, use chemical sprays to alarm and confuse enemies, capture slaves. The families of weaver ants engage in child labor, holding their larvae like shuttles to spin out the thread that sews the leaves together for their fungus gardens. They exchange information ceaselessly. They do everything but watch television.

— Lewis Thomas, "On Societies as Organisms"

Although analogies can be a powerful tool for illuminating a subject, they should be used with caution in arguments. Just because two things may be alike in one respect, we cannot conclude that they are alike in all respects. (See *false analogy*, p. 366.)

Cause and effect

When causes and effects are a matter of argument, they are too complex to be reduced to a simple pattern (see p. 360). However, if a writer wishes merely to describe a cause-and-effect relationship that is generally accepted, then the effect may be stated in the topic sentence, with the causes listed in the body of the paragraph.

> The fantastic water clarity of the Mount Gambier sinkholes results from several factors. The holes are fed from aquifers holding rainwater that fell decades — even centuries — ago, and that has been filtered through miles of limestone. The high level of calcium that limestone adds causes the silty detritus from dead plants and animals to cling together and settle quickly to the bottom. Abundant bottom vegetation in the shallow sinkholes also helps bind the silt. And the rapid turnover of water prohibits stagnation.
>
> — Hillary Hauser, "Exploring a Sunken Realm in Australia"

Or the paragraph may move from cause to effects, as in this paragraph from a student paper on the effects of the industrial revolution on American farms.

> The rise of rail transport in the nineteenth century forever changed American farming — for better and for worse. Farmers who once raised crops and livestock to sustain just their own families could now make a profit by selling their goods in towns and cities miles away. These new markets improved the living standard of struggling farm families and encouraged them to seek out innovations that would increase their profits. On the downside, the competition fostered by the new markets sometimes created hostility among neighboring farm families where there had once been a spirit of cooperation. Those farmers who couldn't compete with their neighbors left farming forever, facing poverty worse than they had ever known.
>
> — Chris Mileski, student

Classification and division

Classification is the grouping of items into categories according to some consistent principle. Philosopher Francis Bacon was using classification when he wrote that "some books are to be tasted, others to be swallowed, and some few to be chewed and digested." Bacon's principle for classifying books is the degree to which they are worthy of our attention, but books of course can be classified according to other principles. For example, an elementary school teacher might classify children's books according to their level of difficulty, or a librarian might group them by subject matter. The principle of classification that a writer chooses ultimately depends on the purpose of the classification.

The following paragraph classifies species of electric fish.

Scientists sort electric fishes into three categories. The first comprises the strongly electric species like the marine electric rays or the freshwater African electric catfish and South American electric eel. Known since the dawn of history, these deliver a punch strong enough to stun a human. In recent years, biologists have focused on a second category: weakly electric fish in the South American and African rivers that use tiny voltages for communication and navigation. The third group contains sharks, nonelectric rays, and catfish, which do not emit a field but possess sensors that enable them to detect the minute amounts of electricity that leak out of other organisms.
— Anne Rudloe and Jack Rudloe, "Electric Warfare: The Fish That Kill with Thunderbolts"

Division takes one item and divides it into parts. As with classification, division should be made according to some consistent principle. Dividing a tree into roots, trunk, branches, and leaves makes sense; listing its components as branches, wood, water, and sap does not, for the categories overlap.

The following passage describes the components that make up a baseball.

Like the game itself, a baseball is composed of many layers. One of the delicious joys of childhood is to take apart a baseball and examine the wonders within. You begin by removing the red cotton thread and peeling off the leather cover — which comes from the hide of a Holstein cow and has been tanned, cut, printed, and punched with holes. Beneath the cover is a thin layer of cotton string, followed by several hundred yards of woolen yarn, which make up the bulk of the ball. Slice into the rubber and you'll find the ball's heart — a cork core. The cork is from Portugal, the rubber from southeast Asia, the covers are American, and the balls are assembled in Costa Rica.
— Dan Gutman, *The Way Baseball Works*

Definition

A definition puts a word or concept into a general class and then provides enough details to distinguish it from others in the same class. For example, in one of its senses the term *grit* names the class of things that birds eat, but it is restricted to those items — such as small pebbles, eggshell, and ashes — that help the bird grind food.

Many definitions may be presented in a sentence or two, but abstract or difficult concepts may require a paragraph or even a full essay of definition. In the following paragraph, the writer defines *envy* as a special kind of desire.

> Envy is so integral and so painful a part of what animates human behavior in market societies that many people have forgotten the full meaning of the word, simplifying it into one of the synonyms of desire. It is that, which may be why it flourishes in market societies: democracies of desire, they might be called, with money for ballots, stuffing permitted. But envy is more or less than desire. It begins with the almost frantic sense of emptiness inside oneself, as if the pump of one's heart were sucking on air. One has to be blind to perceive the emptiness, of course, but that's just what envy is, a selective blindness. *Invidia,* Latin for envy, translates as "nonsight," and Dante had the envious plodding along under cloaks of lead, their eyes sewn shut with leaden wire. What they are blind to is what they have, God-given and humanly nurtured, in themselves.
>
> — Nelson W. Aldrich Jr., *Old Money*

4d Make paragraphs coherent.

When sentences and paragraphs flow from one to another without discernible bumps, gaps, or shifts, they are said to be coherent. Coherence can be improved by strengthening the various ties between old information and new. A number of techniques for strengthening those ties are detailed in this section.

Linking ideas clearly

Readers expect to learn a paragraph's main point in a topic sentence early in the paragraph. Then, as they move into the body of the paragraph, they expect to encounter specific details, facts, or examples that support the topic sentence — either directly or indirectly. In the following paragraph, all of the sentences following the topic sentence directly support it.

> A passenger list of the early years of the Orient Express would read like a *Who's Who of the World,* from art to politics. Sarah Bernhardt and her Italian counterpart Eleonora Duse used the train to thrill the stages of Europe. For musicians there were Toscanini and Mahler. Dancers Nijinsky and Pavlova were there,

while lesser performers like Harry Houdini and the girls of the Ziegfeld Follies also rode the rails. Violinists were allowed to practice on the train, and occasionally one might see trapeze artists hanging like bats from the baggage racks.

— Barnaby Conrad III, "Train of Kings"

If a sentence does not support the topic sentence directly, readers expect it to support another sentence in the paragraph and therefore to support the topic sentence indirectly. The following paragraph begins with a topic sentence. The italicized sentences are direct supports, and the rest of the sentences are indirect supports.

Though the open-space classroom works for many children, it is not practical for my son, David. *First, David is hyperactive.* When he was placed in an open-space classroom, he became distracted and confused. He was tempted to watch the movement going on around him instead of concentrating on his own work. *Second, David has a tendency to transpose letters and numbers, a tendency that can be overcome only by individual attention from the instructor.* In the open classroom he was moved from teacher to teacher, with each one responsible for a different subject. No single teacher worked with David long enough to diagnose the problem, let alone help him with it. *Finally, David is not a highly motivated learner.* In the open classroom, he was graded "at his own level," not by criteria for a certain grade. He could receive a B in reading and still be a grade level behind, because he was doing satisfactory work "at his own level."

— Margaret Smith, student

Repeating key words

Repetition of key words is an important technique for gaining coherence. To prevent repetitions from becoming dull, you can use variations of a key word (*hike, hiker, hiking*), pronouns referring to the word (*gamblers . . . they*), and synonyms (*run, spring, race, dash*). In the following paragraph describing plots among indentured servants in the seventeenth century, historian Richard Hofstadter binds sentences together by repeating the key word *plots* and echoing it with a variety of synonyms (which are italicized).

Plots hatched by several servants to run away together occurred mostly in the plantation colonies, and the few recorded servant *uprisings* were entirely limited to those colonies. Virginia had been forced from its very earliest years to take stringent steps against *mutinous plots,* and severe punishments for *such behavior* were recorded. Most servant *plots* occurred in the seventeenth century: A contemplated *uprising* was nipped in the bud in York County in 1661; apparently led by some left-wing offshoots of the *Great Rebellion,* servants *plotted* an *insurrection* in Gloucester County in 1663, and four leaders were condemned and executed; some discontented servants apparently joined *Bacon's Rebellion* in the 1670s. In the 1680s the planters became newly apprehensive of discontent among the servants "owing to their great necessities and want of clothes," and it was feared that they would *rise up* and *plunder* the storehouses and ships; in 1682 there were plant-cutting *riots* in which servants and laborers, as well as some planters, took part. [Italics added.]

— Richard Hofstadter, *America at 1750*

Using parallel structures

Parallel structures are frequently used within sentences to underscore the similarity of ideas (see 9). They may also be used to bind together a series of sentences expressing similar information. In the following passage describing folk beliefs, anthropologist Margaret Mead presents similar information in parallel grammatical form.

Actually, almost every day, even in the most sophisticated home, something is likely to happen that evokes the memory of some old folk belief. The salt spills. A knife falls to the floor. Your nose tickles. Then perhaps, with a slightly embarrassed smile, the person who spilled the salt tosses a pinch over his left shoulder. Or someone recites the old rhyme, "Knife falls, gentleman calls." Or as you rub your nose you think, That means a letter. I wonder who's writing?

— Margaret Mead, "New Superstitions for Old"

A less skilled writer might have varied the structure, perhaps like this: *The salt gets spilled. Mother drops a knife on the floor. Your nose begins to tickle.* But these sentences are less effective; Mead's parallel structures help tie the passage together.

Maintaining consistency

Coherence suffers whenever a draft shifts confusingly from one point of view to another or from one verb tense to another. (See 13.) In addition, coherence can suffer when new information is introduced with the subject of each sentence. As a rule, a sentence's subject should echo a subject or object in the previous sentence.

The following rough-draft paragraph is needlessly hard to read because so few of the sentences' subjects are tied to earlier subjects or objects. The subjects appear in italics.

> *One* goes about trapping in this manner. At the very outset *one* acquires a "trapping" state of mind. A *library* of books must be read, and preferably *someone* with experience should educate the novice. *Preparing* for the first expedition takes several steps. The *purchase* of traps is first. A *pair* of rubber gloves, waterproof *boots,* and the grubbiest *clothes* capable of withstanding human use come next to outfit the trapper for his adventure. Finally, the *decision* has to be made on just what kind of animals to seek, what sort of bait to use, and where to place the traps.

Although the writer repeats a number of key words, such as *trapping,* the paragraph seems disconnected because new information is introduced with the subject of each sentence.

To improve the paragraph, the writer used the first-person pronoun as the subject of every sentence. The revision is much easier to read.

> *I* went about trapping in this manner. To acquire a "trapping" state of mind, *I* read a library of books and talked at length with an experienced trapper, my father. Then *I* purchased the traps and outfitted myself by collecting a pair of rubber gloves, waterproof boots, and the grubbiest clothes capable of withstanding human use. Finally, *I* decided just what kinds of animals to seek, what sort of bait to use, and where to place my traps.   —John Clyde Thatcher, student

Notice that Thatcher combined some of his original sentences. By doing so, he was able to avoid excessive repetitions of the pronoun *I*. Notice, too, that he varied his sentence openings (most sentences do not begin with *I*) so that readers are not likely to find the repetitions tiresome.

Providing transitions

Transitions are bridges between what has been read and what is about to be read. Transitions help readers move from sentence to sentence; they also alert readers to more global connections of ideas — those between paragraphs or even larger blocks of text.

SENTENCE-LEVEL TRANSITIONS Certain words and phrases signal connections between (or within) sentences. Frequently used transitions are included in the following list.

TO SHOW ADDITION

and, also, besides, further, furthermore, in addition, moreover, next, too, first, second

TO GIVE EXAMPLES

for example, for instance, to illustrate, in fact, specifically

TO COMPARE

also, in the same manner, similarly, likewise

TO CONTRAST

but, however, on the other hand, in contrast, nevertheless, still, even though, on the contrary, yet, although

TO SUMMARIZE OR CONCLUDE

in other words, in short, in summary, in conclusion, to sum up, that is, therefore

TO SHOW TIME— *process essay*

after, as, before, next, during, later, finally, meanwhile, then, when, while, immediately

TO SHOW PLACE OR DIRECTION

above, below, beyond, farther on, nearby, opposite, close, to the left

TO INDICATE LOGICAL RELATIONSHIP

if, so, therefore, consequently, thus, as a result, for this reason, since

Skilled writers use transitional expressions with care, making sure, for example, not to use *consequently* when an *also* would be more precise. They are also careful to select transitions with an appropriate tone, perhaps preferring *so* to *thus* in an informal piece, *in summary* to *in short* for a scholarly essay.

In the following paragraph, taken from an argument that dinosaurs had the "'right-sized' brains for reptiles of their body size," biologist Stephen Jay Gould uses transitions (italicized) with skill.

I don't wish to deny that the flattened, minuscule head of the large-bodied "Stegosaurus" houses little brain from our sub-jective, top-heavy perspective, *but* I do wish to assert that we should not expect more of the beast. *First of all,* large animals have relatively smaller brains than related, small animals. The correlation of brain size with body size among kindred animals (all reptiles, all mammals, *for example*) is remarkably regular. *As* we move from small to large animals, from mice to elephants *or* small lizards to Komodo dragons, brain size increases, *but* not so fast as body size. *In other words,* bodies grow faster than brains, *and* large animals have low ratios of brain weight to body weight. *In fact,* brains grow only about two-thirds as fast as bodies. *Since* we have no reason to believe that large animals are consistently stupider than their smaller relatives, we must conclude that large animals require relatively less brain to do as well as smaller animals. *If* we do not recognize this relationship, we are likely to underestimate the mental power of very large animals, dinosaurs in particular. [Italics added.]

— Stephen Jay Gould, "Were Dinosaurs Dumb?"

CAUTION: Do not be too self-conscious about plugging in transi-tion words while you are drafting sentences; overuse of these signals can seem heavy-handed. Usually, you will use transi-tions quite naturally, just where readers need them. If you (or your reviewers) discover places where readers cannot easily move from sentence to sentence in your rough draft, you can always add transition words as you revise.

ON THE WEB

For an electronic exercise on transitions, go to
dianahacker.com/rules

and click on ▶ **Electronic Writing Exercises**
▶ **E-ex 4-2**

PARAGRAPH-LEVEL TRANSITIONS Paragraph-level transitions usually link the *first* sentence of a new paragraph with the *first* sentence of the previous paragraph. In other words, the topic sentences signal global connections.

Look for opportunities to allude to the subject of a previ-ous paragraph (as summed up in its topic sentence) in the topic sentence of the next one. In his essay "Little Green Lies,"

Jonathan H. Alder uses this strategy in the following topic sentences, which appear in a passage describing the benefits of plastic packaging.

> Consider aseptic packaging, the synthetic packaging for the "juice boxes" so many children bring to school with their lunch. [*Rest of paragraph omitted.*]
>
> What is true for juice boxes is also true for other forms of synthetic packaging. [*Rest of paragraph omitted.*]

TRANSITIONS BETWEEN BLOCKS OF TEXT   In long essays, you will need to alert readers to connections between blocks of text more than one paragraph long. You can do this by inserting transitional sentences or short paragraphs at key points in the essay. Here, for example, is a transitional paragraph from a student research paper. It announces that the first part of her paper has come to a close and the second part is about to begin.

> Although the great apes have demonstrated significant language skills, one central question remains: Can they be taught to use that uniquely human language tool we call grammar, to learn the difference, for instance, between "ape bite human" and "human bite ape"? In other words, can an ape create a sentence?

Another strategy to help readers move from one block of text to another is to insert headings in your essay. Headings, which usually sit above blocks of text, allow you to announce a new topic boldly, without the need for subtle transitions. (See 5b.)

4e   If necessary, adjust paragraph length.

Most readers feel comfortable reading paragraphs that range between one hundred and two hundred words. Shorter paragraphs force too much starting and stopping, and longer ones strain the reader's attention span. There are exceptions to this guideline, however. Paragraphs longer than two hundred words frequently appear in scholarly writing, where they suggest seriousness and depth. Paragraphs shorter than one hundred words occur in newspapers because of narrow columns; in informal essays to quicken the pace; and in business writing and Web sites, where readers routinely skim for main ideas.

In an essay, the first and last paragraphs will ordinarily be the introduction and conclusion. These special-purpose paragraphs are likely to be shorter than the paragraphs in the body of the essay. Typically, the body paragraphs will follow the essay's outline: one paragraph per point in short essays, a group of paragraphs per point in longer ones. Some ideas require more development than others, however, so it is best to be flexible. If an idea stretches to a length unreasonable for a paragraph, you should divide the paragraph, even if you have presented comparable points in the essay in single paragraphs.

Paragraph breaks are not always made for strictly logical reasons. Writers use them for all of the following reasons.

REASONS FOR BEGINNING A NEW PARAGRAPH

— to mark off the introduction and conclusion
— to signal a shift to a new idea
— to indicate an important shift in time or place
— to emphasize a point (by placing it at the beginning or the end, not in the middle, of a paragraph)
— to highlight a contrast
— to signal a change of speakers (in dialogue)
— to provide readers with a needed pause
— to break up text that looks too dense

Beware of using too many short, choppy paragraphs, however. Readers want to see how your ideas connect, and they become irritated when you break their momentum by forcing them to pause every few sentences. Here are some reasons you might have for combining some of the paragraphs in a rough draft.

REASONS FOR COMBINING PARAGRAPHS

— to clarify the essay's organization
— to connect closely related ideas
— to bind together text that looks too choppy

Design

Process

Design

Clarity

Grammar

Punctuation

Mechanics

Argument

Research

Basics

The term *document* is broad enough to describe anything you might write in an English class, in other classes across the curriculum, in the business world, and in everyday life. How you design a document (format it on the page) can affect how readers respond to it.

Instructors have certain expectations about how a college paper should look (see 6a). Employers too expect documents such as business letters and memos to be formatted in standard ways (see 6b). And anyone who reads your e-mail and Web pages will appreciate an effective document design (see 7).

5

Become familiar with the principles of document design.

Good document design promotes readability, but what *readability* means depends on your purpose and audience and perhaps on other elements of your writing situation, such as your subject and any length restrictions. (See the checklist on p. 3.) All of your design choices — word processing options and use of headings, displayed lists, and other visuals — should be made in light of your specific writing situation.

5a Select appropriate format options.

Word processing programs present you with abundant format options. Before you print your final draft, make sure that your margins, line spacing, and alignment are set appropriately. Also decide which font (typeface style and size) is most appropriate for your purposes.

Margins and line spacing

For documents written on $8\frac{1}{2}'' \times 11''$ paper, leave a margin of between one and one and a half inches on all sides of the page. These margins prevent the text from looking too crowded, and they allow room for annotations, such as an instructor's comments or an editor's suggestions.

Most manuscripts-in-progress are double-spaced to allow room for editing. Final copy is often double-spaced as well, since single-spacing is less inviting to read. But at times the advantages of double-spacing are offset by other considerations. For example, most business and technical documents are single-spaced, with double-spacing between paragraphs. Single-spacing promotes quick scanning, and it also saves paper.

Justification (alignment)

Word processing programs give you a choice between left-justified or fully justified text. Left-justified text lines up against the left margin but has a ragged right margin. When text is fully justified, all of the words line up against both the left and the right margins, as they do on a typeset page like the one you are now reading.

Unfortunately, text that has been fully justified on a computer can be hard to read. The problem is that extra space is added between words in some lines, creating "rivers" of white that can be distracting. In addition, fully justified text may create the need for excessive hyphenation at the ends of lines. Unless your computer can create the real look of a typeset page, you will do readers a favor by turning off the full justification feature.

Fonts

If you have a choice of fonts, select a normal size (10 to 12 points) and a style that is not too offbeat. Although unusual styles of type, such as those that look handwritten, may seem attractive, they slow readers down. We all read more efficiently when a text meets our usual expectations.

CAUTION: Never write or type a college essay or any other document in all capital letters. Research shows that readers experience frustration when they are forced to read more than a few consecutive words printed in all capital letters.

5b Consider using headings.

There is little need for headings in short essays, especially if the writer uses paragraphing and clear topic sentences to guide readers. In more complex documents, however, such as research papers, grant proposals, business reports, and long Web documents, headings can be a useful visual cue for readers. Headings help readers see at a glance the organization of a document. If more than one level of heading is used, the headings also indicate the hierarchy of ideas — as they do throughout this book.

Headings serve a number of functions, depending on the needs of different readers. When readers are simply looking up information, headings will help them find it quickly. When readers are scanning, hoping to pick up the gist of things, headings will guide them. Even when readers are committed enough to read every word, headings can help. Efficient readers preview a document before they begin reading; when previewing and while reading, they are guided by any visual cues the writer provides.

CAUTION: Avoid using more headings (or more levels of headings) than you really need. Excessive use of headings can make a text choppy.

Phrasing headings

Headings should be as brief and as informative as possible. Certain styles of headings — the most common being *-ing* phrases, noun phrases, and questions — work better for some purposes, audiences, and subjects than others.

Whatever style you choose, use it consistently for headings on the same level. In other words, headings on the same level of organization should be written in parallel structure (see 9), as in the following examples. The first set of headings appeared in a report written for an environmental think tank, the second in a history textbook, and the third in a mutual fund brochure.

-ING HEADINGS

Safeguarding the earth's atmosphere

Charting the path to sustainable energy

Conserving global forests

Triggering the technological revolution

Strengthening international institutions

NOUN PHRASE HEADINGS

The economics of slavery

The sociology of slavery

The psychological effects of slavery

QUESTIONS AS HEADINGS

How do I buy shares?

How do I redeem shares?

What is the history of the fund's performance?

What are the tax consequences of investing in the fund?

Placing and highlighting headings

Headings on the same level of organization should be positioned and highlighted in a consistent way. For example, you might center your first-level headings and print them in boldface; then you might place the second-level headings flush left (against the left margin) and underline them, like this:

First-level heading

Second-level heading

Headings in college papers are often centered, as in the sample paper on pages 485–94. In business and technical writing, headings are usually placed flush left above flush-left text — without paragraph indents — to create strong alignment among elements on a page (see the memo on p. 76 for an example).

To highlight headings, you might use boldface, italics or underlining, all capital letters, color, a larger or smaller typeface than the text, a different font, or some combination of these:

boldface	color
italics	larger typeface
underlining	smaller typeface
ALL CAPITAL LETTERS	different font

On the whole, it is best to use restraint. Excessive highlighting results in a page that looks too busy, and it defeats its own purpose, since readers have trouble sorting out which headings are more important than others.

Important headings can be highlighted by using white space around them. Less important headings can be downplayed by using less white space or by running them into the text (as with the small all-capitals heading on p. 72).

5c   Consider using displayed lists.

Lists are easy to read or scan when they are displayed rather than run into your text. You might reasonably choose to display the following kinds of lists:

— steps in a process
— materials needed for a project
— parts of an object
— advice or recommendations
— items to be discussed
— criteria for evaluation (as in checklists)

Displayed lists should usually be introduced with an independent clause followed by a colon (see 35a and the preceding list). Periods are not used after items in a displayed list unless the items are sentences.

Lists are most readable when they are presented in parallel grammatical form (see 9). In the preceding list, for instance, the items are all noun phrases. As with headings, some kinds of lists might be more appropriately presented as *-ing* phrases or as questions.

To draw the reader's eye to a list, you might use bullets (circles or squares) or dashes if there is no need to number the items. If there is some reason to number the items, use an arabic number followed by a period for each item.

Although displayed lists can be a useful visual cue, they should not be overdone. Too many of them will give a document a choppy, cluttered look. And lists that are very long (sometimes called "laundry lists") should be avoided as well. Readers can hold only so many ideas in their short-term memory, so if a list grows too long, you should find some way of making it more concise or clustering similar items.

5d   Consider adding visuals.

Visuals such as charts, graphs, tables, diagrams, maps, and photographs convey information concisely and vividly. In a student essay not intended for publication, you can use another person's visuals as long as you credit the source (see 54 and 59).

And with access to computer graphics, you can create your own visuals to enhance an essay, a report, or an electronic document. This section suggests when charts, graphs, tables, and diagrams might be appropriate for your purposes. It also discusses where you might place such visuals.

Using charts, graphs, tables, and diagrams

In documents that help readers follow a process or make a decision, flow charts can be useful; for an example, see page 157 in this book. Pie charts are appropriate for indicating ratios or apportionment, as in the following example.

PIE CHART

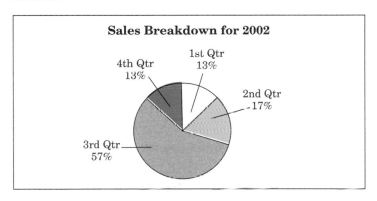

Line graphs and bar graphs illustrate disparities in numerical data. Line graphs (see p. 66) are appropriate when you want to illuminate trends over a period of time, such as trends in sales, in unemployment, or in population growth. Bar graphs (see p. 66) can be used for the same purpose. In addition, bar graphs are useful for highlighting comparisons, such as vote totals for rival political candidates or the number of refugees entering the United States during different time periods.

Tables are not as visually interesting as line graphs or charts, but they allow for inclusion of specific numerical data, such as exact percentages. The table on page 67 presents the responses of students and faculty to one question on a campus-wide questionnaire.

Document Design

LINE GRAPH

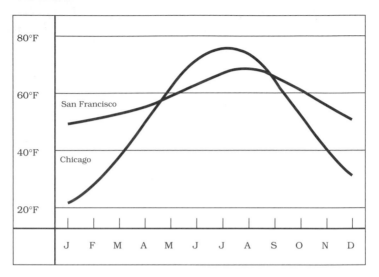

**MONTHLY MEAN TEMPERATURE IN
SAN FRANCISCO AND CHICAGO**

BAR GRAPH

SALES BREAKDOWN BY REGION, 2002

TABLE

Is American education based too much on European history and values?

	PERCENT		
	NO	UNDECIDED	YES
Nonwhite students	21	25	54
White students	55	29	16
Nonwhite faculty	15	20	65
White faculty	57	27	16

Diagrams are useful — and sometimes indispensable — in scientific and technical writing. It is more concise, for example, to use the following diagram than to explain the chemical formula in words.

DIAGRAM

$$(CH_3P)_4$$

Placing visuals

A visual may be placed in the text of a document near a discussion to which it relates, or it can be put in an appendix, labeled, and referred to in the text.

Placing visuals in the text of a document can be tricky. Usually you will want the visual to appear close to the sentences that relate to it, but page breaks won't always allow this placement. At times you may need to insert the visual at a later point and tell readers where they can find it; sometimes, with the help of software, you can make the text flow around the visual.

In newsletters and in business and technical documents, page layout is both an art and a science. The best way to learn how to lay out pages is to work with colleagues who have had experience solving the many problems that can arise.

6

Use standard academic and business formats.

6a Use the manuscript format that is required by your academic discipline.

If your instructor provides formal guidelines for formatting an essay — or a more specialized document such as a lab report, a case study, or a research paper — you should of course follow them. Otherwise, use the manuscript format that is normally recommended for your academic discipline.

In most English and humanities classes, you will be asked to use the MLA (Modern Language Association) format. The sample essay on pages 69–70 illustrates this format. For more detailed advice about MLA manuscript guidelines, along with a sample MLA research paper, see 55. If you have been asked to use APA (American Psychological Association) manuscript guidelines, see 60.

6b Use standard business formats.

This section provides guidelines for preparing business letters, résumés, and memos. For a more detailed discussion of these and other business documents — proposals, reports, executive summaries, and so on — consult a business writing textbook or look at examples currently being written at the organization for which you are writing.

MLA ESSAY FORMAT

½″

Weitzel 1

1″

Tom Weitzel

Dr. Fry

English 101

18 April 2001

Double-spacing
is used
throughout.

Who Goes to the Races?

Title is
centered.

½″ indent   A favorite pastime of mine is observing people, and

my favorite place to observe is at the horse races. After

many encounters with the racing crowd, I have discovered

that there are four distinct groups at the track: the once-

a-year bunch, the professionals, the clubhouse set, and the

unemployed.

1″   The largest group at the track consists of those who   1″

show up once a year. They know little about horses or

betting and rely strictly on racetrack gimmick sheets and

newspaper predictions for selecting possible winners. If

that strategy doesn't work, they use intuition, lucky num-

bers, favorite colors, or appealing names. They bet larger

amounts as the day goes along, gambling on every race,

including long-shot bets on exactas and daily doubles. The

vast majority go home broke and frustrated.

More subtle and quiet are the professionals. They fol-

low the horses from track to track and live in campers and

motor homes. Many are married couples, some are retired,

and all are easily spotted with their lunch sacks, water

jugs, and binoculars. Since most know one another, they

section themselves off in a particular area of the stadium.

1″

MLA ESSAY FORMAT *(continued)*

1″

½″
Weitzel 2

1″

All rely on the racing form and on personal knowledge of each horse, jockey, and track in making the proper bet. They bet only on the smart races, rarely on the favorites. Never do they bet on exactas or daily doubles. More often than not they either break even or go home winners.

Isolated from the others is the clubhouse set. Found either at the cocktail lounge or in the restaurant, usually involved in business transactions, these racing fans rarely see a race in person; instead they do their betting via the waiter. It's difficult to tell whether they go home sad, happy, or in between. They keep their emotions to themselves.

The most interesting members of the racetrack population are the unemployed. They will be found not in the clubhouse, but right down at the rail next to the finish line. Here one can discover the real emotion of the racetrack--the screaming, the cursing, and the pushing. The unemployed are not in it for the sport. Betting is not a game for them, but a battle for survival. If they lose, they must borrow enough money to carry them until the next check comes in, and then, of course, they head right back to the track. This particular group arrives at the track beaten and leaves beaten.

I have probably lost more money than I have won at the track, but observing these four interesting groups of people makes it all worthwhile.

Business letters

In writing a business letter, be direct, clear, and courteous, but do not hesitate to be firm if necessary. State your purpose or request at the beginning of the letter and include only pertinent information in the body. By being as direct and concise as possible, you show that you value your reader's time.

BUSINESS LETTER IN FULL BLOCK FORM

121 Knox Road, #6 ⎤ Return
College Park, MD 20740 ⎟ address
March 4, 2002 ⎦

Linda Hennessee, Managing Editor ⎤
World Discovery ⎟ Inside
1650 K Street, NW ⎟ address
Washington, DC 20036 ⎦

Dear Ms. Hennessee: ⎤—— Salutation

Please accept my application for the summer editorial internship listed with the Career Development Center at the University of Maryland. Currently I am a junior at the University of Maryland, with a double major in English and Latin American studies.

Over the past three years I have gained considerable experience in newspaper and magazine journalism, as you will see on my enclosed résumé. I am familiar with the basic procedures of editing texts and photographs in both traditional and digital media, but my primary — Body interests lie in feature writing and landscape photography. My professional goal is to work as a photojournalist with an international focus, preferably for a major magazine. I cannot imagine a better introduction to that career than a summer at *World Discovery*.

I am available for an interview almost any time and can be reached at 301-555-2651. My e-mail address is jrichard@umdcp.edu.

I look forward to hearing from you.

Sincerely, ———— Close

Jeffrey Richardson ⎤—— Signature
Jeffrey Richardson

Enc.

A sample business letter appears on the previous page. This letter is typed in what is called *full block* style. All elements of the letter are lined up against the left margin, making for a clean, businesslike look. Paragraphs are not indented and an extra line of space is added between paragraphs.

Below the signature, the abbreviation *Enc.* indicates that something is enclosed with the letter. You can also use the abbreviation *cc* followed by a colon and the name of someone who is receiving a copy of the letter.

Résumés

An effective résumé gives relevant information in a clear and concise form. The trick is to present yourself in the best possible light without going on at length and wasting your reader's time.

When you send out your résumé, you should include a letter that tells what position you seek and where you learned about it (see p. 71). The letter should also summarize your education and past experience, relating them to the job you are applying for. End the letter with a suggestion for a meeting, and tell your prospective employer when you will be available.

You may be asked to produce a traditional résumé, a scannable résumé, or a Web résumé. Brief guidelines for each type of résumé appear in this section.

TRADITIONAL RÉSUMÉS Traditional résumés are written on paper, and they are screened by people, not by computers. Because screening committees may face stacks of applications, they often spend very little time looking at each résumé. Therefore you will need to make your résumé as reader-friendly as possible. Here are a few guidelines to follow:

— Limit your résumé to one page if possible, two pages at the most.

— Organize your information into clear categories — Education, Experience, and so on.

— Present your educational and work experience in reverse chronological order to highlight your most recent accomplishments.

— Use bullets to draw the reader's eye to listed information.

— Use strong, active verbs to emphasize your accomplishments. (Use present-tense verbs, such as *manage*, for current activities and past-tense verbs, such as *managed*, for past activities.)

A sample traditional résumé appears below.

TRADITIONAL RÉSUMÉ

Jeffrey Richardson
121 Knox Road, #6
College Park, MD 20740
301-555-2651
jrichard@umdcp.edu

OBJECTIVE   To obtain an editorial internship with a magazine

EDUCATION
Fall 1998 –   University of Maryland
present   • B.A. expected in June 2002
                       • Double major: English and Latin American studies
                       • GPA: 3.7 (on a 4-point scale)

EXPERIENCE
Fall 1999–   Photo editor, *The Diamondback*, college paper
present   • Shoot and print photographs
                       • Select and lay out photographs and other visuals

Summer   Intern, *The Globe*, Fairfax, Virginia
2000   • Wrote stories about local issues and personalities
                       • Interviewed political candidates
                       • Edited and proofread copy
                       • Contributed photographs
                       • Coedited "The Landscapes of Northern Virginia:
                         A Photoessay"

Summers   Tutor, Fairfax County ESL Program
1999, 2000   • Tutored Latino students in English as a Second Language
                       • Trained new tutors

ACTIVITIES   Photographers' Workshop, Spanish Club

REFERENCES   Available upon request

SCANNABLE RÉSUMÉS Scannable résumés are submitted on paper or via e-mail. The prospective employer puts the résumé through a scanner that enters the information from it into a database; the database matches keywords in a job description with keywords in the résumé. If a résumé survives the initial scan, it will later be reviewed by human beings. A scannable résumé must be very simply formatted so that the scanner can accurately pick up its content. In general, follow these guidelines when preparing a scannable résumé:

— Begin the résumé with standard headings (for example, Education, Experience, References), each followed by appropriate information.

— After the standard information, add the heading Keywords and then list words that match your experience to the job description. Use nouns, such as *manager,* not verbs, such as *manage* or *managed.*

— Do not use graphic devices such as boldface or italics. To indicate italics, use an underscore before and after italicized words.

— Do not use word processor formatting, such as tabbed indents, columns, or bullets. Do not insert visuals.

— Use white, 8½" × 11" paper and a laser or an ink-jet printer. Avoid folding or stapling the document.

WEB RÉSUMÉS A Web résumé makes it easy to provide prospective employers with recent information about your employment goals and accomplishments. It also allows you to present a number of details about yourself without overwhelming your readers. You can keep your opening screen simple and provide hyperlinks to take readers farther down the page or to additional pages. Readers can follow up on links as they choose. Although Web résumés can vary considerably in scope and depth, you should generally adhere to the following guidelines:

— Put identifying information — your name, address, phone number, and e-mail address — at the top. Include a link to your e-mail address.

— Be as concise as possible on the opening screen.

— Place links to sections such as Education and Experience high enough on the screen that readers won't need to scroll to see them.

— Present traditional résumé information (key contact information and credentials) on a single, printable home page. Only supplementary materials, such as writing or design samples, should appear on linked internal pages.

— Include a Keywords section. Keywords allow potential employers to find your résumé using a database.

— Keep your résumé current, and list the date on which you last updated it.

ON THE WEB

To view Jeffrey Richardson's résumé in both scannable and Web formats, go to **dianahacker.com/rules**

and click on ▶ **Model Papers**
　　　　　　　▶ **Business Formats**

Memos

Business memos (short for *memorandums*) are a form of communication used within a company or organization. Usually brief and to the point, a memo reports information, makes a request, or recommends an action. The format of a memo, which varies from company to company, is designed for easy distribution, quick reading, and efficient filing.

Most memos display the date, the name of the recipient, the name of the sender, and the subject on separate lines at the top of the page. Many companies have preprinted forms for memos, and some word processing programs allow you to call up a memo template that prints standard memo lines — "To," "cc" (for others receiving a copy of the memo), "From," and "Subject" — at the top of the page.

Because readers of memos are busy people, you cannot assume that they will read your memo word for word. Therefore the subject line should describe the subject as clearly and concisely as possible, and the introductory paragraph should get right to the point. In addition, the body of the memo should be well organized and easy to scan. To promote scanning, use headings where possible and display any items that deserve special attention by setting them off from the text. A sample memo with headings and a displayed list appears on page 76.

BUSINESS MEMO

Commonwealth Press

MEMORANDUM

February 5, 2002

To: Production, promotion, and editorial assistants

cc: Stephen Chapman

From: Helen Brown

Subject: New computers for staff

We will receive the new personal computers next week for the assistants in production, promotion, and editorial. In preparation, I would like you to take part in a training program and to rearrange your work areas to accommodate the new equipment.

Training Program

A computer consultant will teach in-house workshops on how to use our spreadsheet program. If you have already tried the program, be prepared to discuss any problems you have encountered.

Workshops for our three departments will be held in the training room at the following times:

- Production: Monday, March 4, 10:00 a.m. to 2:00 p.m.
- Promotion: Wednesday, March 6, 10:00 a.m. to 2:00 p.m.
- Editorial: Friday, March 8, 10:00 a.m. to 2:00 p.m.

Lunch will be provided in the cafeteria. If you cannot attend, please let me know by March 1.

Allocation and Setup

To give everyone access to a computer, we will set up the new computers as follows: two in the assistants' workspace in production; two in the area outside the conference room for the promotion assistants; and two in the library for the editorial assistants.

Assistants in all three departments should see me before the end of the week to discuss preparation of the spaces for the new equipment.

7

Create effective electronic documents.

7a Follow the conventions of e-mail.

E-mail is fast replacing snail mail in the business world and in most people's personal lives. E-mail is also being used in the academic world for communication between professors and their students and among students in a class.

Especially in business and academic contexts, you will want to show readers of your e-mail that you value their time. Your message may be just one of many that your reader has to wade through. Here are some strategies that you can use to make your messages reader-friendly:

— Fill in the subject line with a meaningful, concise subject to help the reader sort through messages and set priorities.

— Put the most important part of your message where it will be seen on the first screen.

— For long, detailed messages, consider providing a summary at the beginning.

— Write concisely, and keep paragraphs fairly short, especially if your audience is likely to read your message on the screen. (In e-mails meant to be printed out, paragraphs can be somewhat longer.)

— Avoid writing in all capital letters or all lowercase letters, a practice that is easy on the writer but hard on the reader.

— Keep in mind that a recipient's e-mail system may not accept attachments. When possible, include the text of an attachment in the body of the e-mail.

— Proofread for typos and obvious errors that are likely to slow down or annoy the reader.

7b Create effective Web sites.

Web sites in the academic and business worlds are usually aimed at audiences looking for ideas and information, not entertainment. You may have noticed that the most effective informational Web sites give you quick and easy access to what you're looking for.

A Web site consists of a home page and any number of internal pages linked to the home page. Deciding what to put on the home page and how to organize internal pages can present a challenge. When making such crucial decisions, consider your readers' needs and expectations:

— Why are they visiting your site?

— What are they expecting to find?

— What is their level of interest?

— Do they plan to read on-screen or to print hard copy?

The design of your site — from its home page, to its structure, to its page layout and even its writing style — will depend on the answers to such questions.

The home page

A home page consists of text and visuals on an opening screen and any other material that can be reached by scrolling. Because many Web users will resist scrolling — at least initially — you will need to take advantage of the opening screen.

The opening screen of your home page should introduce visitors to the site, give them an overview of its contents, and show them that you have their needs (not your own agenda) in mind. It should also include navigational links, words or visual images that, at the click of the mouse, will send them to other locations or pages within the site. Usually these links are clustered together — often along the top of the screen or on one side — leaving room in the center for the name of the author or sponsor, the title, a relevant visual or two, and an indication of the purpose of the site. The example on page 79 illustrates a well-designed opening screen; the site sponsors community service and teaching internships for students.

SAMPLE HOME PAGE

The sponsoring organization and purpose of the site are clearly defined at the top of the page.

By highlighting the main audiences for the site, this home page allows readers to skip information that is not relevant to their search.

Appealing visual images emphasize the site's three main audiences.

Links to internal pages are consistently placed on the left side of the screen and in the footer to help readers navigate the site.

Structure and navigation

Web sites consisting of more than one page usually have hierarchical structures: General pages link to more specific pages, which in turn may link to even more specific pages. Following is an example of a Web site structure for a chain of fitness centers.

SAMPLE WEB SITE STRUCTURE

How shallow or how deep should your hierarchy be? In other words, how many levels make sense? The answer depends on the complexity of your material and your audience's needs, but two cautions are in order. A structure is too shallow if your readers must deal with long "laundry lists" of choices (unless they can be arranged alphabetically or by date). A structure is too deep if readers are needlessly forced to drill down through several layers of your hierarchy to reach what they need.

Visitors to your site will navigate it in different ways, depending on their interests. They will choose some links and ignore others, landing on internal pages in an order that you can't predict. Indeed, some visitors may arrive at one of your internal pages without having gone through your home page. Because of this unpredictability, provide as much context as possible for each internal page:

— Put key information on each internal page: a title, a link to the home page, and perhaps a list of links to other pages (such lists create context by outlining the site).

— Provide a brief overview that puts the internal page in context; make sure the content of the page can be understood on its own.

— Repeat design elements so that visitors will feel at home: Place navigational aids consistently, and use consistent background colors, fonts, visual motifs, and formatting.

In addition to providing links within your site, you may want to link to other sites. When you decide that an external link enhances the message of your site, create some context for it so that visitors will understand why it is worthwhile and what to expect if they follow it. Because a link to another site is an implicit endorsement of that site, you should evaluate potential sites before linking to them. Also, check your links to external sites periodically to make sure the sites are still functioning.

Page layout and writing style

Don't expect Web site visitors to read in the traditional way: word by word. Most will scan your site, looking for information of interest and ignoring the rest. To keep the attention of a Web audience, make your page layout and writing style as user-friendly as possible.

EXCEPTION: If content on your site is scholarly work meant to be printed out, you can assume that your audience is motivated to read, not just to scan. Even so, visitors will appreciate a reader-friendly page layout and writing style.

PAGE LAYOUT To promote easy scanning, break up your text with headings and displayed lists and, when appropriate, display information with graphics such as clip art, photos, and charts. (See 5b–5d.)

Some common design practices make a site needlessly hard to read. If you are an experienced Web user, you no doubt could have written the following advice:

— Don't stretch lines of text across the full width of the screen. The readers' eye gets lost as it swoops from line to line.

— Limit page width so that readers don't need to scroll sideways.

— Avoid ALL CAPS or *all italic* text. It slows readers down.

— Steer clear of busy backgrounds that make the print illegible.

— Avoid nonstop animations. They are distracting.

Graphics and other media, such as films and sound clips, can enhance a Web site, but they should be used thoughtfully — to support your message. If you've used a lot of graphics, provide a printable version of your text without the graphics; graphics can be slow to load and print and may be irrelevant for your readers' purposes.

WRITING STYLE   Visitors to your Web site value their time. As a rule, they want concise, factual information that they can understand right away. For example, they expect to learn the key idea of a paragraph in its first sentence; if it's not there, they may well move on. They also prefer sentences that waste no words; a verbose, pseudointellectual style will send them elsewhere.

Web users are also sensitive to tone. There is so much promotional hype on the Web that many users have a keen ear for it. The tone of your site will vary, of course, depending on your purpose and audience, but in general aim for an objective — not a promotional — tone.

PROMOTIONAL

Our site tells you everything you want to know about hang gliding! Check out our awesome video clips and click on links to the coolest sites on the Web.

OBJECTIVE

Whether you're a beginning hang glider or a seasoned flier, this site will show you how and where to glide. Visit our Video Window for an animated bird's-eye view.

An objective tone enhances your credibility and makes it likely that readers will trust you enough to stay with you.

ON THE WEB

For links to advice about document design, go to
dianahacker.com/rules

and click on   ▶ **Links Library**
              ▶ **Document Design**

Clarity

Process

Design

Clarity

Grammar

Punctuation

Mechanics

Argument

Research

Basics

8

Prefer active verbs.

As a rule, choose an active verb and pair it with a subject that names the person or thing doing the action. Active verbs express meaning more emphatically and vigorously than their weaker counterparts — forms of the verb *be* or verbs in the passive voice.

PASSIVE   The pumps *were destroyed* by a surge of power.

BE VERB   A surge of power *was* responsible for the destruction of the pumps.

ACTIVE   A surge of power *destroyed* the pumps.

Verbs in the passive voice lack strength because their subjects receive the action instead of doing it. Forms of the verb *be* (*be, am, is, are, was, were, being, been*) lack vigor because they convey no action.

Although passive verbs and forms of *be* have legitimate uses, if an active verb can carry your meaning, use it. Even among active verbs, some are more active — and therefore more vigorous and colorful — than others. Carefully selected verbs can energize a piece of writing.

>   *swept*   *hooked*
> ▶ **The goalie crouched low, ~~reached~~ out his stick, and ~~sent~~ the**
>   ^   ^
> **rebound away from the mouth of the net.**

Some multilingual speakers avoid the passive voice even when it is appropriate. For advice on transforming an active sentence **ESL** to the passive, see 62c.

GRAMMAR CHECKERS are fairly good at flagging passive verbs, such as *were given*. However, because passive verbs are sometimes appropriate, you — not the computer program — must decide whether to make a passive verb active.

8a Use the active voice unless you have a good reason for choosing the passive.

In the active voice, the subject does the action; in the passive voice, the subject receives the action (see also 62c). Although both voices are grammatically correct, the active voice is usually more effective because it is simpler and more direct.

ACTIVE Hernando *caught* the fly ball.

PASSIVE The fly ball *was caught* by Hernando.

In passive sentences, the actor (in this case Hernando) frequently disappears from the sentence: *The fly ball was caught.*

In most cases, you will want to emphasize the actor, so you should use the active voice. To replace a passive verb with an active alternative, make the actor the subject of the sentence.

▶ ~~The transformer was struck by a bolt of lightning~~, plunging us
  A bolt of lightning struck the transformer,
into darkness.

The active verb (*struck*) makes the point more forcefully than the passive verb (*was struck*).

▶ ~~The land was stripped of timber before the settlers realized~~
  The settlers stripped the land of timber before realizing the
the consequences of their actions.

The revision emphasizes the actors (*settlers*) by naming them in the subject.

▶ ~~The~~ Christmas decorations ~~were not taken~~ down until
  We did not take down the
Valentine's Day.

Often the actor does not appear in a passive-voice sentence. To turn such a sentence into the active voice, the writer must decide on an appropriate subject, in this case *We*.

Appropriate uses of the passive

The passive voice is appropriate if you wish to emphasize the receiver of the action or to minimize the importance of the actor.

APPROPRIATE **PASSIVE**	Many native Hawaiians *are forced* to leave their beautiful beaches to make room for hotels and condominiums.
APPROPRIATE **PASSIVE**	As the time for harvest approaches, the tobacco plants *are sprayed* with a chemical to retard the growth of suckers.

The writer of the first sentence wished to emphasize the receiver of the action, *Hawaiians.* The writer of the second sentence wished to focus on the tobacco plants, not on the people spraying them.

In much scientific writing, the passive voice properly emphasizes the experiment or process being described, not the researcher.

APPROPRIATE **PASSIVE**	The solution *was heated* to the boiling point, and then it *was reduced* in volume by 50 percent.

ON THE WEB

Rules on avoiding the passive voice have sparked debates. If you're interested in learning why, go to **dianahacker.com/rules**

and click on ▶ **Language Debates**
                ▶ **Passive voice**

8b   Replace *be* verbs that result in dull or wordy sentences.

Not every *be* verb needs replacing. The forms of *be* (*be, am, is, are, was, were, being, been*) work well when you want to link a subject to a noun that clearly renames it or to an adjective that describes it: *History is a bucket of ashes. Scoundrels are always sociable.* And when used as helping verbs before present participles (*is flying, are disappearing*) to express ongoing action, *be* verbs are fine: *Derrick was plowing the field when his wife went into labor.* (See 29a.)

If using a *be* verb makes a sentence needlessly dull and wordy, however, consider replacing it. Often a phrase following the verb will contain a word (such as *violation*) that suggests a more vigorous, active alternative (*violate*).

violate
▶ Burying nuclear waste in Antarctica would be in violation of
                                                  ^
an international treaty.

Violate is less wordy and more vigorous than *be in violation of.*

resisted
▶ When Rosa Parks was resistant to giving up her seat on the
                          ^
bus, she became a civil rights hero.

Resisted is stronger than *was resistant to.*

EXERCISE 8–1

Revise any weak, unemphatic sentences by replacing *be* verbs or passive verbs with active alternatives. Some sentences are emphatic; do not change them. Revisions of lettered sentences appear in the back of the book. Example:

The ranger doused the campfire before giving us
The campfire was doused by the ranger before we were given
^
a ticket for unauthorized use of a campsite.

a. The Prussians were victorious over the Saxons in 1745.
b. The entire operation is managed by Ahmed, the producer.
c. Yellow flags were thrown down by all the referees.
d. At the crack of rocket and mortar blasts, I jumped from the top bunk and landed on my buddy below, who was crawling on the floor looking for his boots.
e. There were shouting protesters on the courthouse steps.

1. Just as the police were closing in, two shots were fired by the terrorists from the roof of the hotel.
2. Her letter was in acknowledgment of the student's participation in the literacy program.
3. The bomb bay doors rumbled open and freezing air whipped through the plane.
4. Listening to the music of Charlie Parker and John Coltrane was my motivation to take up the saxophone.
5. The only responsibility I was given by my parents was putting gas in the brand-new Mitsubishi they bought me my senior year.

ON THE WEB

For electronic exercises on using active verbs, go to
dianahacker.com/rules

and click on   ▶ **Electronic Grammar Exercises**
                 ▶ **Clarity**
                         ▶ **E-ex 8-1 through 8-3**

9

Balance parallel ideas.

If two or more ideas are parallel, they are easier to grasp when expressed in parallel grammatical form. Single words should be balanced with single words, phrases with phrases, clauses with clauses.

> A kiss can be a comma, a question mark, or an exclamation point.   — Mistinguett

> This novel is not to be tossed lightly aside, but to be hurled with great force.   — Dorothy Parker

> In matters of principle, stand like a rock; in matters of taste, swim with the current.   — Thomas Jefferson

Writers often use parallelism to create emphasis. (See p. 126.)

GRAMMAR CHECKERS do not flag faulty parallelism. Because computer programs have no way of assessing whether two or more ideas are parallel in meaning, they fail to catch the faulty parallelism in sentences such as this: *In my high school, boys were either jocks, preppies, or studied constantly.*

9a Balance parallel ideas in a series.

Readers expect items in a series to appear in parallel grammatical form. When one or more of the items violate readers' expectations, a sentence will be needlessly awkward.

▶ **Abused children commonly exhibit one or more of the follow-**

ing symptoms: withdrawal, rebelliousness, restlessness, and
depression.
~~they are depressed.~~
^

The revision presents all of the items as nouns.

▶ **Hooked on romance novels, I learned that there is nothing**

having
more important than being rich, looking good, and ~~to have~~
^

a good time.

The revision uses *-ing* forms for all items in the series.

▶ **After assuring us that he was sober, Sam drove down the**

went through
middle of the road, ran one red light, and ~~two stop signs.~~
^

The revision adds a verb to make the three items parallel:
drove . . . , ran . . . , went through. . . .

NOTE: In headings and lists, aim for as much parallelism as the content allows. (See 5b and 5c.)

9b Balance parallel ideas presented as pairs.

When pairing ideas, underscore their connection by expressing them in similar grammatical form. Paired ideas are usually connected in one of these ways:

— with a coordinating conjunction such as *and, but,* or *or*
— with a pair of correlative conjunctions such as *either . . . or* or *not only . . . but also*
— with a word introducing a comparison, usually *than* or *as*

Parallel ideas linked with coordinating conjunctions

Coordinating conjunctions (*and, but, or, nor, for, so,* and *yet*) link ideas of equal importance. When those ideas are closely parallel in content, they should be expressed in parallel grammatical form.

▶ At Lincoln High School, vandalism can result in suspension
   expulsion
   or even ~~being expelled~~ from school.
          ^

The revision balances the nouns *suspension* and *expulsion*.

▶ Many states are reducing property taxes for home owners
   extending
   and ~~extend~~ financial aid in the form of tax credits to renters.
       ^

The revision balances two *-ing* verb forms: *reducing* and *extending*.

Parallel ideas linked with correlative conjunctions

Correlative conjunctions come in pairs: *either . . . or, neither . . . nor, not only . . . but also, both . . . and, whether . . . or.* Make sure that the grammatical structure following the second half of the pair is the same as that following the first half.

▶ Thomas Edison was not only a prolific inventor but also ~~was~~ a

   successful entrepreneur.

The words *a prolific inventor* follow *not only,* so *a successful entrepreneur* should follow *but also.* Repeating *was* creates an unbalanced effect.

                                            to
▶ I was advised either to change my flight or ~~take~~ the train.
                                              ^

To change my flight, which follows *either,* should be balanced with *to take the train,* which follows *or.*

Comparisons linked with *than* or *as*

In comparisons linked with *than* or *as,* the elements being compared should be expressed in parallel grammatical structure.

▶ It is easier to speak in abstractions than ~~grounding~~ one's
          to ground
                 ^

thoughts in reality.

▶ Mother could not persuade me that giving is as much a joy as
   receiving.
   ~~to receive.~~
   ^

   To speak in abstractions is balanced with *to ground one's thoughts in reality. Giving* is balanced with *receiving.*

NOTE: Comparisons should also be logical and complete. (See 10c.)

9c Repeat function words to clarify parallels.

Function words such as prepositions (*by, to*) and subordinating conjunctions (*that, because*) signal the grammatical nature of the word groups to follow. Although they can sometimes be omitted, include them whenever they signal parallel structures that might otherwise be missed by readers.

▶ Many smokers try switching to a brand they find distasteful
   to
   or a low tar and nicotine cigarette.
   ^

   In the original sentence the prepositional phrase was too complex for easy reading. The repetition of the preposition *to* prevents readers from losing their way.

EXERCISE 9–1

Edit the following sentences to correct faulty parallelism. Revisions of lettered sentences appear in the back of the book. Example:

   We began the search by calling the Department of Social
                       requesting
   Services and ~~requested~~ a list of licensed day care centers in
                ^

   our area.

a. Police dogs are used for finding lost children, tracking criminals, and the detection of bombs and illegal drugs.
b. Roger explained to the immigration officer that his visa had expired and of his applying to have it renewed.
c. It is more difficult to sustain an exercise program than starting one.
d. During basic training, I was not only told what to do but also what to think.
e. Jan wanted to drive to the wine country or at least Sausalito.

1. Activities on Wednesday afternoons include fishing trips, computer training, and learning to dance.
2. Tony found that it was faster to ride his bike than driving into the city.
3. The streets were not only too steep but also were too narrow for anything other than pedestrian traffic.
4. More plants fail from improper watering than any other cause.
5. The winner of the gluttony contest swallowed six large pancakes, slurped down a cream pie, gobbled six waffles, and four pastries.

ON THE WEB

For electronic exercises on parallelism, go to
dianahacker.com/rules

and click on ▶ **Electronic Grammar Exercises**
▶ **Clarity**
▶ **E-ex 9–1 through 9–3**

10

Add needed words.

Do not omit words necessary for grammatical or logical completeness. Readers need to see at a glance how the parts of a sentence are connected.

ESL Languages sometimes differ in the need for certain words. In particular, be alert for missing verbs, articles, subjects, or expletives. See 29e, 30, and 31a.

GRAMMAR CHECKERS do not flag the vast majority of missing words. They can, however, catch some missing verbs (see 27e). Although they can flag some missing articles (*a, an,* and *the*), they often suggest that an article is missing when in fact it is not. (See also 30.)

10a Add words needed to complete compound structures.

In compound structures, words are often omitted for economy: *Tom is a man who means what he says and [who] says what he means.* Such omissions are perfectly acceptable as long as the omitted words are common to both parts of the compound structure.

If the shorter version defies grammar or idiom because an omitted word is not common to both parts of the compound structure, the word must be put back in.

▶ Some of the regulars are acquaintances whom we see at work
  who
or live in our community.
  ^

The word *who* must be included because *whom . . . live in our community* is not grammatically correct.

                   accepted
▶ Mayor Davis never has and never will accept a bribe.
                          ^

Has . . . accept is not grammatically correct.

                                        in
▶ Many South Pacific islanders still believe and live by ancient
                                           ^
laws.

Believe . . . by is not idiomatic in English. (For a list of common idioms, see 18d.)

10b Add the word *that* if there is any danger of misreading without it.

If there is no danger of misreading, the word *that* may be omitted when it introduces a subordinate clause. *The value of a principle is the number of things [that] it will explain.* Occasionally, however, a sentence might be misread without *that.*

▶ Looking out the family room window, Sarah saw her favorite
^{that}^
tree, which she had climbed so often as a child, was gone.

Sarah didn't see the tree; she saw that the tree was gone.

10c Add words needed to make comparisons logical and complete.

Comparisons should be made between items that are alike. To compare unlike items is illogical and distracting.

▶ The forests of North America are much more extensive than
those of
Europe.
^
Forests must be compared with forests.

Our *graduate at a higher rate*
▶ ~~The graduation rate of our~~ student athletes ~~is higher~~ than the
^ ^
rest of the student population.

A rate cannot logically be compared with a population. The writer could revise the sentence by inserting *that of* after *than,* but the preceding revision is more concise.

▶ Some say that Ella Fitzgerald's renditions of Cole Porter's
singer's.
songs are better than any other ~~singer.~~
^

Ella Fitzgerald's renditions cannot logically be compared with a singer. The revision uses the possessive form *singer's,* with the word *renditions* implied.

Sometimes the word *other* must be inserted to make a comparison logical.

                                  other

▶ Jupiter is larger than any planet in our solar system.

Jupiter cannot be larger than itself.

Sometimes the word *as* must be inserted to make a comparison grammatically complete.

                                  as

▶ The city of Lowell is as old, if not older than, the neighboring

city of Lawrence.

The construction *as old* is not complete without a second *as: as old as . . . the neighboring city of Lawrence.*

Finally, comparisons should be complete enough to ensure clarity. The reader should understand what is being compared.

    INCOMPLETE   Brand X is less salty.

    COMPLETE   Brand X is less salty than Brand Y.

Also, there should be no ambiguity. In the following sentence, two interpretations are possible.

    AMBIGUOUS   Ken helped me more than my roommate.

    CLEAR   Ken helped me more than *he helped* my
                    roommate.

    CLEAR   Ken helped me more than my roommate *did.*

10d Add the articles *a, an,* and *the* where necessary for grammatical completeness.

Articles are sometimes omitted in recipes and other instructions that are meant to be followed while they are being read. Such omissions are inappropriate, however, in nearly all other forms of writing, whether formal or informal.

>   *a*   *an*
> Blood can be drawn only by doctor or by authorized person
>   *the* ^   ^
> who has been trained in procedure.
>   ^

It is not always necessary to repeat articles with paired items: *We bought a computer and printer.* However, if one of the items requires *a* and the other requires *an,* both articles must be included.

>   *an*
> We bought a computer and ink-jet printer.
>   ^

Articles can cause special problems for multilingual speakers. See 30.

ESL

EXERCISE 10–1

Add any words needed for grammatical or logical completeness in the following sentences. Revisions of lettered sentences appear in the back of the book. Example:

>   *that*
> The officer at the desk feared the prisoner in the interroga-
>   ^
> tion room would escape.

  a. A good source of vitamin C is a grapefruit or orange.
  b. The women entering VMI can expect haircuts as short as the male cadets.
  c. The driver went to investigate, only to find one of the supposedly new tires had blown.
  d. Most of the spectators were unhappy and angered by the decision.
  e. Reefs are home to more species than any ecosystem in the sea.

  1. Very few black doctors were allowed to serve in the Civil War, and their qualifications had to be higher than white doctors.
  2. Producers of violent video games are not capable or interested in regulating themselves.
  3. David's cat Machiavelli likes me more than his master.
  4. The inspection team saw many historic old buildings had been damaged by the earthquake.
  5. American English has borrowed more words from Spanish than from any language.

ON THE WEB

For electronic exercises on adding needed words, go to
dianahacker.com/rules

and click on ▶ **Electronic Grammar Exercises**
▶ **Clarity**
▶ **E-ex 10-1 and 10-2**

11

Untangle mixed constructions.

A mixed construction contains parts that do not sensibly fit together. The mismatch may be a matter of grammar or of logic.

> GRAMMAR CHECKERS can flag *is when, is where,* and *reason . . . is because* constructions (11c), but they fail to identify nearly all other mixed constructions, including sentences as tangled as this one: *Depending on the number and strength of drinks, the amount of time that has passed, and one's body weight determines the concentration of alcohol in the blood.*

11a Untangle the grammatical structure.

Once you head into a sentence, your choices are limited by the range of grammatical patterns in English. (See 62 and 63.) You cannot begin with one grammatical plan and switch without warning to another.

MIXED   For most drivers who have a blood alcohol
         content of .05 percent double their risk of causing
         an accident.

REVISED For most drivers who have a blood alcohol
         content of .05 percent, the risk of causing an accident
         is doubled.

> **REVISED** Most drivers who have a blood alcohol content
> of .05 percent double their risk of causing an
> accident.

The writer began with a long prepositional phrase that was destined to be a modifier but then tried to press it into service as the subject of the sentence. This cannot be done. If the sentence is to begin with the prepositional phrase, the writer must finish the sentence with a subject and verb (*risk . . . is doubled*). The writer who wishes to stay with the original verb (*double*) must head into the sentence another way: *Most drivers. . . .*

▶   *Being*
    ~~When an employee is~~ promoted without warning can be
    ^

alarming.

The adverb clause *When an employee is promoted without warning* cannot serve as the subject of the sentence. The revision replaces the adverb clause with a gerund phrase, a word group that can function as the subject. (See 63b and 63c.)

▶ Although the United States is one of the wealthiest nations

in the world, ~~but~~ almost 20 percent of our children live in

poverty.

The *Although* clause is subordinate, so it cannot be linked to an independent clause with the coordinating conjunction *but*.

Occasionally a mixed construction is so tangled that it defies grammatical analysis. When this happens, back away from the sentence, rethink what you want to say, and then say it again as clearly as you can.

> **MIXED** In the whole-word method children learn to recognize
> entire words rather than by the phonics method in
> which they learn to sound out letters and groups of
> letters.

> **REVISED** The whole-word method teaches children to recognize
> entire words; the phonics method teaches them to
> sound out letters and groups of letters.

ESL

English does not allow repeated subjects; nor does it allow an object or an adverb to be repeated in an adjective clause. See 31b and 31c.

▶ The squirrel that came down our chimney ~~it~~ did much damage.

▶ Hearing screams, Serena ran over to the pool that her daughter was swimming in. ~~it.~~
                                                        ^

11b Straighten out the logical connections.

The subject and the predicate should make sense together; when they don't, the error is known as *faulty predication*.

                     Tiffany
▶ We decided that ~~Tiffany's welfare~~ would not be safe living
                           ^

with her mother.

Tiffany, not her welfare, may not be safe.

                              double personal exemption for the
▶ Under the revised plan, the elderly,/ ~~who now receive a~~
                                      ^

~~double personal exemption,~~ will be abolished.

The exemption, not the elderly, will be abolished.

An appositive and the noun to which it refers should be logically equivalent. When they are not, the error is known as *faulty apposition*.

   Tax accounting,
▶ ~~The tax accountant,~~ a very lucrative field, requires
  ^

intelligence, patience, and attention to mathematical

detail.

The tax accountant is a person, not a field.

11c Avoid *is when, is where,* and *reason . . . is because* constructions.

In formal English many readers object to *is when, is where,* and *reason . . . is because* constructions on either grammatical or logical grounds. Grammatically, the verb *is* (as well as *are, was,* and *were*) should be followed by a noun that renames the subject or by an adjective that describes it, not by an adverb clause beginning with *when, where,* or *because.* (See 62b and 63b.) Logically, the words *when, where,* and *because* suggest relations of time, place, and cause — relations that do not always make sense with *is, was,* or *were.*

> *a disorder suffered by people who,*
▶ Anorexia nervosa is ~~where people,~~ believing they are too fat,
⌃
  diet to the point of starvation.

Anorexia nervosa is a disorder, not a place.

▶ ~~The reason~~ I missed the exam ~~is~~ because my motorcycle

  broke down.

The writer might have changed *because* to *that* (*The reason I missed the exam is that my motorcycle broke down*), but the revision above is more concise.

EXERCISE 11–1

Edit the following sentences to untangle mixed constructions. Revisions of lettered sentences appear in the back of the book. Example:

> *L*
> ~~By~~ ∫oosening the soil around your jade plant will help the air
>
> and nutrients penetrate to the roots.

a. Using surgical gloves is a precaution now worn by dentists to prevent contact with patients' blood and saliva.
b. A physician, the career my brother is pursuing, requires at least ten years of challenging work.
c. The reason the pharaohs had bad teeth was because tiny particles of sand found their way into Egyptian bread.

d. The change in quality of service has worsened each year.
e. In this box contains the key to your future.

1. Early diagnosis of prostate cancer is often curable.
2. Depending on the number and strength of drinks, the amount of time that has passed since the last drink, and one's body weight determines the concentration of alcohol in the blood.
3. Dyslexia is where people have a learning disorder that impairs reading ability.
4. Even though Ellen had heard French spoken all her life, yet she could not speak it.
5. By obtaining the correct form is the first step in the application process.

ON THE WEB

For electronic exercises on mixed constructions, go to
dianahacker.com/rules

and click on ▶ **Electronic Grammar Exercises**
▶ **Clarity**
▶ **E-ex 11-1 and 11-2**

12

Repair misplaced and dangling modifiers.

Modifiers, whether they are single words, phrases, or clauses, should point clearly to the words they modify. As a rule, related words should be kept together.

 GRAMMAR CHECKERS can flag split infinitives, such as *to carefully and thoroughly sift* (12d). However, they don't alert you to other misplaced modifiers or dangling modifiers, including danglers like this one: *When a young man, my mother enrolled me in tap dance classes, hoping I would become the next Gregory Hines.*

Clarity

12a Put limiting modifiers in front of the words they modify.

Limiting modifiers such as *only, even, almost, nearly,* and *just* should appear in front of a verb only if they modify the verb: *At first, I couldn't even touch my toes, much less grasp them.* If they limit the meaning of some other word in the sentence, they should be placed in front of that word.

► Lasers ~~only~~ destroy the target, leaving the surrounding

   only (above "destroy")

healthy tissue intact.

Only limits the meaning of *the target,* not *destroy.*

► The turtle ~~only~~ makes progress when it sticks its neck out.

   only (above "progress")

Only limits the meaning of the *when* clause.

The limiting modifier *not* is frequently misplaced, suggesting a meaning the writer did not intend.

► In the United States in 1860, all black southerners were ~~not~~

   not (above)

slaves.

The original sentence says that no black southerners were slaves. The revision makes the writer's real meaning clear: Some (but not all) black southerners were slaves.

12b Place phrases and clauses so that readers can see at a glance what they modify.

Although phrases and clauses can appear at some distance from the words they modify, make sure your meaning is clear. When phrases or clauses are oddly placed, absurd misreadings can result.

MISPLACED   The king returned to the clinic where he had undergone heart surgery in 2000 in a limousine sent by the White House.

REVISED Traveling in a limousine sent by the White House, the king returned to the clinic where he had undergone heart surgery in 2000.

The revision corrects the false impression that the king underwent heart surgery in a limousine.

▶ ~~There~~ are many pictures of comedians who have performed
   On the walls
   ^

at Gavin's. ~~on the walls.~~
          ^

The comedians weren't performing on the walls; the pictures were on the walls.

▶ The robber was described as a six-foot-tall man with a heavy
   150-pound,

mustache. ~~weighing 150 pounds.~~
        ^

The robber, not the mustache, weighed 150 pounds.

Occasionally the placement of a modifier leads to an ambiguity, in which case two revisions will be possible, depending on the writer's intended meaning.

AMBIGUOUS The exchange students we met for coffee occasionally questioned us about our latest slang.

CLEAR The exchange students we occasionally met for coffee questioned us about our latest slang.

CLEAR The exchange students we met for coffee questioned us occasionally about our latest slang.

In the original version, it was not clear whether the meeting or the questioning happened occasionally. The revisions eliminate the ambiguity.

12c Move awkwardly placed modifiers.

As a rule, a sentence should flow from subject to verb to object, without lengthy detours along the way. When a long adverbial element separates a subject from its verb, a verb from its object, or a helping verb from its main verb, the result is often awkward.

▶ ~~Hong Kong,~~ ⌃^A after more than 150 years of British rule, was   ^{Hong Kong}⌃

transferred back to Chinese control in 1997.

There is no reason to separate the subject, *Hong Kong,* from the verb, *was transferred,* with a long phrase.

EXCEPTION: Occasionally a writer may choose to delay a verb or an object to create suspense. In the following passage, for example, Robert Mueller inserts the *after* phrase between the subject *women* and the verb *walk* to heighten the dramatic effect.

> I asked a Burmese why women, after centuries of following their men, now walk ahead. He said there were many unexploded land mines since the war.   — Robert Mueller

---

ESL

English does not allow an adverb to appear between a verb and its object. See 31d.

▶ Yolanda lifted ~~easily~~ the fifty-pound weight⌄/   ^{*easily.*}

12d   Avoid split infinitives when they are awkward.

An infinitive consists of *to* plus a verb: *to think, to breathe, to dance.* When a modifier appears between *to* and the verb, an infinitive is said to be "split": *to carefully balance.*

    When a long word or a phrase appears between the parts of the infinitive, the result is usually awkward.

▶ ~~The~~ patient should try to ~~if possible~~ avoid going up and down ⌃^{*If possible, the*}

stairs.

    Attempts to avoid split infinitives can result in equally awkward sentences. When alternative phrasing sounds unnatural, most experts allow — and even encourage — splitting the infinitive.

AWKWARD We decided actually to enforce the law.

BETTER We decided to actually enforce the law.

At times, neither the split infinitive nor its alternative sounds particularly awkward. In such situations, you may want to unsplit the infinitive, especially in formal writing.

formally.
► The candidate decided to ~~formally~~ launch her campaign./
                                                        ^

ON THE WEB

The rules on avoiding split infinitives have sparked debates. If you are interested in learning why, go to **dianahacker.com/rules**

and click on ► **Language Debates**
              ► **Split infinitives**

EXERCISE 12–1

Edit the following sentences to correct misplaced or awkwardly placed modifiers. Revisions of lettered sentences appear in the back of the book. Example:

in a telephone survey
Answering questions can be annoying. ~~in a telephone survey.~~
                                   ^   ^

a. Our English professor asked us to very carefully reread the sonnet, looking for subtleties we had missed on a first reading.
b. The monarch arrived in a gold carriage at the gate pulled by four white horses.
c. By afternoon, Sam had almost painted the entire dining room.
d. Coronado, after being appointed leader of the expeditionary force by the Spanish viceroy, spent his time recruiting volunteers for the adventure.
e. All fresh vegetables are not salt free.

1. Carlos sat solemnly and didn't even smile once during the comedy.
2. The orderly confessed that he had given a lethal injection to the patient after ten hours of grilling by the police.
3. Several recent studies have encouraged heart patients to more carefully watch their cholesterol levels.
4. The recordings were all done at the studio of the late Jimi Hendrix named Electric Ladyland.
5. The old Marlboro ads depicted a man on a horse smoking a cigarette.

12e Repair dangling modifiers.

A dangling modifier fails to refer logically to any word in the sentence. Dangling modifiers are easy to repair, but they can be hard to recognize, especially in your own writing.

Recognizing dangling modifiers

Dangling modifiers are usually word groups (such as verbal phrases) that suggest but do not name an actor. When a sentence opens with such a modifier, readers expect the subject of the next clause to name the actor. If it doesn't, the modifier dangles.

▶ *When the driver opened*
~~Opening~~ the window to let out a huge bumblebee, the car
  ^

accidentally swerved into an oncoming car.

The car didn't open the window; the driver did.

women have often been denied
▶ After completing seminary training, ~~women's~~ access to the
                                              ^

pulpit. ~~has often been denied.~~
       ^

The women (not their access to the pulpit) complete the training.

The following sentences illustrate four common kinds of dangling modifiers.

DANGLING   *Deciding to join the navy,* the recruiter enthusiastically pumped Joe's hand. [Participial phrase]

DANGLING   *Upon entering the doctor's office,* a skeleton caught my attention. [Preposition followed by a gerund phrase]

DANGLING   *To please the children,* some fireworks were set off a day early. [Infinitive phrase]

DANGLING   *Though only sixteen,* UCLA accepted Martha's application. [Elliptical clause with an understood subject and verb]

These dangling modifiers falsely suggest that the recruiter decided to join the navy, that the skeleton entered the doctor's office, that the fireworks intended to please the children, and that UCLA is only sixteen years old.

Although most readers will understand the writer's intended meaning in such sentences, the inadvertent humor can be distracting, and it can make the writer appear somewhat foolish.

ON THE WEB

The rules on avoiding dangling modifiers have sparked debates. If you're interested in learning why, go to **dianahacker.com/rules**

and click on ▶ **Language Debates**
▶ **Dangling modifiers**

Repairing dangling modifiers

To repair a dangling modifier, you can revise the sentence in one of two ways:

1. Name the actor in the subject of the sentence, or
2. name the actor in the modifier.

Depending on your sentence, one of these revision strategies may be more appropriate than the other.

ACTOR NAMED IN SUBJECT

▶ Upon entering the doctor's office, a skeleton. ~~caught my~~
        I noticed

~~attention.~~

▶ To please the children, some fireworks ~~were set off~~ early.
        we set off

ACTOR NAMED IN MODIFIER

▶ ~~Deciding~~ to join the navy, the recruiter enthusiastically
   When Joe decided

pumped ~~Joe's~~ hand.
         his

> Though only sixteen, UCLA accepted ~~Martha's~~ application.
> *Martha was* *her*
> ⌃ ⌃

NOTE: You cannot repair a dangling modifier just by moving it. Consider, for example, the sentence about the skeleton. If you put the modifier at the end of the sentence (*A skeleton caught my attention upon entering the doctor's office*), you are still suggesting—absurdly, of course—that the skeleton entered the office. The only way to avoid the problem is to put the word *I* in the sentence, either as the subject or in the modifier.

> *I noticed*
> Upon entering the doctor's office, a skeleton. ~~caught my~~
> ⌃ ⌃
>
> ~~attention.~~

> *As I entered*
> ~~Upon entering~~ the doctor's office, a skeleton caught my
> ⌃
>
> attention.

Checking for dangling modifiers

Does an opening phrase suggest an action without naming the actor? → **NO** → No problem

YES ↓

Does the subject of the sentence name the actor? → **YES** → No problem

NO ↓

Revise the dangling modifier.

EXERCISE 12-2

Edit the following sentences to correct dangling modifiers. Most sentences can be revised in more than one way. Revisions of lettered sentences appear in the back of the book. Example:

> *a student must complete*
> To acquire a degree in almost any field, two science courses~~,~~
>   ^   ^
> ~~must be completed.~~

a. At the age of ten, my parents took me on my first balloon ride.
b. To show our appreciation for your patience, enclosed is a coupon that you may redeem for the book of your choice.
c. Nestled in the cockpit, the pounding of the engine was muffled only slightly by my helmet.
d. In choosing her bridesmaids' dresses, cost had to be considered a major factor.
e. When a young man, my mother enrolled me in tap dance classes, hoping I would become the next Gregory Hines.

1. While working as a ranger in Everglades National Park, a Florida panther crossed the road in front of my truck one night.
2. By following this new procedure, our mailing costs will be reduced significantly.
3. As president of the missionary circle, one of Grandmother's duties is to raise money for the church.
4. After becoming eligible to win these bonuses, a sales quota must be maintained for six consecutive months.
5. As a child growing up in Nigeria, my mother taught me to treat all elders with respect.

ON THE WEB

For electronic exercises on misplaced and dangling modifiers, go to **dianahacker.com/rules**

and click on ▶ **Electronic Grammar Exercises**
                  ▶ **Clarity**
                       ▶ **E-ex 12-1 through 12-4**

13

Eliminate distracting shifts.

GRAMMAR CHECKERS do not flag the shifts discussed in this section: shifts in point of view; shifts in verb tense, mood, or voice; and shifts between direct and indirect questions or quotations. Even the most obvious errors like this one will slip right past most grammar checkers: *My three-year-old fell into the pool and to my surprise she swims to the shallow end.*

13a Make the point of view consistent in person and number.

The point of view of a piece of writing is the perspective from which it is written: first person (*I* or *we*), second person (*you*), or third person (*he/she/it/one* or *they*).

The *I* (or *we*) point of view, which emphasizes the writer, is a good choice for informal letters and writing based primarily on personal experience. The *you* point of view, which emphasizes the reader, works well for giving advice or explaining how to do something. The third-person point of view, which emphasizes the subject, is appropriate in formal academic and professional writing.

Writers who are having difficulty settling on an appropriate point of view sometimes shift confusingly from one to another. The solution is to choose a suitable perspective and then stay with it.

▶ One week our class met in a junkyard to practice rescuing a victim trapped in a wrecked car. We learned to dismantle the car with the essential tools. ~~You~~ *We* were graded on ~~your~~ *our* speed and ~~your~~ *our* skill in extricating the victim.

The writer should have stayed with the *we* point of view. *You* is inappropriate because the writer is not addressing readers directly.

You should not be used in a vague sense meaning "anyone." (See also 23d.)

You need
▶ ~~One needs~~ a password and a credit card number to access
  ^

this database. You will be billed at an hourly rate.

Here *You* is an appropriate choice because the writer is giving advice directly to readers.

Police officers are
▶ ~~A police officer is~~ often criticized for always being there when
  ^

they aren't needed and never being there when they are.

Although the writer might have changed *they* to *he or she* (to match the singular *officer*), the revision in the plural is more concise. (See also 17f and 22a.)

EXERCISE 13–1

Edit the following paragraph to eliminate distracting shifts in point of view (person and number).

    Many people my age grew up reading science fiction books that told you about life in the twenty-first century. The lives of the characters in these futuristic tales were often made easier by all kinds of machines, especially robots. Every one of the kids I knew wanted to have their own robot someday. We thought that you wouldn't have to do any chores at home if you had a robot to do the work. Today some kinds of robots exist, but my childhood robot fantasies have not exactly come true. There are no robots like Rosie, the mechanized maid on the cartoon *The Jetsons*. Instead, robots for consumer use are more likely to be toys. For example, a child today might have their own Furby, an animatronic stuffed animal. A Furby is kind of amusing, I admit, but I'm still a little disappointed. They can talk and move, but they won't clean your room.

13b   Maintain consistent verb tenses.

Consistent verb tenses clearly establish the time of the actions being described. When a passage begins in one tense and then shifts without warning and for no reason to another, readers are distracted and confused.

▶ There was no way I could fight the current and win. Just as I
was losing hope, a stranger ~~jumps~~ off a passing boat and ~~swims~~
                           jumped   *swam*

toward me.

Writers often encounter difficulty with verb tenses when
writing about literature. Because fictional events occur outside
the time frames of real life, the past tense and the present tense
may seem equally appropriate. The literary convention, however, is to describe fictional events consistently in the present
tense.

▶ The scarlet letter is a punishment sternly placed upon Hester's
breast by the community, and yet it ~~was~~ an extremely fanciful
                                          is
and imaginative product of Hester's own needlework.

EXERCISE 13–2

Edit the following paragraphs to eliminate distracting shifts in tense.

    The English colonists who settled in Massachusetts received
assistance at first from the local Indian tribes, but by 1675 there
had been friction between the English and the Indians for many
years. On June 20 of that year, Metacomet, whom the colonists
called Philip, leads the Wampanoag tribe in the first of a series of
attacks on the colonial settlements. The war, known today as King
Philip's War, rages on for over a year and leaves three thousand
Indians and six hundred colonists dead. Metacomet's attempt to
retain power in his native land failed. Finally he too is killed, and
the victorious colonists sell his wife and children into slavery.
    The Indians did not leave records of their unfortunate
encounters with the English settlers, but the settlers recorded
some of their experiences at the hands of the Indians. One of the
few accounts to survive was written by a captured colonist, Mrs.
Mary Rowlandson. She is a minister's wife who is kidnapped by
an Indian war party and held captive for eleven weeks in 1676.
Her history, *A Narrative of the Captivity and Restoration of Mrs.
Mary Rowlandson,* tells the story of her experiences with the
Wampanoags. Although it did not paint a completely balanced
picture of the Indians, Rowlandson's narrative, which is considered a classic early American text, showed its author to be a keen
observer of life in an Indian camp.

13c Make verbs consistent in mood and voice.

Unnecessary shifts in the mood of a verb can be as distracting as needless shifts in tense. There are three moods in English: the *indicative,* used for facts, opinions, and questions; the *imperative,* used for orders or advice; and the *subjunctive,* used in certain contexts to express wishes or conditions contrary to fact (see 28b).

The following passage shifts confusingly from the indicative to the imperative mood.

▶ The officers advised us against allowing anyone into our
   They also suggested that we
   homes without proper identification. ~~Also,~~ alert neighbors to
   ^

   vacation schedules.

Since the writer's purpose was to report the officers' advice, the revision puts both sentences in the indicative.

A verb may be in either the active voice (with the subject doing the action) or the passive voice (with the subject receiving the action). (See 8a.) If a writer shifts without warning from one to the other, readers may be left wondering why.

▶ When the tickets are ready, the travel agent notifies the
         lists each ticket
   client./, ~~Each ticket is then listed~~ on a daily register form, and
   files ^   ^
   a copy of the itinerary. ~~is filed.~~
   ^   ^

The passage began in the active voice (*agent notifies*) and then switched to the passive (*ticket is listed, copy is filed*). Because the active voice is clearer and more direct, the writer changed all the verbs to the active voice.

13d Avoid sudden shifts from indirect to direct questions or quotations.

An indirect question reports a question without asking it: *We asked whether we could take a swim.* A direct question asks directly: *Can we take a swim?* Sudden shifts from indirect to direct questions are awkward. In addition, sentences containing such shifts are impossible to punctuate because indirect questions must end with a period and direct questions must end with a question mark. (See 38b.)

▶ I wonder whether the sister knew of the theft and, if so, ~~did~~

  whether she reported
  ~~she report~~ it to the police.
  ^

The revision poses both questions indirectly. The writer could also ask both questions directly: *Did the sister know of the theft and, if so, did she report it to the police?*

An indirect quotation reports someone's words without quoting word for word: *Annabelle said that she is a Virgo.* A direct quotation presents the exact words of a speaker or writer, set off with quotation marks: *Annabelle said, "I am a Virgo."* Unannounced shifts from indirect to direct quotations are distracting and confusing, especially when the writer fails to insert the necessary quotation marks, as in the following example.

                                                  asked me not to
▶ Mother said that she would be late for dinner and ~~please do~~
                                                         ^
                                          came
  ~~not~~ leave for choir practice until Dad ~~comes~~ home.
                                            ^

The revision reports all of the mother's words. The writer could also quote directly: *Mother said, "I will be late for dinner. Please do not leave for choir practice until Dad comes home."*

EXERCISE 13–3

Edit the following sentences to eliminate distracting shifts. Revisions of lettered sentences appear in the back of the book. Example:

                                            they
  For most people, quitting smoking is not easy once ~~you~~ are
                                                      ^
  hooked.

a. A courtroom lawyer has more than a touch of theater in their blood.
b. The interviewer asked if we had brought our proof of birth and citizenship and did we bring our passports.
c. A single parent often has only their ingenuity to rely on.

d. When the director travels, you will make the hotel and airline reservations and arrange for a rental car. A detailed itinerary must also be prepared.

e. Madame Defarge is a sinister figure in Dickens's *A Tale of Two Cities*. On a symbolic level, she represents fate; like the Greek Fates, she knitted the fabric of individual destiny.

1. Everyone should protect yourself from the sun, especially on the first day of extensive exposure.

2. Our neighbors told us that the island was being evacuated because of the coming storm. Also, take the northern route to the mainland.

3. Rescue workers put water on her face and lifted her head gently onto a pillow. Finally, she opens her eyes.

4. The polygraph examiner will ask you if you have ever stolen goods on the job, if you have ever taken drugs, and have you ever killed or threatened to kill anyone.

5. The artist has often been seen as a threat to society, especially when they refuse to conform to conventional standards of taste.

ON THE WEB

For electronic exercises on distracting shifts, go to
dianahacker.com/rules

and click on ▶ **Electronic Grammar Exercises**
▶ **Clarity**
▶ **E-ex 13-1 through 13-4**

14

Emphasize key ideas.

Within each sentence, emphasize your point by expressing it in the subject and verb of an independent clause, the words that receive the most attention from readers (see 14a–e).

Within longer stretches of prose, you can draw attention to ideas deserving special emphasis by using a variety of techniques, often involving an unusual twist or some element of surprise (see 14f).

14a Coordinate equal ideas; subordinate minor ideas.

When combining two or more ideas in one sentence, you have two choices: coordination or subordination. Choose coordination to indicate that the ideas are equal or nearly equal in importance. Choose subordination to indicate that one idea is less important than another.

 GRAMMAR CHECKERS do not catch the problems with coordination and subordination discussed in this section. Not surprisingly, computer programs have no way of sensing the relative importance of ideas.

Coordination

Coordination draws attention equally to two or more ideas. To coordinate single words or phrases, join them with a coordinating conjunction or with a pair of correlative conjunctions (see 61g). To coordinate independent clauses — word groups that could stand alone as a sentence — join them with a comma and a coordinating conjunction or with a semicolon:

, and	, but	, or	, nor
, for	, so	, yet	;

The semicolon is often accompanied by a conjunctive adverb such as *furthermore, therefore,* or *however* or by a transitional phrase such as *for example, in other words,* or *as a matter of fact.* (See the chart on p. 117 for a more complete list.)

Assume, for example, that your intention is to draw equal attention to the following two ideas.

Grandmother lost her sight. Her hearing sharpened.

To coordinate these ideas, you can join them with a comma and the coordinating conjunction *but* or with a semicolon and the conjunctive adverb *however.*

Grandmother lost her sight, but her hearing sharpened.

Grandmother lost her sight; however, her hearing sharpened.

It is important to choose a coordinating conjunction or conjunctive adverb appropriate to your meaning. In the preceding example, the two ideas contrast with one another, calling for *but* or *however.*

Using coordination to combine sentences of equal importance

1. Consider using a comma and a coordinating conjunction. (See 32a.)

   , and   , but   , or   , nor

   , for   , so   , yet

► In Orthodox Jewish funeral ceremonies, the shroud is a simple
   and the
   linen vestment,/.~~The~~ coffin is plain wood with no adornment.
   ^

2. Consider using a semicolon and a conjunctive adverb or transitional phrase. (See 34b.)

also	in addition	now
as a result	in fact	of course
besides	in other words	on the other hand
consequently	in the first place	otherwise
finally	meanwhile	still
for example	moreover	then
for instance	nevertheless	therefore
furthermore	next	thus
however		

   ; moreover, she
► Alicia scored well on the SAT,/ ~~She also~~ had excellent high school
   ^
   grades and a record of community service.

3. Consider using a semicolon alone. (See 34a.)

   in
► In youth we learn,/; ~~In~~ age we understand.
   ^

Subordination

To give unequal emphasis to two or more ideas, express the major idea in an independent clause and place any minor ideas in subordinate clauses or phrases. (For specific subordination strategies, see the chart on p. 119.)

Deciding which idea to emphasize is not a matter of right and wrong but is determined by the meaning you intend. Consider the two ideas about Grandmother's sight and hearing.

> Grandmother lost her sight. Her hearing sharpened.

If your purpose is to stress your grandmother's acute hearing rather than her blindness, subordinate the idea about her blindness.

> *As she lost her sight,* Grandmother's hearing sharpened.

To focus on your grandmother's growing blindness, subordinate the idea about her hearing.

> *Though her hearing sharpened,* Grandmother gradually lost her sight.

14b Combine choppy sentences.

Short sentences demand attention, so you should use them primarily for emphasis. Too many short sentences, one after the other, make for a choppy style.

If an idea is not important enough to deserve its own sentence, try combining it with a sentence close by. Put any minor ideas in subordinate structures such as phrases or subordinate clauses.

▶ We keep our use of insecticides, herbicides, and fungicides

               because we

to a minimum./ ~~We~~ are concerned about their effect on the

             ^

environment.

A minor idea is now expressed in a subordinate clause beginning with *because.*

Using subordination to combine sentences of unequal importance

1. Consider putting the less important idea in a subordinate clause beginning with one of the following words. (See 63b.)

after	before	that	which
although	even though	unless	while
as	if	until	who
as if	since	when	whom
because	so that	where	whose

▶ *When my*
~~My~~ son asked his great-grandmother if she had been a
^
she
slave/, ~~She~~ became very angry.
^

▶ My sister owes much of her recovery to a bodybuilding
that she
program/ ~~She~~ began ~~the program~~ three years ago.
^

2. Consider putting the less important idea in an appositive phrase. (See 63d.)

▶ Karate,~~is~~ a discipline based on the philosophy of nonviolence/,
^   ^
~~It~~ teaches the art of self-defense.

3. Consider putting the less important idea in a participial phrase. (See 63c.)

▶ *Noticing*
~~I noticed~~ that smoke had filled the backyard/, I ran out to see where
^   ^
it was coming from.

▶ *E*
~~Alvin was~~ ~~e~~ncouraged by his professor to apply for the
^
Alvin
job/, ~~He~~ filed an application on Monday morning.
^

▶ The Chesapeake and Ohio Canal,⌃is a 184-mile waterway

constructed in the 1800s,/,⌃It was a major source of

transportation for goods during the Civil War.

A minor idea is now expressed in an appositive phrase (*a 184-mile waterway constructed in the 1800s*).

                E
▶ ~~Sister Consilio was~~ ⌃nveloped in a black robe with only her
                  Sister Consilio
face and hands visible,/,⌃~~She~~ was an imposing figure.

A minor idea is now expressed in a participial phrase beginning with *Enveloped.*

Although subordination is ordinarily the most effective technique for combining short, choppy sentences, coordination is appropriate when the ideas are equal in importance.

▶ The hospital decides when patients will sleep and wake,/,⌃~~It~~
                           and
dictates what and when they will eat,/,⌃~~It~~ tells them when

they may be with family and friends.

Equivalent ideas are expressed in a coordinate series.

ESL

When combining sentences, do not repeat the subject of the sentence; also do not repeat an object or adverb in an adjective clause. See 31b and 31c.

▶ The apartment that we moved into ~~it~~ needed many

repairs.

▶ Tanya climbed into the tree house that the boys were

playing in. ⌃~~it.~~

EXERCISE 14–1

Combine the following sentences by subordinating minor ideas or by coordinating ideas of equal importance. You must decide which ideas are minor because the sentences are given out of context. Revisions of lettered sentences appear in the back of the book. Example:

Agnes, ~~was~~ another girl I worked with~~.~~ ~~She~~ was a hyperactive

child.

a. The lift chairs were going around very fast. They were bumping the skiers into their seats.
b. Our waitress was costumed in a kimono. She had painted her face white. She had arranged her hair in an upswept lacquered beehive.
c. Student volunteers from Baltimore City Community College help the younger children with reading and math. These are the children's weakest subjects.
d. Shore houses were flooded up to the first floor. Beaches were washed away. Brant's Lighthouse was swallowed by the sea.
e. Mary will graduate from high school in June. She has not yet decided on a college.

1. I noticed that the sky was glowing orange and red. I bent down to crawl into the bunker.
2. The Market Inn is located at 2nd and E Streets. It doesn't look very impressive from the outside. The food, however, is excellent.
3. He walked up to the pitcher's mound. He dug his toe into the ground. He swung his arm around backward and forward. Then he threw the ball and struck the batter out.
4. On one of my solo runs, I met a six-year-old boy. His name was Timmy. He was in the hospital for treatment of leukemia.
5. The first football card set was released by the Goudey Gum Company in 1933. The set featured only three football players. They were Red Grange, Bronko Nagurski, and Knute Rockne.

ON THE WEB

For electronic exercises on combining choppy sentences, go to
dianahacker.com/rules

and click on ▶ **Electronic Grammar Exercises**
    ▶ **Clarity**
        ▶ **E-ex 14–1 and 14–2**

14c Avoid ineffective or excessive coordination.

Coordinate structures are appropriate only when you intend to draw the reader's attention equally to two or more ideas: *Professor Naake praises loudly, and she criticizes softly.* If one idea is more important than another — or if a coordinating conjunction does not clearly signal the relation between the ideas — you should subordinate the less important idea.

> **INEFFECTIVE** Closets were taxed as rooms, and most colonists stored their clothes in chests or clothes presses.

> **IMPROVED** Because closets were taxed as rooms, most colonists stored their clothes in chests or clothes presses.

The revision subordinates the less important idea by putting it in a subordinate clause. Notice that the subordinating conjunction *Because* signals the relation between the ideas more clearly than the coordinating conjunction *and.*

Because it is so easy to string ideas together with *and,* writers often rely too heavily on coordination in their rough drafts. The cure for excessive coordination is simple: Look for opportunities to tuck minor ideas into subordinate clauses or phrases.

▶ *When*
Jason walked over to his new Miata, ~~and~~ he saw that its windshield had been smashed.

The minor idea has become a subordinate clause beginning with *When.*

▶ *noticing*
My uncle, ~~noticed~~ my frightened look, ~~and~~ told me that Grandma had to feel my face because she was blind.

The less important idea has become a participial phrase modifying the noun *uncle.*

▶ *After four hours,*
~~Four hours went by, and~~ a rescue truck finally arrived, but by that time we had been evacuated in a helicopter.

Three independent clauses were excessive. The least important idea has become a prepositional phrase.

EXERCISE 14–2

In the following sentences, ideas have been coordinated (joined with a coordinating conjunction or a semicolon). Restructure the sentences by subordinating minor ideas. You must decide which ideas are minor because the sentences are given out of context. Revisions of lettered sentences appear in the back of the book. Example:

where they
The crew team finally returned to shore, and had a party on
to celebrate
the beach and celebrated the start of the season.

a. These particles are known as "stealth liposomes," and they can hide in the body for a long time without detection.

b. Cocaine is an addictive drug; it can seriously harm you both physically and mentally, if death doesn't get you first.

c. Students, textile workers, and labor unions have loudly protested sweatshop abuses, so apparel makers have been forced to examine their labor practices.

d. IRC (Internet Relay Chat) was developed in a European university; it was created as a way for a group of graduate students to talk about projects from their dorm rooms.

e. The cafeteria's new menu has an international flavor, and it includes everything from enchiladas and pizza to pad thai and sauerbraten.

1. We arrived at the Capital Center, and to my dismay we had to pay five dollars for parking.

2. Iguanas are dependent on ultraviolet rays from the sun, so in the winter months they must be put under ultraviolet-coated lights that can be purchased at most pet stores.

3. The Civil War Trust was founded in 1991; it spearheads a nationwide campaign to protect America's Civil War battlefields.

4. We did not expect to receive so many large orders so quickly, and we are short on inventory.

5. I am certain that Mother spread her love equally among us all, but she had a way of making each of us feel very special in our own way.

14d Do not subordinate major ideas.

If a sentence buries its major idea in a subordinate construction, readers may not give the idea enough attention. Express the major idea in an independent clause and subordinate any minor ideas.

> *had polio as a child,*
> Lanie, who now walks with the help of braces,/. ~~had polio as~~
> ~~a child.~~

The writer wanted to focus on Lanie's ability to walk, but the original sentence buried this information in an adjective clause. The revision puts the major idea in an independent clause and tucks the less important idea into an adjective clause (*who had polio as a child*).

> *As*
> I was driving home from my new job, heading down Ranchitos
> Road, ~~when~~ my car suddenly overheated.

The writer wanted to emphasize that the car overheated, not the fact of driving home. The revision expresses the major idea in an independent clause, the less important idea in an adverb clause (*As I was driving home from my new job*).

14e Do not subordinate excessively.

In attempting to avoid short, choppy sentences, writers sometimes go to the opposite extreme, putting more subordinate ideas into a sentence than its structure can bear. If a sentence collapses of its own weight, occasionally it can be restructured. More often, however, such sentences must be divided.

> Our job is to stay between the stacker and the tie machine
> *If they do,*
> watching to see if the newspapers jam,/. ~~in which case~~ we
> pull the bundles off and stack them on a skid, because
> otherwise they would back up in the stacker.

EXERCISE 14–3

In each of the following sentences, the idea that the writer wished to emphasize is buried in a subordinate construction. Restructure each sentence so that the independent clause expresses the major idea and lesser ideas are subordinated. Revisions of lettered sentences appear in the back of the book. Example:

Although
Catherine has weathered many hardships, ~~although~~ she has
^

rarely become discouraged. [*Emphasize that Catherine has*

rarely become discouraged.]

a. Gina worked as an aide for the relief agency, distributing food and medical supplies. [*Emphasize distributing food and medical supplies.*]
b. For the past three years, Ms. Brooks has been an attorney at Pepco, where she has done an excellent job. [*Emphasize that Ms. Brooks has done an excellent job.*]
c. The visiting period was nearly over when the prison guard tapped me on the shoulder. [*Emphasize the guard's tapping the writer on the shoulder.*]
d. My grandfather, who raised his daughters the old-fashioned way, was born eighty years ago in Puerto Rico. [*Emphasize how the grandfather raised his daughters.*]
e. The Narcan reversed the depressive effect of the drug, saving the patient's life. [*Emphasize that the patient's life was saved.*]

1. The ivy-covered dormitories, located about a mile from most of the classrooms, date from the early nineteenth century. [*Emphasize where the dormitories are located.*]
2. I was losing consciousness when my will to live kicked in. [*Emphasize the will to live.*]
3. Louis's team worked with the foreign mission by building new churches and restoring those damaged by hurricanes. [*Emphasize the building and restoring.*]
4. The rotor hit, gouging a hole about an eighth of an inch deep in my helmet. [*Emphasize that the rotor gouged a hole in the helmet.*]
5. Sophia's country kitchen, which overlooks a field where cattle graze among old tombstones, was formerly a lean-to porch. [*Emphasize that the kitchen overlooks the field.*]

ON THE WEB

For an electronic exercise on subordination, go to
dianahacker.com/rules

and click on ▶ **Electronic Grammar Exercises**
　　　　　　　 ▶ **Clarity**
　　　　　　　　 ▶ **E-ex 14-3**

14f Experiment with techniques for gaining special emphasis.

By experimenting with certain techniques, usually involving some element of surprise, you can draw attention to ideas that deserve special emphasis. Use such techniques sparingly, however, or they will lose their punch. The writer who tries to emphasize everything ends up emphasizing nothing.

Using sentence endings for emphasis

You can highlight an idea simply by withholding it until the end of a sentence. The technique works something like a punch line. In the following example, the sentence's meaning is not revealed until its very last word.

> The only completely consistent people are the dead.
>
> — Aldous Huxley

Using parallel structure for emphasis

Parallel grammatical structure draws special attention to paired ideas or to items in a series. (See 9.) When parallel ideas are paired, the emphasis falls on words that underscore comparisons or contrasts, especially when they occur at the end of a phrase or clause.

> We must *stop talking* about the *American dream* and *start listening* to the *dreams of Americans.*   — Reubin Askew

In a parallel series, the emphasis falls at the end, so it is generally best to end with the most dramatic or climactic item in the series.

> Sister Charity enjoyed passing out writing punishments: translate the Ten Commandments into Latin, type a thousand-word essay on good manners, copy the New Testament with a quill pen.   — Marie Visosky, student

Using punctuation for emphasis

Obviously the exclamation point can add emphasis, but you should not overuse it. As a rule, the exclamation point is more appropriate in dialogue than in ordinary prose.

I oozed a glob of white paint onto my palette, whipped some medium into it, loaded my brush, and announced to the class, "Move over, Michelangelo. Here I come!"

— Carolyn Goff, student

A dash or a colon may be used to draw attention to word groups worthy of special attention. (See 35a, 35b, and 39a.)

The middle of the road is where the white line is — and that's the worst place to drive.   — Robert Frost

I turned to see what the anemometer read: The needle had pegged out at 106 knots.   — Jonathan Shilk, student

Using an occasional short sentence for emphasis

Too many short sentences in a row will fast become monotonous (see 14b), but an occasional short sentence, when played off against longer sentences in the same passage, will draw attention to an idea.

The great secret, known to internists and learned early in marriage by internists' wives [or husbands], but still hidden from the general public, is that most things get better by themselves. Most things, in fact, are better by morning.   — Lewis Thomas

15

Provide some variety.

When a rough draft is filled with too many same-sounding sentences, try injecting some variety — as long as you can do so without sacrificing clarity or ease of reading.

GRAMMAR CHECKERS are of little help with sentence variety. It takes a human ear to know when and why sentence variety is needed.

Some programs tell you when you have used the same word to open several sentences, but sometimes it is a good idea to do so — if you are trying to highlight parallel ideas, for example (see p. 54).

15a Vary your sentence openings.

Most sentences in English begin with the subject, move to the verb, and continue along to the object, with modifiers tucked in along the way or put at the end. For the most part, such sentences are fine. Put too many of them in a row, however, and they become monotonous.

Adverbial modifiers, being easily movable, can often be inserted ahead of the subject. Such modifiers might be single words, phrases, or clauses.

> *Eventually a*
> ▶ ~~A~~ few drops of sap ~~eventually~~ began to trickle into the
> ^
> bucket.

Like most adverbs, *eventually* does not need to appear close to the verb it modifies (*began*).

> *Just as the sun was coming up, a*
> ▶ ~~A~~ pair of black ducks flew over the blind, ~~just as the sun was~~
> ^   ^
> ~~coming up.~~

The adverb clause, which modifies the verb *flew,* is as clear at the beginning of the sentence as it is at the end.

Adjectives and participial phrases can frequently be moved to the beginning of a sentence without loss of clarity.

> *Dejected and withdrawn,*
> ▶ Edward, ~~dejected and withdrawn,~~ nearly gave up his search
> ^
> for a job.

>   *A*   *John and I*
> ▶ ~~John and I,~~ anticipating a peaceful evening, sat down at the
> ^   ^
> campfire to brew a cup of coffee.

CAUTION: When beginning a sentence with an adjective or a participial phrase, make sure that the subject of the sentence names the person or thing described in the introductory phrase. If it doesn't, the phrase will dangle. (See 12e.)

15b Use a variety of sentence structures.

A writer should not rely too heavily on simple sentences and compound sentences, for the effect tends to be both monotonous and choppy. (See 14b and 14c.) Too many complex or compound-complex sentences, however, can be equally monotonous. If your style tends to one or the other extreme, try to achieve a better mix of sentence types. For a discussion of sentence types, see 64a.

15c Try inverting sentences occasionally.

A sentence is inverted if it does not follow the normal subject-verb-object pattern (see 62c). Many inversions sound artificial and should be avoided except in the most formal contexts. But if an inversion sounds natural, it can provide a welcome touch of variety.

▶ *Opposite the produce section is a*
A̶ refrigerated case of mouth-watering cheeses,̶ ̶i̶s̶ ̶o̶p̶p̶o̶s̶i̶t̶e̶ ̶t̶h̶e̶
     ^   ^

p̶r̶o̶d̶u̶c̶e̶ ̶s̶e̶c̶t̶i̶o̶n̶;̶ a friendly attendant will cut off just the

amount you want.

The revision inverts the normal subject-verb order by moving the verb, *is,* ahead of its subject, *case.*

▶ *Set at the top two corners of the stage were huge*
H̶u̶g̶e̶ lavender hearts outlined in bright white lights.̶w̶e̶r̶e̶ ̶s̶e̶t̶
   ^   ^

a̶t̶ ̶t̶h̶e̶ ̶t̶o̶p̶ ̶t̶w̶o̶ ̶c̶o̶r̶n̶e̶r̶s̶ ̶o̶f̶ ̶t̶h̶e̶ ̶s̶t̶a̶g̶e̶.̶

In the revision the subject, *hearts,* appears after the verb, *were set.* Notice that the two parts of the verb are also inverted — and separated from one another — without any awkwardness or loss of meaning.

EXERCISE 15–1

Edit the following paragraph to increase sentence variety.

I have spent thirty years of my life on a tobacco farm, and I cannot understand why people smoke. The whole process of raising tobacco involves deadly chemicals. The ground is treated for mold and chemically fertilized before the tobacco seed is ever planted. The seed is planted and begins to grow, and then the bed is treated with weed killer. The plant is then transferred to the field. It is sprayed with poison to kill worms about two months later. Then the time for harvest approaches, and the plant is sprayed once more with a chemical to retard the growth of suckers. The tobacco is harvested and hung in a barn to dry. These barns are havens for birds. The birds defecate all over the leaves. After drying, these leaves are divided by color, and no feces are removed. They are then sold to the tobacco companies. I do not know what the tobacco companies do after they receive the tobacco. I do not need to know. They cannot remove what I know is in the leaf and on the leaf. I don't want any of it to pass through my mouth.

16

Tighten wordy sentences.

Long sentences are not necessarily wordy, nor are short sentences always concise. A sentence is wordy if it can be tightened without loss of meaning.

GRAMMAR CHECKERS can flag some, but not all, wordy constructions. Most programs alert you to common redundancies, such as *true fact,* and empty or inflated phrases, such as *in my opinion* or *in order that.* In addition, they alert you to wordiness caused by passive verbs, such as *is determined.* (See also 8a.) They are less helpful in identifying sentences with needlessly complex structures.

16a   Eliminate redundancies.

Writers often repeat themselves unnecessarily. Afraid, perhaps, that they won't be heard the first time, they insist that a teacup is small *in size* or yellow *in color,* that married people should cooperate *together,* that a fact is not just a fact but a *true* fact. Such redundancies may seem at first to add emphasis. In reality they do just the opposite, for they divide the reader's attention.

▶ Black slaves were ~~thought of or~~ stereotyped as lazy even

though they were the main labor force of the South.

works
▶ Daniel ~~is now employed~~ at a private rehabilitation center
⌃

~~working~~ as a registered physical therapist.

Though modifiers ordinarily add meaning to the words they modify, occasionally they are redundant.

▶ Sylvia ~~very hurriedly~~ scribbled her name, address, and phone

number on the back of a greasy napkin.

▶ Joel was determined ~~in his mind~~ to lose weight.

The words *scribbled* and *determined* already contain the notions suggested by the modifiers *very hurriedly* and *in his mind.*

16b Avoid unnecessary repetition of words.

Though words may be repeated deliberately, for effect, repetitions will seem awkward if they are clearly unnecessary. When a more concise version is possible, choose it.

▶ Our fifth patient, in room six, is ⱡ mentally ill. ~~patient.~~
⌃

grow
▶ The best teachers help each student to ~~become a better~~
⌃

~~student~~ both academically and emotionally.

16c Cut empty or inflated phrases.

An empty phrase can be cut with little or no loss of meaning. Common examples are introductory word groups that apologize or hedge: *in my opinion, I think that, it seems that, one must admit that,* and so on.

Clarity

▶ <del>In my opinion,</del> ~~O~~ ̸our current immigration policy is misguided

on several counts.

Readers understand without being told that they are hearing the writer's opinion.

Inflated phrases can be reduced to a word or two without loss of meaning.

INFLATED	CONCISE
along the lines of	like
as a matter of fact	in fact
at all times	always
at the present time	now, currently
at this point in time	now, currently
because of the fact that	because
by means of	by
by virtue of the fact that	because
due to the fact that	because
for the purpose of	for
for the reason that	because
have the ability to	be able to, can
in light of the fact that	because
in order to	to
in spite of the fact that	although, though
in the event that	if
in the final analysis	finally
in the nature of	like
in the neighborhood of	about
until such time as	until

▶ We will file the appropriate papers *if* <del>in the event that</del> we are

unable to meet the deadline.

16d Simplify the structure.

If the structure of a sentence is needlessly indirect, try simplifying it. Look for opportunities to strengthen the verb.

▶ The CEO claimed that because of volatile market conditions she could not make~~ an~~ estimate ~~of~~ the company's future profits.

The verb *estimate* is more vigorous and more concise than *make an estimate of.*

The colorless verbs *is, are, was,* and *were* frequently generate excess words.

▶ The secretary ~~is responsible for~~ *monitors and balances* ~~monitoring and balancing~~ the budgets for travel, contract services, and personnel.

The revision is more direct and concise. Actions originally appearing in subordinate structures have become verbs replacing *is.*

The expletive constructions *there is* and *there are* (or *there was* and *there were*) can also generate excess words. The same is true of expletive constructions beginning with *it.* (See 62c.)

▶ ~~There is~~ *A* another module ~~that~~ tells the story of Charles Darwin and introduces the theory of evolution.

▶ ~~It is imperative that all~~ *All* police officers *must* follow strict procedures when apprehending a suspect.

Expletive constructions do have legitimate uses, however. For example, they are appropriate when a writer has a good reason for delaying the subject. (See 62c.)

Finally, verbs in the passive voice may be needlessly indirect. When the active voice expresses your meaning as well, use it. (See 8a.)

▶ All too often, athletes with marginal academic skills *our coaches have recruited*.have ~~been recruited by our coaches.~~

16e Reduce clauses to phrases, phrases to single words.

Word groups functioning as modifiers can often be made more compact. Look for any opportunities to reduce clauses to phrases or phrases to single words.

▶ We took a side trip to Monticello, ~~which was~~ the home of

Thomas Jefferson.

> *silk*
▶ For her birthday we gave Jess a stylish vest. ~~made of silk.~~
> ⌃ ⌃

EXERCISE 16–1

Edit the following sentences for wordiness. Revisions of lettered sentences appear in the back of the book. Example:

> *even though*
> The Wilsons moved into the house ~~in spite of the fact that~~
> ⌃
>
> the back door was only ten yards from the train tracks.

a. Martin Luther King Jr. was a man who set a high standard for future leaders to meet.
b. Coach Becker loves to work with the young people of today.
c. In my opinion, Bloom's race for the governorship is a futile exercise.
d. What a casualty call officer does is assist the bereaved family in many ways.
e. Your task will be the deliverance of correspondence to all employees in the company.

1. Seeing the barrels, the driver immediately slammed on his brakes.
2. The thing data sets are used for is communicating with other computers.
3. The opening words of the Declaration of Independence, which sum up in total America's entire rationale for its very existence, were the subject of considerable debate in 1776.
4. A typical autocross course consists of at least two straightaways, and the rest of the course is made up of numerous slaloms and several sharp turns.
5. You will be the departmental travel coordinator for all members of the department.

ON THE WEB

For electronic exercises on wordiness, go to
dianahacker.com/rules

and click on ▶ **Electronic Grammar Exercises**
▶ **Clarity**
▶ **E-ex 16–1 through 16–3**

17

Choose appropriate language.

Language is appropriate when it suits your subject, engages your audience, and blends naturally with your own voice.

To some extent, your choice of language will be governed by the conventions of the genre in which you are writing. When in doubt about the conventions of a particular genre — lab reports, informal essays, business memos, and so on — take a look at models written by experts in the field.

17a Stay away from jargon.

Jargon is specialized language used among members of a trade, profession, or group. Use jargon only when readers will be familiar with it; even then, use it only when plain English will not do as well.

Sentences filled with jargon are likely to be long and lumpy. To revise such sentences, you must rewrite them, usually in fewer words.

> **JARGON** For years the indigenous body politic of South Africa attempted to negotiate legal enfranchisement without result.

> **REVISED** For years the indigenous people of South Africa negotiated in vain for the right to vote.

Though a political scientist might feel comfortable with the original version, jargon such as *body politic* and *legal enfranchisement* is needlessly complicated for ordinary readers.

Broadly defined, jargon includes puffed-up language designed more to impress readers than to inform them. The following are common examples from business, government, higher education, and the military, with plain English translations in parentheses.

ameliorate (improve)   indicator (sign)
commence (begin)   optimal (best, most favorable)
components (parts)   parameters (boundaries, limits)
endeavor (try)   peruse (read, look over)
exit (leave)   prior to (before)
facilitate (help)   utilize (use)
factor (consideration, cause)   viable (workable)
impact (v.) (affect)

Sentences filled with jargon are hard to read, and they are often wordy as well.

▶ All ~~employees functioning in the capacity of~~ work-study
                must prove that they are currently enrolled.
   students ~~are required to give evidence of current enrollment.~~
          ^

                        begin
▶ Mayor Summers will ~~commence~~ his term of office by
   improving   ^   *poor neighborhoods.*
   ~~ameliorating~~ living conditions in ~~economically deprived zones.~~
   ^   ^

17b Avoid pretentious language, most euphemisms, and "doublespeak."

Hoping to sound profound or poetic, some writers embroider their thoughts with large words and flowery phrases, language that in fact sounds pretentious. Pretentious language is so ornate and often so wordy that it obscures the thought that lies beneath.

          parents become old,
▶ When our ~~progenitors reach their silver-haired and golden~~
          ^   *entomb*   *old-age homes*
   ~~years,~~ we frequently ~~ensepulcher~~ them in ~~homes for~~
                            ^   ^
                                              dead.
   ~~senescent beings~~ as if they were already among the ~~deceased.~~
                                                           ^

Related to pretentious language are emphemisms, nice-sounding words or phrases substituted for words thought to sound harsh or ugly. Like pretentious language, euphemisms are wordy and indirect. Unlike pretentious language, they are sometimes appropriate. It is our social custom, for example, to use euphemisms when speaking or writing about death (*Her sister passed on*), excretion (*I have to go to the bathroom*), sexual intercourse (*They did not sleep together until they were married*), and the like. We may also use euphemisms out of concern for someone's feelings. Telling parents, for example, that their daughter is "unmotivated" is more sensitive than saying she's lazy. Tact or politeness, then, can justify an occasional euphemism.

Most euphemisms, however, are needlessly evasive or even deceitful. Like pretentious language, they obscure the intended meaning.

EUPHEMISM	PLAIN ENGLISH
adult entertainment	pornography
preowned automobile	used car
economically deprived	poor
selected out	fired
negative savings	debts
strategic withdrawal	retreat or defeat
revenue enhancers	taxes
chemical dependency	drug addiction
downsize	lay off
correctional facility	prison

The term *doublespeak,* coined by George Orwell in his novel *1984,* applies to any deliberately evasive or deceptive language, including euphemisms. Doublespeak is especially common in politics, where missiles are named "Peacekeepers," airplane crashes are termed "uncontrolled contact with the ground," and a military retreat is described as "tactical redeployment." Business also gives us its share of doublespeak. When the manufacturer of a pacemaker writes that its product "may result in adverse health consequences in pacemaker-dependent patients as a result of sudden 'no output' failure," it takes an alert reader to grasp the message: The pacemakers might suddenly stop functioning and cause a heart attack or even death.

GRAMMAR CHECKERS can be helpful in identifying jargon and pretentious language. For example, they commonly advise against using words such as *utilize, finalize, facilitate,* and *effectuate.* You may find, however, that a program advises you to "simplify" language that is not jargon or pretentious language and may in fact be appropriate in academic writing. Sometimes you can direct the program to change the style level from standard to formal.

EXERCISE 17–1

Edit the following sentences to eliminate jargon, pretentious or flowery language, euphemisms, and doublespeak. You may need to make substantial changes in some sentences. Revisions of lettered sentences appear in the back of the book. Example:

> *mastered*
> After two weeks in the legal department, Sue has ~~worked~~
>
> *office*   *performance has*
> ~~into~~ the routine, ~~of the office,~~ and her ~~functional and self-~~
>
> ~~management skills have~~ exceeded all expectations.

a. In my youth, my family was under the constraints of difficult material circumstances.

b. In order that I may increase my expertise in the area of delivery of services to clients, I feel that participation in this conference will be beneficial.

c. Have you ever been accused of flagellating a deceased equine?

d. Health educators facilitate lifestyle changes in their recipients of service.

e. Passengers should endeavor to finalize the customs declaration form prior to exiting the aircraft.

1. We learned that the mayor had been engaging in a creative transfer of city employees' pension funds.

2. As I approached the edifice of confinement where my brother was incarcerated, several inmates loudly vocalized a number of lewd remarks.

3. The nurse announced that there had been a negative patient-care outcome due to a therapeutic misadventure on the part of the surgeon.

4. Dan's early work hours leave him free to utilize afternoons for errands and for helping the children with their homework.

5. The bottom line is that the company is experiencing a negative cash flow.

ON THE WEB

For an electronic exercise on eliminating jargon, go to
dianahacker.com/rules
and click on ► **Electronic Grammar Exercises**
    ► **Clarity**
      ► **E-ex 17-1**

17c Avoid obsolete and invented words.

Although dictionaries list obsolete words such as *recomfort* and *reechy,* these words are not appropriate for current use. Invented words (also called *neologisms*) are too recently created to be part of standard English. Many invented words fade out of use without becoming standard. *Palimony* and *technobabble* are neologisms that may not last. *Printout* and *flextime* are no longer neologisms; they have become standard English. Avoid using invented words in formal writing unless they are given in the dictionary as standard or unless no other word expresses your meaning.

17d In most contexts, avoid slang, regional expressions, and nonstandard English.

Slang is an informal and sometimes private vocabulary that expresses the solidarity of a group such as teenagers, rock musicians, or football fans; it is subject to more rapid change than standard English. For example, the slang teenagers use to express approval changes every few years; *cool, groovy, neat, awesome, phat,* and *money* have replaced one another within the last three decades. Sometimes slang becomes so widespread that it is accepted as standard vocabulary. *Jazz,* for example, started out as slang but is now generally accepted to describe a style of music.

Although slang has a certain vitality, it is a code that not everyone understands, and it is very informal. Therefore, it is inappropriate in most writing.

► If we don't begin studying for the final, a whole semester's

   will be wasted.
   work ~~is going down the tubes.~~
              ^

                                                      disgust you.
► The government's "filth" guidelines for food will ~~gross you out.~~
                                                              ^

Regional expressions are common to a group in a geographical area. *Let's talk with the bark off* (for *Let's speak frankly*) is an expression in the southern United States, for example. Regional expressions have the same limitations as slang and are therefore inappropriate in most writing.

► John was four blocks from the house before he remembered

   turn on
   to ~~cut~~ the headlights.~~on.~~
      ^   ^

► I'm not ~~for~~ sure, but I think the dance has been postponed

   until tomorrow.

Standard English is the language used in all academic, business, and professional fields. Nonstandard English is spoken by people with a common regional or social heritage. Although nonstandard English may be appropriate when spoken within a close group, it is out of place in most formal and informal writing.

                  has
► The counselor ~~have~~ so many problems in her own life that
   doesn't   ^
   she ~~don't~~ know how to advise anyone else.
       ^

If you speak a nonstandard dialect, try to identify the ways in which your dialect differs from standard English. Look especially for the following features of nonstandard English, which commonly cause problems in writing.

Misuse of verb forms such as *began* and *begun* (See 27a.)

Omission of *-s* endings on verbs (See 27c.)

Omission of *-ed* endings on verbs (See 27d.)

Omission of necessary verbs (See 27e.)

Double negatives (See 26d.)

17e Choose an appropriate level of formality.

In deciding on a level of formality, consider both your subject and your audience. Does the subject demand a dignified treatment, or is a relaxed tone more suitable? Will readers be put off if you assume too close a relationship with them, or might you alienate them by seeming too distant?

For most college and professional writing, some degree of formality is appropriate. In a letter applying for a job, for example, it is a mistake to sound too breezy and informal.

TOO INFORMAL   I'd like to get that receptionist job you've got in the paper.

MORE FORMAL   I would like to apply for the receptionist position listed in the *Peoria Journal Star*.

Informal writing is appropriate for private letters, personal e-mail, and business correspondence between close associates. Like spoken conversation, it allows contractions (*don't, I'll*) and colloquial words (*kids, buddy*). Vocabulary and sentence structure are rarely complex.

In choosing a level of formality, above all be consistent. When a writer's voice shifts from one level of formality to another, readers receive mixed messages.

▶ Once a pitcher for the Cincinnati Reds, Bob shared with me
the secrets of his trade. His lesson ~~commenced~~ *began* with his
famous curveball, ~~implemented~~ *thrown* by tucking the little finger
behind the ball instead of holding it straight out. Next he
~~elucidated~~ *revealed* the mysteries of the sucker pitch, a slow ball
coming behind a fast windup.

Words such as *commenced* and *elucidated* are inappropriate for the subject matter, and they clash with informal terms such as *sucker pitch* and *fast windup*.

Clarity

GRAMMAR CHECKERS can flag slang and some informal language. Be aware, though, that they tend to be conservative on the matter of using contractions. If your ear tells you that a contraction such as *isn't* or *doesn't* strikes the right tone, stay with it.

17f Avoid sexist language.

Sexist language is language that stereotypes or demeans men or women, usually women. Using nonsexist language is a matter of courtesy — of respect for and sensitivity to the feelings of others.

Recognizing sexist language

Some sexist language is easy to recognize because it reflects genuine contempt for women: referring to a woman as a "broad," for example, or calling a lawyer a "lady lawyer," or saying in an advertisement, "If our new sports car were a lady, it would get its bottom pinched."

Other forms of sexist language are less blatant. The following practices, while they may not result from conscious sexism, reflect stereotypical thinking: referring to nurses as women and doctors as men, using different conventions when naming or identifying women and men, or assuming that all of one's readers are men.

STEREOTYPICAL LANGUAGE

After the nursing student graduates, *she* must face a difficult state board examination. [Not all nursing students are women.]

Running for city council are Jake Stein, an attorney, and *Mrs. Cynthia Jones*, a professor of English and *mother of three*. [The title *Mrs.* and the phrase *mother of three* are irrelevant.]

Wives of senior government officials are required to report any gifts they receive that are valued at more than $100. [Not all senior government officials are men.]

Still other forms of sexist language result from outmoded traditions. The pronouns *he, him,* and *his,* for instance, were traditionally used to refer generically to persons of either sex.

GENERIC *HE* OR *HIS*

When a senior physician is harassed by managed care professionals, *he* may be tempted to leave the profession.

A journalist is stimulated by *his* deadline.

Today, however, such usage is widely viewed as sexist because it excludes women and encourages sex-role stereotyping — the view that men are somehow more suited than women to be doctors, journalists, and so on.

Like the pronouns *he, him,* and *his,* the nouns *man* and *men* were once used indefinitely to refer to persons of either sex. Current usage demands gender-neutral terms for references to both men and women.

INAPPROPRIATE	APPROPRIATE
chairman	chairperson, moderator, chair, head
clergyman	member of the clergy, minister, pastor
congressman	member of Congress, representative, legislator
fireman	firefighter
foreman	supervisor
mailman	mail carrier, postal worker, letter carrier
mankind	people, humans
manpower	personnel
policeman	police officer
salesman	salesperson, sales associate, salesclerk, sales representative
to man	to operate, to staff
weatherman	weather forecaster, meteorologist
workman	worker, laborer

GRAMMAR CHECKERS are good at flagging sexist words, such as *mankind,* but they may also flag words, such as *girl* and *woman,* when they aren't being used in a sexist manner. It's sexist to call a woman a girl or a doctor a woman doctor, but you don't need to avoid the words *girl* and *woman* entirely and replace them with needlessly abstract terms like *female* and *individual.* All in all, just use your common sense. It's usually easy to tell when a word is offensive — and when it is not.

Although grammar checkers can flag sexist words, they cannot flag other kinds of sexist language, such as inconsistent treatment of men and women.

ON THE WEB

The rules on avoiding sexist language have sparked debates. If you're interested in learning why, go to
dianahacker.com/rules

and click on ▶ **Language Debates**
▶ **Sexist language**

Revising sexist language

When revising sexist language, be sparing in your use of the wordy constructions *he or she* and *his or her.* Although these constructions are fine in small doses, they become awkward when repeated throughout an essay. A better revision strategy, many writers have discovered, is to write in the plural; yet another strategy is to recast the sentence so the problem does not arise.

SEXIST

When a senior physician is harassed by managed care professionals, *he* may be tempted to leave the profession.

A journalist is stimulated by *his* deadline.

ACCEPTABLE BUT WORDY

When a senior physician is harassed by managed care professionals, *he or she* may be tempted to leave the profession.

A journalist is stimulated by *his or her* deadline.

BETTER: USING THE PLURAL

When senior *physicians* are harassed by managed care professionals, *they* may be tempted to leave the profession.

Journalists are stimulated by *their* deadlines.

BETTER: RECASTING THE SENTENCE

When harassed by managed care professionals, *a senior physician* may be tempted to leave the profession.

A journalist is stimulated by *a* deadline.

For more examples of these revision strategies, see 22.

EXERCISE 17–2

Edit the following sentences to eliminate sexist language or sexist assumptions. Revisions of lettered sentences appear in the back of the book. Example:

> *Scholarship athletes*   *their*
> A scholarship athlete must be as concerned about ~~his~~
>   ^   *they are*   *their*   ^
> academic performance as ~~he is~~ about ~~his~~ athletic
>   ^   ^
>
> performance.

  a. Mrs. Geralyn Farmer, who is the mayor's wife, is the chief surgeon at University Hospital. Dr. Paul Green is her assistant.
  b. Every applicant wants to know how much he will make.
  c. An elementary school teacher should understand the concept of nurturing if she intends to be a success.
  d. The vice president for community affairs asked Elizabeth and Joseph to serve as cochairmen for the Red Cross blood drive.
  e. If man does not stop polluting his environment, mankind will perish.

  1. A fireman must always be on call even when he is off duty.
  2. If a high school graduate makes a career in the armed forces, he can retire with a comfortable pension before the age of fifty.
  3. In the gubernatorial race, Lena Weiss, a defense lawyer and mother of two, easily defeated Harvey Towei, an architect.
  4. My brother hired a lady lawyer who is a partner in the firm of Harris and Porter.
  5. A secretary must be willing to sacrifice some of her spare time in the evenings and on the weekends if she expects to advance within this company.

ON THE WEB

For an electronic exercise on avoiding sexist language, go to
dianahacker.com/rules

and click on ▶ **Electronic Grammar Exercises**
                    ▶ **Clarity**
                           ▶ **E-ex 17–2**

17g Revise language that may offend groups of people.

Obviously it is impolite to use offensive terms such as *Polack* or *redneck.* But biased language can take more subtle forms. Because language evolves over time, names once thought acceptable may become offensive. When describing groups of people, choose names that the groups currently use to describe themselves.

► North Dakota takes its name from the ~~Indian~~ word meaning
   Lakota
   ∧
   "friend" or "ally."

► Many ~~Oriental~~ immigrants have recently settled in our small
   Asian
   ∧
   town in Tennessee.

Negative stereotypes (such as "drives like a teenager" or "haggard as an old crone") are of course offensive. But you should avoid stereotyping a person or a group even if you believe your generalization to be positive.

► It was no surprise that Greer, ~~a Chinese American,~~ was
   an excellent math and science student,
   ∧
   selected for the honors chemistry program at the University

   of Illinois.

18

Find the exact words.

Two reference works (or their online equivalents) will help you find words to express your meaning exactly: a good dictionary, such as *Webster's New World Dictionary of the American Language* or *The American Heritage Dictionary,* and a book of synonyms and antonyms, such as *Roget's International Thesaurus.*

CAUTION: Do not turn to a thesaurus in search of exotic, fancy words — such as *halcyon* or *eschew* — with which to embellish your essays. Look instead for words that exactly express your meaning. Most of the time these words — such as *tranquil* or *avoid* — will be familiar to both you and your readers.

GRAMMAR CHECKERS can flag some nonstandard idioms, such as *comply to,* and many clichés, such as *leave no stone unturned.* In addition, they can flag commonly confused words such as *principal* and *principle* or *affect* and *effect,* although you must decide which word is correct in your context. Grammar checkers are less helpful with the other problems discussed in section 18: choosing words with appropriate connotations, using concrete language, and using figures of speech appropriately.

18a Select words with appropriate connotations.

In addition to their strict dictionary meanings (or *denotations*), words have *connotations,* emotional colorings that affect how readers respond to them. The word *steel* denotes "made of or resembling commercial iron that contains carbon," but it also calls up a cluster of images associated with steel, such as the sensation of touching it. These associations give the word its connotations — cold, smooth, unbending.

If the connotation of a word does not seem appropriate for your purpose, your audience, or your subject matter, you should change the word. When a more appropriate synonym does not come quickly to mind, consult a dictionary or a thesaurus.

▶ The model was ~~skinny~~ *slender* and fashionable.

The connotation of the word *skinny* is too negative.

▶ As I covered the boats with marsh grass, the ~~perspiration~~ *sweat* I had worked up evaporated in the wind, and the cold morning air seemed even colder.

The term *perspiration* is too dainty for the context, which suggests vigorous exercise.

18b Prefer specific, concrete nouns.

Unlike general nouns, which refer to broad classes of things, specific nouns point to definite and particular items. *Film,* for example, names a general class, *science fiction film* names a narrower class, and *Jurassic Park* is more specific still. Other examples: *team, football team, Denver Broncos; music, symphony, Beethoven's Ninth.*

Unlike abstract nouns, which refer to qualities and ideas (*justice, beauty, realism, dignity*), concrete nouns point to immediate, often sensory experience and to physical objects (*steeple, asphalt, lilac, stone, garlic*).

Specific, concrete nouns express meaning more vividly than general or abstract ones. Although general and abstract language is sometimes necessary to convey your meaning, ordinarily prefer specific, concrete alternatives.

▶ The senator spoke about the challenges of the future:
  problems ~~concerning the environment and world peace.~~
  of famine, pollution, dwindling resources, and terrorism.

Nouns such as *thing, area, aspect, factor,* and *individual* are especially dull and imprecise.

▶ A career in transportation management offers many ~~things.~~ *rewards.*

▶ Try pairing a trainee with an ~~individual with technical experience.~~ *experienced technician.*

18c Do not misuse words.

If a word is not in your active vocabulary, you may find yourself misusing it, sometimes with embarrassing consequences. Imagine the chagrin of the young woman who wrote that the "aroma of pumpkin pie and sage stuffing acted as an *aphrodisiac*" when she learned that aphrodisiacs are drugs or foods stimulating sexual desire. Such blunders are easily prevented: When in doubt, check the dictionary.

climbing
▶ The fans were ~~migrating~~ up the bleachers in search of seats.
                    ^

avail.
▶ Mrs. Johnson tried to fight but to no ~~prevail.~~
                                          ^

permeated
▶ Drugs have so ~~diffused~~ our culture that they touch all
                 ^

segments of society.

Be especially alert for misused word forms — using a noun such as *absence, significance,* or *persistence,* for example, when your meaning requires the adjective *absent, significant,* or *persistent.*

persistent
▶ Most dieters are not ~~persistence~~ enough to make a permanent
                        ^

change in their eating habits.

EXERCISE 18–1

Edit the following sentences to correct misused words. Revisions of lettered sentences appear in the back of the book. Example:

all-absorbing.
The training required for a ballet dancer is ~~all-absorbent.~~
                                              ^

a. We regret this delay; thank you for your patients.
b. Ada's plan is to require education and experience to prepare herself for a position as property manager.
c. Tiger Woods, the penultimate competitor, has earned millions of dollars just in endorsements.
d. When Robert Frost died at age eighty-eight, he left a legacy of poems that will make him immoral.
e. I would not advice anyone to pass up a chance to study geology.

1. Waste, misuse of government money, security and health violations, and even pilfering have become major dilemmas at the FBI.
2. Did you understand the significant of the list?
3. Grand Isle State Park is surrounded on three sides by water.
4. The Old World nuance of the restaurant intrigued us.
5. Trifle, a popular English dessert, contains a ménage of ingredients that do not always appeal to American tastes.

ON THE WEB

For an electronic exercise on misused words, go to
dianahacker.com/rules

and click on ▶ **Electronic Grammar Exercises**
▶ **Clarity**
▶ **E-ex 18–1**

18d Use standard idioms.

Idioms are speech forms that follow no easily specified rules. The English say "Maria went *to hospital*," an idiom strange to American ears, which are accustomed to hearing *the* in front of *hospital*. Native speakers of a language seldom have problems with idioms, but prepositions sometimes cause trouble, especially when they follow certain verbs and adjectives. When in doubt, consult a dictionary.

UNIDIOMATIC	IDIOMATIC
abide with (a decision)	abide by (a decision)
according with	according to
agree to (an idea)	agree with (an idea)
angry at (a person)	angry with (a person)
capable to	capable of
comply to	comply with
desirous to	desirous of
different than (a person or thing)	different from (a person or thing)
intend on doing	intend to do
off of	off
plan on doing	plan to do
preferable than	preferable to
prior than	prior to
superior than	superior to
sure and	sure to
try and	try to
type of a	type of

ESL Because idioms follow no particular rules, you must learn them individually. You may find it helpful to keep a list of idioms that you frequently encounter in conversation and in reading.

EXERCISE 18-2

Edit the following sentences to eliminate errors in the use of idioms. If a sentence is correct, write "correct" after it. Answers to lettered sentences appear in the back of the book. Example:

>   *by*
> We agreed to abide ~~with~~ the decision of the judge.
>   ^

a. Queen Anne was so angry at Sarah Churchill that she refused to see her again.
b. Prior to the Russians' launching of *Sputnik, -nik* was not an English suffix.
c. The parade moved off of the street and onto the beach.
d. For the frightened refugees, the dangerous trek across the mountains was preferable than life in a war zone.
e. What type of a wedding are you planning?

1. Be sure and report on the danger of releasing genetically engineered bacteria into the atmosphere.
2. Why do you assume that embezzling bank assets is so different than robbing the bank?
3. Most of the class agreed to Sylvia's view that domestic terrorism is a very dangerous problem.
4. I refuse to abide by a decision I had no part in making.
5. Andrea intends on joining the Peace Corps after graduation.

ON THE WEB

For an electronic exercise on standard idioms, go to
dianahacker.com/rules

and click on ▶ **Electronic Grammar Exercises**
       ▶ **Clarity**
          ▶ **E-ex 18-2**

18e Do not rely heavily on clichés.

The frontiersman who first announced that he had "slept like a log" no doubt amused his companions with a fresh and unlikely comparison. Today, however, that comparison is a cliché, a saying that has lost its dazzle from overuse. No longer can it surprise.

To see just how dully predictable clichés are, put your hand over the right-hand column below and then finish the phrases on the left.

cool as a	cucumber
beat around	the bush
blind as a	bat
busy as a	bee, beaver
crystal	clear
dead as a	doornail
out of the frying pan and	into the fire
light as a	feather
like a bull	in a china shop
playing with	fire
nutty as a	fruitcake
selling like	hotcakes
starting out at the bottom	of the ladder
water under the	bridge
white as a	sheet, ghost
avoid clichés like the	plague

The cure for clichés is frequently simple: Just delete them. When this won't work, try adding some element of surprise. One student, for example, who had written that she had butterflies in her stomach, revised her cliché like this:

> If all of the action in my stomach is caused by butterflies, there must be a horde of them, with horseshoes on.

The image of butterflies wearing horseshoes is fresh and unlikely, not dully predictable like the original cliché.

ON THE WEB

The rules on avoiding clichés have sparked debates. If you're interested in learning why, go to **dianahacker.com/rules**

and click on ▶ **Language Debates**
           ▶ **Clichés**

18f Use figures of speech with care.

A figure of speech is an expression that uses words imaginatively (rather than literally) to make abstract ideas concrete. Most often, figures of speech compare two seemingly unlike things to reveal surprising similarities.

In a *simile,* the writer makes the comparison explicitly, usually by introducing it with *like* or *as:* "By the time cotton had to be picked, grandfather's neck was as red as the clay he plowed." In a *metaphor,* the *like* or *as* is omitted, and the comparison is implied. For example, in the Old Testament Song of Solomon, a young woman compares the man she loves to a fruit tree: "With great delight I sat in his shadow, and his fruit was sweet to my taste."

Although figures of speech are useful devices, writers sometimes use them without thinking through the images they evoke. This can result in a *mixed metaphor,* the combination of two or more images that don't make sense together.

▶ Crossing Utah's salt flats in his new Corvette, my father flew
  at jet speed.
  ~~under a full head of steam.~~
  ^

  Flew suggests an airplane, while *under a full head of steam* suggests a steamboat or a train. To clarify the image, the writer should stick with one comparison or the other.

▶ Our office had decided to put all controversial issues on a

  back burner.~~in a holding pattern.~~
       ^

  Here the writer is mixing stoves and airplanes. Simply deleting one of the images corrects the problem.

EXERCISE 18–3

Edit the following sentences to replace worn-out expressions and clarify mixed figures of speech. Revisions of lettered sentences appear in the back of the book. Example:

                                      the color drained from his face.
  When he heard about the accident, ~~he turned white as a~~
                                     ^

  ~~sheet.~~

a. John stormed into the room like a bull in a china shop.

b. The president thought that the scientists were using science as a sledgehammer to grind their political axes.

c. The Cubs easily beat the Mets, who were in the soup early in the game today at Wrigley Field.

d. We ironed out the sticky spots in our relationship.

e. Sasha told us that he wasn't willing to put his neck out on a limb.

1. Once she had sunk her teeth into it, Helen burned through the assignment.

2. The interrogators were raking him over the ropes.

3. The dean of students acted like a big fish in a little pond.

4. There are too many cooks in the broth here at corporate headquarters.

5. Juanita told Kyle that keeping skeletons in the closet would be playing with fire.

ON THE WEB

For an electronic exercise on clichés and figures of speech, go to
dianahacker.com/rules

and click on ▶ **Electronic Grammar Exercises**
　　　　　　　▶ **Clarity**
　　　　　　　　　▶ **E-ex 18-3**

Process

Design

Clarity

Grammar

Grammar

Punctuation

Mechanics

Argument

Research

Basics

19

Repair sentence fragments.

A sentence fragment is a word group that pretends to be a sentence. Sentence fragments are easy to recognize when they appear out of context, like these:

> On the old wooden stool in the corner of my grandmother's kitchen.

> And immediately popped their flares and life vests.

When fragments appear next to related sentences, however, they are harder to spot.

> On that morning I sat in my usual spot. On the old wooden stool in the corner of my grandmother's kitchen.

> The pilots ejected from the burning plane, landing in the water not far from the ship. And immediately popped their flares and life vests.

Recognizing sentence fragments

To be a sentence, a word group must consist of at least one full independent clause. An independent clause has a subject and a verb, and it either stands alone or could stand alone.

To test a word group for sentence completeness, use the flow chart on page 157. For example, by using the flow chart, you can see exactly why *On the old wooden stool in the corner of my grandmother's kitchen* is a fragment: It lacks both a subject and a verb. *And immediately popped their flares and life vests* is a fragment because it lacks a subject.

 Unlike some languages, English does not allow omission of subjects (except in imperative sentences); nor does it allow
ESL omission of verbs. See 31a and 29e.

Test for sentence completeness

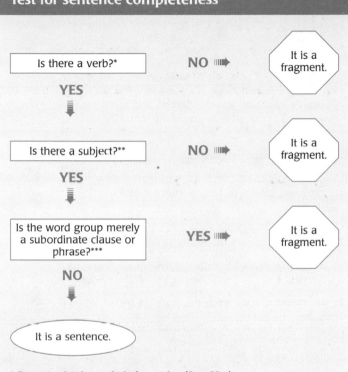

Is there a verb?*   NO ⟹ It is a fragment.

YES ⬇

Is there a subject?**   NO ⟹ It is a fragment.

YES ⬇

Is the word group merely a subordinate clause or phrase?***   YES ⟹ It is a fragment.

NO ⬇

It is a sentence.

* Do not mistake verbals for verbs. (See 63c.)
** The subject of a sentence may be *you,* understood. (See 62a.)
*** A sentence may open with a subordinate clause, but the sentence must also include an independent clause. (See 63c.)

If you find any fragments, try one of these methods of revision:

1. Attach the fragment to a nearby sentence.
2. Turn the fragment into a sentence.

Subordinate clauses function within sentences as adjectives, as adverbs, or as nouns. They cannot stand alone. (See 63b.) Most fragmented clauses beg to be pulled into a sentence nearby.

▶ Normally the bride-price consists of cattle and sheep./
because
~~Because~~ money has little value to these isolated people.
^

Because introduces a subordinate clause. (For punctuation of a subordinate clause appearing at the end of a sentence, see 33f.)

at
▶ Although we seldom get to see wildlife in the city/, ~~At~~ the zoo
^
we can still find some of our favorites.

Although introduces a subordinate clause. (For punctuation of subordinate clauses appearing at the beginning of a sentence, see 32b.)

If a fragmented clause cannot be attached to a nearby sentence or if you feel that attaching it would be awkward, try turning the clause into a sentence. The simplest way to do this is to delete the opening word or words that mark it as subordinate:

▶ Population increases and uncontrolled development are
In
taking a deadly toll on the environment. ~~So that in~~ many
^
parts of the world, fragile ecosystems are collapsing.

19b Attach fragmented phrases or turn them into sentences.

Like subordinate clauses, phrases function within sentences as adjectives, as adverbs, or as nouns. They cannot stand alone. Fragmented phrases are often prepositional or verbal phrases; sometimes they are appositives, words or word groups that rename nouns or pronouns. (See 63a, 63c, and 63d.)

Often a fragmented phrase may simply be pulled into a nearby sentence.

▶ The archaeologists worked slowly./, ~~Examining~~ and labeling

                                  examining

every pottery shard they uncovered.

The word group beginning with *Examining* is a verbal phrase.

▶ Mary is suffering from agoraphobia./, ~~A~~ fear of the outside

                                         a

world.

A fear of the outside world is an appositive renaming the noun *agoraphobia*. (For punctuation of appositives, see 32e.)

If a fragmented phrase cannot be pulled into a nearby sentence effectively, turn the phrase into a sentence. You may need to add a subject, a verb, or both.

▶ In the computer training session, Eugene explained how to

                         He also taught us

install our new software. ~~Also~~ how to organize our files,

connect to the Internet, and back up our hard drives.

The revision turns the fragmented phrase into a sentence by adding a subject and a verb.

19c   Attach other fragmented word groups or turn them into sentences.

Other word groups that are commonly fragmented include parts of compound predicates, lists, and examples introduced by *such as, for example,* or similar expressions.

Parts of compound predicates

A predicate consists of a verb and its objects, complements, and modifiers (see 62b). A compound predicate includes two or more predicates joined by a coordinating conjunction such as *and, but,* or *or.* Because the parts of a compound predicate share the same subject, they should appear in the same sentence.

▶ The woodpecker finch of the Galápagos Islands carefully

selects a twig of a certain size and shape./ ~~And~~ then uses this

and

tool to pry out grubs from trees.

Notice that no comma appears between the parts of a compound predicate. (See 33a.)

Lists

When a list is mistakenly fragmented, it can often be attached to a nearby sentence with a colon or a dash. (See 35a and 39a.)

▶ It has been said that there are only three indigenous

American art forms./: ~~Musical~~ comedy, jazz, and soap opera.

musical

Examples introduced by such as, for example, or similar expressions

Expressions that introduce examples (or explanations) can lead to unintentional fragments. Although you may begin a sentence with some of the following words or phrases, make sure that what you have written is a sentence, not a fragment.

also	for instance	or
and	in addition	such as
but	like	that is
especially	mainly	
for example	namely	

Sometimes fragmented examples can be attached to the preceding sentence.

▶ The South has produced some of our greatest twentieth-

century writers./, ~~Such~~ as Flannery O'Connor, William

such

Faulkner, Alice Walker, Tennessee Williams, and Thomas

Wolfe.

At times, however, it may be necessary to turn the fragment into a sentence.

▶   If Eric doesn't get his way, he goes into a fit of rage. For

example, ~~lying~~ *he lies* on the floor screaming or ~~opening~~ *opens* the cabinet
         ^   ^
doors and then ~~slamming~~ *slams* them shut.
                           ^

The writer corrected this fragment by adding a subject — he — and substituting verbs for the verbals *lying, opening,* and *slamming.*

19d   Exception: Occasionally a fragment may be used deliberately, for effect.

Skilled writers occasionally use sentence fragments for the following special purposes.

FOR EMPHASIS   Following the dramatic Americanization of their children, even my parents grew more publicly confident. *Especially my mother.*
                                                      — Richard Rodriguez

TO ANSWER   Are these new drug tests 100 percent
A QUESTION   reliable? *Not in the opinion of most experts.*

AS TRANSITION   *And now the opposing arguments.*

EXCLAMATIONS   *Not again!*

IN ADVERTISING   *Fewer calories. Improved taste.*

Although fragments are sometimes appropriate, writers and readers do not always agree on when they are appropriate. That's why you will find it safer to write in complete sentences.

EXERCISE 19–1

Repair any fragment by attaching it to a nearby sentence or by rewriting it as a complete sentence. If a word group is correct, write "correct" after it. Revisions of lettered sentences appear in the back of the book. Example:

                                                              a
One Greek island that should not be missed is Mykonos/. A
                                                          ^
vacation spot for Europeans and a playpen for the rich.

a. The shock of bereavement is often followed by a succession of emotions. Denial, sorrow, anger, despair, guilt, remorse, and longing.
b. Cortés and his soldiers were astonished when they looked down from the mountains and saw Tenochtitlán. The magnificent capital of the Aztecs.
c. Although my spoken Spanish is not very good. I can read the language with ease.
d. There are several reasons for not eating meat. One reason being that dangerous chemicals are used throughout the various stages of meat production.
e. To give my family a comfortable, secure home life. That is my most important goal.

1. The panther lay quite motionless behind the rock. Waiting silently for its prey.
2. Mother loved to play all our favorite games. Crazy eights, Monopoly, hide-and-seek, and even kick-the-can.
3. With machetes, the explorers cut their way through the tall grasses to the edge of the canyon. Then they began to lay out the tapes for the survey.
4. The geologists were interested in visiting the Seychelles. The only midocean islands in the world that are formed of granite.
5. If a woman from the desert tribe showed anger toward her husband, she was whipped in front of the whole village. And shunned by the rest of the women.

EXERCISE 19–2

Repair each fragment in the following paragraphs by attaching it to a sentence nearby or by rewriting it as a complete sentence.

Surfing the Internet now competes with watching television as our national pastime. People, it seems, have a natural ability to sit for hour upon hour. Passively watching images flit before their eyes. Whether these appear on a TV screen or a computer screen doesn't seem to make much difference. What counts are the images themselves. Not where they come from.

Web surfing is the cyber-age equivalent of channel surfing. Both of which appeal to us because of their constant promise of something better around the corner. When 1950s TV viewers got bored with Howdy Doody, they turned off the set. Or switched to a channel with no programming and stared at the test pattern. Today, with more than one hundred channels to choose from, the demanding spectator is no longer forced to watch anything uninteresting. The Internet is the next logical step in this constant broadening of choice. Taking us from a finite number of channels to a seemingly infinite number of screens.

But there is at least one major risk of a culture based on images. That the written word may become an endangered species. As our brains eventually adapt to greater and greater levels of stimulation. Will we continue to be able to focus on a page of print? Already, members of the TV generation have a much harder time reading than their parents did. What, many people are wondering, will become of the Internet generation?

Before we send out too many alarms, however, we should remember that the Internet is still in its infancy. Already, Web browsers are helping us limit the dizzying number of choices that face us on the World Wide Web. By giving us powerful search tools that zero in on whatever aspect of a topic we are most interested in. And there is some evidence that those who spend time surfing the Net are doing more, not less, reading. Unlike TV viewers. Some Net surfers prefer to run their eyes over the words on the screen. An activity that is, after all, reading. Others download information and read the printouts. While it is true that television has reduced our nation's level of literacy, the Internet could well advance it. Only the future will tell.

ON THE WEB

For electronic exercises on sentence fragments, go to
dianahacker.com/rules

and click on ▶ **Electronic Grammar Exercises**
　　　　　　　▶ **Grammar**
　　　　　　　　▶ **E-ex 19-1 through 19-3**

20

Revise run-on sentences.

Run-on sentences are independent clauses that have not been joined correctly. An independent clause is a word group that can stand alone as a sentence. (See 64a.) When two independent clauses appear in one sentence, they must be joined in one of these ways:

— with a comma and a coordinating conjunction (*and, but, or, nor, for, so, yet*)

— with a semicolon (or occasionally with a colon or a dash)

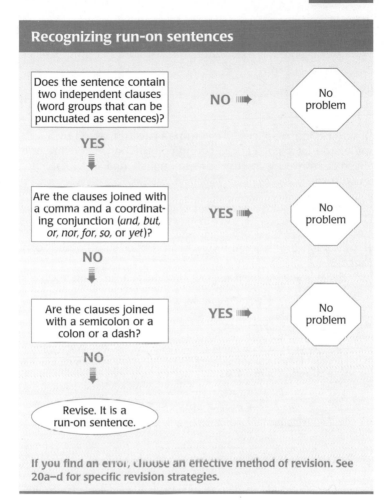

Recognizing run-on sentences

Does the sentence contain two independent clauses (word groups that can be punctuated as sentences)?

NO ⟹ No problem

YES

Are the clauses joined with a comma and a coordinating conjunction (*and, but, or, nor, for, so,* or *yet*)?

YES ⟹ No problem

NO

Are the clauses joined with a semicolon or a colon or a dash?

YES ⟹ No problem

NO

Revise. It is a run-on sentence.

If you find an error, choose an effective method of revision. See 20a–d for specific revision strategies.

Recognizing run-on sentences

There are two types of run-on sentences. When a writer puts no mark of punctuation and no coordinating conjunction between independent clauses, the result is called a *fused sentence.*

┌──────── INDEPENDENT CLAUSE ────────┐
FUSED Gestures are a means of communication for everyone

┌──────── INDEPENDENT CLAUSE ───────┐
they are essential for the hearing-impaired.

A far more common type of run-on sentence is the *comma splice* — two or more independent clauses joined by a comma without a coordinating conjunction. In some comma splices, the comma appears alone.

COMMA   Gestures are a means of communication for everyone,
SPLICE   they are essential for the hearing-impaired.

In other comma splices, the comma is accompanied by a joining word that is *not* a coordinating conjunction. There are only seven coordinating conjunctions in English: *and, but, or, nor, for, so,* and *yet.*

COMMA   Gestures are a means of communication for everyone,
SPLICE   however, they are essential for the hearing-impaired.

However is a transitional expression, not a coordinating conjunction (see 20b).

To review your writing for possible run-on sentences, use the flow chart on page 165.

ON THE WEB

The rules on avoiding comma splices have sparked debates. If you're interested in learning why, go to
dianahacker.com/rules

and click on ▶ **Language Debates**
▶ **Comma splices**

GRAMMAR CHECKERS can flag only about 20 to 50 percent of the run-on sentences in a sample. The programs tend to be cautious, telling you that you "may have" a run-on sentence; you will almost certainly get a number of "false positives," sentences that have been flagged but are not run-ons. For example, a grammar checker flagged the following acceptable sentence as a possible run-on: *They believe that requiring gun owners to purchase a license is sufficient.*

If you have a problem with run-ons, you will need to proofread for them even after using a grammar checker. Also, if your program spots a "possible" run-on, you should check to see if it is in fact a run-on, perhaps by using the flow chart on page 165.

Revising run-on sentences

To revise a run-on sentence, you have four choices.

1. Use a comma and a coordinating conjunction (*and, but, or, nor, for, so, yet*).

   ▶ Gestures are a means of communication for everyone, ^*but* they are essential for the hearing-impaired.

2. Use a semicolon (or, if appropriate, a colon or a dash). A semicolon may be used alone; it can also be accompanied by a transitional expression.

   ▶ Gestures are a means of communication for everyone ^*;* they are essential for the hearing-impaired.

   ▶ Gestures are a means of communication for everyone ^*; however,* they are essential for the hearing-impaired.

3. Make the clauses into separate sentences.

   ▶ Gestures are a means of communication for everyone ^*. They* ~~they~~ are essential for the hearing-impaired.

4. Restructure the sentence, perhaps by subordinating one of the clauses.

   ▶ *Although gestures* ^~~Gestures~~ are a means of communication for everyone, they are essential for the hearing-impaired.

One of these revision techniques usually works better than the others for a particular sentence. The fourth technique, the one requiring the most extensive revision, is often the most effective.

20a Consider separating the clauses with a comma and a coordinating conjunction.

There are seven coordinating conjunctions in English: *and, but, or, nor, for, so,* and *yet.* When a coordinating conjunction joins independent clauses, it is usually preceded by a comma. (See 32a.)

▶ The paramedic asked where I was hurt, *and* as soon as I told him,

he cut up the leg of my favorite pair of jeans.

▶ Many government officials privately admit that the polygraph

is unreliable, ~~however~~, *yet* they continue to use it as a security

measure.

However is a transitional expression, not a coordinating conjunction, so it cannot be used with only a comma to join independent clauses. (See 20b.)

20b Consider separating the clauses with a semicolon (or, if appropriate, with a colon or a dash).

When the independent clauses are closely related and their relation is clear without a coordinating conjunction, a semicolon is an acceptable method of revision. (See 34a.)

▶ Tragedy depicts the individual confronted with the fact of

death*;* comedy depicts the adaptability and ongoing survival

of human society.

A semicolon is required between independent clauses that have been linked with a transitional expression (such as *however, therefore, moreover, in fact,* or *for example*). For a longer list, see 34b.

▶ The timber wolf looks much like a large German shepherd/;
^
however, the wolf has longer legs, larger feet, a wider head,

and a long, bushy tail.

▶ Everyone in my outfit had a specific job/; as a matter of fact,
^
most of the officers had three or four duties.

If the first independent clause introduces the second or if
the second clause summarizes or explains the first, a colon or
a dash may be an appropriate method of revision. (See 35b and
39a.) In formal writing, the colon is usually preferred to the
dash.

: This
▶ Nuclear waste is hazardous ~~this~~ is an indisputable fact.
^

▶ The female black widow spider is often a widow of her own
—
making/ she has been known to eat her partner after mating.
^

If the first independent clause introduces a quoted sentence, a colon is an appropriate method of revision.

▶ Carolyn Heilbrun has this to say about the future/: "Today's
^
shocks are tomorrow's conventions."

20c Consider making the clauses into separate sentences.

▶ Why should we spend money on expensive space
We
exploration/? ~~we~~ have enough underfunded programs here
^
on Earth.

Since one independent clause is a question and the other is a statement, they should be separate sentences.

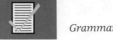 *Grammar*

▶ I gave the necessary papers to the police officer. ~~then~~ *Then* he said

I would have to accompany him to the police station, where

a counselor would talk with me and call my parents.

Because the second independent clause is quite long, a sensible revision is to use separate sentences.

NOTE: When two quoted independent clauses are divided by explanatory words, make each clause its own sentence.

▶ "It's always smart to learn from your mistakes," quipped my

supervisor~~,~~ *"It's* ~~"it's~~ even smarter to learn from the mistakes of

others."

20d Consider restructuring the sentence, perhaps by subordinating one of the clauses.

If one of the independent clauses is less important than the other, turn it into a subordinate clause or phrase. (For more about subordination, see 14, especially the chart on p. 119.)

▶ Of the many geysers in Yellowstone National Park, the most

famous is Old Faithful, *which* ~~it~~ sometimes reaches 150 feet in height.

Although many
▶ ~~Many~~ scholars dismiss the abominable snowman of the

Himalayas as a myth, others claim it may be a kind of ape.

▶ Mary McLeod Bethune, ~~was~~ the seventeenth child of former

slaves, ~~she~~ founded the National Council of Negro Women in

1935.

Minor ideas in these sentences are now expressed in subordinate clauses or phrases.

EXERCISE 20–1

Revise any run-on sentences using the method of revision suggested in brackets. Revisions of lettered sentences appear in the back of the book. Example:

Because
Orville had been obsessed with his weight as a teenager, he
  ^
rarely ate anything sweet and delicious. [*Restructure the*

sentence.]

a. The city had one public swimming pool, it stayed packed with children all summer long. [*Restructure the sentence.*]
b. The building is being renovated, therefore at times we have no heat, water, or electricity. [*Use a comma and a coordinating conjunction.*]
c. The neighborhood was ruled by gangs, what kind of environment was this for my ten-year-old son? [*Make two sentences.*]
d. Suddenly there was a loud silence, the shelling had stopped. [*Use a semicolon.*]
e. The car was hardly worth trading, the frame was twisted and the block was warped. [*Restructure the sentence.*]

1. The city government had good reason to fear a major earthquake, most of the business district was built on a landfill. [*Restructure the sentence.*]
2. The next time an event is canceled because of bad weather, don't blame the meteorologist, blame nature. [*Make two sentences.*]
3. Mr. Romero is an excellent linguist he has been studying Chinese dialects for twenty years. [*Restructure the sentence.*]
4. The president of Algeria was standing next to the podium he was waiting to be introduced. [*Restructure the sentence.*]
5. There was one major reason for John's wealth, his grandfather had been a multimillionaire. [*Use a colon.*]

EXERCISE 20–2

Revise any run-on sentences using a technique that you find effective. If a sentence is correct, write "correct" after it. Revisions of lettered sentences appear in the back of the book. Example:

Crossing so many time zones on an eight-hour flight, I knew
                                              but
I would be tired when I arrived, ~~however~~, I was too excited
                                         ^
to sleep on the plane.

a. Wind power for the home is a supplementary source of energy, it can be combined with electricity, gas, or solar energy.
b. The duck hunter set out his decoys in the shallow bay and then settled in to wait for the first real bird to alight.
c. In the Middle Ages, the streets of London were dangerous places, it was safer to travel by boat along the Thames.
d. "He's not drunk," I said, "he's in a state of diabetic shock."
e. Are you able to endure boredom, isolation, and potential violence, then the army may well be the adventure for you.

1. Death Valley National Monument, located in southern California and Nevada, is one of the hottest places on earth, temperatures in this desert area have soared as high as 134 degrees Fahrenheit.
2. If one of the dogs should happen to fall through the ice, it would be cut loose from the team and left to its fate, the sled drivers could not endanger the rest of the team for just one dog.
3. Nuclear power plants produce energy by fission, a process that generates radioactive waste.
4. The center of the French Quarter of New Orleans is Jackson Square, this square is one of the most beautiful urban spaces in the United States.
5. The neurosurgeon explained that the medication could have one side effect, it might cause me to experience a temporary memory loss.

ON THE WEB

For electronic exercises on run-on sentences, go to
dianahacker.com/rules

and click on   ▶ **Electronic Grammar Exercises**
                      ▶ **Grammar**
                          ▶ **E-ex 20-1 through 20-3**

21

Make subjects and verbs agree.

Native speakers of standard English know by ear that *he talks, she has,* and *it doesn't* (not *he talk, she have,* and *it don't*) are standard subject-verb combinations. For such speakers, problems with subject-verb agreement arise only in certain tricky situations, which are detailed in 21b–21k.

If you don't trust your ear — perhaps because you speak English as a second language, perhaps because you speak or hear nonstandard English in your community — you will need to learn the standard forms explained in 21a. Even if you do trust your ear, take a quick look at 21a to see what "subject-verb agreement" means.

21a Consult this section for standard subject-verb combinations.

In the present tense, verbs agree with their subjects in number (singular or plural) and in person (first, second, or third). The present-tense ending -s (or -es) is used on a verb if its subject is third-person singular; otherwise the verb takes no ending. Consider, for example, the present-tense forms of the verb *love,* given at the beginning of the chart on the next page.

The verb *be* varies from this pattern; unlike any other verb, it has special forms in *both* the present and the past tense. These forms appear at the end of the chart on the next page.

If you aren't confident that you know the standard forms, use the charts on pages 174 and 175 as you proofread for subject-verb agreement. You may also want to take a look at 27c, which discusses -s endings in detail.

GRAMMAR CHECKERS attempt to flag faulty subject-verb agreement, but they have mixed success. They fail to flag many problems; in addition, they flag a number of correct sentences, usually because they have misidentified the subject, the verb, or both. For example, one program flagged the following correct sentence: *Nearly everyone on the panel favors the health care reform proposal.* The program identified the subject as *care* and the verb as *reform;* in fact, the subject is *everyone* and the verb is *favors.*

Subject-verb agreement at a glance

**PRESENT-TENSE FORMS OF *LOVE*
(A TYPICAL VERB)**

	SINGULAR		PLURAL	
FIRST PERSON	I	love	we	love
SECOND PERSON	you	love	you	love
THIRD PERSON	he/she/it	loves	they	love

PRESENT-TENSE FORMS OF *HAVE*

	SINGULAR		PLURAL	
FIRST PERSON	I	have	we	have
SECOND PERSON	you	have	you	have
THIRD PERSON	he/she/it	has	they	have

PRESENT-TENSE FORMS OF *DO*

	SINGULAR		PLURAL	
FIRST PERSON	I	do/don't	we	do/don't
SECOND PERSON	you	do/don't	you	do/don't
THIRD PERSON	he/she/it	does/doesn't	they	do/don't

**PRESENT-TENSE AND PAST-TENSE
FORMS OF *BE***

	SINGULAR		PLURAL	
FIRST PERSON	I	am/was	we	are/were
SECOND PERSON	you	are/were	you	are/were
THIRD PERSON	he/she/it	is/was	they	are/were

21b Make the verb agree with its subject, not with a word that comes between.

Word groups often come between the subject and the verb. Such word groups, usually modifying the subject, may contain a noun that at first appears to be the subject. By mentally stripping away such modifiers, you can isolate the noun that is in fact the subject.

The *samples* on the tray in the lab *need* testing.

When to use the *-s* (or *-es*) form of a present-tense verb

Is the verb's subject *he, she, it,* or *one*?   YES ⟹ Use the -s form (*loves, has, does, doesn't*).

NO ⬇

Is the subject a singular noun (such as *parent*)?   YES ⟹ Use the -s form.

NO ⬇

Is the subject a singular indefinite pronoun — *anybody, anyone, each, either, everybody, everyone, everything, neither, no one, someone,* or *something*?   YES ⟹ Use the -s form.

NO ⬇

Use the base form of the verb (such as *love, have, do, don't*).

EXCEPTION: Choosing the correct present-tense form of *be* (*am, is,* or *are*) is not quite so simple. See the chart on page 174 for both present- and past-tense forms of *be*.

ESL CAUTION: Do not use the *-s* form of a verb when it follows a helping verb such as *can, must,* or *should*. (See 29a.)

▶ High levels of air pollution causes damage to the respiratory

tract.

The subject is *levels,* not *pollution.* Strip away the phrase *of air pollution* to hear the correct verb: *levels cause.*

has
▶ The slaughter of pandas for their pelts ~~have~~ caused the panda
    ^

population to decline drastically.

The subject is *slaughter,* not *pandas* or *pelts.*

NOTE: Phrases beginning with the prepositions *as well as, in addition to, accompanied by, together with,* and *along with* do not make a singular subject plural.

was
▶ The governor, as well as his press secretary, ~~were~~ shot.
    ^

To emphasize that two people were shot, the writer could use *and* instead: *The governor and his press secretary were shot.*

21C Treat most subjects joined with *and* as plural.

A subject with two or more parts is said to be compound. If the parts are connected by *and,* the subject is nearly always plural.

Leon and Jan often *jog* together.

have
▶ Jill's natural ability and her desire to help others ~~has~~ led to a
    ^

career in the ministry.

Ability and desire is a plural subject, so its verb should be *have.*

EXCEPTIONS: When the parts of the subject form a single unit or when they refer to the same person or thing, treat the subject as singular.

Strawberries and cream was a last-minute addition to the menu.

Sue's friend and adviser was surprised by her decision.

When a compound subject is preceded by *each* or *every,* treat it as singular.

Each tree, shrub, and vine needs to be sprayed.

Every car, truck, and van is required to pass inspection.

This exception does not apply when a compound subject is followed by *each: Alan and Marcia each have different ideas.*

21d With subjects joined with *or* or *nor* (or by *either . . . or* or *neither . . . nor*), make the verb agree with the part of the subject nearer to the verb.

A driver's *license* or credit *card is* required.

A driver's *license* or two credit *cards are* required.

▶ If a relative or neighbor ~~are~~ *is* abusing a child, notify the police immediately.

▶ Neither the lab assistant nor the students ~~was~~ *were* able to download the information.

The verb must be matched with the part of the subject closer to it: *neighbor is* in the first sentence, *students were* in the second.

NOTE: If one part of the subject is singular and the other is plural, put the plural one last to avoid awkwardness.

21e Treat most indefinite pronouns as singular.

Indefinite pronouns are pronouns that do not refer to specific persons or things. The following commonly used indefinite pronouns are singular:

anybody	each	everyone	nobody	somebody
anyone	either	everything	no one	someone
anything	everybody	neither	nothing	something

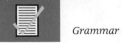
Many of these words appear to have plural meanings, and they are often treated as such in casual speech. In formal written English, however, they are nearly always treated as singular.

Everyone on the team *supports* the coach.

▶ Each of the furrows ~~have~~ ^has^ been seeded.

▶ Everybody who signed up for the ski trip ~~were~~ ^was^ taking lessons.

The subjects of these sentences are *Each* and *Everybody.* These indefinite pronouns are third-person singular, so the verbs must be *has* and *was.*

A few indefinite pronouns (*all, any, none, some*) may be singular or plural depending on the noun or pronoun they refer to.

Some of our *luggage was* lost. *None* of his *advice makes* sense.

Some of the *rocks are* slippery. *None* of the *eggs were* broken.

NOTE: When the meaning of *none* is emphatically "not one," *none* may be treated as singular: *None* [meaning "Not one"] *of the eggs was broken.* However, some experts advise using *not one* instead: *Not one of the eggs was broken.*

ON THE WEB

The rules on whether to treat *none* as singular or plural have sparked debates. If you're interesed in learning why, go to
dianahacker.com/rules

and click on ▶ **Language Debates**
        ▶ *none*

21f Treat collective nouns as singular unless the meaning is clearly plural.

Collective nouns such as *jury, committee, audience, crowd, class, troop, family,* and *couple* name a class or a group. In American English, collective nouns are nearly always treated as singular: They emphasize the group as a unit. Occasionally, when there is some reason to draw attention to the individual members of the group, a collective noun may be treated as plural. (Also see 22b.)

SINGULAR   The *class respects* the teacher.

PLURAL   The *class are* debating among themselves.

To underscore the notion of individuality in the second sentence, many writers would add a clearly plural noun such as *members.*

PLURAL   The class *members are* debating among themselves.

▶ The board of trustees ~~meet~~ meets in Denver on the first Tuesday of each month.

The board as a whole meets; there is no reason to draw attention to its individual members.

▶ A young couple ~~was~~ were arguing about politics while holding hands.

The meaning is clearly plural. Only individuals can argue and hold hands.

NOTE: The phrase *the number* is treated as singular, *a number* as plural.

SINGULAR   *The number* of school-age children *is* declining.

PLURAL   *A number* of children *are* attending the wedding.

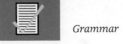

NOTE: When units of measurement are used collectively, treat them as singular; when they refer to individual persons or things, treat them as plural.

SINGULAR   *Three-fourths* of the pie *has* been eaten.

PLURAL   *One-fourth* of the drivers *were* drunk.

21g   **Make the verb agree with its subject even when the subject follows the verb.**

Verbs ordinarily follow subjects. When this normal order is reversed, it is easy to become confused. Sentences beginning with *There is* or *There are* (or *There was* or *There were*) are inverted; the subject follows the verb.

There *are* surprisingly few *children* in our neighborhood.

▶ There ~~was~~ *were* a social worker and a crew of twenty volunteers at

the scene of the accident.

The subject *worker and crew* is plural, so the verb
must be *were*.

Occasionally you may decide to invert a sentence for variety or effect. When you do so, check to make sure that your subject and verb agree.

▶ At the back of the room ~~is~~ *are* a small aquarium and an enormous

terrarium.

The subject *aquarium and terrarium* is plural, so the verb must be *are*. If the correct sentence seems awkward, begin with the subject: *A small aquarium and an enormous terrarium are at the back of the room.*

21h Make the verb agree with its subject, not with a subject complement.

One basic sentence pattern in English consists of a subject, a linking verb, and a subject complement: *Jack is a securities lawyer.* Because the subject complement names or describes the subject (*Jack*), it is sometimes mistaken for the subject. (See 62b on subject complements.)

These *exercises are* a way to test your physical stamina.

▶ A tent and a sleeping bag is the required equipment for all
   are
   ^
   campers.

Tent and bag is the subject, not *equipment.*

▶ A major force in today's economy are women — as earners,
   is
   ^
   consumers, and investors.

Force is the subject, not *women.* If the corrected version seems awkward, make *women* the subject: *Women are a major force in today's economy — as earners, consumers, and investors.*

21i *Who, which,* and *that* take verbs that agree with their antecedents.

Like most pronouns, the relative pronouns *who, which,* and *that* have antecedents, nouns or pronouns to which they refer. Relative pronouns used as subjects of subordinate clauses take verbs that agree with their antecedents.

Take a *suit that travels* well.

Constructions such as *one of the students who* [or *one of the things that*] cause problems for writers. Do not assume that the antecedent must be *one.* Instead, consider the logic of the sentence.

▶ Our ability to use language is one of the things that set*s̶* us

apart from animals.

The antecedent of *that* is *things*, not *one*. Several things set us apart from animals.

When the word *only* comes before *one*, you are safe in assuming that *one* is the antecedent of the relative pronoun.

▶ Dr. Barker knew that Frank was the only one of his sons who
was
w̶e̶r̶e̶ responsible enough to handle the estate.
^

The antecedent of *who* is *one*, not *sons*. Only one son was responsible enough.

ON THE WEB

The rules on *one of those who* constructions have sparked debates. If you're interested in learning why, go to
dianahacker.com/rules

and click on ▶ **Language Debates**
▶ ***one of those who*** (or ***that***)

21j Words such as *athletics, economics, mathematics, physics, statistics, measles, mumps,* and *news* are usually singular, despite their plural form.

is
▶ Statistics a̶r̶e̶ among the most difficult courses in our program.
^

EXCEPTION: When they describe separate items rather than a collective body of knowledge, words such as *athletics, mathematics, physics,* and *statistics* are plural: *The statistics on school retention rates are impressive.*

21k Titles of works, company names, words mentioned as words, and gerund phrases are singular.

describes
▶ *Lost Cities* d̶e̶s̶c̶r̶i̶b̶e̶ the discoveries of many ancient
^
civilizations.

specializes
▶ Delmonico Brothers ~~specialize~~ in organic produce and
               ^

additive-free meats.

       is
▶ *Controlled substances* ~~are~~ a euphemism for illegal drugs.
                       ^

A gerund phrase consists of an *-ing* verb form followed by
any objects, complements, or modifiers (see 63c). Treat gerund
phrases as singular.

                  is
▶ Encountering busy signals ~~are~~ troublesome to our clients, so
                        ^

we have hired two new switchboard operators.

EXERCISE 21-1

Underline the subject (or compound subject) and then select the verb
that agrees with it. (If you have difficulty identifying the subject, consult 62a.) Answers to lettered sentences appear in the back of the book.
Example:

> <u>Someone</u> in the audience ((has)/ have) volunteered to partici-
>
> pate in the experiment.

a. Your friendship over the years and your support on a wide variety of issues (has / have) meant a great deal to us.
b. Shelters for teenage runaways (offers / offer) a wide variety of services.
c. The main source of income for Trinidad (is / are) oil and pitch.
d. The chances of your being promoted (is / are) excellent.
e. There (was / were) a *Peanuts* cartoon and a few Mother Goose
   rhymes pinned to the bulletin board.

1. Neither the professor nor his assistants (was / were) able to solve
   the mystery of the eerie glow in the laboratory.
2. Four years of research (has / have) gone into making our software
   suitable for the Japanese market.
3. Discovered in the soil of our city garden (was / were) a button dating from the Civil War and three marbles dating from the turn of
   the century.
4. Every year, during the midsummer festival, the smoke of village
   bonfires (fills / fill) the sky.
5. When food supplies (was / were) scarce, the slaves had to make do
   with the less desirable parts of the animals.

ON THE WEB

For electronic exercises on subject-verb agreement, go to
dianahacker.com/rules

and click on ▶ **Electronic Grammar Exercises**
　　　　　　　　▶ **Grammar**
　　　　　　　　　　▶ **E-ex 21-1 through 21-3**

EXERCISE 21-2

Edit the following sentences to eliminate problems with subject-verb agreement. If a sentence is correct, write "correct" after it. Answers to lettered sentences appear in the back of the book. Example:

were

Jack's first days in the infantry ~~was~~ grueling.
　　　　　　　　　　　　　　　　　^

a. One of the main reasons for elephant poaching are the profits received from selling the ivory tusks.
b. Not until my interview with Dr. Hwang were other possibilities opened to me.
c. Of those who die in single-car wrecks, a majority is drunk.
d. Crystal chandeliers, polished floors, and a new oil painting has transformed Sandra's apartment.
e. The board of directors, ignoring the wishes of the neighborhood, has voted to allow further development.

1. Measles is a contagious childhood disease.
2. Of particular concern are penicillin and tetracycline, antibiotics used to make animals more resistant to disease.
3. The presence of certain bacteria in our bodies is one of the factors that determines our overall health.
4. Sheila is the only one of the many applicants who has the ability to step into this job.
5. Neither the explorer nor his companions was ever seen again.

22

Make pronouns and antecedents agree.

A pronoun is a word that substitutes for a noun. (See 61b.) Many pronouns have antecedents, nouns or pronouns to which they refer. A pronoun and its antecedent agree when they are both singular or both plural.

SINGULAR *Dr. Samantha McQueen* finished *her* rounds.

PLURAL The hospital *interns* finished *their* rounds.

ESL

The pronouns *he, his, she, her, it,* and *its* must agree in gender (masculine, feminine, or neuter) with their antecedents, not with the words they modify.

Steve visited *his* [not *her*] sister in Seattle.

GRAMMAR CHECKERS do not flag problems with pronoun-antecedent agreement. It takes a human eye to see that a plural pronoun, such as *their,* does not agree with a singular noun, such as *logger,* in a sentence like this: *The logger in the North-west relies on the old forest growth for their living.*

22a Do not use plural pronouns to refer to singular antecedents.

Writers are frequently tempted to use plural pronouns to refer to two kinds of singular antecedents: indefinite pronouns and generic nouns.

Indefinite pronouns

Indefinite pronouns refer to nonspecific persons or things. Even though some of the following indefinite pronouns may seem to have plural meanings, treat them as singular in formal English.

anybody	either	neither	somebody
anyone	everybody	nobody	someone
anything	everyone	no one	something
each	everything		

In class *everyone* performs at *his or her* [not *their*] own level.

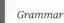

When a plural pronoun refers mistakenly to a singular indefinite pronoun, you can usually choose one of three options for revision:

1. Replace the plural pronoun with *he or she* (or *his or her*).
2. Make the antecedent plural.
3. Rewrite the sentence so that no problem of agreement exists.

▶ When someone has been drinking, ~~they are~~ likely to speed.
  he or she is

▶ When ~~someone has~~ been drinking, they are likely to speed.
  drivers have

▶ ~~When someone~~ has been drinking/ ~~they are~~ likely to speed.
  A driver who   *is*

Because the *he or she* construction is wordy, often the second or third revision strategy is more effective. Be aware that the traditional use of *he* (or *his*) to refer to persons of either sex is now widely considered sexist. (See 17f.)

Generic nouns

A generic noun represents a typical member of a group, such as a typical student, or any member of a group, such as any lawyer. Although generic nouns may seem to have plural meanings, they are singular.

Every *runner* must train rigorously if *he or she wants* [not *they want*] to excel.

When a plural pronoun refers mistakenly to a generic noun, you will usually have the same three revision options as just mentioned for indefinite pronouns.

▶ A medical student must study hard if ~~they want~~ to succeed.
  he or she wants

▶ ~~A medical student~~ must study hard if they want to succeed.
  Medical students

▶ A medical student must study hard ~~if they want~~ to succeed.

Choosing a revision strategy that avoids sexist language

Because many readers object to sexist language, avoid the use of *he, him,* and *his* to refer to both men and women. Also try to be sparing in your use of the wordy expressions *he or she* and *his or her.* Where possible, seek out more graceful alternatives.

USE AN OCCASIONAL *HE OR SHE* (OR *HIS OR HER*).

▶ In our office, everyone works at ~~their~~ *his or her* own pace.

MAKE THE ANTECEDENT PLURAL.

▶ ~~An employee~~ *Employees* on extended leave may continue their life

insurance.

RECAST THE SENTENCE.

▶ The amount of annual leave a federal worker may accrue

depends on ~~their~~ length of service.

▶ ~~If a~~ *A* child ~~is~~ born to parents who are both bipolar ~~/ they have~~ *has* a

high chance of being bipolar.

▶ A year later someone finally admitted ~~that they were~~ *to being* involved

in the kidnapping.

▶ I was taught that no one *who wanted to reach heaven* could escape the fires of purgatory.

~~if they wanted to reach heaven.~~

ON THE WEB

The rules on pronoun-antecedent agreement have sparked debates. If you're interested in learning why, go to **dianahacker.com/rules**

and click on ▶ **Language Debates**
                ▶ **Pronoun-antecedent agreement**

22b Treat collective nouns as singular unless the meaning is clearly plural.

Collective nouns such as *jury, committee, audience, crowd, class, troop, family, team,* and *couple* name a class or a group. Ordinarily the group functions as a unit, so the noun should be treated as singular; if the members of the group function as individuals, however, the noun should be treated as plural. (See also 21f.)

AS A UNIT   The *committee* granted *its* permission to build.

AS INDIVIDUALS   The *committee* put *their* signatures on the document.

▶ The jury has reached ~~their~~ *its* decision.

There is no reason to draw attention to the individual members of the jury, so *jury* should be treated as singular. Notice also that the writer treated the noun as singular when choosing the verb *has,* so for consistency the pronoun must be *its.*

▶ The audience shouted "Bravo" and stamped ~~its~~ *their* feet.

It is difficult to see how the audience as a unit can stamp *its* feet. The meaning here is clearly plural, requiring *their.*

22c Treat most compound antecedents connected by *and* as plural.

Jill and John moved to Luray, where *they* built a cabin.

22d With compound antecedents connected by *or* or *nor* (or by *either . . . or* or *neither . . . nor*), make the pronoun agree with the nearer antecedent.

Either *Bruce* or *Tom* should receive first prize for *his* poem.

Neither the *mouse* nor the *rats* could find *their* way through the maze.

NOTE: If one of the antecedents is singular and the other plural, put the plural one last to avoid awkwardness.

EXCEPTION: If one antecedent is male and the other female, do not follow the traditional rule. The sentence *Either Bruce or Ann should receive first prize for her poem* makes no sense. The best solution is to recast the sentence: *The prize for best poem should go to Bruce or Ann.*

EXERCISE 22–1

Edit the following sentences to eliminate problems with pronoun-antecedent agreement. Most of the sentences can be revised in more than one way, so experiment before choosing a solution. If a sentence is correct, write "correct" after it. Revisions of lettered sentences appear in the back of the book. Example:

> Recruiters
> ~~The recruiter~~ may tell the truth, but there is much that they
> ^
> choose not to tell.

a. Every presidential candidate must appeal to a wide variety of ethnic and social groups if they want to win the election.
b. David lent his motorcycle to someone who allowed their friend to use it.
c. The instructor has asked everyone to bring their tools to carpentry class.
d. The parade committee was unanimous in its decision to allow all groups and organizations to join the festivities.
e. The applicant should be bilingual if they want to qualify for this position.

1. If a driver refuses to take a blood or breath test, he or she will have their licenses suspended for six months.
2. Why should we care about the timber wolf? One answer is that they have proven beneficial to humans by killing off weakened prey.

3. The National Rifle Association argues that current gun laws should be enforced. In the past, however, they have opposed nearly all proposed legislation affecting guns.
4. Eight highly qualified firefighters applied for the forestry position in Durango, each hoping for a career move that would allow them to hone their skills in battling and preventing forest fires.
5. If anyone notices any suspicious activity, they should report it to the police.

EXERCISE 22–2

Edit the following paragraph to eliminate problems with pronoun-antecedent agreement or sexist language.

A common practice in businesses is to put each employee in their own cubicle. A typical cubicle resembles an office, but their walls don't reach the ceiling. Many office managers feel that a cubicle floor plan has its advantages. Cubicles make a large area feel spacious. In addition, they can be moved around so that each new employee can be accommodated in his own work area. Of course, the cubicle model also has problems. The typical employee is not as happy with a cubicle as they would be with a traditional office. Also, productivity can suffer. Neither a manager nor a frontline worker can ordinarily do their best work in a cubicle because of noise and lack of privacy. Each worker can hear his neighbors tapping on computer keyboards, making telephone calls, and muttering under their breath.

ON THE WEB

For electronic exercises on pronoun-antecedent agreement, go to
dianahacker.com/rules

and click on ▶ **Electronic Grammar Exercises**
▶ **Grammar**
▶ **E-ex 22–1 through 22–3**

23

Make pronoun references clear.

Pronouns substitute for nouns; they are a kind of shorthand. In a sentence like *After Andrew intercepted the ball, he kicked it as hard as he could,* the pronouns *he* and *it* substitute for the nouns *Andrew* and *ball.* The word a pronoun refers to is called its *antecedent.*

GRAMMAR CHECKERS do not flag problems with faulty pronoun reference. Although a computer program can identify pronouns, it has no way of knowing which words, if any, they refer to. For example, grammar checkers miss the fact that the pronoun *it* has an ambiguous reference in the following sentence: *The thief stole the woman's purse and her car and then destroyed it.* Did the thief destroy the purse or the car? It takes human judgment to realize that readers might be confused.

23a Avoid ambiguous or remote pronoun reference.

Ambiguous pronoun reference occurs when the pronoun could refer to two possible antecedents.

> *The pitcher broke when Gloria set it*
> ~~When Gloria set the pitcher~~ on the glass-topped table~~,~~ ~~it~~
>   ^   ^
> ~~broke.~~

>   *"You have*
> Tom told James~~,~~ ~~that he had~~ won the lottery~~.~~*"*
>   ^   ^

What broke — the table or the pitcher? Who won the lottery — Tom or James? The revisions eliminate the ambiguity.

Remote pronoun reference occurs when a pronoun is too far away from its antecedent for easy reading.

> After the court ordered my ex-husband to pay child support,
>
> he refused. Eight months later, we were back in court. This
>
> time the judge ordered him to send checks to the Support
>
> and Collections Unit, which would then pay me. For six
>
> months I received payments, but then they stopped. Again
> *my ex-husband*
> ~~he~~ was summoned to appear in court; he did not respond.
>   ^

The pronoun *he* was too distant from its antecedent, *ex-husband*, which appeared several sentences earlier.

23b Generally, avoid broad reference of *this, that, which,* and *it.*

For clarity, the pronouns *this, that, which,* and *it* should ordinarily refer to specific antecedents rather than to whole ideas or sentences. When a pronoun's reference is needlessly broad, either replace the pronoun with a noun or supply an antecedent to which the pronoun clearly refers.

▶ More and more often, especially in large cities, we are finding

ourselves victims of serious crimes. We learn to accept ~~this~~ *our fate*
^

with minor gripes and groans.

For clarity the writer substituted a noun (*fate*) for the pronoun *this,* which referred broadly to the idea expressed in the preceding sentence.

▶ Romeo and Juliet were both too young to have acquired much
a fact
wisdom, which accounts for their rash actions.
^

The writer added an antecedent (*fact*) that the pronoun *which* clearly refers to.

EXCEPTION: Many writers view broad reference as acceptable when the pronoun refers clearly to the sense of an entire clause.

If you pick up a starving dog and make him prosperous, he will not bite you. *This* is the principal difference between a dog and a man. — Mark Twain

23c Do not use a pronoun to refer to an implied antecedent.

A pronoun should refer to a specific antecedent, not to a word that is implied but not present in the sentence.

the braids
▶ After braiding Ann's hair, Sue decorated ~~them~~ with ribbons.
^

The pronoun *them* referred to Ann's braids (implied by the term *braiding*), but the word *braids* did not appear in the sentence.

Modifiers, such as possessives, cannot serve as antecedents. A modifier may strongly imply the noun that the pronoun might logically refer to, but it is not itself that noun.

Euripides
▶ In ~~Euripides'~~ *Medea,* ~~he~~ describes the plight of a woman
^

rejected by her husband.

The pronoun *he* cannot refer logically to the possessive modifier *Euripides'.* The revision substitutes the noun *Euripides* for the pronoun *he,* thereby eliminating the problem.

23d Avoid the indefinite use of *they, it,* and *you.*

Do not use the pronoun *they* to refer indefinitely to persons who have not been specifically mentioned. *They* should always refer to a specific antecedent.

Congress
▶ Last year ~~they~~ shut down all government agencies for more
^

than a month until the budget crisis was finally resolved.

The word *it* should not be used indefinitely in constructions such as "It is said on television . . ." or "In the article it says that . . ."

The
▶ ~~In the~~ encyclopedia ~~it~~ states that male moths can smell
^

female moths from several miles away.

The pronoun *you* is appropriate when the writer is addressing the reader directly: *Once you have kneaded the dough, let it rise in a warm place for at least twenty-five minutes.* Except in informal contexts, however, the indefinite *you* (meaning "anyone in general") is inappropriate. (See page 177.)

▶ Ms. Pickersgill's *Guide to Etiquette* stipulates that ~~you~~ should
                                                          a guest
not arrive at a party too early or leave too late.

The writer could have replaced *you* with *one*, but in American English the pronoun *one* can seem stilted.

ON THE WEB

The rule on avoiding the indefinite *you* has sparked debates. If you're interested in learning why, go to
dianahacker.com/rules

and click on   ▶ **Language Debates**
                     ▶ *you*

23e To refer to persons, use *who, whom,* or *whose,* not *which* or *that.*

In most contexts, use *who, whom,* or *whose* to refer to persons, *which* or *that* to refer to animals or things. *Which* is reserved only for animals or things, so it is impolite to use it to refer to persons.

                                                        whom
▶ When he heard about my seven children, four of ~~which~~ live

at home, Ron smiled and said, "I love children."

Although *that* is sometimes used to refer to persons, many readers will find such references dehumanizing. It is more polite to use a form of *who* — a word reserved only for people.

                                              who
▶ Fans wondered how an out-of-shape old man ~~that~~ walked

with a limp could play football.

NOTE: Occasionally *whose* may be used to refer to animals and things to avoid the awkward *of which* construction.

                          whose
▶ A major corporation, ~~the name of which~~ will be in tomorrow's

paper, has been illegally dumping toxic waste in the harbor.

ON THE WEB

The rule on avoiding *that* to refer to people has sparked debates.
If you're interested in learning why, go to
dianahacker.com/rules

and click on ▶ **Language Debates**
▶ *who* versus *which* or *that*

EXERCISE 23–1

Edit the following sentences to correct errors in pronoun reference. In
some cases you will need to decide on an antecedent that the pronoun
might logically refer to. Revisions of lettered sentences appear in the
back of the book. Example:

Following the breakup of AT&T, many other companies began

The competition
to offer long-distance phone service. ~~This~~ has led to lower
                                       ^

long-distance rates.

a. They say that the *Challenger* disaster set the space program back
   five years.
b. She had decorated her living room with posters from chamber
   music festivals. This led her date to believe that she was interested
   in classical music, but actually she preferred rock.
c. In Ethiopia, you don't need much property to be considered well-off.
d. Marianne told Jenny that she was worried about her mother's
   illness.
e. Though Lewis cried for several minutes after scraping his knee,
   eventually it subsided.

1. Our German conversation group is made up of six people, three
   of which I had never met before.
2. Many people believe that the polygraph test is highly reliable if
   you employ a licensed examiner.
3. France receives nearly 80 percent of its electrical needs from nuclear power. They have not had a serious mishap to date, but will
   their luck continue?
4. Because of Paul Robeson's outspoken attitude toward fascism, he
   was labeled a Communist.
5. In the report it points out that lifting the ban on Compound
   1080 would prove detrimental, possibly even fatal, to the bald
   eagle.

ON THE WEB

For electronic exercises on pronoun reference, go to
dianahacker.com/rules

and click on ▶ **Electronic Grammar Exercises**
▶ **Grammar**
▶ **E-ex 23-1 through 23-3**

24

Distinguish between pronouns such as *I* and *me*.

The personal pronouns in the following chart change what is known as case form according to their grammatical function in a sentence. Pronouns functioning as subjects (or subject complements) appear in the *subjective* case; those functioning as objects appear in the *objective* case; and those showing ownership appear in the *possessive* case.

	SUBJECTIVE CASE	OBJECTIVE CASE	POSSESSIVE CASE
SINGULAR	I	me	my
	you	you	your
	he/she/it	him/her/it	his/her/its

	SUBJECTIVE CASE	OBJECTIVE CASE	POSSESSIVE CASE
PLURAL	we	us	our
	you	you	your
	they	them	their

Pronouns in the subjective and objective case are frequently confused. Most of the rules in this section specify when to use one or the other of these cases (*I* or *me, he* or *him,* and so on). Rule 24g details a special use of pronouns and nouns in the possessive case.

GRAMMAR CHECKERS can flag some incorrect pronouns and explain the rules for using *I* or *me, he* or *him, she* or *her, we* or *us,* and *they* or *them.* For example, one grammar checker program correctly flagged *we* in the following sentence and advised using *us* instead: *I say it is about time for we parents to revolt.*

You should not assume, however, that a computer program will catch all incorrect pronouns. For example, grammar checkers did not flag *more than I* in this sentence, where the writer's meaning requires *me: I get a little jealous that our dog likes my neighbor more than I.*

24a Use the subjective case (*I, you, he, she, it, we, they*) for subjects and subject complements.

When personal pronouns are used as subjects, ordinarily your ear will tell you the correct pronoun. Problems sometimes arise, however, with compound word groups containing a pronoun, so it is not always safe to trust your ear.

▶ Joel ran away from home because his stepfather and ~~him~~ *he* had

quarreled.

His stepfather and he is the subject of the verb *had quarreled.* If we strip away the words *his stepfather and,* the correct pronoun becomes clear: *he had quarreled* (not *him had quarreled*).

When a pronoun is used as a subject complement (a word following a linking verb), your ear may mislead you, since the incorrect form is frequently heard in casual speech. (See subject complement, 62b.)

▶ During the Lindbergh trial, Bruno Hauptmann repeatedly

denied that the kidnapper was ~~him.~~ *he.*

If *kidnapper was he* seems too stilted, rewrite the sentence: *During the Lindbergh trial, Bruno Hauptmann repeatedly denied that he was the kidnapper.*

Grammar

24b Use the objective case (*me, you, him, her, it, us, them*) for all objects.

When a personal pronoun is used as a direct object, an indirect object, or the object of a preposition, ordinarily your ear will lead you to the correct pronoun. When an object is compound, however, you may occasionally become confused.

▶ Janice was indignant when she realized that the salesclerk

                                her.
   was insulting her mother and ~~she.~~
                              ^

Her mother and her is the direct object of the verb *was insulting.* Strip away the words *her mother and* to hear the correct pronoun: *was insulting her* (not *was insulting she*).

                                          me
▶ The most traumatic experience for her father and ~~I~~ occurred

                                           ^
   long after her operation.

Her father and me is the object of the preposition *for.* Strip away the words *her father and* to test for the correct pronoun: *for me* (not *for I*).

When in doubt about the correct pronoun, some writers try to avoid making the choice by using the reflexive pronoun *myself.* Such evasions are nonstandard, even though they are used by some educated persons.

                                       me
▶ The Egyptian cab driver gave my husband and ~~myself~~ some

                                           ^
   good tips on traveling in North Africa.

My husband and me is the indirect object of the verb *gave.* For correct uses of *myself,* see the Glossary of Usage.

ON THE WEB

The rule on avoiding *myself* as a substitute for *I* or *me* has sparked debates. If you're interested in learning why, go to
dianahacker.com/rules

and click on ▶ **Language Debates**
                      ▶ ***myself***

24c Put an appositive and the word to which it refers in the same case.

Appositives are noun phrases that rename nouns or pronouns. A pronoun used as an appositive has the same function (usually subject or object) as the word(s) the appositive renames.

▶ The chief strategists, Dr. Bell and ~~me~~, could not agree on a

 I,

plan.

> The appositive *Dr. Bell and I* renames the subject, *strategists*. Test: *I could not agree* (not *me could not agree*).

▶ The reporter interviewed only two witnesses, the shopkeeper

 me.

and ~~I.~~

> The appositive *the shopkeeper and me* renames the direct object, *witnesses*. Test: *interviewed me* (not *interviewed I*).

24d Following *than* or *as,* choose the pronoun that expresses your meaning.

When a comparison begins with *than* or *as,* your choice of a pronoun will depend on your intended meaning. Consider, for example, the difference in meaning between these sentences.

> My husband likes football better than I.
>
> My husband likes football better than me.

Finish each sentence mentally and its meaning becomes clear: *My husband likes football better than I [do]. My husband likes football better than [he likes] me.*

▶ Even though he is sometimes ridiculed by the other boys,

 they.

Norman is much better off than ~~them.~~

> *They* is the subject of the verb *are,* which is understood: *Norman is much better off than they [are].* If the correct English seems too formal, you can always add the verb.

▶ We respected no other candidate for the city council as

her.
much as ~~she.~~
^

This sentence means that we respected no other candidate as much as *we respected her.* *Her* is the direct object of an understood verb.

24e When deciding whether *we* or *us* should precede a noun, choose the pronoun that would be appropriate if the noun were omitted.

We
▶ ~~Us~~ tenants would rather fight than move.
^

us
▶ Management is short-changing ~~we~~ tenants.
^

No one would say *Us would rather fight than move* or *Management is short-changing we.*

24f Use the objective case for subjects and objects of infinitives.

An infinitive is the word *to* followed by the base form of a verb. (See 63c.) Subjects of infinitives are an exception to the rule that subjects must be in the subjective case. Whenever an infinitive has a subject, it must be in the objective case. Objects of infinitives also are in the objective case.

me   *her*
▶ Ms. Wilson asked John and ~~I~~ to drive the senator and ~~she~~ to
^   ^
the airport.

John and me is the subject of the infinitive *to drive; senator and her* is the direct object of the infinitive.

24g Use the possessive case to modify a gerund.

A pronoun that modifies a gerund or a gerund phrase should appear in the possessive case (*my, our, your, his/her/its, their*). A gerund is a verb form ending in *-ing* that functions as a noun. Gerunds frequently appear in phrases, in which case the whole gerund phrase functions as a noun. (See 63c.)

▶ The chances of ~~you~~ $\overset{your}{}$ being hit by lightning are about two

million to one.

Your modifies the gerund phrase *being hit by lightning.*

Nouns as well as pronouns may modify gerunds. To form the possessive case of a noun, use an apostrophe and an *-s* (*a victim's rights*) or just an apostrophe (*victims' rights*). (See 36a.)

▶ The old order in France paid a high price for the ~~aristocracy~~ $\overset{aristocracy's}{}$

exploiting the lower classes.

The possessive noun *aristocracy's* modifies the gerund phrase *exploiting the lower classes.*

Gerund phrases should not be confused with participial phrases, which function as adjectives, not as nouns: *We saw Brenda driving a yellow convertible.* Here *driving a yellow convertible* is a participial phrase modifying the noun *Brenda.* (See 63c.)

Sometimes the choice between the objective or the possessive case conveys a subtle difference in meaning:

We watched *them* dancing.

We watched *their* dancing.

In the first sentence the emphasis is on the people; *dancing* is a participle modifying the pronoun *them.* In the second sentence the emphasis is on the dancing; *dancing* is a gerund, and *their* is a possessive pronoun modifying the gerund.

NOTE: Do not use the possessive if it creates an awkward effect. Try to reword the sentence instead.

AWKWARD	The president agreed to the applications' being reviewed by a faculty committee.
REVISED	The president agreed that the applications could be reviewed by a faculty committee.
REVISED	The president agreed that a faculty committee could review the applications.

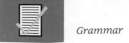

Grammar

ON THE WEB

The rule on using a possessive before a gerund has sparked debates. If you're interested in learning why, go to
dianahacker.com/rules

and click on ▶ **Language Debates**
              ▶ **Possessive before a gerund**

EXERCISE 24–1

Edit the following sentences to eliminate errors in case. If a sentence is correct, write "correct" after it. Answers to lettered sentences appear in the back of the book. Example:

> **Grandfather cuts down trees for neighbors much younger**
> *he.*
> **than ~~him.~~**
>   ^

a. Rick applied for the job even though he heard that other candidates were more experienced than he.
b. The jury could not agree that the murderer was he.
c. She appreciated him telling the truth in such a difficult situation.
d. The director has asked you and I to draft a proposal for a new recycling plan.
e. Five close friends and myself rented a station wagon, packed it with food, and drove to Mardi Gras on a three-day weekend.

1. The chain stores are threatening the survival of us shopkeepers.
2. The mysterious old woman handed Natasha and he a gold coin each.
3. The patient began suffering from the delusion that him and his family were constantly being followed and observed.
4. My adjustment to a new career was compounded by me becoming a single parent.
5. The swirling cyclone caused he and his horse to race for shelter.

EXERCISE 24–2

Choose the correct pronoun in each set of parentheses.

> (We/Us) adults who grew up watching *Sesame Street* are familiar with the practice of using one product to sell another. Big Bird might not have been interrupted by ads, but wasn't he for sale at the local toy store? We may blame television, but in

fact merchandising that capitalizes on a character's popularity with children predates television by decades. Raggedy Ann began as a child's rag doll, and a few years later books about (she/her) and her brother, Raggedy Andy, were published. A cartoonist named Johnny Gruelle painted a cloth face on a family doll and applied for a patent in 1915. Later Gruelle began writing and illustrating stories about Raggedy Ann, and in 1918 (he/him) and a publisher teamed up to publish the books and sell the dolls. He was not the only one to try to sell products linked to children's stories. Beatrix Potter created the beloved Peter Rabbit picture books, and no one was better than (she/her) at making a living from spin-offs. After Peter Rabbit and Benjamin Bunny became popular, Potter began putting pictures of (they/them) and their little animal friends on merchandise. Potter had fans all over the world, and she understood (them/their) wanting to see Peter Rabbit not only in books but also on teapots and plates and lamps and other furnishings for the nursery. Potter and Gruelle, like countless others before and since, knew that entertaining children could be a profitable business.

ON THE WEB

For electronic exercises on pronoun case, go to
dianahacker.com/rules

and click on ▶ **Electronic Grammar Exercises**
      ▶ **Grammar**
         ▶ **E-ex 24–1 and 24–2**

25

Distinguish between *who* and *whom.*

The choice between *who* and *whom* (or *whoever* and *whomever*) occurs primarily in subordinate clauses and in questions. *Who* and *whoever,* subjective-case pronouns, are used for subjects and subject complements. *Whom* and *whomever,* objective-case pronouns, are used for objects. (See 25a and 25b.)

An exception to this general rule occurs when the pronoun functions as the subject of an infinitive (see 25c).

GRAMMAR CHECKERS can flag some sentences with a misused *who* or *whom* and explain the nature of the error. For example, some grammar checkers flagged the subject pronoun *who* in the following sentence, suggesting correctly that the context calls for the object pronoun *whom: One of the women who Martinez hired became the most successful lawyer in the agency.*

However, at times the programs skip past a misused *who* or *whom*, as they did with this sentence: *Now that you have studied with both musicians, whom in your opinion is the better teacher?* The programs could not tell that the object pronoun *whom* functions as the subject of the verb *is.*

25a In subordinate clauses, use *who* and *whoever* for subjects or subject complements, *whom* and *whomever* for all objects.

When *who* and *whom* (or *whoever* and *whomever*) introduce subordinate clauses, their case is determined by their function *within the clause they introduce.* To choose the correct pronoun, you must isolate the subordinate clause and then decide how the pronoun functions within it. (See subordinate clauses, 63b.)

In the following two examples, the pronouns *who* and *whoever* function as the subjects of the clauses they introduce.

> ▶ The prize goes to the runner ~~whom~~ ^who^ collects the most points.

The subordinate clause is *who collects the most points.* The verb of the clause is *collects,* and its subject is *who.*

> ▶ He tells that story to ~~whomever~~ ^whoever^ will listen.

The writer selected the pronoun *whomever,* thinking that it was the object of the preposition *to.* However, the object of the preposition is the entire subordinate clause *whoever will listen.* The verb of the clause is *will listen,* and its subject is *whoever.*

Who occasionally functions as a subject complement in a subordinate clause. Subject complements occur with linking verbs (usually *be, am, is, are, was, were, being,* and *been*). (See 62b.)

> *who*
> ▶ The receptionist knows ~~whom~~ you are.
>   ^

The subordinate clause is *who you are.* Its subject is *you,* and its subject complement is *who.*

When functioning as an object in a subordinate clause, *whom* (or *whomever*) appears out of order, before both the subject and the verb. To choose the correct pronoun, you must mentally restructure the clause.

> *whom*
> ▶ You will work with our senior industrial engineers, ~~who~~ you
>   ^
>
> will meet later.

The subordinate clause is *whom you will meet later.* The subject of the clause is *you,* the verb is *will meet,* and *whom* is the direct object of the verb. This becomes clear if you mentally restructure the clause: *you will meet whom.*

When functioning as the object of a preposition in a subordinate clause, *whom* is often separated from its preposition.

> *whom*
> ▶ The tutor ~~who~~ I was assigned to was very
>   ^
>
> supportive.

Whom is the object of the preposition *to.* In this sentence, the writer might choose to drop *whom: The tutor I was assigned to was very supportive.*

NOTE: Inserted expressions such as *they know, I think,* and *she says* should be ignored in determining whether to use *who* or *whom.*

> ▶ All of the show-offs, bullies, and tough guys in school
>   *who*
> want to take on a big guy ~~whom~~ they know will not hurt
>   ^
> them.

Who is the subject of *will hurt,* not the object of *know.*

Grammar

25b In questions, use *who* and *whoever* for subjects, *whom* and *whomever* for all objects.

When *who* and *whom* (or *whoever* and *whomever*) are used to open questions, their case is determined by their function within the question. In the following example, *who* functions as the subject of the question.

> *Who*
> ▶ ~~Whom~~ was responsible for creating that computer virus?
>   ^

When *whom* functions as the object of a verb or the object of a preposition in a question, it appears out of normal order. To choose the correct pronoun, you must mentally restructure the question.

> *Whom*
> ▶ ~~Who~~ did the Democratic Party nominate in 1976?
>   ^

> *Whom* is the direct object of the verb *did nominate*. This becomes clear if you restructure the question: *The Democratic Party did nominate whom in 1976?*

> *Whom*
> ▶ ~~Who~~ did you enter into the contract with?
>   ^

> *Whom* is the object of the preposition *with,* as is clear if you recast the question: *You did enter into the contract with whom?*

25c Use *whom* for subjects or objects of infinitives.

An infinitive is the word *to* followed by the base form of a verb. (See 63c.) Subjects of infinitives are an exception to the rule that subjects must be in the subjective case. Whenever an infinitive has a subject, it must be in the objective case. Objects of infinitives also are in the objective case.

> *whom*
> ▶ On the subject of health care, I don't know ~~who~~ to believe.
>   ^

USAGE NOTE: In spoken English, *who* is frequently used when the correct *whom* sounds too stuffy. Even educated speakers are likely to say *Who* [not *Whom*] *did Joe replace?* Although some readers will accept such constructions in informal written English, it is safer to use *whom* in formal English: *Whom did Joe replace?*

ON THE WEB

The rules on using *who* and *whom* have sparked debates. If you're interested in learning why, go to
dianahacker.com/rules

and click on ▶ **Language Debates**
           ▶ *who* **versus** *whom*

EXERCISE 25-1

Edit the following sentences to eliminate errors in the use of *who* and *whom* (or *whoever* and *whomever*). If a sentence is correct, write "correct" after it. Answers to lettered sentences appear in the back of the book. Example:

>   *whom*
> What is the name of the person ~~who~~ you are sponsoring for
>   ^
> membership in the club?

a. The roundtable featured several scholars who I had never heard of.
b We had no idea who had shot whom.
c. Whom did you support in the last presidential election?
d. Daniel always gives a holiday donation to whomever needs it most.
e. So many of the candidates were overqualified that it was difficult to decide who to choose.

1. When medicine is scarce and expensive, physicians must give it to whomever has the best chance to survive.
2. Who was accused of receiving Mafia funds?
3. According to the Greek myth, the Sphinx devoured those who could not answer her riddles.
4. The only interstate travelers who get pulled over for speeding are the ones whom cannot afford a radar detector.
5. Who did the committee select?

ON THE WEB

For an electronic exercise on using *who* and *whom*, go to
dianahacker.com/rules

and click on ▶ **Electronic Grammar Exercises**
           ▶ **Grammar**
                     ▶ **E-ex 25-1**

26

Choose adjectives and adverbs with care.

Adjectives ordinarily modify nouns or pronouns; occasionally they function as subject complements following linking verbs. Adverbs modify verbs, adjectives, or other adverbs. (See 61d and 61e.)

Many adverbs are formed by adding *-ly* to adjectives (*normal, normally; smooth, smoothly*). But don't assume that all words ending in *-ly* are adverbs or that all adverbs end in *-ly.* Some adjectives end in *-ly* (*lovely, friendly*) and some adverbs don't (*always, here, there*). When in doubt, consult a dictionary.

ESL

In English, adjectives are not pluralized to agree with the words they modify: *The red* [not *reds*] *roses were a wonderful surprise.*

GRAMMAR CHECKERS can flag a number of problems with adjectives and adverbs: some misuses of *bad* or *badly* and *good* or *well;* some double comparisons, such as *more meaner;* some absolute comparisons, such as *most unique;* and some double negatives, such as *can't hardly.* However, the programs slip past more problems than they find. Programs ignored errors like these: *could have been handled more professional* and *hadn't been bathed regular.*

26a Use adverbs, not adjectives, to modify verbs, adjectives, and adverbs.

When adverbs modify verbs (or verbals), they nearly always answer the question When? Where? How? Why? Under what conditions? How often? or To what degree? When adverbs modify adjectives or other adverbs, they usually qualify or intensify the meaning of the word they modify. (See 61e.)

The incorrect use of adjectives in place of adverbs to modify verbs occurs primarily in casual or nonstandard speech.

▶ The arrangement worked out ~~perfect~~ for everyone.
  perfectly
  ^

▶ The manager must see that the office runs ~~smooth~~ and
  smoothly
  ~~efficient.~~
  efficiently.
  ^

The adverb *perfectly* modifies the verb *worked out;* the adverbs *smoothly* and *efficiently* modify the verb *runs.*

The incorrect use of the adjective *good* in place of the adverb *well* is especially common in casual and nonstandard speech.

▶ We were glad that Nemo had done ~~good~~ on the CPA exam.
  well
  ^

The adverb *well* (not the adjective *good*) should be used to modify the verb *had done.*

NOTE: The word *well* is an adjective when it means "healthy," "satisfactory," or "fortunate": *I am very well, thank you. All is well. It is just as well.*

Adjectives are sometimes used incorrectly to modify adjectives or adverbs.

▶ In the early 1970s, chances for survival of the bald eagle
  really
  looked ~~real~~ slim.
  ^

Only adverbs can be used to modify adjectives or other adverbs *Really* intensifies the meaning of the adjective *slim.*

ESL Placement of adjectives and adverbs can be a tricky matter for multilingual speakers. See 31d.

26b Use adjectives, not adverbs, as subject complements.

A subject complement follows a linking verb and completes the meaning of the subject. (See 62b.) When an adjective functions as a subject complement, it describes the subject.

Justice is *blind.*

Problems can arise with verbs such as *smell, taste, look,* and *feel,* which sometimes, but not always, function as linking verbs. If the word following one of these verbs describes the subject, use an adjective; if it modifies the verb, use an adverb.

> **ADJECTIVE**   The detective looked *cautious.*
>
> **ADVERB**   The detective looked *cautiously* for fingerprints.

The adjective *cautious* describes the detective; the adverb *cautiously* modifies the verb *looked.*

Linking verbs suggest states of being, not actions. Notice, for example, the different meanings of *looked* in the preceding examples. To look cautious suggests the state of being cautious; to look cautiously is to perform an action in a cautious way.

▶ The lilacs in our backyard smell especially ~~sweetly~~ *sweet* this year.

▶ Lori looked ~~well~~ *good* in her new raincoat.

The verbs *smell* and *looked* suggest states of being, not actions. Therefore, they should be followed by adjectives, not adverbs. (Contrast with action verbs: *We smelled the flowers. Lori looked for her raincoat.*)

When the verb *feel* refers to the state of a person's health or emotions, it is a linking verb and should be followed by an adjective.

▶ We felt ~~badly~~ *bad* upon hearing of your grandmother's death.

Another adjective, such as *saddened,* could be used in place of *bad.*

ON THE WEB

The rules on using *bad* and *badly* have sparked debates. If you're interested in learning why, go to **dianahacker.com/rules**

and click on   ▶ **Language Debates**
                 ▶ ***bad* versus *badly***

26C Use comparatives and superlatives with care.

Most adjectives and adverbs have three forms: the positive, the comparative, and the superlative.

POSITIVE	COMPARATIVE	SUPERLATIVE
soft	softer	softest
fast	faster	fastest
careful	more careful	most careful
bad	worse	worst
good	better	best

Comparative versus superlative

Use the comparative to compare two things, the superlative to compare three or more.

▶ Which of these two brands of toothpaste is ~~best~~? *better?*

▶ Though Shaw and Jackson are impressive, Hobbs is the ~~more~~ *most* qualified of the three candidates running for mayor.

Form of comparatives and superlatives

To form comparatives and superlatives of most one- and two-syllable adjectives, use the endings *-er* and *-est: smooth, smoother, smoothest; easy, easier, easiest.* With longer adjectives, use *more* and *most* (or *less* and *least* for downward comparisons): *exciting, more exciting, most exciting; helpful, less helpful, least helpful.*

Some one-syllable adverbs take the endings *-er* and *-est* (*fast, faster, fastest*), but longer adverbs and all of those ending in *-ly* form the comparative and superlative with *more* and *most* (or *less* and *least*).

The comparative and superlative forms of the following adjectives and adverbs are irregular: *good, better, best; well, better, best; bad, worse, worst; badly, worse, worst.*

▶ The Kirov is the ~~talentedest~~ *most talented* ballet company we have seen.

▶ Lloyd's luck couldn't have been ~~worser~~ *worse* than David's.

Grammar

Double comparatives or superlatives

Do not use double comparatives or superlatives. When you have added *-er* or *-est* to an adjective or adverb, do not also use *more* or *most* (or *less* or *least*).

▶ Of all her family, Julia is the ~~most~~ happiest about the move.

likely
▶ All the polls indicated that Dewey was more ~~likelier~~ to win
^
than Truman.

Absolute concepts

Avoid expressions such as *more straight, less perfect, very round,* and *most unique.* Either something is unique or it isn't. It is illogical to suggest that absolute concepts come in degrees.

unusual
▶ That is the most ~~unique~~ wedding gown I have ever seen.
^

valuable
▶ The painting would have been even more ~~priceless~~ had it
^
been signed.

ON THE WEB

The rule on avoiding absolute concepts in comparisons has sparked debates. If you're interested in learning why, go to
dianahacker.com/rules

and click on ▶ **Language Debates**
▶ **Absolute concepts such as *unique***

26d Avoid double negatives.

Standard English allows two negatives only if a positive meaning is intended: *The orchestra was not unhappy with its performance.* Double negatives used to emphasize negation are nonstandard.

Negative modifiers such as *never, no,* and *not* should not be paired with other negative modifiers or with negative words such as *neither, none, no one, nobody,* and *nothing.*

anything
▶ Management is not doing ~~nothing~~ to see that the trash is
                      ^

picked up.

The double negative *not . . . nothing* is nonstandard.

The modifiers *hardly, barely,* and *scarcely* are considered negatives in standard English, so they should not be used with other negatives such as *not, no one,* or *never.*

can
▶ Maxine is so weak she ~~can't~~ hardly climb stairs.
                       ^

EXERCISE 26–1

Edit the following sentences to eliminate errors in the use of adjectives and adverbs. If a sentence is correct, write "correct" after it. Answers to lettered sentences appear in the back of the book. Example:

When I watched Carl run the race on Saturday, I was amazed
well
at how good he paced himself.

a. Did you do good on last week's chemistry exam? *well*
b. With the budget deadline approaching, our office has not hardly had time to handle routine correspondence.
c. Some flowers smell surprisingly bad.
d. The customer complained that he hadn't been treated nicely.
e. Of all my relatives, Uncle Roberto is the most cleverest. *cleverest*
1. When answering the phone, you should speak clearly and courteously. *most*
2. Who was more upset about the loss? Was it the coach or the quarterback or the owner of the team? *really*
3. The green bagels looked and tasted real peculiar.
4. After checking to see how bad I had been hurt, my sister dialed 911. *badly*
5. If the college's Web page had been updated more regular, students would have learned about the new course offerings. *regularly*

ON THE WEB

For electronic exercises on using adjectives and adverbs, go to
dianahacker.com/rules

and click on ▶ **Electronic Grammar Exercises**
▶ **Grammar**
▶ **E-ex 26~1 and 26~2**

27

Choose standard English verb forms.

In nonstandard English, spoken by those who share a regional or cultural heritage, verb forms sometimes differ from those of standard English. In writing, use standard English verb forms unless you are quoting nonstandard speech or using nonstandard forms for literary effect. (See 17d.)

Except for the verb *be,* all verbs in English have five forms. The following chart lists the five forms and provides a sample sentence in which each might appear.

BASE FORM	Usually I (*walk, ride*).
PAST TENSE	Yesterday I (*walked, rode*).
PAST PARTICIPLE	I have (*walked, ridden*) many times before.
PRESENT PARTICIPLE	I am (*walking, riding*) right now.
-S FORM	He/she/it (*walks, rides*) regularly.

Both the past-tense and past-participle forms of regular verbs end in *-ed* (*walked, walked*). Irregular verbs form the past tense and past participle in other ways (*rode, ridden*).

The verb *be* has eight forms instead of the usual five: *be, am, is, are, was, were, being, been.*

GRAMMAR CHECKERS can flag some misused irregular verbs in sentences, such as *I had drove the car only twice before* or *Lucia swum across the lake,* but they miss about twice as many errors as they find.

27a Use the correct forms of irregular verbs.

For all regular verbs, the past-tense and past-participle forms are the same (ending in *-ed* or *-d*), so there is no danger of confusion. This is not true, however, for irregular verbs, such as the following.

BASE FORM	PAST TENSE	PAST PARTICIPLE
go	went	gone
fight	fought	fought
fly	flew	flown

The past-tense form, which never has a helping verb, expresses action that occurred entirely in the past. The past participle is used with a helping verb — either with *has, have,* or *had* to form one of the perfect tenses or with *be, am, is, are, was, were, being,* or *been* to form the passive voice.

PAST TENSE	Last July, we *went* to Paris.
PAST PARTICIPLE	We have *gone* to Paris twice.

When you aren't sure which verb form to choose (*went* or *gone, began* or *begun,* and so on), consult the list of common irregular verbs that starts on page 216. Choose the past-tense form if the verb in your sentence doesn't have a helping verb; choose the past-participle form if it does.

In nonstandard English speech, the past-tense and past-participle forms may differ from those of standard English, as in the following sentences.

▶ Yesterday we ~~seen~~ *saw* an unidentified flying object.

▶ The reality of the situation finally ~~sunk~~ *sank* in.

The past-tense forms *saw* and *sank* are required because there are no helping verbs.

> The truck was apparently s̶t̶o̶l̶e̶ *stolen* while the driver ate lunch.
> ^

> By the end of the day, the stock market had f̶e̶l̶l̶ *fallen* two hundred
> ^
>
> points.

Because of the helping verbs, the past-participle forms are required: *was stolen, had fallen.*

When in doubt about the standard English forms of irregular verbs, consult the following list or look up the base form of the verb in the dictionary, which also lists any irregular forms. (If no additional forms are listed in the dictionary, the verb is regular, not irregular.)

Common irregular verbs

BASE FORM	PAST TENSE	PAST PARTICIPLE
arise	arose	arisen
awake	awoke, awaked	awaked, awoke
be	was, were	been
beat	beat	beaten, beat
become	became	become
begin	began	begun
bend	bent	bent
bite	bit	bitten, bit
blow	blew	blown
break	broke	broken
bring	brought	brought
build	built	built
burst	burst	burst
buy	bought	bought
catch	caught	caught
choose	chose	chosen
cling	clung	clung
come	came	come
cost	cost	cost
deal	dealt	dealt
dig	dug	dug
dive	dived, dove	dived

BASE FORM	PAST TENSE	PAST PARTICIPLE
do	did	done
drag	dragged	dragged
draw	drew	drawn
dream	dreamed, dreamt	dreamed, dreamt
drink	drank	drunk
drive	drove	driven
eat	ate	eaten
fall	fell	fallen
fight	fought	fought
find	found	found
fly	flew	flown
forget	forgot	forgotten, forgot
freeze	froze	frozen
get	got	gotten, got
give	gave	given
go	went	gone
grow	grew	grown
hang (suspend)	hung	hung
hang (execute)	hanged	hanged
have	had	had
hear	heard	heard
hide	hid	hidden
hurt	hurt	hurt
keep	kept	kept
know	knew	known
lay (put)	laid	laid
lead	led	led
lend	lent	lent
let (allow)	let	let
lie (recline)	lay	lain
lose	lost	lost
make	made	made
prove	proved	proved, proven
read	read	read
ride	rode	ridden
ring	rang	rung
rise (get up)	rose	risen
run	ran	run
say	said	said
see	saw	seen
send	sent	sent
set (place)	set	set
shake	shook	shaken
shoot	shot	shot

BASE FORM	PAST TENSE	PAST PARTICIPLE
shrink	shrank	shrunk
sing	sang	sung
sink	sank	sunk
sit (be seated)	sat	sat
slay	slew	slain
sleep	slept	slept
speak	spoke	spoken
spin	spun	spun
spring	sprang	sprung
stand	stood	stood
steal	stole	stolen
sting	stung	stung
strike	struck	struck, stricken
swear	swore	sworn
swim	swam	swum
swing	swung	swung
take	took	taken
teach	taught	taught
throw	threw	thrown
wake	woke, waked	waked, woken
wear	wore	worn
wring	wrung	wrung
write	wrote	written

27b Distinguish among the forms of *lie* and *lay*.

Writers and speakers frequently confuse the various forms of *lie* (meaning "to recline or rest on a surface") and *lay* (meaning "to put or place something"). *Lie* is an intransitive verb; it does not take a direct object: *The tax forms lie on the table.* The verb *lay* is transitive; it takes a direct object: *Please lay the tax forms on the table.* (See 62b.)

In addition to confusing the meaning of *lie* and *lay*, writers and speakers are often unfamiliar with the standard English forms of these verbs.

BASE FORM	PAST TENSE	PAST PARTICIPLE	PRESENT PARTICIPLE
lie	lay	lain	lying
lay	laid	laid	laying

        lay
▶ Sue was so exhausted that she ~~laid~~ down for a nap.
           ^

The past-tense form of *lie* ("to recline") is *lay*.

> *lain*
> The patient had ~~laid~~ in an uncomfortable position all night.
>   ∧

The past-participle form of *lie* ("to recline") is *lain*. If the correct English seems too stilted, recast the sentence: *The patient had been lying in an uncomfortable position all night.*

> *laid*
> The prosecutor ~~lay~~ the pistol on a table close to the jurors.
>   ∧

The past-tense form of *lay* ("to place") is *laid*.

> *lying*
> Letters dating from the Civil War were ~~laying~~ in the corner of
>   ∧
> the chest.

The present participle of *lie* ("to rest on a surface") is *lying*.

ON THE WEB

The rules on using *lie* and *lay* have sparked debates. If you're interested in learning why, go to **dianahacker.com/rules**

and click on ▶ **Language Debates**
        ▶ ***lie* versus *lay***

EXERCISE 27–1

Edit the following sentences to eliminate problems with irregular verbs. If a sentence is correct, write "correct" after it. Answers to lettered sentences appear in the back of the book. Example:

> *saw*
> Was it you I ~~seen~~ last night at the concert?
>   ∧

a. When I get the urge to exercise, I lay down until it passes.

b. Grandmother had drove our new jeep to the sunrise church service on Savage Mountain, so we were left with the station wagon.

c. A pile of dirty rags was laying at the bottom of the stairs.

d. How did the detective know that the suspect had went to the office on the night of the murder?

e. Lincoln took good care of his legal clients; the contracts he drew for the Illinois Central Railroad could never be broke.

1. The burglar must have gone immediately upstairs, grabbed what looked good, and took off.
2. Have you ever dreamed that you were falling from a cliff or flying through the air?
3. I locked my brakes, leaned the motorcycle to the left, and laid it down to keep from slamming into the fence.
4. In her junior year, Cindy run the 440-yard dash in 51.1 seconds.
5. Larry claimed that he had drank a bad soda, but Esther suspected the truth.

ON THE WEB

For an electronic exercise on irregular verbs, go to
dianahacker.com/rules

and click on ▶ **Electronic Grammar Exercises**
　　　　　　 ▶ **Grammar**
　　　　　　　　 ▶ **E-ex 27–1**

27c Use *-s* (or *-es*) endings on present-tense verbs that have third-person singular subjects.

All singular nouns (*child, tree*) and the pronouns *he, she,* and *it* are third-person singular; indefinite pronouns such as *everyone* and *neither* are also third-person singular. When the subject of a sentence is third-person singular, its verb takes an *-s* or *-es* ending in the present tense. (See also 21.)

	SINGULAR		PLURAL	
FIRST PERSON	I	know	we	know
SECOND PERSON	you	know	you	know
THIRD PERSON	he/she/it	knows	they	know
	child	knows	parents	know
	everyone	knows		

In nonstandard speech, the *-s* ending required by standard English is sometimes omitted.

　　　　　　　 turns　　　　　　　　*dissolves*　　　　　 *eats*
▶ Sulfur dioxide ~~turn~~ leaves yellow, ~~dissolve~~ marble, and ~~eat~~
　　　　　　　 ^　　　　　　　　　　 ^　　　　　　　 ^

away iron and steel.

The subject *sulfur dioxide* is third-person singular, so the verbs must end in *-s.*

CAUTION: Do not add the *-s* ending to the verb if the subject is not third-person singular. The writers of the following sentences, knowing they sometimes dropped *-s* endings from verbs, overcorrected by adding the endings where they don't belong.

▶ I prepares program specifications and logic diagrams.

The writer mistakenly concluded that the *-s* ending belongs on present-tense verbs used with *all* singular subjects, not just *third-person* singular subjects. The pronoun *I* is first-person singular, so its verb does not require the *-s.*

▶ The dirt floors requires continual sweeping.

The writer mistakenly thought that the *-s* ending on the verb indicated plurality. The *-s* goes on present-tense verbs used with third-person *singular* subjects.

Has *versus* have

In the present tense, use *has* with third person singular subjects; all other subjects require *have.*

	SINGULAR		PLURAL	
FIRST PERSON	I	have	we	have
SECOND PERSON	you	have	you	have
THIRD PERSON	he/she/it	has	they	have

In some dialects, *have* is used with all subjects. But standard English requires *has* for third-person singular subjects.

▶ This respected musician almost always ~~have~~ *has* a message to convey in his work.

▶ As for the retirement income program, it ~~have~~ *has* finally been established.

The subjects *musician* and *it* are third-person singular, so the verb should be *has* in each case.

CAUTION: Do not use *has* if the subject is not third-person singular. The writers of the following sentences were aware that they often wrote *have* when standard English requires *has*. Here they are using what appears to them to be the "more correct" form, but in an inappropriate context.

▶ My business law classes ~~has~~ *have* helped me to understand more

about contracts.

▶ I ~~has~~ *have* much to be thankful for.

The subjects of these sentences — *classes* and *I* — are third-person plural and first-person singular, so standard English requires *have*. *Has* is used with third-person singular subjects only.

Does *versus* do *and* doesn't *versus* don't

In the present tense, use *does* and *doesn't* with third-person singular subjects; all other subjects require *do* and *don't*.

	SINGULAR		PLURAL	
FIRST PERSON	I	do / don't	we	do / don't
SECOND PERSON	you	do / don't	you	do / don't
THIRD PERSON	he / she / it	does / doesn't	they	do / don't

The use of *don't* instead of the standard English *doesn't* is a feature of many dialects in the United States. Use of *do* for *does* is rarer.

▶ Grandfather really ~~don't~~ *doesn't* have a place to call home.

▶ ~~Do~~ *Does* she know the correct procedure for setting up the

experiment?

Grandfather and *she* are third-person singular, so the verbs should be *doesn't* and *does*.

Am, is, *and* are; was *and* were

The verb *be* has three forms in the present tense (*am, is, are*) and two in the past tense (*was, were*). Use *am* and *was* with first-person singular subjects; use *is* and *was* with third-person singular subjects. With all other subjects, use *are* and *were*.

	SINGULAR		PLURAL	
FIRST PERSON	I	am / was	we	are / were
SECOND PERSON	you	are / were	you	are / were
THIRD PERSON	he / she / it	is / was	they	are / were

▶ Judy wanted to borrow Tim's notes, but she ~~were~~ too shy to

                                                         was

ask for them.

The subject *she* is third-person singular, so the verb should be *was*.

▶ Did you think you ~~was~~ going to drown?

                     were

The subject *you* is second-person singular, so the verb should be *were*.

GRAMMAR CHECKERS can catch some missing -*s* endings on verbs and some misused -*s* forms of the verb. Unfortunately, they flag quite a few correct sentences, so you need to know how to interpret what the programs tell you. (See the grammar checker advice on p. 173 for more detailed information.)

27d Do not omit -*ed* endings on verbs.

Speakers who do not fully pronounce -*ed* endings sometimes omit them unintentionally in writing. Failure to pronounce -*ed* endings is common in many dialects and in informal speech even in standard English. In the following frequently used words and phrases, for example, the -*ed* ending is not always fully pronounced.

advised	developed	prejudiced	supposed to
asked	fixed	pronounced	used to
concerned	frightened	stereotyped	

When a verb is regular, both the past tense and the past participle are formed by adding *-ed* to the base form of the verb.

Past tense

Use an *-ed* or *-d* ending to express the past tense of regular verbs. The past tense is used when the action occurred entirely in the past.

▶ Over the weekend, Ed ~~fix~~ his brother's skateboard and tuned
                  fixed
                  ^

up his mother's 1955 Thunderbird.

▶ Last summer my counselor ~~advise~~ me to ask my chemistry
                    advised
                  ^

instructor for help.

Past participles

Past participles are used in three ways: (1) following *have, has,* or *had* to form one of the perfect tenses; (2) following *be, am, is, are, was, were, being,* or *been* to form the passive voice; and (3) as adjectives modifying nouns or pronouns. The perfect tenses are listed on page 228, and the passive voice is discussed in 8a. For a discussion of participles functioning as adjectives, see 63c.

▶ Robin has ~~ask~~ me to go to California with her.
          asked

Has asked is present perfect tense (*have* or *has* followed by a past participle).

▶ Though it is not a new phenomenon, domestic violence is
   publicized
   ~~publicize~~ more frequently than before.
   ^

Is publicized is a verb in the passive voice (a form of *be* followed by a past participle).

▶ All aerobics classes end in a cool-down period to stretch
   tightened
   ~~tighten~~ muscles.
   ^

The past participle *tightened* functions as an adjective modifying the noun *muscles*.

GRAMMAR CHECKERS can catch some missing -ed endings, but they tend to slip past as many as they catch. For example, although some programs flagged *was accustom,* they ignored *has change* and *was pass.*

27e Do not omit needed verbs.

Although standard English allows some linking verbs and helping verbs to be contracted, at least in informal contexts, it does not allow them to be omitted.

Linking verbs, used to link subjects to subject complements, are frequently a form of *be: be, am, is, are, was, were, being, been.* (See 62b.) Some of these forms may be contracted (*I'm, she's, we're, you're, they're*), but they should not be omitted altogether.

▶ When we *are* out there in the evening, we often hear the
  ^

helicopters circling above.

▶ Alvin *is* a man who can defend himself.
  ^

Helping verbs, used with main verbs, include forms of *be, do,* and *have* or the words *can, will, shall, could, would, should, may, might,* and *must.* (See 61c.) Some helping verbs may be contracted (*he's leaving, we'll celebrate, they've been told*), but they should not be omitted altogether.

▶ We *have* been in Chicago since last Thursday.
  ^

▶ Do you know someone who *would* be good for the job?
  ^

Multilingual speakers sometimes have problems with omitted verbs and correct use of helping verbs. See 29e and 29a.

ESL

> GRAMMAR CHECKERS are fairly good at flagging omitted verbs, but they do not catch all of them. For example, programs caught the missing verb in this sentence: *He always talking.* But in the following, more complicated sentence, they did not catch the missing verb: *We often don't know whether he angry or just talking.*

EXERCISE 27-2

Edit the following sentences to eliminate problems with *-s* and *-ed* verb forms and with omitted verbs. If a sentence is correct, write "correct" after it. Answers to lettered sentences appear in the back of the book. Example:

> The Pell Grant sometimes cover̞ the student's full tuition.

a. The cops was after my hot rod Lincoln. We was passing cars like they was standing still.
b. The museum visitors were not suppose to touch the exhibits.
c. Our church has all the latest technology, even a close-circuit television.
d. Christos didn't know about Marlo's promotion because he never listens. He always talking.
e. Most psychologists agree that no one performs well under stress.

1. Have there ever been a time in your life when you were too depressed to get out of bed?
2. My days in this department have taught me to do what I'm told without asking questions.
3. Last year, Darlene planned to major in computer science; this year she has change to accounting.
4. The training for security checkpoint screeners, which took place in an empty airplane hangar, consist of watching out-of-date videos.
5. How would you feel if a love one had been a victim of a crime like this?

ON THE WEB

For an electronic exercise on verb forms, go to
dianahacker.com/rules

and click on ▶ **Electronic Grammar Exercises**
▶ **Grammar**
▶ **E-ex 27-2**

28

Use verbs in the appropriate tense and mood.

28a Choose the appropriate verb tense.

Tenses indicate the time of an action in relation to the time of the speaking or writing about that action.

The most common problem with tenses — shifting confusingly from one tense to another — is discussed in 13. Other problems with tenses are detailed in this section, after the following survey of tenses.

> GRAMMAR CHECKERS do not flag the problems with tense discussed in this section. Although some programs may tell you that *had had* is incorrect, in fact it is often correct. See page 231.

Survey of tenses

English has three simple tenses (past, present, and future) and three perfect tenses (present perfect, past perfect, and future perfect). In addition, there is a progressive form of each of these six tenses.

SIMPLE TENSES   The simple present tense is used primarily to describe habitual actions (*Jane walks to work*) or to refer to actions occurring at the time of speaking (*I see a cardinal in our maple tree*). It is also used to state facts or general truths and to describe fictional events in a literary work (see p. 230). The present tense may even be used to express future actions that are to occur at some specified time (*The semester begins tomorrow*).

The simple past tense is used for actions completed entirely in the past (*Yesterday Jane walked to work*).

The simple future tense is used for actions that will occur in the future (*Tomorrow Jane will walk to work*) or for actions that are predictable, given certain causes (*Meat will spoil if not properly refrigerated*).

In the following chart, the simple tenses are given for the regular verb *walk*, the irregular verb *ride*, and the highly irregular verb *be*.

Grammar

SIMPLE PRESENT

SINGULAR		PLURAL	
I	walk, ride, am	we	walk, ride, are
you	walk, ride, are	you	walk, ride, are
he / she / it	walks, rides, is	they	walk, ride, are

SIMPLE PAST

SINGULAR		PLURAL	
I	walked, rode, was	we	walked, rode, were
you	walked, rode, were	you	walked, rode, were
he / she / it	walked, rode, was	they	walked, rode, were

SIMPLE FUTURE

I, you, he / she / it, we, they   will walk, ride, be

PERFECT TENSES   More complex time relations are indicated by the perfect tenses (which consist of a form of *have* plus the past participle). The present perfect tense is used for an action that began in the past and is still going on in the present (*Jane has walked to work for years*) or an action that began in the past and is finished by the time of speaking or writing (*Jane has discovered a new restaurant on Elm Street*).

The past perfect tense is used for an action already completed by the time of another past action (*Jane hailed a cab after she had walked several blocks in the rain*) or for an action already completed at some specific past time (*By 8:30, Jane had walked two miles*). (See also p. 231.)

The future perfect tense is used for an action that will be completed before or by a certain future time (*Jane will have left town by the time Jo arrives*).

PRESENT PERFECT

I, you, we, they	have walked, ridden, been
he/she/it	has walked, ridden, been

PAST PERFECT

I, you, he/she/it, we, they	had walked, ridden, been

FUTURE PERFECT

I, you, he/she/it, we, they	will have walked, ridden, been

PROGRESSIVE FORMS   The simple and perfect tenses already discussed have progressive forms that describe actions in progress. The present progressive form is used for actions currently in progress (*Jane is writing a letter*) or for future actions that are to occur at some specified time (*Jane is leaving for Chicago on Monday*).

The past progressive is used for past actions in progress (*Jane was writing a letter last night*).

The future progressive is used for future actions in progress (*Jane will be traveling next week*).

PRESENT PROGRESSIVE

I	am walking, riding, being
he/she/it	is walking, riding, being
you, we, they	are walking, riding, being

PAST PROGRESSIVE

I, he/she/it	was walking, riding, being
you, we, they	were walking, riding, being

FUTURE PROGRESSIVE

I, you, he/she/it, we, they	will be walking, riding, being

Like the simple tenses, the perfect tenses have progressive forms. The perfect progressive forms express the length of time an action is, was, or will be in progress: *Jane has been walking to work for five years* (present perfect progressive). *Jane had been walking to work until she was mugged* (past perfect progressive). *Jane will have been walking to work for five years by the end of this month* (future perfect progressive).

PRESENT PERFECT PROGRESSIVE

I, you, we, they	have been walking, riding, being
he/she/it	has been walking, riding, being

PAST PERFECT PROGRESSIVE

I, you, he/she/it, we, they	had been walking, riding, being

FUTURE PERFECT PROGRESSIVE

I, you, he/she/it, we, they	will have been walking, riding, being

ESL

The progressive forms are not normally used with mental activity verbs such as *believe*. See page 238.

Special uses of the present tense

Use the present tense when writing about events in a literary work, when expressing general truths, and when quoting, summarizing, or paraphrasing an author's views.

When writing about a work of literature, you may be tempted to use the past tense. The convention, however, is to describe fictional events in the present tense. (See also 13b.)

> In Masuji Ibuse's *Black Rain*, a child ~~reached~~ *reaches* for a pome-
> granate in his mother's garden, and a moment later he ~~was~~ *is* dead, killed by the blast of the atomic bomb.

Scientific principles or general truths should appear in the present tense, unless such principles have been disproved.

> Galileo taught that the earth ~~revolved~~ *revolves* around the sun.

Since Galileo's teaching has not been discredited, the verb should be in the present tense. The following sentence, however, is acceptable: *Ptolemy taught that the sun revolved around the earth.*

When you are quoting, summarizing, or paraphrasing the author of a nonliterary work, use present-tense verbs such as *writes, reports, asserts,* and so on. (See p. 408 for a more complete list.) This convention is usually followed even when the author is dead (unless a date specifies the time of writing).

> Baron Bowan of Colwood ~~wrote~~ *writes* that a metaphysician is "one who goes into a dark cellar at midnight without a light, looking for a black cat that is not there."

EXCEPTION: When you are documenting a paper with the APA (American Psychological Association) style of in-text citations, which include a date after the author's name, use past-tense verbs such as *reported* or *demonstrated* or present perfect verbs such as *has reported* or *has demonstrated.* (See p. 463.)

E. Wilson (1996) reported that positive reinforcement alone was a less effective teaching technique than a mixture of positive reinforcement and constructive criticism.

The past perfect tense

The past perfect tense consists of a past participle preceded by *had* (*had worked, had gone, had had*). (See p. 228.) This tense is used for an action already completed by the time of another past action or for an action already completed at some specific past time.

> Everyone *had spoken* by the time I arrived.

> Everyone *had spoken* by 10:00 A.M.

Writers sometimes use the simple past tense when they should use the past perfect.

▶ We built our cabin high on a pine knoll, forty feet above an

had been

abandoned quarry that ~~was~~ flooded in 1920 to create a lake.

^

The building of the cabin and the flooding of the quarry both occurred in the past, but the flooding was completed before the time of building.

had

▶ By the time we arrived at the party, the guest of honor left.

^

The past perfect tense is needed because the action of leaving was completed at a specific past time (*by the time we arrived*).

Some writers tend to overuse the past perfect tense. Do not use the past perfect if two past actions occurred at the same time.

▶ When we arrived in Paris, Pauline ~~had~~ met us at the train

station.

Sequence of tenses with infinitives and participles

An infinitive is the base form of a verb preceded by *to*. (See 63c.) Use the present infinitive to show action at the same time as or later than the action of the verb in the sentence.

>   *raise*
> ► The club had hoped to ~~have raised~~ a thousand dollars by
>   ^
>
> April 1.

The action expressed in the infinitive (*to raise*) occurred later than the action of the sentence's verb (*had hoped*).

Use the perfect form of an infinitive (*to have* followed by the past participle) for an action occurring earlier than that of the verb in the sentence.

>   *have joined*
> ► Dan would like to ~~join~~ the navy, but he did not pass the
>   ^
>
> physical.

The liking occurs in the present; the joining would have occurred in the past.

Like the tense of an infinitive, the tense of a participle is also governed by the tense of the sentence's verb. Use the present participle (ending in *-ing*) for an action occurring at the same time as that of the sentence's verb.

Hiking the Appalachian Trail in early spring, we spotted many wildflowers.

Use the past participle (such as *given* or *helped*) or the present perfect participle (*having* plus the past participle) for an action occurring before that of the verb.

Discovered off the coast of Florida, the *Atocha* yielded many treasures.

Having worked her way through college, Melanie graduated debt-free.

28b Use the subjunctive mood in the few contexts that require it.

There are three moods in English: the *indicative,* used for facts, opinions, and questions; the *imperative,* used for orders or advice; and the *subjunctive,* used in certain contexts to express wishes, requests, or conditions contrary to fact. Of these moods, only the subjunctive causes problems for writers.

Forms of the subjunctive

In the subjunctive mood, present-tense verbs do not change form to indicate the number and person of the subject (see 21). Instead, the subjunctive uses the base form of the verb (*be, drive, employ*) with all subjects.

It is important that you *be* [not *are*] prepared for the interview.

We asked that she *drive* [not *drives*] more slowly.

Also, in the subjunctive mood, there is only one past-tense form of *be: were* (never *was*).

If I *were* [not *was*] you, I'd proceed more cautiously.

Uses of the subjunctive

The subjunctive mood appears only in a few contexts: in contrary-to-fact clauses beginning with *if* or expressing a wish; in *that* clauses following verbs such as *ask, insist, recommend, request,* and *suggest;* and in certain expressions.

IN CONTRARY-TO-FACT CLAUSES BEGINNING WITH *IF* When a subordinate clause beginning with *if* expresses a condition contrary to fact, use the subjunctive mood.

> were
> ▶ If I ~~was~~ a member of Congress, I would vote for that bill.
>   ^

> were
> ▶ We could be less cautious if Jake ~~was~~ more trustworthy.
>   ^

The verbs in these sentences express conditions that do not exist: The writer is not a member of Congress, and Jake is not trustworthy.

Do not use the subjunctive mood in *if* clauses expressing conditions that exist or may exist.

If Dana *wins* the contest, she will leave for Barcelona in June.

IN CONTRARY-TO-FACT CLAUSES EXPRESSING A WISH In formal English, the subjunctive is used in clauses expressing a wish or desire; in informal speech, however, the indicative is more common.

FORMAL   I wish that Dr. Kurtinitis *were* my professor.

INFORMAL   I wish that Dr. Kurtinitis *was* my professor.

IN *THAT* CLAUSES FOLLOWING VERBS SUCH AS *ASK, INSIST, REQUEST,* AND *SUGGEST*   Because requests have not yet become reality, they are expressed in the subjunctive mood.

▶ Professor Moore insists that her students ~~are~~ on time.
                                             be
                                                ^

▶ We recommend that Lambert ~~files~~ form 1050 soon.
                               file
                               ^

IN CERTAIN EXPRESSIONS   The subjunctive mood, once more widely used, remains in certain expressions: *Be that as it may, as it were, far be it from me,* and so on.

GRAMMAR CHECKERS rarely flag problems with the subjunctive mood. They may at times question your correct use of the subjunctive, since your correct use will seem to violate the rules of subject-verb agreement (see 21). For example, a program advised using *was* instead of *were* in this correct sentence: *This isn't my dog; if it were, I would feed it.*

EXERCISE 28–1

Edit the following sentences to eliminate errors in verb tense or mood. If a sentence is correct, write "correct" after it. Answers to lettered sentences appear in the back of the book. Example:

                 had been
After the path ~~was~~ plowed, we were able to walk through the
              ^

park.

a. The palace of Knossos in Crete is believed to have been destroyed by fire around 1375 B.C.E.
b. Watson and Crick discovered the mechanism that controlled inheritance in all life: the workings of the DNA molecule.
c. When Hitler decided to kill the Jews in 1941, did he know that Himmler and his SS had mass murder in mind since 1938?
d. This isn't the Waldorf; if it were, we wouldn't be here.
e. As soon as my aunt applied for the position of pastor, the post was filled by an inexperienced seminary graduate who had been so hastily snatched that his mortarboard was still in midair.

1. Don Quixote, in Cervantes's novel, was an idealist ill suited for life in the real world.
2. The hurricane tore up the palm trees, lifted them over the hotel roof, and had dropped them into the swimming pool.
3. I would like to have been on the *Mayflower* but not to have lived through the first winter.
4. When the doctor said "It's a girl," I was stunned. For nine months I dreamed about playing baseball with my son.
5. If men and women were angels, no government would be necessary.

ON THE WEB

For an electronic exercise on verb tense and mood, go to
dianahacker.com/rules

and click on ▶ **Electronic Grammar Exercises**
▶ **Grammar**
▶ **E-ex 28-1**

ESL GRAMMAR

Sections 29, 30, and 31 of *Rules for Writers* have a special audience: speakers of English as a second language (ESL) who have learned English but continue to have problems in a few trouble spots.

29

Be alert to special problems with verbs.

Both native and nonnative speakers of English encounter the following problems with verbs, which are treated elsewhere in this handbook:

problems with active and passive voice (8)

problems with subject-verb agreement (21)

misuse of verb forms (27)

problems with tense and mood (28)

This section focuses on features of the English verb system that cause special problems for multilingual speakers.

29a   Match helping verbs and main verbs appropriately.

Only certain combinations of helping verbs and main verbs are allowed in English. The correct combinations are discussed in this section, after the following review of helping verbs and main verbs.

Review of helping verbs and main verbs

Helping verbs always appear before main verbs. (See 61c.)

> HV   MV   HV   MV
> We *will leave* for the picnic at noon. *Do* you *want* a ride?

Some helping verbs — *have, do,* and *be* — change form to indicate tense; others, known as modals, do not.

FORMS OF *HAVE, DO,* AND *BE*

have, has, had
do, does, did
be, am, is, are, was, were, being, been

MODALS

can, could, may, might, must, shall, should, will, would (*also* ought to)

Every main verb has five forms (except *be,* which has eight forms). The following list shows these forms for the regular verb *help* and the irregular verb *give.* (See 27a for a list of common irregular verbs.)

BASE FORM	help, give
PAST TENSE	helped, gave
PAST PARTICIPLE	helped, given
PRESENT PARTICIPLE	helping, giving
-S FORM	helps, gives

Modal + base form

After the modals *can, could, may, might, must, shall, should, will,* and *would,* use the base form of the verb.

▶ My cousin will send~~s~~ us photographs from her wedding.

        speak
▶ We could ~~spoke~~ Spanish when we were young.
          ^

CAUTION: Do not use *to* in front of a main verb that follows a modal. (*Ought to* is an exception.)

▶ Gina can ~~to~~ drive us home if we miss the bus.

Do, does, *or* did + *base form*

After helping verbs that are a form of *do*, use the base form of the verb.

The helping verbs *do*, *does*, and *did* are used in three ways: (1) to express a negative meaning with the adverb *not* or *never*, (2) to ask a question, and (3) to emphasize a main verb used in a positive sense.

▶ Mariko does not want~~s~~ any more dessert.

        buy
▶ Did Janice ~~bought~~ the gift for Katherine?
          ^

        hope
▶ We do ~~hoping~~ that you will come to the retirement party.
       ^

Have, has, *or* had + *past participle (perfect tenses)*

After the helping verb *have*, *has*, or *had*, use the past participle to form one of the perfect tenses. (See 28a.) Past participles usually end in -ed, -d, -en, -n, or -t. (See 27a.)

                        offered
▶ On cold nights many churches in the city have ~~offer~~ shelter
                               ^

   to the homeless.

            spoken
▶ An-Mei has not ~~speaking~~ Chinese since she was young.
          ^

The helping verb *have* is sometimes preceded by a modal helping verb such as *will*: *By nightfall, we will have driven five hundred miles.* (See also perfect tenses, 28a.)

Form of be + present participle (progressive forms)

After the helping verb *be, am, is, are, was, were,* or *been,* use the present participle to express a continuing action. (See progressive forms, 28a.)

>   *building*
> ▶ Carlos is ~~build~~ his house on a cliff overlooking the Pacific
>   ^
> Ocean.

>   *driving*
> ▶ Uncle Roy was ~~driven~~ a brand-new red Corvette.
>   ^

The helping verb *be* must be preceded by a modal (*can, could, may, might, must, shall, should, will,* or *would*): *Edith will be going to Germany soon.* The helping verb *been* must be preceded by *have, has,* or *had: Andy has been studying English for five years.* (See also progressive forms, 28a.)

CAUTION: Certain verbs are not normally used in the progressive sense in English. In general, these verbs express a state of being or mental activity, not a dynamic action. Common examples are *appear, believe, belong, contain, have, hear, know, like, need, see, seem, taste, think, understand,* and *want.*

>   *want*
> ▶ I ~~am wanting~~ to see August Wilson's *Fences* at Arena Stage.
>   ^

Some of these verbs, however, have special uses in which progressive forms are normal. (*We are thinking about going to the Bahamas.*) You will need to make a note of exceptions as you encounter them.

Form of be + past participle (passive voice)

When a sentence is written in the passive voice, the subject receives the action instead of doing it: *Melissa was given a special award.* (See 8a.)

To form the passive voice, use *be, am, is, are, was, were, being,* or *been* followed by a past participle (usually ending in *-ed, -d, -en, -n,* or *-t*).

>   *written*
> ▶ *Bleak House* was ~~write~~ by Charles Dickens.
>   ^

> *honored*
> The scientists were ~~honor~~ for their work with dolphins.
>   ^

When the helping verb is *be, being,* or *been,* it must be preceded by another helping verb. *Be* must be preceded by a modal such as *will: Senator Dixon will be defeated. Being* must be preceded by *am, is, are, was,* or *were: The child was being teased. Been* must be preceded by *have, has,* or *had: I have been invited to a party.*

CAUTION: Although they may seem to have passive meanings, verbs such as *occur, happen, sleep, die,* and *fall* may not be used to form the passive voice because they are intransitive. Only transitive verbs, those that take direct objects, may be used to form the passive voice. (See transitive and intransitive verbs, 62b.)

> The earthquake ~~was~~ occurred last Wednesday.

EXERCISE 29-1

Revise any sentences in which helping and main verbs do not match. You may need to look at the list of irregular verbs in 27a to determine the correct form of some irregular verbs. Answers to lettered sentences appear in the back of the book. Example:

> **Maureen should finds' an apartment closer to campus.**

a. We will making this a better country.
b. There is nothing in the world that TV has not touch on.
c. Did the landlord told you that he's going to raise the rent?
d. If we can afford to, we will to spend our vacation in Canada next summer.
e. The child's innocent world has been taking away from him.

1. The swimming pool was fill early this year, on May 1.
2. A serious accident was happened at the corner of Main Street and First Avenue last night.
3. My family has going to Sam's restaurant ever since we moved to this neighborhood.
4. I have ate Thai food only once before.
5. How often does Sandy takes her daughter to the doctor?

ON THE WEB

For an electronic exercise on helping verbs and main verbs, go to
dianahacker.com/rules

and click on   ▶ **Electronic Grammar Exercises**
                  ▶ **Grammar**
                        ▶ **E-ex 29-1**

GRAMMAR CHECKERS can catch some mismatches of helping and main verbs. They can tell you, for example, that the base form of the verb should be used after certain helping verbs, such as *did* and *could,* in incorrect sentences like these: *Did you understood my question? Could Alan comes with us?*

Programs can also catch some, but not all, problems with main verbs following forms of *have* or *be.* For example, grammar checkers flagged *have spend,* explaining that the past participle *spent* is required. However, programs failed to flag problems in many sentences, such as these: *Sasha has change her major three times. The provisions of the contract were broke by both parties.*

29b In conditional sentences, choose verbs with care.

Conditional sentences state that one set of circumstances depends on whether another set of circumstances exists. Choosing verbs in such sentences can be tricky, partly because two clauses are involved: usually an *if* or a *when* or an *unless* clause and an independent clause.

Three kinds of conditional sentences are discussed in this section: factual, predictive, and speculative.

Factual

Factual conditional sentences express factual relationships. These relationships might be scientific truths, in which case the present tense is used in both clauses.

> If water cools to 32°, it *freezes.*

Or they might be present or past relationships that are habitually true, in which case the same tense is used in both clauses.

When Sue *bicycles* along the canal, her dog *runs* ahead of her.

Whenever the coach *asked* for help, I *volunteered*.

Predictive

Predictive conditional sentences are used to predict the future or to express future plans or possibilities. In such a sentence, an *if* or *unless* clause contains a present-tense verb; the verb in the independent clause usually consists of the modal *will, can, may, should,* or *might* followed by the base form of the verb.

If you *practice* regularly, your tennis game *will improve*.

We *will lose* our remaining wetlands unless we *act* now.

Speculative

Speculative conditional sentences are used for three purposes: (1) to speculate about unlikely possibilities in the present or future, (2) to speculate about events that did not happen in the past, and (3) to speculate about conditions that are contrary to fact. Each of these purposes requires its own combination of verbs.

UNLIKELY POSSIBILITIES Somewhat confusingly, English uses the past tense in an *if* clause to speculate about a possible but unlikely condition in the present or future. The verb in the independent clause consists of *would, could,* or *might* plus the base form of the verb.

If I *had* the time, I *would travel* to Senegal.

If Stan *studied* harder, he *could master* calculus.

In the *if* clause, the past-tense form *were* is used with subjects that would normally take *was: Even if I were* [not *was*] *invited, I wouldn't go to the picnic.* (See also 28b.)

EVENTS THAT DID NOT HAPPEN English uses the past perfect tense in an *if* clause to speculate about an event that did not happen in the past or to speculate about a state of being that was unreal in the past. (See past perfect tense, 28a.) The verb in the independent clause consists of *would have, could have,* or *might have* plus the past participle.

If I *had saved* enough money, I *would have traveled* to Senegal last year.

If Aunt Grace *had been* alive for your graduation, she *would have been* very proud.

CONDITIONS CONTRARY TO FACT   To speculate about conditions that are currently unreal or contrary to fact, English usually uses the past-tense verb *were* (never *was*) in an *if* clause. (See 28b.) The verb in the independent clause consists of *would, could,* or *might* plus the base form of the verb.

If Grandmother *were* alive today, she *would be* very proud of you.

I *would make* children's issues a priority if I *were* president.

GRAMMAR CHECKERS do not flag problems with conditional sentences. The programs miss even obvious errors, such as this one: *Whenever I washed my car, it rains.*

EXERCISE 29–2

Edit the following conditional sentences for problems with verbs. In some cases, more than one revision is possible. Suggested revisions of lettered sentences appear in the back of the book. Example:

    had
If I ~~have~~ time, I would study both French and Russian next
      ^

semester.

a. He would have won the election if he went to the inner city to campaign.
b. If Verena wins a scholarship, she would go to graduate school.
c. Whenever there is a fire in our neighborhood, everybody came out to watch.
d. We will lose our most valuable client unless we would update our computer system.
e. If I live in California, I wouldn't need to buy a winter coat.

1. If our daughter was an angel, we wouldn't need to discipline her.
2. If everyone has voted in the last election, the results would have been very different.
3. The tenants will not pay the rent unless the landlord fixed the furnace.

4. When dark gray clouds appeared on a hot summer afternoon, a thunderstorm often follows.

5. Our daughter would have drowned if Officer Blake didn't risk his life to save her.

ON THE WEB

For an electronic exercise on conditional verbs, go to
dianahacker.com/rules

and click on ▶ **Electronic Grammar Exercises**
▶ **Grammar**
▶ **E-ex 29-2**

29c Become familiar with verbs that may be followed by gerunds or infinitives.

A gerund is a verb form that ends in *-ing* and is used as a noun: *sleeping, dreaming.* (See 63c.) An infinitive is the base form of the verb preceded by the word *to: to sleep, to dream.* The word *to* is not a preposition in this use but an infinitive marker. (See 63c.)

A few verbs may be followed by either a gerund or an infinitive; still others may be followed by an infinitive (either directly or with a noun or pronoun intervening) but not by a gerund.

Verb + gerund or infinitive

These commonly used verbs may be followed by a gerund or an infinitive, with little or no difference in meaning:

begin	continue	like	start
can't stand	hate	love	

I love *skiing.*   I love *to ski.*

With a few verbs, however, the choice of a gerund or infinitive changes the meaning dramatically:

forget	remember	stop	try

She stopped *speaking* to Lucia. [She no longer spoke to Lucia.]

She stopped *to speak* to Lucia. [She paused so that she could speak to Lucia.]

Verb + gerund

These verbs may be followed by a gerund but not by an infinitive:

admit	enjoy	postpone	resist
appreciate	escape	practice	risk
avoid	finish	put off	suggest
deny	imagine	quit	tolerate
discuss	miss	recall	

Have you finished *decorating* [not *to decorate*] the tree?

Bill enjoys *playing* [not *to play*] the piano.

Verb + infinitive

These verbs may be followed by an infinitive but not by a gerund:

agree	decide	manage	pretend	want
ask	expect	mean	promise	wish
beg	have	offer	refuse	
claim	hope	plan	wait	

We plan *to visit* [not *visiting*] the Yucatán next week.

Jill has offered *to water* [not *watering*] the plants while we are away.

Verb + noun or pronoun + infinitive

With certain verbs in the active voice, a noun or pronoun must come between the verb and the infinitive that follows it. The noun or pronoun usually names a person who is affected by the action.

advise	command	have	persuade	tell
allow	convince	instruct	remind	urge
cause	encourage	order	require	warn

The dean encourages *you to apply* for the scholarship.

The class asked *Luis to tell* the story of his escape.

A few verbs may be followed either by an infinitive directly or by an infinitive preceded by a noun or pronoun.

ask   expect   need   want   would like

We asked *to speak* to the congregation.

We asked *Rabbi Abrams to speak* to our congregation.

Verb + noun or pronoun + unmarked infinitive

An unmarked infinitive is an infinitive without *to*. A few verbs (known as "causative verbs") may be followed by a noun or pronoun and an unmarked (but not a marked) infinitive.

have ("cause")   let ("allow")   make ("force")

Absence makes *the heart grow* [not *to grow*] fonder.

Please let *me pay* [not *to pay*] for the tickets.

GRAMMAR CHECKERS can flag some, but not all, problems with gerunds and infinitives following verbs. For example, programs flagged many sentences with misused infinitives, such as this one: *Chris enjoys to play tennis.* Programs were less successful at flagging sentences with misused present participles, skipping past incorrect sentences like this one: *We want traveling to Hawaii next spring.*

EXERCISE 29–3

Form sentences by adding gerund or infinitive constructions to the following sentence openings. In some cases, more than one kind of construction may be possible. Possible sentences for lettered items appear in the back of the book. Example:

Please remind *your sister to call me.*

a. I enjoy
b. Will you help Samantha
c. The team hopes
d. Ricardo and his brothers miss
e. The babysitter let

1. Pollen makes
2. The club president asked
3. Next summer we plan
4. Waverly intends
5. Please stop

ON THE WEB

For an electronic exercise on verbs followed by gerunds or infinitives, go to **dianahacker.com/rules**

and click on ▶ **Electronic Grammar Exercises**
▶ **Grammar**
▶ **E-ex 29–3**

29d Become familiar with commonly used two-word verbs.

Many verbs in English consist of a verb followed by a preposition or adverb known as a *particle*. (See 61c.) A two-word verb
(also known as a *phrasal verb*) often expresses an idiomatic
meaning that cannot be understood literally. Consider the verbs
in the following sentences, for example:

> We *ran across* Professor Magnotto on the way to the bookstore.

> Calvin *dropped in* on his adviser this morning.

> Regina told me to *look* her *up* when I got to Seattle.

As you probably know, *ran across* means "encountered," *dropped in* means "paid an unexpected visit," and *look up* means "get
in touch with." When you were first learning English, however,
these two-word verbs must have suggested strange meanings.

Some two-word verbs are intransitive; they do not take
direct objects. (See 62b.)

> This morning I *got up* at dawn.

Transitive two-word verbs (those that take direct objects)
have particles that are separable or inseparable. Separable particles may be separated from the verb by the direct object.

> Lucy *called* the wedding *off.*

When the direct object is a noun, a separable particle may also
follow the verb immediately.

At the last minute, Lucy *called off* the wedding.

When the direct object is a pronoun, however, the particle must be separated from the verb.

Why was there no wedding? Lucy *called* it *off* [not *called off* it].

Inseparable particles must follow the verb immediately. A direct object cannot come between the verb and the particle.

The police will *look into* the matter [not *look* the matter *into*].

29e Do not omit needed verbs.

Some languages allow the omission of the verb when the meaning is clear without it; English does not.

▶ Jim $\overset{is}{\underset{\wedge}{}}$ exceptionally intelligent.

▶ Many streets in San Francisco $\overset{are}{\underset{\wedge}{}}$ very steep.

30

Use the articles *a, an,* and *the* appropriately.

Except for occasional difficulty in choosing between *a* and *an*, native speakers of English encounter few problems with articles. To speakers whose native language is not English, however, articles can prove troublesome, for the rules governing their use are surprisingly complex. This section summarizes those rules.

The definite article *the* and the indefinite articles *a* and *an* signal that a noun is about to appear. The noun may follow the article immediately or modifiers may intervene (see 61a and 61d).

the candidate, the exceptionally well qualified *candidate*

a sunset, a spectacular *sunset*

an apple, an appetizing *apple*

Articles are not the only words used to mark nouns. Other markers (sometimes called *determiners*) include possessive nouns (*Helen's*), numbers, and the following pronouns: *my, your, his, her, its, our, their, whose, this, that, these, those, all, any, each, either, every, few, many, more, most, much, neither, several, some.*

Usually an article is not used with another noun marker. Common exceptions include expressions such as *a few, the most,* and *all the.*

GRAMMAR CHECKERS can flag some missing or misused articles, pointing out, for example, that an article usually precedes a word such as *paintbrush* or *vehicle* or that the articles *a* and *an* are not used before a noncount noun such as *sugar* or *advice.*

However, the programs fail to flag many missing or misused articles. For example, in two paragraphs with eleven missing or misused articles, grammar checkers caught only two of the problems. In addition, the programs frequently suggest that an article is missing when it is not. For example, one program suggested that an article might be needed before *teacher* in this correct sentence: *My social studies teacher entered me in a public-speaking contest.*

30a Use *a* (or *an*) with singular count nouns whose specific identity is not known to the reader.

Count nouns refer to persons, places, or things that can be counted: *one girl, two girls; one city, three cities; one apple, four apples.* Noncount nouns refer to entities or abstractions that cannot be counted: *water, steel, air, furniture, patience, knowledge.* It is important to remember that noncount nouns vary from language to language. To see what nouns English categorizes as noncount nouns, refer to the list on page 250.

If a singular count noun names something not known to the reader — perhaps because it is being mentioned for the first time, perhaps because its specific identity is unknown even to the writer — the noun should be preceded by *a* or *an* unless it has been preceded by another noun marker. *A* (or *an*) usually means "one among many" but can also mean "any one."

▶ Mary Beth arrived in ^*a* limousine.

▶ We are looking for ^*an* apartment close to the lake.

NOTE: *A* is used before a consonant sound: *a banana, a tree, a picture, a hand, a happy child. An* is used before a vowel sound: *an eggplant, an occasion, an uncle, an hour, an honorable person.* Notice that words beginning with *h* can have either a consonant sound (*hand, happy*) or a vowel sound (*hour, honorable*). (See also the Glossary of Usage: *a, an*.)

30b Do not use *a* (or *an*) with noncount nouns.

A (or *an*) is not used to mark noncount nouns, such as *sugar, gold, honesty,* or *jewelry.* A list of commonly used noncount nouns is given in the chart on page 250.

▶ Claudia asked her mother for ~~an~~ advice.

To express an approximate amount, you can often use one of the following quantifiers with a noncount noun.

QUANTIFIER	NONCOUNT NOUN
a great deal of	candy, courage
a little	salt, rain
any	sugar, homework
enough	bread, wood, money
less	meat, violence
little (*or* a little)	knowledge, time
more	coffee, information
much (*or* a lot of)	snow, pollution
plenty of	paper, lumber
some	tea, news, work

To express a more specific amount, you can often precede a noncount noun with a unit word that is typically associated with it. Here are some common combinations.

A OR *AN* + UNIT + *OF*	NONCOUNT NOUNS
a bottle of	water, vinegar
a carton of	ice cream, milk, yogurt
an ear of	corn
a head of	cabbage, lettuce
a loaf of	bread
a piece of	meat, furniture, advice
a pound of	butter, sugar

Commonly used noncount nouns

FOOD AND DRINK

bacon, beef, bread, broccoli, butter, cabbage, candy, cauliflower, celery, cereal, cheese, chicken, chocolate, coffee, corn, cream, fish, flour, fruit, ice cream, lettuce, meat, milk, oil, pasta, rice, salt, spinach, sugar, tea, water, wine, yogurt

NONFOOD SUBSTANCES

air, cement, coal, dirt, gasoline, gold, paper, petroleum, plastic, rain, silver, snow, soap, steel, wood, wool

ABSTRACT NOUNS

advice, anger, beauty, confidence, courage, employment, fun, happiness, health, honesty, information, intelligence, knowledge, love, poverty, satisfaction, truth, wealth

OTHER

biology (and other areas of study), clothing, equipment, furniture, homework, jewelry, luggage, lumber, machinery, mail, money, news, poetry, pollution, research, scenery, traffic, transportation, violence, weather, work

NOTE: A few noncount nouns may also be used as count nouns, especially in informal English: *Bill loves chocolate; Bill offered me a chocolate. I'll have coffee; I'll have a coffee.*

| a quart of | milk, ice cream |
| a slice of | bread, bacon |

CAUTION: Noncount nouns do not have plural forms, and they should not be used with numbers or words suggesting plurality (such as *several, many, a few, a couple of, a number of*).

▶ We need some information~~s~~ about rain forests.

   much
▶ Do you have ~~many~~ money with you?
    ^

30c Use *the* with most nouns whose specific identity is known to the reader.

The definite article *the* is used with most nouns whose identity is known to the reader. (For exceptions, see 30d.) Usually the identity will be clear to the reader for one of the following reasons:

— The noun has been previously mentioned.
— A phrase or a clause following the noun restricts its identity.
— A superlative such as *best* or *most intelligent* makes the noun's identity specific.
— The noun describes a unique person, place, or thing.
— The context or situation makes the noun's identity clear.

▶ A truck loaded with dynamite cut in front of our van.
　　　the
When truck skidded a few seconds later, we almost plowed
　　　^
into it.

The noun *truck* is preceded by *A* when it is first mentioned. When the noun is mentioned again, it is preceded by *the* since readers now know the specific truck being discussed.

　　　　　　　　　　the
▶ Bob warned me that gun on the top shelf of the cupboard
　　　　　　　　　^
was loaded.

The phrase *on the top shelf of the cupboard* identifies the specific gun.

　　　　　　　　　the
▶ Our petite daughter dated tallest boy in her class.
　　　　　　　　　　^
The superlative *tallest* restricts the identity of the noun *boy*.

　　　　　　　　　　　the
▶ During an eclipse, one should not look directly at sun.
　　　　　　　　　　　　^
There is only one sun in our solar system, so its identity is clear.

　　　　　　the
▶ Please don't slam door when you leave.
　　　　^
Both the speaker and the listener know which door is meant.

Geographical names

WHEN TO OMIT *THE*

streets, squares, parks	Ivy Street, Union Square, Denali National Park
cities, states, counties	Miami, Idaho, Bee County
most countries	Italy, Nigeria, China
continents	South America, Africa
bays, single lakes	Tampa Bay, Lake Geneva
single mountains, islands	Mount Everest, Crete

WHEN TO USE *THE*

united countries	the United States, the Republic of China
large regions, deserts	the East Coast, the Sahara
peninsulas	the Iberian Peninsula
oceans, seas, gulfs	the Pacific, the Dead Sea, the Persian Gulf
canals and rivers	the Panama Canal, the Amazon
mountain ranges	the Rocky Mountains, the Alps
groups of islands	the Solomon Islands

30d Do not use *the* with plural or noncount nouns meaning "all" or "in general"; do not use *the* with most singular proper nouns.

When a plural or a noncount noun means "all" or "in general," it is not marked with *the*.

▶ ~~The~~ F̂ountains are an expensive element of landscape design.

▶ In some parts of the world, ~~the~~ rice is preferred to all other grains.

As you probably know, proper nouns—which name specific people, places, or things—are capitalized. Although there are many exceptions, *the* is not used with most singular proper nouns, such as *Judge Hennessey, Spring Street,* or *Lake Huron.*

However, *the* is used with plural proper nouns, such as *the United Nations, the Bahamas,* and *the Finger Lakes.*

Geographical names create problems because there are so many exceptions to the rules. When in doubt, consult the chart on the previous page or ask a native speaker.

EXERCISE 30–1

Articles have been omitted from the following story, adapted from *Zen Flesh, Zen Bones,* compiled by Paul Reps. Insert the articles *a, an,* and *the* where English requires them and be prepared to explain the reasons for your choices.

Moon Cannot Be Stolen

Ryokan, who was Zen master, lived simple life in little hut at foot of mountain. One evening thief visited hut only to discover there was nothing in it to steal.

Ryokan returned and caught him. "You may have come long way to visit me," he told prowler, "and you should not return empty-handed. Please take my clothes as gift." Thief was bewildered. He took Ryokan's clothes and slunk away. Ryokan sat naked, watching moon. "Poor fellow," he mused, "I wish I could give him this beautiful moon."

ON THE WEB

For an electronic exercise on articles, go to
dianahacker.com/rules

and click on   ▶ **Electronic Grammar Exercises**
              ▶ **Grammar**
                ▶ **E-ex 30–1**

31

Be aware of other potential trouble spots.

31a Do not omit subjects or the expletive *there* or *it.*

English requires a subject for all sentences except imperatives, in which the subject *you* is understood (*Give to the poor*). (See

62a.) If your native language allows the omission of an explicit subject in other sentences or clauses, be especially alert to this requirement in English.

I have
▶ ~~Have~~ a large collection of baseball cards.
 ^

 she
▶ Your Aunt Geraldine is very energetic; seems young for
 ^

 her age.

When the subject has been moved from its normal position before the verb, English sometimes requires an expletive (*there* or *it*) at the beginning of the sentence or clause. (See 62c.) *There* is used at the beginning of a sentence or clause to draw the reader's (or listener's) attention to the location or existence of something.

There is
▶ ~~Is~~ an apple in the refrigerator.
 ^

 there
▶ As you know, are many religious sects in India.
 ^

Notice that the verb agrees with the subject that follows it: *apple is, sects are.* (See 21g.)

In one of its uses, the word *it* functions as an expletive, to call attention to a subject following the verb.

It is
▶ ~~Is~~ healthy to eat fruit and grains.
 ^
It is
▶ ~~Is~~ clear that we must change our approach.
 ^

The subjects of these sentences are *to eat fruit and grains* (an infinitive phrase) and *that we must change our approach* (a noun clause). (See 63c and 63b.)

As you probably know, the word *it* is also used as the subject of sentences describing the weather or temperature, stating the time, indicating distance, or suggesting an environmental fact.

It is raining in the valley, and it is snowing in the mountains.

In July, it is very hot in Arizona.

It is 9:15 A.M.

It is three hundred miles to Chicago.

It gets noisy in our dorm on weekends.

> GRAMMAR CHECKERS can flag some sentences with a missing expletive (*there* or *it*), but they often misdiagnose the problem, suggesting that if a sentence opens with a word such as *Is* or *Are*, it may need a question mark at the end. Consider this sentence, which grammar checkers flagged: *Are two grocery stores on Elm Street.* Clearly, the sentence doesn't need a question mark. What it needs is an expletive: *There are two grocery stores on Elm Street.*

31b Do not repeat the subject of a sentence.

English does not allow a subject to be repeated in its own clause.

▶ The doctor ~~she~~ advised me to cut down on salt.

The pronoun *she* repeats the subject *doctor.*

The subject of a sentence should not be repeated even if a word group intervenes between the subject and the verb.

▶ The car that had been stolen ~~it~~ was found.

The pronoun *it* repeats the subject *car.*

31c Do not repeat an object or an adverb in an adjective clause.

In some languages an object or an adverb is repeated later in the adjective clause in which it appears; in English such repetitions are not allowed. Adjective clauses begin with relative pronouns (*who, whom, whose, which, that*) or relative adverbs (*when, where*), and these words always serve a grammatical function within the clauses they introduce. (See 63b.) Another word in the clause cannot also serve that same grammatical function.

When a relative pronoun functions as the object of a verb or the object of a preposition, do not add another word with the same function later in the clause.

▶ The puppy ran after the car that we were riding in. ~~it.~~
∧

The relative pronoun *that* is the object of the preposition *in,* so the object *it* is not allowed.

Even when the relative pronoun has been omitted, do not add another word with its same function.

▶ The puppy ran after the car we were riding in. ~~it.~~
∧

The relative pronoun *that* is understood even though it is not present in the sentence.

Like a relative pronoun, a relative adverb should not be echoed later in its clause.

▶ The place where I work ~~there~~ is one hour from my apartment

in the city.

The adverb *there* should not echo the relative adverb *where.*

GRAMMAR CHECKERS usually fail to flag sentences with repeated subjects or objects. One program flagged some sentences with repeated subjects, such as this one: *The roses that they brought home they cost three dollars each.* However, the program misdiagnosed the problem, calling the sentence a run-on. The sentence is not a run-on; the problem is that the second *they* repeats the subject *roses.*

EXERCISE 31–1

In the following sentences, add needed subjects or expletives and delete any repeated subjects, objects, or adverbs. Answers to lettered sentences appear in the back of the book. Example:

Nancy is the woman whom I talked to ~~her~~ last week.

a. Are some cartons of ice cream in the freezer.
b. I don't use the subway because am afraid.
c. The prime minister she is the most popular leader in my country.
d. We tried to get in touch with the same manager whom we spoke to him earlier.
e. Recently have been a number of earthquakes in Turkey.

1. We visited an island where several ancient ruins are being excavated there.
2. In this city is difficult to find a high-paying job.
3. Foreign tourists sometimes unhappy about the high prices here.
4. Is a banyan tree in our backyard.
5. The neighbor whom we trusted he was a thief.

ON THE WEB

For an electronic exercise on omitted and repeated words, go to **dianahacker.com/rules**

and click on ▶ **Electronic Grammar Exercises**
▶ **Grammar**
▶ **E-ex 31-1**

31d Place adjectives and adverbs with care.

Adjectives modify nouns or pronouns; adverbs modify verbs, adjectives, or other adverbs. (See 61d and 61e.) Both native and nonnative speakers encounter problems in the use of adjectives and adverbs. (See 26.) For nonnative speakers, the placement of adjectives and adverbs can also be troublesome.

Placement of adjectives

No doubt you have already learned that in English adjectives usually precede the nouns they modify and that they may also appear following linking verbs. (See 26b and 62b.)

Janine wore a *new* necklace. Janine's necklace was *new*.

When adjectives pile up in front of a noun, however, you may sometimes have difficulty arranging them. English is quite particular about the order of cumulative adjectives, those not separated by commas. (See 32d.)

> Janine was wearing a *beautiful antique silver* necklace [not *silver antique beautiful* necklace].

The chart on page 259 shows the order in which cumulative adjectives ordinarily appear in front of the noun they modify. This list is just a general guide; don't be surprised when you encounter exceptions.

NOTE: Long strings of cumulative adjectives tend to be awkward. As a rule, use no more than two or three of them between the article (or other noun marker) and the noun modified. Here are several examples:

a beautiful old pine table	Susan's large round painting
two enormous French urns	some small blue medicine
an exotic purple jungle flower	bottles

Placement of adverbs

Adverbs modifying verbs appear in various positions: at the beginning or end of the sentence, before or after the verb, or between a helping verb and its main verb.

> *Slowly,* we drove along the rain-slick road.

> Mia handled the teapot *very carefully.*

> Martin *always* wins our tennis matches.

> Christina is *rarely* late for our lunch dates.

> My daughter has *often* spoken of you.

An adverb may not, however, be placed between a verb and its direct object.

> ► Mother wrapped ~~carefully~~ the gift/
>   ^
>   *carefully.*

> The adverb *carefully* may be placed at the beginning or at the end of this sentence or before the verb. It cannot appear after the verb because the verb is followed by the direct object *the gift.*

Usual order of cumulative adjectives

ARTICLE OR OTHER NOUN MARKER

a, an, the, her, Joe's, two, many, some

EVALUATIVE WORD

attractive, dedicated, delicious, ugly, disgusting

SIZE

large, enormous, small, little

LENGTH OR SHAPE

long, short, round, square

AGE

new, old, young, antique

COLOR

yellow, blue, crimson

NATIONALITY

French, Scandinavian, Vietnamese

RELIGION

Catholic, Protestant, Jewish, Muslim

MATERIAL

silver, walnut, wool, marble

NOUN/ADJECTIVE

tree (as in *tree* house), kitchen (as in *kitchen* table)

THE NOUN MODIFIED

house, sweater, bicycle, bread, woman, priest

GRAMMAR CHECKERS do not flag problems with the placement of adjectives and adverbs. They can, however, flag a few other problems with adjectives and adverbs. See the grammar checker advice on page 208.

EXERCISE 31-2

Using the chart on page 259, arrange the following modifiers and nouns in their proper order. Answers to lettered items appear in the back of the book. Example:

> *two new French racing bicycles*
> **new, French, two, bicycles, racing**

a. woman, young, an, Vietnamese, attractive
b. dedicated, a, priest, Catholic
c. old, her, sweater, blue, wool
d. delicious, Joe's, Scandinavian, bread
e. many, cages, bird, antique, beautiful

1. round, two, marble, tables, large
2. several, yellow, tulips, tiny
3. a, sports, classic, car
4. courtyard, a, square, small, brick
5. charming, restaurants, Italian, several

ON THE WEB

For an electronic exercise on the order of cumulative adjectives, go to **dianahacker.com/rules**

and click on ▶ **Electronic Grammar Exercises**
  ▶ **Grammar**
    ▶ **E-ex 31-2**

31e Distinguish between present participles and past participles used as adjectives.

Both present and past participles may be used as adjectives. The present participle always ends in *-ing*. Past participles usually end in *-ed, -d, -en, -n,* or *-t.* (See 27a.)

PRESENT PARTICIPLES   confusing, speaking

PAST PARTICIPLES   confused, spoken

Participles used as adjectives can precede the nouns they modify; they can also follow linking verbs, in which case they describe the subject of the sentence. (See 62b.)

It was a *depressing* movie. Jim was a *depressed* young man.

The essay was *confusing*. The student was *confused*.

A present participle should describe a person or thing causing or stimulating an experience; a past participle should describe a person or thing undergoing an experience.

> The lecturer was *boring* [not *bored*].

> The audience was *bored* [not *boring*].

In the first example, the lecturer is causing boredom, not experiencing it. In the second example, the audience is experiencing boredom, not causing it.

The participles that cause the most trouble for nonnative speakers are those describing mental states:

annoying / annoyed	exhausting / exhausted
boring / bored	fascinating / fascinated
confusing / confused	frightening / frightened
depressing / depressed	satisfying / satisfied
exciting / excited	surprising / surprised

GRAMMAR CHECKERS do not flag problems with present and past participles used as adjectives. Not surprisingly, the programs have no way of knowing the meaning a writer intends. For example, both of the following sentences could be correct, depending on the writer's meaning: *My roommate was annoying.* *My roommate was annoyed.*

EXERCISE 31–3

Edit the following sentences for proper use of present and past participles. If a sentence is correct, write "correct" after it. Answers to lettered sentences appear in the back of the book. Example:

excited
Danielle and Monica were very ~~exciting~~ to be going to a
^
Broadway show for the first time.

a. Listening to everyone's complaints all day was irritated.
b. During the long lecture, many students appeared boring.
c. His skill at chess is amazing.
d. After a great deal of research, the scientist made a fascinated discovery.
e. That blackout was one of the most frightened experiences I've ever had.

1. I couldn't concentrate on my homework because I was distracted.
2. The directions to the new board game seem extremely complicating.
3. How interested are you in visiting Civil War battlefields?
4. The statistics on childhood poverty in the United States were depressing.
5. Even after the lecturer went over the main points again, the students were still confusing.

ON THE WEB

For an electronic exercise on present and past participles, go to
dianahacker.com/rules

and click on ▶ **Electronic Grammar Exercises**
▶ **Grammar**
▶ **E-ex 31-3**

31f   Become familiar with common prepositions that show time and place.

The most frequently used prepositions in English are *at, by, for, from, in, of, on, to,* and *with.* Each of these prepositions has a variety of uses that must be learned gradually, in context.

Prepositions that indicate time and place can be difficult to master because the differences among them are subtle and idiomatic. The chart on page 263 limits itself to four troublesome prepositions that show time and place: *at, on, in,* and *by.*

Not every possible use is listed in the chart, so don't be surprised when you encounter exceptions and idiomatic uses that

at, on, in, and *by* to show time and place

Showing time

AT   *at* a specific time: *at* 7:20, *at* dawn, *at* dinner

ON   *on* a specific day or date: *on* June 4

IN   *in* a part of a 24-hour period: *in* the afternoon, *in* the day-time [but *at* night]

  in a year or month: *in* 1999, *in* July

  in a period of time: finished *in* three hours

BY   *by* a specific time or date: *by* 4:15, *by* Christmas

Showing place

AT   *at* a meeting place or location: *at* home, *at* the club

  at the edge of something: sitting *at* the desk

  at the corner of something: turning *at* the intersection

  at a target: throwing the snowball *at* Lucy

ON   *on* a surface: placed *on* the table, hanging *on* the wall

  on an electronic medium: *on* television, *on* the Internet

IN   *in* an enclosed space: *in* the garage, *in* the envelope

  in a geographic location: *in* San Diego, *in* Texas

  in a print medium: *in* a book, *in* a magazine

BY   *by* a landmark: *by* the fence, *by* the flagpole

you must learn one at a time. For example, in English we ride *in* a car but *on* a bus, train, or subway. And when we fly *on* (not *in*) a plane, we are not sitting on top of the plane.

EXERCISE 31–4

In the following sentences, replace prepositions that are not used correctly. If a sentence is correct, write "correct" after it. Answers to lettered sentences appear in the back of the book. Example:

  at
The play begins ~~on~~ 7:20 P.M.
  ^

a. Whenever we eat at the Centerville Diner, we sit at a small table on the corner of the room.
b. In the 1980s, the gap between the rich and the poor in the United States became wider.
c. In Wednesdays he leaves work early so he can lift weights at his health club.
d. Our rabbi moved to the Northwest in 1994 and has been with our temple at Seattle since 1996.

1. I don't feel safe walking on my neighborhood in night.
2. If the train is on time, it will arrive on six o'clock at the morning.
3. In the corner of the room there is a large bookcase with a pair of small Russian dolls standing at the top shelf.
4. She licked the stamp, stuck it in the envelope, put the envelope on her pocket, and walked to the nearest mailbox.
5. The mailbox was in the intersection of Laidlaw Avenue and Williams Street.

ON THE WEB

For an electronic exercise on prepositions showing time and place, go to **dianahacker.com/rules**

and click on ▶ **Electronic Grammar Exercises**
　　　　　　　▶ **Grammar**
　　　　　　　　　▶ **E-ex 31-4**

Punctuation

Process

Design

Clarity

Grammar

Punctuation

Mechanics

Argument

Research

Basics

32

The comma

The comma was invented to help readers. Without it, sentence parts can collide into one another unexpectedly, causing misreadings.

CONFUSING   If you cook Elmer will do the dishes.

CONFUSING   While we were eating a rattlesnake approached our campsite.

Add commas in the logical places (after *cook* and *eating*), and suddenly all is clear. No longer is Elmer being cooked, the rattlesnake being eaten.

Various rules have evolved to prevent such misreadings and to speed readers along through complex grammatical structures. Those rules are detailed in this section.

32a   Use a comma before a coordinating conjunction joining independent clauses.

When a coordinating conjunction connects two or more independent clauses — word groups that could stand alone as separate sentences — a comma must precede it. There are seven coordinating conjunctions in English: *and, but, or, nor, for, so,* and *yet.*

A comma tells readers that one independent clause has come to a close and that another is about to begin.

▶   Nearly everyone has heard of love at first sight, but I fell in
    ⌃
love at first dance.

EXCEPTION: If the two independent clauses are short and there is no danger of misreading, the comma may be omitted.

The plane took off and we were on our way.

GRAMMAR CHECKERS have mixed success in flagging missing or misused commas. They can tell you that a comma is usually used before *which* but not before *that* (see 32e), and they can flag some missing commas after an introductory word or word group or between items in a series. In general, however, the programs are unreliable. For example, in an essay with ten missing commas and five misused ones, a grammar checker spotted only one missing comma (after the word *therefore*).

CAUTION: As a rule, do *not* use a comma to separate coordinate word groups that are not independent clauses. (See 33a.)

▶ A good money manager controls expenses/ and invests

surplus dollars to meet future needs.

The word group following *and* is not an independent clause; it is the second half of a compound predicate.

32b Use a comma after an introductory clause or phrase.

The most common introductory word groups are clauses and phrases functioning as adverbs. Such word groups usually tell when, where, how, why, or under what conditions the main action of the sentence occurred. (See 63a–63c.)

A comma tells readers that the introductory clause or phrase has come to a close and that the main part of the sentence is about to begin.

▶ When Irwin was ready to eat, his cat jumped onto the table.
        ^

Without the comma, readers may imagine Irwin eating his cat. The comma signals that *his cat* is the subject of a new clause, not part of the introductory one.

▶ Near a small stream at the bottom of the canyon, the park
                                              ^

rangers discovered an abandoned mine.

The comma tells readers that the introductory prepositional phrase has come to a close.

EXCEPTION: The comma may be omitted after a short adverb clause or phrase if there is no danger of misreading.

In no time we were at 2,800 feet.

Sentences also frequently begin with participial phrases describing the noun or pronoun immediately following them (see 63c). The comma tells readers that they are about to learn the identity of the person or thing described; therefore, the comma is usually required even when the phrase is short.

▶ Thinking his motorcade drive through Dallas was routine,
  President Kennedy smiled and waved at the crowds.

▶ Buried under layers of younger rocks, the earth's oldest
  rocks contain no fossils.

NOTE: Other introductory word groups include transitional expressions and absolute phrases (see 32f).

EXERCISE 32–1

Add or delete commas where necessary in the following sentences. If a sentence is correct, write "correct" after it. Answers to lettered sentences appear in the back of the book. Example:

Because it rained all Labor Day, our picnic was rather soggy.

  a. Alisa brought the injured bird home, and fashioned a splint out of Popsicle sticks for its wing.

  b. Considered the first Western philosopher Thales believed that water was the elemental principle underlying all things.

  c. If you complete the enclosed card, and return it within two weeks, you will receive a free breakfast during your stay.

  d. After retiring from the New York City Ballet in 1965, legendary dancer Maria Tallchief went on to found the Chicago City Ballet.

  e. Uncle Swen's dulcimers disappeared as soon as he put them up for sale but he always kept one for himself.

  1. When the runaway race car crashed the gas tank exploded.

2. He pushed the car beyond the tollgate, and poured a bucket of water on the smoking hood.
3. Lighting the area like a second moon the helicopter circled the scene.
4. As the concert began, we heard a tremendous explosion.
5. Many musicians of Bach's time played several instruments but few mastered them as early or played with as much expression as Bach.

32c Use a comma between all items in a series.

When three or more items are presented in a series, those items should be separated from one another with commas. Items in a series may be single words, phrases, or clauses.

▶ Bubbles of air, leaves, ferns, bits of wood, and insects are

often found trapped in amber.

ON THE WEB

The rules on using commas with items in a series have sparked debates. If you're interested in learning why, go to
dianahacker.com/rules

and click on ▶ **Language Debates**
          ▶ **Commas with items in a series**

Although some writers view the comma between the last two items as optional, most experts advise using the comma because its omission can result in ambiguity.

▶ Uncle David willed me all of his property, houses, and

warehouses.

Did Uncle David will his property *and* houses *and* warehouses — or simply his property, consisting of houses and warehouses? If the former meaning is intended, a comma is necessary to prevent ambiguity.

32d Use a comma between coordinate adjectives not joined with *and*. Do not use a comma between cumulative adjectives.

When two or more adjectives each modify a noun separately, they are coordinate.

> Roberto is a *warm, gentle, affectionate* father.

Adjectives are coordinate if they can be joined with *and* (warm *and* gentle *and* affectionate).

Adjectives that do not modify the noun separately are cumulative.

> *Three large gray* shapes moved slowly toward us.

We cannot insert the word *and* between cumulative adjectives (three *and* large *and* gray shapes).

COORDINATE ADJECTIVES

▶ Patients with severe, irreversible brain damage should not be
put on life support systems.

CUMULATIVE ADJECTIVES

▶ Ira ordered a rich/ chocolate/ layer cake.

EXERCISE 32–2

Add or delete commas where necessary in the following sentences. If a sentence is correct, write "correct" after it. Answers to lettered sentences appear in the back of the book. Example:

> We gathered our essentials, took off for the great outdoors,
> and ignored the fact that it was Friday the 13th.

a. The cold impersonal atmosphere of the university was unbearable.
b. An ambulance threaded its way through police cars, fire trucks and irate citizens.
c. The 1812 Overture is a stirring, magnificent piece of music.
d. After two broken arms, three cracked ribs and one concussion, Ken quit the varsity football team.

e. My cat's pupils had constricted to small black shining dots.

1. We prefer our staff to be orderly, prompt and efficient.
2. For breakfast the children ordered cornflakes, English muffins with peanut butter and cherry Cokes.
3. It was a small, unimportant part, but I was happy to have it.
4. Cyril was clad in a luminous orange rain suit and a brilliant white helmet.
5. Anne Frank and thousands like her were forced to hide in attics, cellars and secret rooms in an effort to save their lives.

32e Use commas to set off nonrestrictive elements. Do not use commas to set off restrictive elements.

Word groups describing nouns or pronouns (adjective clauses, adjective phrases, and appositives) are restrictive or nonrestrictive. A *restrictive* element defines or limits the meaning of the word it modifies and is therefore essential to the meaning of the sentence. Because it contains essential information, a restrictive element is not set off with commas.

RESTRICTIVE   The children needed clothes *that were washable.*

If you remove a restrictive element from a sentence, the meaning changes significantly, becoming more general than you intended. The writer of the example sentence does not mean that the children needed clothes in general. The intended meaning is more limited: the children needed *washable* clothes.

A *nonrestrictive* element describes a noun or pronoun whose meaning has already been clearly defined or limited. Because it contains nonessential or parenthetical information, a nonrestrictive element is set off with commas.

NONRESTRICTIVE   The children needed sturdy shoes, *which were expensive.*

If you remove a nonrestrictive element from a sentence, the meaning does not change dramatically. Some meaning is lost, to be sure, but the defining characteristics of the person or thing described remain the same as before. The children needed *sturdy shoes,* and these happened to be expensive.

NOTE: Often it is difficult to tell whether a word group is restrictive or nonrestrictive without seeing it in context and considering the writer's meaning. Both of the following sentences are grammatically correct, but their meaning is slightly different.

The dessert made with fresh raspberries was delicious.

The dessert, made with fresh raspberries, was delicious.

In the example without commas, the phrase *made with fresh raspberries* tells readers which of two or more desserts the writer is referring to. In the example with commas, the phrase merely adds information about the particular dessert served with the meal.

Adjective clauses

Adjective clauses are patterned like sentences, containing subjects and verbs, but they function within sentences as modifiers of nouns or pronouns. They always follow the word they modify, usually immediately. Adjective clauses begin with a relative pronoun (*who, whom, whose, which, that*) or with a relative adverb (*where, when*).

Nonrestrictive adjective clauses are set off with commas; restrictive adjective clauses are not.

NONRESTRICTIVE CLAUSE

▶ Ed's house‚ which is located on thirteen acres‚ was completely
          ^   ^

   furnished with bats in the rafters and mice in the kitchen.

The adjective clause *which is located on thirteen acres* does not restrict the meaning of *Ed's house,* so the information is nonessential.

RESTRICTIVE CLAUSE

▶ An office manager for a corporation/ that had government

   contracts/ asked her supervisor whether she could

   reprimand her co-workers for smoking.

Because the adjective clause *that had government contracts* identifies the corporation, the information is essential.

NOTE: Use *that* only with restrictive clauses. Many writers prefer to use *which* only with nonrestrictive clauses, but usage varies.

ON THE WEB

The rules on using *that* versus *which* have sparked debates. If you're interested in learning why, go to
dianahacker.com/rules

and click on ▶ **Language Debates**
▶ *that* **versus** *which*

Phrases functioning as adjectives

Prepositional or verbal phrases functioning as adjectives may be restrictive or nonrestrictive. Nonrestrictive phrases are set off with commas; restrictive phrases are not.

NONRESTRICTIVE PHRASE

▶ The helicopter, with its 100,000-candlepower spotlight
^

illuminating the area, circled above.
^

The *with* phrase is nonessential because its purpose is not to specify which of two or more helicopters is being discussed.

RESTRICTIVE PHRASE

▶ One corner of the attic was filled with newspapers, dating

from the turn of the century.

Dating from the turn of the century restricts the meaning of *newspapers,* so the comma should be omitted.

Appositives

An appositive is a noun or noun phrase that renames a nearby noun. Nonrestrictive appositives are set off with commas; restrictive appositives are not.

NONRESTRICTIVE APPOSITIVE

▶ Darwin's most important book, *On the Origin of Species*, was
   ⌃   ⌃
the result of many years of research.

Most important restricts the meaning to one book, so the appositive *On the Origin of Species* is nonrestrictive.

RESTRICTIVE APPOSITIVE

▶ The song/ "Fire It Up/" was blasted out of amplifiers ten feet

tall.

Once they've read *song,* readers still don't know precisely which
song the writer means. The appositive following *song* restricts its
meaning.

EXERCISE 32–3

Add or delete commas where necessary in the following sentences. If a
sentence is correct, write "correct" after it. Answers to lettered sentences appear in the back of the book. Example:

My youngest sister, who plays left wing on the team, now
          ⌃   ⌃
lives at The Sands, a beach house near Los Angeles.
              ⌃

a. Choreographer Alvin Ailey's best-known work *Revelations* is more
   than just a crowd pleaser.
b. Twyla Tharp's contemporary ballet *Push Comes to Shove* was made
   famous by Russian dancer Baryshnikov. [Tharp has written more
   than one contemporary ballet.]
c. The woman running for the council seat in the fifth district has a
   long history of community service.
d. A member of an organization, that provides housing for AIDS patients, was also appointed to the commission.
e. A 1911 fire at the Triangle Shirtwaist Company which killed 146
   sweatshop workers led to reforms in working conditions.

1. I had the pleasure of talking to a woman who had just returned
   from India where she had lived for ten years.
2. Sally's best friend Sid Phillips has been playing the guitar since
   the age of seven.

3. The gentleman waiting for the prescription is Mr. Rhee.
4. *Where the Wild Things Are,* the 1964 Caldecott Medal winner, is my nephew's favorite book.
5. The flame crawled up a few blades of grass to reach a low-hanging palmetto branch which quickly ignited.

32f Use commas to set off transitional and parenthetical expressions, absolute phrases, and elements expressing contrast.

Transitional expressions

Transitional expressions serve as bridges between sentences or parts of sentences. They include conjunctive adverbs such as *however, therefore,* and *moreover* and transitional phrases such as *for example, as a matter of fact,* and *in other words.* (For more complete lists, see also 34b.)

When a transitional expression appears between independent clauses in a compound sentence, it is preceded by a semicolon and is often followed by a comma. (See also 34b.)

▶ Minh did not understand our language; moreover, he was

unfamiliar with our customs.

When a transitional expression appears at the beginning or in the middle of an independent clause, it is usually set off with commas.

▶ As a matter of fact, American football was established by

fans who wanted to play a more organized game of rugby.

▶ Natural foods are not always salt free; celery, for example,

contains more sodium than most people would imagine.

EXCEPTION: If a transitional expression blends smoothly with the rest of the sentence, calling for little or no pause in reading, it does not need to be set off with a comma. Expressions such as *also, at least, certainly, consequently, indeed, of course, moreover, no doubt, perhaps, then,* and *therefore* do not always call for a pause.

> Alice's bicycle is broken; *therefore* you will need to borrow Sue's.

Parenthetical expressions

Expressions that are distinctly parenthetical should be set off with commas. Providing supplemental information, they interrupt the flow of a sentence or appear at the end as afterthoughts.

▶ Evolution, as far as we know, doesn't work this way.

▶ The bass weighed about twelve pounds, give or take a few

ounces.

Absolute phrases

An absolute phrase, which modifies the whole sentence, usually consists of a noun followed by a participle or participial phrase. (See 63e.) Absolute phrases may appear at the beginning or at the end of a sentence. Wherever they appear, they should be set off with commas.

▶ Our grant having been approved, we were at last able to

begin the archaeological dig.

▶ Elvis Presley made music industry history in the 1950s, his

records having sold more than ten million copies.

CAUTION: Do not insert a comma between the noun and participle of an absolute construction.

▶ The next day/ being a school day, we turned down the

invitation.

Contrasted elements

Sharp contrasts beginning with words such as *not, never,* and *unlike* are set off with commas.

▶ The Epicurean philosophers sought mental‚ not bodily‚

pleasures.

▶ Unlike Robert‚ Celia loved dance contests.

32g   Use commas to set off nouns of direct address, the words *yes* and *no*, interrogative tags, and mild interjections.

▶ Forgive us‚ Dr. Spock‚ for reprimanding Jason.

▶ Yes‚ the loan will probably be approved.

▶ The film was faithful to the book‚ wasn't it?

▶ Well‚ cases like these are difficult to decide.

32h   Use commas with expressions such as *he said* to set off direct quotations. (See also 37f.)

▶ Naturalist Arthur Cleveland Bent remarked‚ "In part the peregrine declined unnoticed because it is not adorable."

▶ "Convictions are more dangerous foes of truth than lies,"

wrote philosopher Friedrich Nietzsche.

32i   Use commas with dates, addresses, titles, and numbers.

Dates

In dates, the year is set off from the rest of the sentence with a pair of commas.

▶ On December 12, 1890, orders were sent out for the arrest of
   Sitting Bull.

EXCEPTIONS: Commas are not needed if the date is inverted or if only the month and year are given.

The recycling plan went into effect on 15 April 2003.

January 2003 was an extremely cold month.

Addresses

The elements of an address or place name are separated by commas. A zip code, however, is not preceded by a comma.

▶ John Lennon was born in Liverpool, England, in 1940.

▶ Please send the package to Greg Tarvin at 708 Spring Street, Washington, Illinois 61571.

Titles

If a title follows a name, separate it from the rest of the sentence with a pair of commas.

▶ Sandra Belinsky, M.D., has been appointed to the board of trustees.

Numbers

In numbers more than four digits long, use commas to separate the numbers into groups of three, starting from the right. In numbers four digits long, a comma is optional.

> 3,500 [*or* 3500]
> 100,000
> 5,000,000

EXCEPTIONS: Do not use commas in street numbers, zip codes, telephone numbers, or years.

32j   Use a comma to prevent confusion.

In certain contexts, a comma is necessary to prevent confusion. If the writer has omitted a word or phrase, for example, a comma may be needed to signal the omission.

▶ To err is human; to forgive, divine.

If two words in a row echo each other, a comma may be needed for ease of reading.

▶ All of the catastrophes that we had feared might happen,

happened.

Sometimes a comma is needed to prevent readers from grouping words in ways that do not match the writer's intention.

▶ Patients who can, walk up and down the halls several times

a day.

EXERCISE 32–4: Major uses of the comma

This exercise covers the major uses of the comma listed in the chart on page 280. Add or delete commas where necessary. If a sentence is correct, write "correct" after it. Answers to lettered sentences appear in the back of the book. Example:

Although we invited him to the party, Gerald decided to

spend another late night in the computer room.

a. Cricket, which originated in England is also popular in Australia, South Africa and India.
b. At the sound of a starting pistol the horses surged forward toward the first obstacle, a sharp incline three feet high.
c. After the passage of the Civil Rights Act of 1964 the Ku Klux Klan went underground for a few years but the group's racist views did not change.
d. Jan's costume was completed with bright red, snakeskin sandals.

Major uses of the comma

BEFORE A COORDINATING CONJUNCTION JOINING INDEPENDENT CLAUSES (32a)

No grand idea was ever born in a conference, but a lot of foolish ideas have died there.   —F. Scott Fitzgerald

AFTER AN INTRODUCTORY CLAUSE OR PHRASE (32b)

If thought corrupts language, language can also corrupt thought.   —George Orwell

BETWEEN ALL ITEMS IN A SERIES (32c)

All the things I really like to do are either immoral, illegal, or fattening.   —Alexander Woollcott

BETWEEN COORDINATE ADJECTIVES (32d)

There is a mighty big difference between good, sound reasons and reasons that sound good.   —Burton Hillis

TO SET OFF NONRESTRICTIVE ELEMENTS (32E)

Silence, which will save me from shame, will also deprive me of fame.   —Igor Stravinsky

     e. Computers must be manufactured in clean climate-controlled rooms.

1. Research on Andean condors has shown that high levels of the chemical pesticide chlorinated hydrocarbon can cause the thinning of eggshells.
2. Founded in 1868 Hampton University was one of the first colleges for African Americans.
3. Aunt Emilia was an impossible demanding guest.
4. The French Mirage, the fastest airplane in the Colombian air force, was an astonishing machine to fly.
5. In the showroom sat a brand-new, red convertible Porsche, a car no driver can resist.

EXERCISE 32–5: All uses of the comma

Add or delete commas where necessary in the following sentences. If a sentence is correct, write "correct" after it. Answers to lettered sentences appear in the back of the book. Example:

"Yes, Virginia, there is a Santa Claus," wrote the editor.
   ^

a. On January 15, 1996 our office moved to 29 Commonwealth Avenue, Mechanicsville Virginia 19607.
b. The coach having bawled us out thoroughly, we left the locker room with his harsh words ringing in our ears.
c. Ms. Carlson you are a valued customer whose satisfaction is very important to us.
d. Mr. Mundy was born on July 22, 1939 in Arkansas, where his family had lived for four generations.
e. Swords flashing, our heroes dashed into action.

1. President Lincoln's original intention was to save the Union, not to destroy slavery.
2. For centuries people believed that Greek culture had developed in isolation from the world. Today however scholars are acknowledging the contributions made by Egypt and the Middle East.
3. Eating raw limpets, I found out, is like trying to eat art gum erasers.
4. Fortunately science is creating many alternatives to research performed on animals.
5. While the machine was printing the oversized paper jammed.

ON THE WEB

For electronic exercises on using commas, go to
dianahacker.com/rules

and click on   ▶ **Electronic Grammar Exercises**
                 ▶ **Punctuation**
                   ▶ **E-ex 32-1 through 32-3**

33

Unnecessary commas

Many common misuses of the comma result from an incomplete understanding of the major comma rules presented in 32. In particular, writers frequently form misconceptions about rules 32a–32e, either extending the rules inappropriately or misinterpreting them. Such misconceptions can lead to the errors described in 33a–33e; rules 33f–33h list other common misuses of the comma.

33a Do not use a comma between compound elements that are not independent clauses.

Though a comma should be used before a coordinating conjunction joining independent clauses (see 32a), this rule should not be extended to other compound word groups.

▶ Marie Curie discovered radium⁄ and later applied her work

on radioactivity to medicine.

And links two verbs in a compound predicate: *discovered* and *applied.*

▶ Jake still doesn't realize that his illness is serious⁄ and that

he will have to alter his diet to improve his chances of survival.

And links two subordinate clauses, each beginning with *that.*

33b Do not use a comma after a phrase that begins an inverted sentence.

Though a comma belongs after most introductory phrases (see 32b), it does not belong after phrases that begin an inverted sentence. In an inverted sentence, the subject follows the verb, and a phrase that ordinarily would follow the verb is moved to the beginning (see 62c).

▶ At the bottom of the sound⁄ lies a ship laden with treasure.

33c Do not use a comma before the first or after the last item in a series.

Though commas are required between items in a series (32c), do not place them either before or after the whole series.

▶ Other causes of asthmatic attacks are/ stress, change in

temperature, humidity, and cold air.

▶ Ironically, this job that appears so glamorous, carefree, and

easy/ carries a high degree of responsibility.

33d **Do not use a comma between cumulative adjectives, between an adjective and a noun, or between an adverb and an adjective.**

Commas are required between coordinate adjectives (those that can be joined with *and*), but they do not belong between cumulative adjectives (those that cannot be joined with *and*). (For a full discussion, see 32d.)

▶ In the corner of the closet we found an old/ maroon hatbox

from Sears.

A comma should never be used between an adjective and the noun that follows it.

▶ It was a senseless, dangerous/ mission.

Nor should a comma be used between an adverb and an adjective that follows it.

▶ The Hurst Home is unsuitable as a mental facility for

severely/ disturbed youths.

33e **Do not use commas to set off restrictive or mildly parenthetical elements.**

Restrictive elements are modifiers or appositives that restrict the meaning of the nouns they follow. Because they are essential to the meaning of the sentence, they are not set off with commas. (For a full discussion of both restrictive and nonre-strictive elements, see 32e.)

▶ Drivers/ who think they own the road/ make cycling a

dangerous sport.

The modifier *who think they own the road* restricts the meaning of *Drivers* and is therefore essential to the meaning of the sentence. Putting commas around the *who* clause falsely suggests that all drivers think they own the road.

▶ Margaret Mead's book/ *Coming of Age in Samoa/* stirred up

considerable controversy when it was published.

Since Mead wrote more than one book, the appositive contains information essential to the meaning of the sentence.

Although commas should be used with distinctly paren-thetical expressions (see 32f), do not use them to set off ele-ments that are only mildly parenthetical.

▶ Charisse believes that the Internet is/ essentially/ a bastion

of advertising.

33f Do not use a comma to set off a concluding adverb clause that is essential to the meaning of the sentence.

When adverb clauses introduce a sentence, they are nearly al-ways followed by a comma (see 32b). When they conclude a sentence, however, they are not set off by commas if their con-tent is essential to the meaning of the earlier part of the sen-tence. Adverb clauses beginning with *after, as soon as, because, before, if, since, unless, until,* and *when* are usually essential.

▶ Don't visit Paris at the height of the tourist season/ unless

you have booked hotel reservations.

Without the *unless* clause, the meaning of the sentence might at first seem broader than the writer intended.

When a concluding adverb clause is nonessential, it should be preceded by a comma. Clauses beginning with *although, even though, though,* and *whereas* are usually nonessential.

▶ The lecture seemed to last only a short time, although the
  ^
clock said it had gone on for more than an hour.

33g Do not use a comma to separate a verb from its subject or object.

A sentence should flow from subject to verb to object without unnecessary pauses. Commas may appear between these major sentence elements only when a specific rule calls for them.

▶ Zoos large enough to give the animals freedom to roam/ are

becoming more popular.

▶ Francesca explained to him/ that she was busy and would

see him later.

In the first sentence, the comma should not separate the subject, *Zoos,* from the verb, *are becoming.* In the second sentence, the comma should not separate the verb, *explained,* from its object, the subordinate clause *that she was busy and would see him later.*

33h Avoid other common misuses of the comma.

Do not use a comma in the following situations.

AFTER A COORDINATING CONJUNCTION (*AND, BUT, OR, NOR, FOR, SO, YET*)

▶ Occasionally soap operas are performed live, but/ more often

they are taped.

AFTER *SUCH AS* OR *LIKE*

▶ Many shade-loving plants, such as/ begonias, impatiens, and coleus, can add color to a shady garden.

BEFORE *THAN*

▶ Touring Crete was more thrilling for us/ than visiting the Greek islands frequented by rich Europeans.

AFTER *ALTHOUGH*

▶ Although/ the air was balmy, the water was too cold for swimming.

BEFORE A PARENTHESIS

▶ At MCI Sylvia began at the bottom/ (with only three and a half walls and a swivel chair), but within five years she had been promoted to supervisor.

TO SET OFF AN INDIRECT (REPORTED) QUOTATION

▶ Samuel Goldwyn once said/ that a verbal contract isn't worth the paper it's written on.

WITH A QUESTION MARK OR AN EXCLAMATION POINT

▶ "Why don't you try it?/" she coaxed. "You can't do any worse than the rest of us."

EXERCISE 33–1

Delete commas where necessary in the following sentences. If a sentence is correct, write "correct" after it. Answers to lettered sentences appear in the back of the book. Example:

> Loretta Lynn has paved the way for artists such as/ Shania
>
> Twain and the Dixie Chicks.

a. As a child growing up in Jamaica, I often daydreamed about life in the United States.
b. He wore a thick, black, wool coat over army fatigues.
c. Often public figures, (Greta Garbo was a good example) go to great lengths to guard their private lives.
d. She loved early spring flowers such as, crocuses, daffodils, forsythia, and irises.
e. On Pam's wrist, was a tattoo of a dragon chasing a tiger.

1. Mesquite, the hardest of the softwoods, grows primarily in the Southwest.
2. Male supremacy was assumed by my father, and accepted by my mother.
3. The lieutenant reported to his captain, that all of his men were present and accounted for.
4. The streets that three hours later would be bumper to bumper with commuters, were quiet and empty except for a few prowling cats.
5. Most of the citizens in the United States, expect their elected officials to be truthful.

ON THE WEB

For an electronic exercise on the use and misuse of commas, go to
dianahacker.com/rules

and click on   ▶ **Electronic Grammar Exercises**
                    ▶ **Punctuation**
                         ▶ **E-ex 33-1**

34

The semicolon

The semicolon is used to connect major sentence elements of equal grammatical rank.

GRAMMAR CHECKERS flag some, but not all, misused semicolons (34d). In addition, they can alert you to some run-on sentences (34a). However, they miss more run-on sentences than they identify, and they sometimes flag correct sentences as possible run-ons. (See also the grammar checker advice on p. 166.)

34a Use a semicolon between closely related independent clauses not joined with a coordinating conjunction.

When related independent clauses appear in one sentence, they are ordinarily linked with a comma and a coordinating conjunction (*and, but, or, nor, for, so, yet*). The coordinating conjunction signals the relation between the clauses. If the clauses are closely related and the relation is clear without a conjunction, they may be linked with a semicolon instead.

> Injustice is relatively easy to bear; what stings is justice.
> — H. L. Mencken

A semicolon must be used whenever a coordinating conjunction has been omitted between independent clauses. To use merely a comma creates a kind of run-on sentence known as a comma splice. (See 20.)

▶ In 1800, a traveler needed six weeks to get from New York

City to Chicago/; in 1860, the trip by railroad took only
         ^

two days.

CAUTION: Do not overuse the semicolon as a means of revising run-on sentences. For other revision strategies, see 20a, 20c, and 20d.

34b Use a semicolon between independent clauses linked with a transitional expression.

Transitional expressions include conjunctive adverbs and transitional phrases.

CONJUNCTIVE ADVERBS

accordingly	indeed	subsequently
also	instead	then
anyway	likewise	therefore
besides	meanwhile	thus
certainly	moreover	
consequently	nevertheless	
conversely	next	
finally	nonetheless	
furthermore	otherwise	
hence	similarly	
however	specifically	
incidentally	still	

TRANSITIONAL PHRASES

after all	even so	in fact
as a matter of fact	for example	in other words
as a result	for instance	in the first place
at any rate	in addition	on the contrary
at the same time	in conclusion	on the other hand

When a transitional expression appears between two independent clauses, it is preceded by a semicolon and usually followed by a comma.

▶ Many corals grow very gradually/; in fact, the creation of a
 ^

coral reef can take centuries.

When a transitional expression appears in the middle of the second independent clause, the semicolon goes between the clauses.

▶ Most singers gain fame through hard work and dedication/;
 ^

Evita, however, found other means.

Transitional expressions should not be confused with the coordinating conjunctions *and, but, or, nor, for, so,* and *yet,* which are preceded by a comma when they link independent clauses. (See 32a.)

34c Use a semicolon between items in a series containing internal punctuation.

▶ Classic science fiction sagas are *Star Trek,* with Mr. Spock

and his large pointed ears̷;̷ *Battlestar Galactica,* with its
     ^

Cylon Raiders̷;̷ and *Star Wars,* with Han Solo, Luke
     ^

Skywalker, and Darth Vader.

Without the semicolons, the reader would have to sort out the major groupings, distinguishing between important and less important pauses according to the logic of the sentence. By inserting semicolons at the major breaks, the writer does this work for the reader.

34d Avoid common misuses of the semicolon.

Do not use a semicolon in the following situations.

BETWEEN A SUBORDINATE CLAUSE AND THE REST OF THE SENTENCE

▶ Unless you brush your teeth within ten or fifteen minutes

after eating̷,̷ brushing does almost no good.
     ^

BETWEEN AN APPOSITIVE AND THE WORD IT REFERS TO

▶ The scientists were fascinated by the species *Argyroneta*

aquatica̷,̷ a spider that lives underwater.
     ^

TO INTRODUCE A LIST

▶ Some of my favorite film stars have home pages on the

Web̷:̷ John Travolta, Susan Sarandon, and Leonardo
   ^

DiCaprio.

BETWEEN INDEPENDENT CLAUSES JOINED BY *AND, BUT, OR, NOR, FOR, SO,* OR *YET*

▶ Five of the applicants had worked with spreadsheets, but

only one was familiar with database management.

EXCEPTIONS: If at least one of the independent clauses contains internal punctuation, you may use a semicolon even though the clauses are joined with a coordinating conjunction.

> As a vehicle [the model T] was hard-working, commonplace, and heroic; and it often seemed to transmit those qualities to the person who rode in it. — E. B. White

Although a comma would also be correct in this sentence, the semicolon is more effective, for it indicates the relative weights of the pauses.

Occasionally, a semicolon may be used to emphasize a sharp contrast or a firm distinction between clauses joined with a coordinating conjunction.

> We hate some persons because we do not know them; and we will not know them because we hate them.
> Charles Caleb Colton

EXERCISE 34–1

Add commas or semicolons where needed in the following quotations. If a sentence is correct, write "correct" after it. Answers to lettered sentences appear in the back of the book. Example:

> If an animal does something, we call it instinct; if we do the
>
> same thing, we call it intelligence. — Will Cuppy

> a. Do not ask me to be kind just ask me to act as though I were.
> — Jules Renard
> b. When men talk about defense they always claim to be protecting women and children but they never ask the women and children what they think. — Pat Schroeder
> c. When I get a little money I buy books if any is left I buy food and clothes. — Desiderius Erasmus
> d. America is a country that doesn't know where it is going but is determined to set a speed record getting there. — Lawrence J. Peter

e. Wit has truth in it wisecracking is simply calisthenics with words.
— Dorothy Parker

1. Everyone is a genius at least once a year a real genius has his [or her] original ideas closer together.   — G. C. Lichtenberg
2. When choosing between two evils, I always like to try the one I've never tried before.   — Mae West
3. Once the children were in the house the air became more vivid and more heated every object in the house grew more alive.
— Mary Gordon
4. We don't know what we want but we are ready to bite someone to get it.   — Will Rogers
5. I've been rich and I've been poor rich is better.
— Sophie Tucker

EXERCISE 34–2

Edit the following sentences to correct errors in the use of the comma and the semicolon. If a sentence is correct, write "correct" after it. Answers to lettered sentences appear in the back of the book. Example:

Love is blind; envy has its eyes wide open.
    ^

a. Strong black coffee will not sober you up, the truth is that time is the only way to get alcohol out of your system.
b. It is not surprising that our society is increasingly violent, after all, television desensitizes us to brutality at a very early age.
c. There is often a fine line between right and wrong; good and bad; truth and deception.
d. At Weight Watchers, we believe that being fat is not hereditary; it is a choice.
e. Severe, unremitting pain is a ravaging force; especially when the patient tries to hide it from others.

1. Another delicious dish is the chef's special; a roasted duck rubbed with spices and stuffed with wild rice.
2. Martin Luther King Jr. had not intended to be a preacher, initially, he had planned to become a lawyer.
3. We all assumed that the thief had been Jean's boyfriend; even though we had seen him only from the back.
4. The Victorians avoided the subject of sex but were obsessed with death, our contemporaries are obsessed with sex but avoid thinking about death.
5. Some educators believe that African American history should be taught in separate courses, others prefer to see it integrated into survey courses.

ON THE WEB

For electronic exercises on using semicolons, go to
dianahacker.com/rules

and click on ▶ **Electronic Grammar Exercises**
            ▶ **Punctuation**
                    ▶ **E-ex 34-1 and 34-2**

35

The colon

The colon is used primarily to call attention to the words that follow it. In addition, the colon has some conventional uses.

GRAMMAR CHECKERS do not flag missing or misused colons. For example, they failed to catch the misused colon in this sentence: *Uncle Carlos left behind: his watch, his glasses, and his favorite pen.* Occasionally grammar checkers flag misused semicolons in contexts where a colon is required.

35a Use a colon after an independent clause to direct attention to a list, an appositive, or a quotation.

A LIST

The daily routine should include at least the following: twenty knee bends, fifty sit-ups, fifteen leg lifts, and five minutes of running in place.

AN APPOSITIVE

My roommate is guilty of two of the seven deadly sins: gluttony and sloth.

A QUOTATION

Consider the words of John F. Kennedy: "Ask not what your country can do for you; ask what you can do for your country."

For other ways of introducing quotations, see "Introducing quoted material" on pages 304–05.

35b Use a colon between independent clauses if the second summarizes or explains the first.

Faith is like love: It cannot be forced.

NOTE: When an independent clause follows a colon, it may begin with a lowercase or a capital letter.

35c Use a colon after the salutation in a formal letter, to indicate hours and minutes, to show proportions, between a title and subtitle, and between city and publisher in bibliographic entries.

Dear Sir or Madam:

5:30 P.M. (or p.m.)

The ratio of women to men was 2:1.

The Glory of Hera: Greek Mythology and the Greek Family

Boston: Bedford, 2001

NOTE: In biblical references, a colon is ordinarily used between chapter and verse (Luke 2:14). The Modern Language Association recommends a period instead (Luke 2.14).

35d Avoid common misuses of the colon.

A colon must be preceded by a full independent clause. Therefore, avoid using it in the following situations.

BETWEEN A VERB AND ITS OBJECT OR COMPLEMENT

▶ Some important vitamins found in vegetables are: vitamin A, thiamine, niacin, and vitamin C.

BETWEEN A PREPOSITION AND ITS OBJECT

▶ The heart's two pumps each consist of̸ an upper chamber, or atrium, and a lower chamber, or ventricle.

AFTER *SUCH AS, INCLUDING,* OR *FOR EXAMPLE*

▶ The trees on our campus include many fine Japanese specimens such as̸ black pines, ginkgos, and weeping cherries.

EXERCISE 35-1

Edit the following sentences to correct errors in the use of the comma, the semicolon, or the colon. If a sentence is correct, write "correct" after it. Answers to lettered sentences appear in the back of the book. Example:

> Smiling confidently, the young man stated his major goal in
> life̸: to be secretary of agriculture before he was thirty.
>   ^

a. Minds are like parachutes: They function only when open.
b. If we have come to fight, we are far too few, if we have come to die, we are far too many.
c. The travel package includes: a round-trip ticket to Athens, a cruise through the Cyclades, and all hotel accommodations.
d. The media like to portray my generation as lazy; although polls show that we work as hard as the twentysomethings before us.
e. Fran Lebowitz has this advice for parents, "Never allow your child to call you by your first name. He hasn't known you long enough."

1. Kay survived for one reason, the medics got to her in time.
2. While traveling through France, Fiona visited: the Loire Valley, Chartres, the Louvre, and the McDonald's stand at the foot of the Eiffel Tower.
3. There are three types of leave; annual leave, used for vacations, sick leave, used for medical appointments and illness, and personal leave, used for a variety of personal reasons.
4. Carl Sandburg once asked three important questions, "Who paid for my freedom? What was the price? And am I somehow beholden?"
5. Robin sorts the crabs into three groups: males, females, and crabs about to molt.

ON THE WEB

For an electronic exercise on using colons, go to
dianahacker.com/rules

and click on ▶ **Electronic Grammar Exercises**
                    ▶ **Punctuation**
                        ▶ **E-ex 35-1**

36

The apostrophe

GRAMMAR CHECKERS can flag some, but not all, missing or mis-used apostrophes. They can catch missing apostrophes in common contractions, such as *don't*. They can also flag some problems with possessives, although they miss others. The programs usually phrase their advice cautiously, telling you that you have a "possible possessive error" in a phrase such as *a days work* or *sled dogs feet*. Therefore, you — not the grammar checker — must decide whether to add an apostrophe and, if so, whether to put it before or after the *-s*.

36a Use an apostrophe to indicate that a noun is possessive.

Possessive nouns usually indicate ownership, as in *Tim's hat* or *the lawyer's desk*. Frequently, however, ownership is only loosely implied: *the tree's roots, a day's work*. If you are not sure whether a noun is possessive, try turning it into an *of* phrase: *the roots of the tree, the work of a day*.

When to add -'s

1. If the noun does not end in *-s,* add *-'s.*

Roy managed to climb out on the driver's side.

Thank you for refunding the children's money.

2. If the noun is singular and ends in -s, add -'s.

Lois's sister spent last year in India.

EXCEPTION: If pronunciation would be awkward with the added -'s, some writers use only the apostrophe. Either use is acceptable.

Sophocles' plays are among my favorites.

When to add only an apostrophe

If the noun is plural and ends in -s, add only an apostrophe.

Both diplomats' briefcases were stolen.

Joint possession

To show joint possession, use -'s or (-s') with the last noun only; to show individual possession, make all nouns possessive.

Have you seen Joyce and Greg's new camper?

John's and Marie's expectations of marriage couldn't have been more different.

In the first sentence, Joyce and Greg jointly own one camper. In the second sentence, John and Marie individually have different expectations.

Compound nouns

If a noun is compound, use -'s (or -s') with the last element.

My father-in-law's sculpture won first place.

36b Use an apostrophe and -s to indicate that an indefinite pronoun is possessive.

Indefinite pronouns refer to no specific person or thing: *everyone, someone, no one, something.* (See 61b.)

Someone's raincoat has been left behind.

36C Use an apostrophe to mark omissions in contractions and numbers.

In contractions the apostrophe takes the place of missing letters.

It's a shame that Frank can't go on the tour.

It's stands for *it is, can't* for *cannot*.

The apostrophe is also used to mark the omission of the first two digits of a year (*the class of '95*) or years (*the '60s generation*).

We'll never forget the blizzard of '96.

36d An apostrophe is often optional in plural numbers, letters, abbreviations, and words mentioned as words.

Traditionally, an apostrophe has been used to pluralize numbers, letters, abbreviations, and words mentioned as words. The trend, however, is toward omitting the apostrophe. Either use is correct, but be consistent.

PLURAL NUMBERS AND ABBREVIATIONS To pluralize a number or an abbreviation, you may add *-s* or *-'s*.

Peggy skated nearly perfect figure 8s [*or* 8's].

We collected only four IOUs [*or* IOU's] out of forty.

NOTE: To pluralize decades, most current writers omit the apostrophe: 1920s (*not* 1920's).

PLURAL LETTERS Italicize the letter and use roman type for the *-s* ending. Use of an apostrophe is usually optional; the Modern Language Association continues to recommend the apostrophe.

Two large *J*s [*or J*'s] were painted on the door.

PLURALS OF WORDS MENTIONED AS WORDS Italicize the word and use roman type for the *-s* ending. Use of an apostrophe is optional.

We've heard enough *maybes* [*or maybe*'s].

Words mentioned as words may also appear in quotation marks. When you choose this option, use the apostrophe: We've heard enough "maybe's."

36e Avoid common misuses of the apostrophe.

Do not use an apostrophe in the following situations.

WITH NOUNS THAT ARE NOT POSSESSIVE

> *outpatients*
> Some ~~outpatient's~~ are given special parking permits.
> ^

IN THE POSSESSIVE PRONOUNS *ITS, WHOSE, HIS, HERS, OURS, YOURS,* AND *THEIRS*

> *its*
> Each area has ~~it's~~ own conference room.
> ^

It's means "it is." The possessive pronoun *its* contains no apostrophe despite the fact that it is possessive.

> *whose*
> This course was taught by a professional florist ~~who's~~
> ^
> technique was Japanese.

Who's means "who is." The possessive pronoun is *whose*.

EXERCISE 36–1

Edit the following sentences to correct errors in the use of the apostrophe. If a sentence is correct, write "correct" after it. Answers to lettered sentences appear in the back of the book. Example:

> Marietta lived above the only bar in town, Smiling
> *Jack's.*
> ~~Jacks.~~
> ^

a. This diet will improve almost anyone's health.
b. The deed must be transferred to the purchasers name.
c. Each days menu features a different European country's dish.
d. Sue worked overtime to increase her families earnings.
e. Ms. Jacobs is unwilling to listen to students complaints about computer failures and damaged disks.

1. Siddhartha sat by the river and listened to its many voices.
2. Three teenage son's can devour about as much food as four full-grown field hands. The only difference is that they dont do half as much work.
3. We handle contracts with NASA and many other government agency's.
4. Luck is an important element in a rock musicians career.
5. My sister-in-law's quilts are being shown at the Fendrick Gallery.

ON THE WEB

For an electronic exercise on using apostrophes, go to
dianahacker.com/rules

and click on ▶ **Electronic Grammar Exercises**
▶ **Punctuation**
▶ **E-ex 36-1**

37

Quotation marks

 GRAMMAR CHECKERS can tell you to put commas and periods inside quotation marks; they can also flag "unbalanced quotes," an opening quotation mark that is not balanced with a closing quotation mark. The programs can't tell you, however, when you should or shouldn't use quotation marks.

37a Use quotation marks to enclose direct quotations.

Direct quotations of a person's words, whether spoken or written, must be in quotation marks.

> "A foolish consistency is the hobgoblin of little minds," wrote Ralph Waldo Emerson.

CAUTION: Do not use quotation marks around indirect quotations. An indirect quotation reports someone's ideas without using that person's exact words.

Ralph Waldo Emerson believed that consistency for its own sake is the mark of a small mind.

NOTE: In dialogue, begin a new paragraph to mark a change in speaker.

"Mom, his name is Willie, not William. A thousand times I've told you, it's *Willie.*"

"Willie is a derivative of William, Lester. Surely his birth certificate doesn't have Willie on it, and I like calling people by their proper names."

"Yes, it does, ma'am. My mother named me Willie K. Mason." —Gloria Naylor

If a single speaker utters more than one paragraph, introduce each paragraph with quotation marks, but do not use closing quotation marks until the end of the speech.

37b Set off long quotations of prose or poetry by indenting.

MLA and APA styles have different guidelines for setting off long quotations (see pp. 410 and 464). The guidelines given in this section are those of the Modern Language Association (MLA).

When a quotation of prose runs to more than four typed lines in your paper, set it off by indenting one inch (or ten spaces) from the left margin. Quotation marks are not required because the indented format tells readers that the quotation is taken word for word from a source. Long quotations are ordinarily introduced by a sentence ending with a colon.

After making an exhaustive study of the historical record, James Horan evaluates Billy the Kid like this:

The portrait that emerges of [the Kid] from the thousands of pages of affidavits, reports, trial transcripts, his letters, and his testimony is neither the mythical Robin Hood nor the stereotyped adenoidal moron and pathological killer. Rather Billy appears as a disturbed, lonely young man, honest, loyal to his friends, dedicated to his beliefs, and betrayed by our institutions and the corrupt, ambitious, and compromising politicians in his time. (158)

The number in parentheses is a citation handled according to MLA style (see 54a).

NOTE: When you quote two or more paragraphs from the source, indent the first line of each paragraph an additional one-half inch (or five spaces).

When you quote more than three lines of a poem, set the quoted lines off from the text by indenting one inch (or ten spaces) from the left margin. Use no quotation marks unless they appear in the poem itself. (To quote two or three lines of poetry, see 39e.)

> Although many anthologizers "modernize" her punctuation, Emily Dickinson relied heavily on dashes, using them, perhaps, as a musical device. Here, for example, is the original version of the opening stanza from "The Snake":
>
> > A narrow Fellow in the Grass
> >
> > Occasionally rides—
> >
> > You may have met Him—did you not
> >
> > His notice sudden is—

37c Use single quotation marks to enclose a quotation within a quotation.

According to Paul Eliott, Eskimo hunters "chant an ancient magic song to the seal they are after: 'Beast of the sea! Come and place yourself before me in the early morning!' "

37d Use quotation marks around the titles of short works: newspaper and magazine articles, poems, short stories, songs, episodes of television and radio programs, and subdivisions of books or web sites.

Katherine Mansfield's "The Garden Party" provoked a lively discussion in our short-story class last night.

NOTE: Titles of books, plays, Web sites, television and radio programs, films, magazines, and newspapers are put in italics or underlined. (See 42a.)

37e Quotation marks may be used to set off words used as words.

Although words used as words are ordinarily underlined or italicized (see 42d), quotation marks are also acceptable. Just be sure to be consistent throughout a paper.

> The words "accept" and "except" are frequently confused.

> The words *accept* and *except* are frequently confused.

37f Use punctuation with quotation marks according to convention.

This section describes the conventions used by American publishers in placing various marks of punctuation inside or outside quotation marks. It also explains how to punctuate when introducing quoted material.

Periods and commas

Place periods and commas inside quotation marks

> "This is a stick-up," said the well-dressed young couple. "We want all your money."

This rule applies to single quotation marks as well as double quotation marks. (See 37c.) It also applies to all uses of quotation marks: for quoted material, for titles of works, and for words used as words.

EXCEPTION: In the Modern Language Association's style of parenthetical in-text citations (see 54a), the period follows the citation in parentheses.

> James M. McPherson comments, approvingly, that the Whigs "were not averse to extending the blessings of American liberty, even to Mexicans and Indians" (48).

Colons and semicolons

Put colons and semicolons outside quotation marks.

Harold wrote, "I regret that I am unable to attend the fundraiser for AIDS research"; his letter, however, came with a substantial contribution.

Question marks and exclamation points

Put question marks and exclamation points inside quotation marks unless they apply to the whole sentence.

> Contrary to tradition, bedtime at my house is marked by "Mommy, can I tell you a story now?"

> Have you heard the old proverb "Do not climb the hill until you reach it"?

In the first sentence, the question mark applies only to the quoted question. In the second sentence, the question mark applies to the whole sentence.

NOTE: Modern Language Association parenthetical citations create a special problem. According to MLA, the question mark or exclamation point should appear before the quotation mark, and a period should follow the parenthetical citation.

> Rosie Thomas asks, "Is nothing in life ever straight and clear, the way children see it?" (77).

Introducing quoted material

After a word group introducing a quotation, choose a colon, a comma, or no punctuation at all, whichever is appropriate in context.

FORMAL INTRODUCTION   If a quotation has been formally introduced, a colon is appropriate. A formal introduction is a full independent clause, not just an expression such as *he said* or *she remarked.*

> Morrow views personal ads in the classifieds as an art form: "The personal ad is like a haiku of self-celebration, a brief solo played on one's own horn."

EXPRESSION SUCH AS *HE SAID*   If a quotation is introduced with an expression such as *he said* or *she remarked* — or if it is followed by such an expression — a comma is needed.

Stephan Leacock once said, "I am a great believer in luck, and I find the harder I work the more I have of it."

"You can be a little ungrammatical if you come from the right part of the country," writes Robert Frost.

BLENDED QUOTATION   When a quotation is blended into the writer's own sentence, either a comma or no punctuation is appropriate, depending on the way in which the quotation fits into the sentence structure.

The future champion could, as he put it, "float like a butterfly and sting like a bee."

Charles Hudson notes that the prisoners escaped "by squeezing through a tiny window eighteen feet above the floor of their cell."

BEGINNING OF SENTENCE   If a quotation appears at the beginning of a sentence, set it off with a comma unless the quotation ends with a question mark or an exclamation point.

"We shot them like dogs," boasted Davy Crockett, who was among Jackson's troops.

"What is it?" I asked, bracing myself.

INTERRUPTED QUOTATION   If a quoted sentence is interrupted by explanatory words, use commas to set off the explanatory words.

"A great many people think they are thinking," observed William James, "when they are merely rearranging their prejudices."

If two successive quoted sentences from the same source are interrupted by explanatory words, use a comma before the explanatory words and a period after them.

"I was a flop as a daily reporter," admitted E. B. White. "Every piece had to be a masterpiece — and before you knew it, Tuesday was Wednesday."

37g   Avoid common misuses of quotation marks.

Do not use quotation marks to draw attention to familiar slang, to disown trite expressions, or to justify an attempt at humor.

▶ Between Thanksgiving and Super Bowl Sunday, many Ameri-

can wives become /football widows./

Do not use quotation marks around indirect quotations.
(See also 37a.)

▶ After leaving the scene of the domestic quarrel, the officer

said that /he was due for a coffee break./

Do not use quotation marks around the title of your own
essay.

ON THE WEB

For an electronic exercise on using quotation marks, go to
dianahacker.com/rules

and click on   ▶ **Electronic Grammar Exercises**
                ▶ **Punctuation**
                ▶ **E-ex 37-1**

EXERCISE 37–1

Add or delete quotation marks as needed and make any other necessary changes in punctuation in the following sentences. If a sentence is
correct, write "correct" after it. Answers to lettered sentences appear in
the back of the book. Example:

> Bill Cosby once said, "I don't know the key to success, but
>   ^
> the key to failure is trying to please everyone."
>   ^

a. As for the advertisement "Sailors have more fun", if you consider
   chipping paint and swabbing decks fun, then you will have plenty
   of it.
b. Even after forty minutes of discussion, our class could not agree
   on an interpretation of Robert Frost's "The Road Not Taken."
c. After winning the lottery, Juanita said that "she would give half the
   money to charity."

d. After the movie Vicki said, "The reviewer called this flick "trash of the first order." I guess you can't believe everything you read."

e. "Cleaning your house while your kids are still growing," quipped Phyllis Diller, "is like shoveling the walk before it stops snowing."

1. "Order in the court! Order in the court!", shouts the judge, banging her wooden spoon on the kitchen table.

2. "Kick the tires and light the fires" exclaimed the pilot, giving me my cue to start the engines.

3. Gloria Steinem once twisted an old proverb like this, "A woman without a man is like a fish without a bicycle."

4. "Even when freshly washed and relieved of all obvious confections," says Fran Lebowitz, "children tend to be sticky."

5. Have you heard the Cowboy Junkies' rendition of Hank Williams's "I'm So Lonesome I Could Cry?"

38

End punctuation

38a The period

Use a period to end all sentences except direct questions or genuine exclamations. Also use periods in abbreviations according to convention.

To end sentences

Everyone knows that a period should be used to end most sentences. The only problems that arise concern the choice between a period and a question mark or between a period and an exclamation point.

If a sentence reports a question instead of asking it directly, it should end with a period, not a question mark.

▶ Celia asked whether the picnic would be canceled?.

If a sentence is not a genuine exclamation, it should end with a period, not an exclamation point.

▶ After years of working her way through school, Pat finally

graduated with high honors.

In abbreviations

A period is conventionally used in abbreviations such as these:

Mr.	B.A.	i.e.	B.C.	A.M. (or a.m.)
Mrs.	M.A.	e.g.	B.C.E.	P.M. (or p.m.)
Ms.	Ph.D.	etc.	A.D.	
Dr.	R.N.		C.E.	

A period is not used with U.S. Postal Service abbreviations for states: MD, TX, CA.

Ordinarily a period is not used in abbreviations of organization names:

NATO	UNESCO	UCLA	PUSH	IBM
TVA	IRS	AFL-CIO	NBA	FTC
USA (*or* U.S.A.)	NAACP	SEC	FCC	NIH

Usage varies, however. When in doubt, consult a dictionary, a style manual, or a publication by the agency in question. Even the yellow pages can help.

NOTE: If a sentence ends with a period marking an abbreviation, do not add a second period.

38b The question mark

Obviously a direct question should be followed by a question mark.

What is the horsepower of a 747 engine?

If a polite request is written in the form of a question, it may be followed by a period.

Would you please send me your catalog of lilies.

CAUTION: Do not use a question mark after an indirect question, one that is reported rather than asked directly. Use a period instead.

▶ He asked me who was teaching the mythology course?.
                                                      ^

NOTE: Questions in a series may be followed by question marks even when they are not complete sentences.

> We wondered where Calamity had hidden this time. Under the sink? Behind the furnace? On top of the bookcase?

38c The exclamation point

Use an exclamation point after a word group or sentence that expresses exceptional feeling or deserves special emphasis.

> When Gloria entered the room, I switched on the lights and we all yelled, "Surprise!"

CAUTION: Do not overuse the exclamation point.

▶ Whenever I see Venus lunging forward to put away an

   overhead smash, it might as well be me!. She does it just
                                         ^

   the way that I would!

> The first exclamation point should be deleted so that the second one will have more force.

39

Other punctuation marks: the dash, parentheses, brackets, the ellipsis mark, the slash

39a The dash

When typing, use two hyphens to form a dash (--). Do not put spaces before or after the dash. (If your word processing program has what is known as an "em-dash," you may use it instead, with no space before or after it.) Dashes are used for the following purposes.

To set off parenthetical material that deserves emphasis

Everything that went wrong — from the peeping Tom at her window last night to my head-on collision today — was blamed on our move.

To set off appositives that contain commas

An appositive is a noun or noun phrase that renames a nearby noun. Ordinarily most appositives are set off with commas (32e), but when the appositive contains commas, a pair of dashes helps readers see the relative importance of all the pauses.

In my hometown, basic needs — food, clothing, and shelter — are less costly than in Los Angeles.

To prepare for a list, a restatement, an amplification, or a dramatic shift in tone or thought

Along the wall are the bulk liquids — sesame seed oil, honey, safflower oil, and that half-liquid "peanuts only" peanut butter.

Consider the amount of sugar in the average person's diet — 104 pounds per year, 90 percent more than that consumed by our ancestors.

Everywhere we looked there were little kids — a box of Cracker Jack in one hand and mommy's or daddy's sleeve in the other.

Kiere took a few steps back, came running full speed, kicked a mighty kick — and missed the ball.

In the first two examples, the writer could also use a colon. (See 35a.) The colon is more formal than the dash and not quite as dramatic.

CAUTION: Unless there is a specific reason for using the dash, avoid it. Unnecessary dashes create a choppy effect.

▶ Insisting that students use computers as instructional

tools ⟡ for information retrieval ⟡ makes good sense.

Herding them ⟡ sheeplike ⟡ into computer technology

does not.

39b Parentheses

Use parentheses to enclose supplemental material, minor digressions, and afterthoughts.

> After taking her temperature, pulse, and blood pressure (routine vital signs), the nurse made Becky as comfortable as possible.

> The weights James was first able to move (not lift, mind you) were measured in ounces.

Use parentheses to enclose letters or numbers labeling items in a series.

> Regulations stipulated that only the following equipment could be used on the survival mission: (1) a knife, (2) thirty feet of parachute line, (3) a book of matches, (4) two ponchos, (5) an *E* tool, and (6) a signal flare.

CAUTION: Do not overuse parentheses. Rough drafts are likely to contain more afterthoughts than necessary.

from ten to fifty million
▶ Researchers have said that ~~ten million (estimates run as~~
                                    ^
~~high as fifty million)~~ Americans have hypoglycemia.

39c Brackets

Use brackets to enclose any words or phrases that you have inserted into an otherwise word-for-word quotation.

> *Audubon* reports that "if there are not enough young to balance deaths, the end of the species [California condor] is inevitable."

The *Audubon* article did not contain the words *California condor* in the sentence quoted, since the context made clear what species was meant. Out of context, however, the words *California condor* are needed.

The Latin word "sic" in brackets indicates that an error in a quoted sentence appears in the original source.

> According to the review, k. d. lang's performance was brilliant, "exceeding [sic] the expectations of even her most loyal fans."

Do not overuse "sic," however, since calling attention to others' mistakes can appear snobbish. The preceding quotation, for example, might have been paraphrased instead: *According to the review, even k. d. lang's most loyal fans were surprised by the brilliance of her performance.*

39d The ellipsis mark

The ellipsis mark consists of three spaced periods. Use an ellipsis mark to indicate that you have deleted words from an otherwise word-for-word quotation.

> Reuben reports that "when the amount of cholesterol circulating in the blood rises over . . . 300 milligrams per 100, the chances of a heart attack increase dramatically."

If you delete a full sentence or more in the middle of a quoted passage, use a period before the three ellipsis dots.

> "Most of our efforts," writes Dave Erikson, "are directed toward saving the bald eagle's wintering habitat along the Mississippi River. . . . It's important that the wintering birds have a place to roost, where they can get out of the cold wind."

CAUTION: Do not use the ellipsis mark at the beginning of a quotation; do not use it at the end of a quotation unless you have cut some words from the end of the final sentence quoted. (See also pp. 409–10.)

In quoted poetry, use a full line of ellipsis dots to indicate that you have dropped a line or more from the poem.

> Had we but world enough, and time,
> This coyness, lady, were no crime.
> ....
>
> But at my back I always hear
> Time's winged chariot hurrying near;   — Andrew Marvell

The ellipsis mark may also be used to indicate a hesitation or interruption in speech or to suggest unfinished thoughts.

> Before falling into a coma, the victim whispered, "It was a man with a tattoo on his . . ."

39e The slash

Use the slash to separate two or three lines of poetry that have been run into your text. Add a space both before and after the slash.

> In the opening lines of "Jordan," George Herbert pokes gentle fun at popular poems of his time: "Who says that fictions only and false hair / Become a verse? Is there in truth no beauty?"

More than three lines of poetry should be handled as an indented quotation. (See 37b.)

The slash may occasionally be used to separate paired terms such as *pass/fail* and *producer/director.* Do not use a space before or after the slash.

> Roger, the producer/director, announced a casting change.

Be sparing, however, in this use of the slash. In particular, avoid the use of *and/or, he/she,* and *his/her.*

EXERCISE 39–1

Edit the following sentences to correct errors in punctuation, focusing especially on appropriate use of the dash, parentheses, brackets, ellipsis mark, and slash. If a sentence is correct, write "correct" after it. Answers to lettered sentences appear in the back of the book. Example:

> **Social insects/— bees, for example/— are able to**
>
> **communicate quite complicated messages to one another.**

a. A client has left his/her cell phone in our conference room.
b. The thousand dollars that we invested in the stock market — just ten years ago — has tripled in value.
c. Samantha selected the pass/fail option for Chemistry 101.
d. The child sang her way through the alphabet — A, B, C, . . . Z — and then waited for our applause.
e. Of the three basic schools of detective fiction, the tea-and-crumpet, the hardboiled detective, and the police procedural, I find the quaint, civilized quality of the tea-and-crumpet school the most appealing.

1. The old Valentine verse we used to chant says it all: "Sugar is sweet, / And so are you."

2. In studies in which mothers gazed down at their infants in their cribs but remained facially unresponsive, for example, not smiling, laughing, or showing any change of expression, the infants responded with intense weariness and eventual withdrawal.

3. There are three points of etiquette in poker: 1. always allow someone to cut the cards, 2. don't forget to ante up, and 3. never stack your chips.

4. In *Lifeboat,* Alfred Hitchcock appears [some say without his knowledge] in a newspaper advertisement for weight loss.

5. When he was informed that fewer than 20 percent of the panelists scheduled for the 1986 PEN conference were women, Norman Mailer gave this explanation: "There are more men who are deeply interested in intellectual matters than women. . . . [If we put more women on the panel], all we'd be doing is lowering the level of discussion."

ON THE WEB

For an electronic exercise on using the dash, parentheses, brackets, the ellipsis mark, and the slash, go to
dianahacker.com/rules

and click on   ▶ **Electronic Grammar Exercises**
                    ▶ **Punctuation**
                        ▶ **E-ex 39-1**

Mechanics

Process

Design

Clarity

Grammar

Punctuation

Mechanics

Argument

Research

Basics

40

Abbreviations

GRAMMAR CHECKERS can flag a few inappropriate abbreviations, such as *Xmas* and *e.g.*, but do not assume that a program will catch all problems with abbreviations.

40a Use standard abbreviations for titles immediately before and after proper names.

TITLES BEFORE PROPER NAMES	TITLES AFTER PROPER NAMES
Mr. Rafael Zabala	William Albert Sr.
Ms. Nancy Linehan	Thomas Hines Jr.
Mrs. Edward Horn	Anita Lor, Ph.D.
Dr. Margaret Simmons	Robert Simkowski, M.D.
the Rev. John Stone	Margaret Chin, LL.D.
Prof. James Russo	Polly Stein, D.D.S.

Do not abbreviate a title if it is not used with a proper name.

           professor
▶ My history ~~prof.~~ was an expert on America's use of the
             ^

atomic bomb in World War II.

Avoid redundant titles such as *Dr. Amy Day, M.D.* Choose one title or the other: *Dr. Amy Day* or *Amy Day, M.D.*

40b Use abbreviations only when you are sure your readers will understand them.

Familiar abbreviations, often written without periods, are acceptable:

CIA	FBI	AFL-CIO	NAACP
NBA	UPI	NEA	CD-ROM
YMCA	CBS	USA (*or* U.S.A.)	ESL

While in Washington the schoolchildren toured the FBI.

The YMCA has opened a new gym close to my office.

NOTE: When using an unfamiliar abbreviation (such as NASW for National Association of Social Workers) throughout a paper, write the full name followed by the abbreviation in parentheses at the first mention of the name. Then use the abbreviation throughout the rest of the paper.

40c Use B.C., A.D., A.M., P.M., No., and $ only with specific dates, times, numbers, and amounts.

The abbreviation B.C. ("before Christ") follows a date, and A.D. ("*anno Domini*") precedes a date. Many writers prefer the abbreviations B.C.E. ("before the common era") and C.E. ("common era"), both of which follow a date.

40 B.C. (or 40 B.C.E.)	4:00 A.M. (or a.m.)	No. 12 (or no. 12)
A.D. 44 (or 44 C.E.)	6:00 P.M. (or p.m.)	$150

Avoid using A.M., P.M., No., or $ when not accompanied by a specific figure.

> We set off for the lake early in the A.M.
>   *morning.*
>   ^

40d Be sparing in your use of Latin abbreviations.

Latin abbreviations are acceptable in footnotes and bibliographies and in informal writing for comments in parentheses.

cf. (Latin *confer*, "compare")
e.g. (Latin *exempli gratia*, "for example")
et al. (Latin *et alia*, "and others")
etc. (Latin *et cetera*, "and so forth")
i.e. (Latin *id est*, "that is")
N.B. (Latin *nota bene*, "note well")

Harold Simms et al., *The Race for Space*

Alfred Hitchcock directed many classic thrillers (e.g., *Psycho, Rear Window*, and *Vertigo*).

In formal writing use the appropriate English phrases.

▶ Many obsolete laws remain on the books, ~~e.g.,~~ a law in
   for example,
       ^

Vermont forbidding an unmarried man and woman to sit

closer than six inches apart on a park bench.

40e Avoid inappropriate abbreviations.

In formal writing, abbreviations for the following are not commonly accepted: personal names, units of measurement, days of the week, holidays, months, courses of study, divisions of written works, states, and countries (except in addresses and except Washington, DC). Do not abbreviate *Company* and *Incorporated* unless their abbreviated forms are part of an official name.

PERSONAL NAME Charles (not Chas.)

UNITS OF MEASUREMENT pound (not lb.)

DAYS OF THE WEEK Monday (not Mon.)

HOLIDAYS Christmas (not Xmas)

MONTHS January, February, March (not Jan., Feb., Mar.)

COURSES OF STUDY political science (not poli. sci.)

DIVISIONS OF WRITTEN WORKS chapter, page (not ch., p.)

STATES AND COUNTRIES Massachusetts (not MA or Mass.)

PARTS OF A BUSINESS NAME Adams Lighting Company (not Adams Lighting Co.); Kim and Brothers, Inc. (not Kim and Bros., Inc.)

▶ Eliza promised to buy me one ~~lb.~~ of Godiva chocolate for my
                     pound
birthday, which was last ~~Fri.~~
            Friday.
          ^

EXERCISE 40–1

Edit the following sentences to correct errors in abbreviations. If a sentence is correct, write "correct" after it. Answers to lettered sentences appear in the back of the book. Example:

Christmas   Tuesday.
This year X̶m̶a̶s̶ will fall on a T̶u̶e̶s̶.
         ^   ^

a. Since its inception, the BBC has maintained a consistently high standard of radio and television broadcasting.
b. A no. of govt. officials have been reviewing the records of some small brokerage firms in the area.
c. "Mahatma" Gandhi has inspired many modern leaders, including Martin Luther King Jr.
d. How many lb. have you lost since you began running four miles a day?
e. Denzil spent all night studying for his psych. exam.

1. My favorite prof., Dr. Barker, is on sabbatical this semester.
2. When she arrived in Poughkeepsie to work at IBM, Pauline was overwhelmed by the sophistication and variety of product prototypes.
3. Some historians think that the New Testament was completed by A.D. 100.
4. My mother's birthday was on Fri. the 13th this year.
5. Many girls fall prey to a cult worship of great entertainers — e.g., in my mother's generation, girls worshiped the Beatles.

ON THE WEB

For an electronic exercise on using abbreviations, go to
dianahacker.com/rules

and click on ▶ **Electronic Grammar Exercises**
▶ **E-ex 40-1**

41

Numbers

GRAMMAR CHECKERS can tell you to spell out certain numbers, such as *thirty-three* and numbers that begin a sentence, but they won't help you understand when it is acceptable to use figures.

41a Spell out numbers of one or two words or those that begin a sentence. Use figures for numbers that require more than two words to spell out.

▶ Now, some ~~8~~ *eight* years later, Muffin is still with us.

▶ I counted ~~one hundred seventy-six~~ *176* CDs on the shelf.

If a sentence begins with a number, spell out the number or rewrite the sentence.

▶ ~~150~~ *One hundred fifty* children in our program need expensive dental treatment.

Rewriting the sentence will also correct the error and may be less awkward if the number is long: *In our program 150 children need expensive dental treatment.*

EXCEPTIONS: In technical and some business writing, figures are preferred even when spellings would be brief, but usage varies. When in doubt, consult the style guide of the organization for which you are writing.

When several numbers appear in the same passage, many writers choose consistency rather than strict adherence to the rule.

When one number immediately follows another, spell out one and use figures for the other: *three 100-meter events, 125 four-poster beds.*

41b Generally, figures are acceptable for dates, addresses, percentages, fractions, decimals, scores, statistics and other numerical results, exact amounts of money, divisions of books and plays, pages, identification numbers, and the time.

DATES July 4, 1776, 56 B.C., A.D. 30

ADDRESSES 77 Latches Lane, 519 West 42nd Street

PERCENTAGES 55 percent (or 55%)

FRACTIONS, DECIMALS ½, 0.047

SCORES   7 to 3, 21–18

STATISTICS   average age 37, average weight 180

SURVEYS   4 out of 5

EXACT AMOUNTS OF MONEY $105.37, $106,000

DIVISIONS OF BOOKS   volume 3, chapter 4, page 189

DIVISIONS OF PLAYS   act 3, scene 3 (or act III, scene iii)

IDENTIFICATION NUMBERS   serial number 10988675

TIME OF DAY   4:00 P.M., 1:30 A.M.

▶ Several doctors put up ~~two hundred fifty-five thousand dollars~~ *$255,000*

for the construction of a golf course.

NOTE: When not using A.M. or P.M., write out the time in words (*two o'clock in the afternoon, twelve noon, seven in the morning*).

EXERCISE 41–1

Edit the following sentences to correct errors in the use of numbers. If a sentence is correct, write "correct" after it. Answers to lettered sentences appear in the back of the book. Example:

By the end of the evening Ashanti had only ~~three dollars and~~ *$3.06*

~~six cents~~ left.

a. We have ordered 4 azaleas, 3 rhododendrons, and 2 mountain laurels for the back area of the garden.
b. The program's cost is well over one billion dollars.
c. The score was tied at 5–5 when the momentum shifted and carried the Standards to a decisive 12–5 win.
d. 8 students in the class had been labeled "learning disabled."
e. The Vietnam Veterans Memorial in Washington, DC, had fifty-eight thousand one hundred thirty-two names inscribed on it when it was dedicated in 1982.

1. One of my favorite scenes in Shakespeare is the property division scene in act 1 of *King Lear.*
2. The botany lecture will begin at precisely 3:30 P.M.
3. 12 percent of all American marriages occur in June.

4. In nineteen hundred and forty-one, the United States entered World War II.
5. On a normal day, I spend at least 4 to 5 hours surfing the Internet.

ON THE WEB

For an electronic exercise on using numbers, go to
dianahacker.com/rules

and click on ▶ **Electronic Grammar Exercises**
▶ **Mechanics**
▶ **E-ex 41-1**

42

Italics (underlining)

Italics, a slanting typeface used in printed material, can be produced by word processing programs. In handwritten or typed papers, <u>underlining</u> is used instead. Some instructors prefer underlining even though their students can produce italics.

NOTE: Some e-mail systems do not allow for italics or underlining. Many people indicate words that should be italicized by preceding and ending them with underscore marks or asterisks. Punctuation should follow the coding.

> I am planning to write my senior thesis on _Anna Karenina_.

In less formal e-mail messages, normally italicized words aren't marked at all.

> I finally finished reading Anna Karenina—what a masterpiece!

CAUTION: In World Wide Web documents, underlining indicates a hot link. When creating a Web document, use italics, not underlining, for the conventions described in this section.

 GRAMMAR CHECKERS do not flag problems with italics or underlining. (For a general discussion of what grammar checkers can and cannot do, see p. 29.)

42a Underline or italicize the titles of works according to convention.

Titles of the following works should be underlined or italicized.

BOOKS *The Great Gatsby, A Distant Mirror*

MAGAZINES *Time, Scientific American*

NEWSPAPERS the *St. Louis Post-Dispatch*

PAMPHLETS *Common Sense, Facts about Marijuana*

LONG POEMS *The Waste Land, Paradise Lost*

PLAYS *King Lear, A Raisin in the Sun*

FILMS *Casablanca, The Matrix*

TELEVISION PROGRAMS *Survivor, 60 Minutes*

RADIO PROGRAMS *All Things Considered*

MUSICAL COMPOSITIONS Gershwin's *Porgy and Bess*

CHOREOGRAPHIC WORKS Twyla Tharp's *Brief Fling*

WORKS OF VISUAL ART Rodin's *The Thinker*

COMIC STRIPS *Dilbert*

SOFTWARE *WordPerfect, Acrobat Reader*

WEB SITES *Barron's Online, ZDNet*

The titles of other works, such as short stories, essays, episodes of radio and television programs, songs, and short poems, are enclosed in quotation marks. (See 37d.)

NOTE: Do not use underlining or italics when referring to the Bible, titles of books in the Bible (Genesis, not *Genesis*), or titles of legal documents (the Constitution, not the *Constitution*). Do not underline the title of your own paper.

42b Underline or italicize the names of spacecraft, aircraft, ships, and trains.

Challenger, Spirit of St. Louis, Queen Elizabeth II, Silver Streak

▶ The success of the Soviets' Sputnik galvanized the U.S.

space program.

Mechanics

42c Underline or italicize foreign words used in an English sentence.

▶ Although Joe's method seemed to be successful, I decided to

establish my own <u>modus operandi</u>.

EXCEPTION: Do not underline or italicize foreign words that have become a standard part of the English language — "laissez-faire," "fait accompli," "habeas corpus," and "per diem," for example.

42d Underline or italicize words mentioned as words, letters mentioned as letters, and numbers mentioned as numbers.

▶ Tim assured us that the howling probably came from

his bloodhound, Hill Billy, but his <u>probably</u> stuck in

our minds.

▶ Sarah called her father by his given name, Johnny, but she

was unable to pronounce <u>J</u>.

▶ A big <u>3</u> was painted on the door.

NOTE: Quotation marks may be used instead of underlining or italics to set off words mentioned as words. (See 37e.)

42e Avoid excessive underlining or italics for emphasis.

Underlining or italicizing to emphasize words or ideas is distracting and should be used sparingly.

▶ In-line skating is a popular sport that has become almost

an addiction.
~~~~~~~~~~~~

EXERCISE 42–1

Edit the following sentences to correct errors in the use of italics. If a sentence is correct, write "correct" after it. Answers to lettered sentences appear in the back of the book. Example:

> Leaves of Grass by Walt Whitman was quite controversial
>
> when it was published over a century ago.

a. Howard Hughes commissioned the Spruce Goose, a beautifully built but thoroughly impractical wooden aircraft.
b. The old man *screamed* his anger, *shouting* to all of us, "I will not leave my money to you worthless layabouts!"
c. I learned the Latin term ad infinitum from an old nursery rhyme about fleas: "Great fleas have little fleas upon their back to bite 'em, / Little fleas have lesser fleas and so on ad infinitum."
d. Cinema audiences once gasped at hearing the word *damn* in *Gone with the Wind.*
e. "The City and the Pillar" is an early novel by Gore Vidal.

1. Bernard watched as Eileen stood transfixed in front of Vermeer's painting Head of a Young Girl.
2. The monastery walls were painted with scenes described in the book of Genesis.
3. My per diem allowance was two hundred dollars.
4. In her first calligraphy lesson, Suzanne learned how to make a Romanesque B.
5. Redford and Newman in the movie "The Sting" were amateurs compared to the seventeen-year-old con artist who lives at our house.

┌─ **ON THE WEB** ──────────────────────────────

For an electronic exercise on using italics, go to
dianahacker.com/rules

and click on ▶ **Electronic Grammar Exercises**
              ▶ **Mechanics**
                ▶ **E-ex 42–1**

43

Spelling

You learned to spell from repeated experience with words in both reading and writing, but especially writing. Words have a look, a sound, and even a feel to them as the hand moves across the page. As you proofread, you can probably tell if a word doesn't look quite right. In such cases, the solution is obvious: Look up the word in the dictionary.

SPELL CHECKERS AND GRAMMAR CHECKERS are useful alternatives to a dictionary, but only to a point. A spell checker will not tell you how to spell words not listed in its dictionary; nor will it help you catch words commonly confused, such as *accept* and *except,* or some typographical errors, such as *own* for *won.* You will still need to proofread, and for some words you may need to turn to the dictionary.

Grammar checkers can flag commonly confused words such as *accept* and *except* or *principal* and *principle,* but they often do this when you have used the correct word. You will still need to think about the meaning you intend.

43a Become familiar with your dictionary.

A good desk dictionary — such as *The American Heritage Dictionary of the English Language, The Random House College Dictionary, Merriam-Webster's Collegiate Dictionary,* or *Webster's New World Dictionary of the American Language* — is an indispensable writer's aid.

A sample dictionary entry, taken from *The American Heritage Dictionary,* appears on the next page. Labels show where various kinds of information about a word can be found in that dictionary.

Spelling, word division, pronunciation

The main entry (*re•gard* in the sample entry) shows the correct spelling of the word. When there are two correct spellings of a

Pronunciation — Grammatical label

Word division | Part of speech label | Word endings (inflections) | Meanings

Spelling —— **re•gard** (rĭ-gärd′) *v.* **-gard•ed, -gard•ing, -gards** —*tr.* **1.** To look at attentively; observe closely. **2.** To look upon or consider in a particular way: *I regard him as a fool.* **3.** To hold in esteem or respect: *She regards her teachers highly.* **4.** To relate or refer to; concern: *This item regards their liability.* **5.** To take into account; consider. **6.** *Obsolete* To take care of. —*intr.* **1.** To look or gaze. **2.** To give heed; pay attention. ❖ *n.* **1.** A look or gaze. **2.** Careful thought or attention; heed: *She gives little regard to her sister's teasing.* **3a.** Respect, affection, or esteem: *He has high regard for your work.* **b. regards** Good wishes expressing such sentiment: *Give the family my best regards.* **4.** A particular point or aspect; respect: *She was lucky in that regard.* **5.** Basis for action; motive. **6.** *Obsolete* Appear-
Idioms —— ance or aspect. —***idioms:* as regards** Concerning. **in (or with) regard to** With respect to. [Middle English *regarden*, from Old French *regarder* : *re-*, re- + *guarder*, to guard (of Germanic origin; see GUARD).]

Synonyms *regard, esteem, admiration, respect* These nouns refer to a feeling based on perception of and approval for the worth of a person or thing. *Regard* is the most general: "*I once thought you had a kind of regard for her*" (George Borrow). *Esteem* connotes considered appraisal and pos-
Synonyms — itive regard: "*The near-unanimity of esteem he enjoyed during his lifetime has by no means been sustained since*" (Will Crutchfield). *Admiration* is a feeling of keen approbation: "*Greatness is a spiritual condition worthy to excite love, interest, and admiration*" (Matthew Arnold). *Respect* implies appreciative, often deferential regard resulting from careful assessment: "*I have a great respect for any man who makes his own way in life*" (Winston Churchill). See also synonyms at **consider**.

Usage Note *Regard* is traditionally used in the singular in the phrase *in regard* (not *in regards*) *to. Regarding* and *as regards* are also standard in
Usage note — the sense "with reference to." In the same sense *with respect to* is acceptable, but *respecting* is not. • *Respects* is sometimes considered preferable to *regards* in the sense of "particulars": *In some respects* (not *regards*) *the books are alike.*

Word origin (etymology)

word (as in *collectible, collectable,* for example), both are given, with the preferred spelling usually appearing first.

The main entry also shows how the word is divided into syllables. The dot between *re* and *gard* separates the word's two syllables and indicates where the word should be divided if it can't fit at the end of a line of type (see 44f). When a word is compound, the main entry shows how to write it: as one word (*crossroad*), as a hyphenated word (*cross-stitch*), or as two words (*cross section*).

The word's pronunciation is given just after the main entry. The accents indicate which syllables are stressed; the other

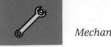
marks are explained in the dictionary's pronunciation key. In some dictionaries this key appears at the bottom of every page or every other page.

Word endings and grammatical labels

When a word takes endings to indicate grammatical functions (called *inflections*), the endings are listed in boldface, as with *-garded, -garding,* and *-gards* in the sample entry.

Labels for the parts of speech and for other grammatical terms are abbreviated. The most commonly used abbreviations are these:

n.	noun	adj.	adjective
pl.	plural	adv.	adverb
sing.	singular	pron.	pronoun
v.	verb	prep.	preposition
tr.	transitive verb	conj.	conjunction
intr.	intransitive verb	interj.	interjection

Meanings, word origin, synonyms, and antonyms

Each meaning for the word is given a number. Occasionally a word's use is illustrated in a quoted sentence.

Sometimes a word can be used as more than one part of speech (*regard,* for instance, can be used as either a verb or a noun). In such a case, all the meanings for one part of speech are given before all the meanings for another, as in the sample entry. The entry also gives idiomatic uses of the word.

The origin of the word, called its *etymology,* appears in brackets after all the meanings (in some dictionaries it appears before the meanings).

Synonyms, words similar in meaning to the main entry, are frequently listed. In the sample entry, the dictionary draws distinctions in meaning among the various synonyms. Antonyms, which do not appear in the sample entry, are words having a meaning opposite from that of the main entry.

Usage

Usage labels indicate when, where, or under what conditions a particular meaning for a word is appropriately used. Common labels are _informal_ (or _colloquial_), _slang, nonstandard, dialect, obsolete, archaic, poetic,_ and _British._ In the sample entry, two meanings of _regard_ are labeled _obsolete_ because they are no longer in use.

Dictionaries sometimes include usage notes as well. In the sample entry, the dictionary offers advice on several uses of _regard_ not specifically covered by the meanings. Such advice is based on the opinions of many experts and on actual usage in current magazines, newspapers, and books.

ON THE WEB

For links to online dictionaries and other resources that will help you with grammar, style, and punctuation, go to
dianahacker.com/rules

and click on ▶ **Links Library**
▶ **Grammar, Style, and Punctuation**

43b Discriminate between words that sound alike but have different meanings.

Words that sound alike or nearly alike but have different meanings and spellings are called homophones. The following sets of words are so commonly confused that a good proofreader will double-check their every use.

affect (verb: "to exert an influence")
effect (verb: "to accomplish"; noun: "result")

its (possessive pronoun: "of or belonging to it")
it's (contraction for "it is")

loose (adjective: "free, not securely attached")
lose (verb: "to fail to keep, to be deprived of")

principal (adjective: "most important"; noun: "head of a school")
principle (noun: "a general or fundamental truth")

their (possessive pronoun: "belonging to them")
they're (contraction for "they are")
there (adverb: "that place or position")

who's (contraction for "who is")
whose (possessive form of "who")

your (possessive form of "you")
you're (contraction of "you are")

To check for correct use of these and other commonly confused words, consult the Glossary of Usage, which begins on page 531.

43c Become familiar with the major spelling rules.

i before *e* except after *c*

Use *i* before *e* except after *c* or when sounded like *ay,* as in *neighbor* and *weigh.*

I BEFORE E   relieve, believe, sieve, niece, fierce, frieze

E BEFORE I   receive, deceive, sleigh, freight, eight

EXCEPTIONS   seize, either, weird, height, foreign, leisure

Suffixes

FINAL SILENT -E   Generally, drop a final silent -*e* when adding a suffix that begins with a vowel. Keep the final -*e* if the suffix begins with a consonant.

combine, combination   achieve, achievement
desire, desiring   care, careful
prude, prudish   entire, entirety
remove, removable   gentle, gentleness

Words such as *changeable, judgment, argument,* and *truly* are exceptions.

FINAL -Y   When adding -*s* or -*d* to words ending in -*y,* ordinarily change -*y* to -*ie* when the -*y* is preceded by a consonant but not when it is preceded by a vowel.

comedy, comedies   monkey, monkeys
dry, dried   play, played

With proper names ending in -*y,* however, do not change the -*y* to -*ie* even if it is preceded by a consonant: *the Dougherty family, the Doughertys.*

FINAL CONSONANTS If a final consonant is preceded by a single vowel *and* the consonant ends a one-syllable word or a stressed syllable, double the consonant when adding a suffix beginning with a vowel.

bet, betting   occur, occurrence
commit, committed

ESL

Spelling varies slightly among English-speaking countries. This can prove particularly confusing for multilingual speakers, who may have learned British or Canadian English. Following is a list of some common words spelled differently in American and British English. Consult a dictionary for others.

AMERICAN	BRITISH
canceled, traveled	cancelled, travelled
color, humor	colour, humour
judgment	judgement
check	cheque
realize, apologize	realise, apologise
defense	defence
anemia, anesthetic	anaemia, anaesthetic
theater, center	theatre, centre
fetus	foetus
mold, smolder	mould, smoulder
civilization	civilisation
connection, inflection	connexion, inflexion
licorice	liquorice

Plurals

-S **OR** *-ES* Add *-s* to form the plural of most nouns; add *-es* to singular nouns ending in *-s, -sh, -ch,* and *-x.*

table, tables   church, churches
paper, papers   dish, dishes

Ordinarily add *-s* to nouns ending in *-o* when the *-o* is preceded by a vowel. Add *-es* when it is preceded by a consonant.

radio, radios   hero, heroes
video, videos   tomato, tomatoes

OTHER PLURALS To form the plural of a hyphenated compound word, add the *-s* to the chief word even if it does not appear at the end.

mother-in-law, mothers-in-law

English words derived from other languages such as Latin or French sometimes form the plural as they would in their original language.

medium, media   chateau, chateaux
criterion, criteria

43d Be alert to commonly misspelled words.

absence	candidate	exhaust	marriage
academic	cemetery	existence	mathematics
accidentally	changeable	extraordinary	mischievous
accommodate	column	extremely	necessary
achievement	commitment	familiar	noticeable
acknowledge	committed	fascinate	occasion
acquaintance	committee	February	occurred
acquire	competitive	foreign	occurrence
address	conceivable	forty	pamphlet
all right	conferred	fourth	parallel
amateur	conqueror	friend	particularly
analyze	conscience	government	pastime
answer	conscientious	grammar	permissible
apparently	conscious	guard	perseverance
appearance	criticism	harass	phenomenon
arctic	criticize	height	physically
argument	decision	humorous	picnicking
arithmetic	definitely	incidentally	playwright
arrangement	descendant	incredible	practically
ascend	dictionary	indispensable	precede
athlete	disastrous	inevitable	preference
athletics	eighth	intelligence	preferred
attendance	eligible	irrelevant	prejudice
basically	embarrass	irresistible	prevalent
beginning	emphasize	knowledge	privilege
believe	entirely	license	proceed
benefited	environment	lightning	professor
bureau	especially	loneliness	pronunciation
business	exaggerated	maintenance	quiet
calendar	exercise	maneuver	quite

quizzes	seize	subtly	unnecessarily
receive	separate	succeed	usually
referred	sergeant	surprise	vacuum
restaurant	siege	thorough	vengeance
rhythm	similar	tragedy	villain
roommate	sincerely	transferred	weird
sandwich	sophomore	tries	whether
schedule	strictly	truly	writing

EXERCISE 43-1

The following memo has been run through a spell checker. Proofread it carefully, editing the spelling and typographical errors that remain.

November 1, 2001

To: Patricia Wise

cc: Richard Chang

Form: Constance Mayhew

Subject: Express Tours annual report

Thank you for agreeing to draft the annual report for Express Tours. Before you begin you're work, let me outline the initial steps.

First, its essential for you to include brief profiles of top management. Early next week, I'll provide profiles for all manages accept Samuel Heath, who's biographical information is being revised. You should edit these profiles carefully, than format them according to the enclosed instructions. We may ask you to include other employee's profiles at some point.

Second, you should arrange to get complete financial information for fiscal year 2001 from our comptroller, Richard Chang. (Helen Boyes, to, can provide the necessary figures.) When you get this information, precede according tot he plans we discuss in yesterday's meeting. By the way, you will notice from the figures that the sale of our Charterhouse division did not significantly effect net profits.

Third, you should submit first draft of the report by December 15. I assume that you won a laser printer, but if you don't, you can submit a disk and we'll print out a draft here. Of coarse, you should proofread you writing.

I am quiet pleased that you can take on this project. If I or anyone else at Express Tours can answers questions, don't hesitate to call.

Mechanics

44

The hyphen

GRAMMAR CHECKERS can flag some, but not all, missing or mis-used hyphens. For example, the programs can often tell you that a hyphen is needed in compound numbers, such as *sixty-four*. They can also tell you how to spell certain compound words, such as *breakup* (not *break-up*).

44a Consult the dictionary to determine how to treat a compound word.

The dictionary will tell you whether to treat a compound word as a hyphenated compound (*water-repellent*), one word (*waterproof*), or two words (*water table*). If the compound word is not in the dictionary, treat it as two words.

▶ The prosecutor chose not to cross‑examine any witnesses.

▶ Grandma kept a small note book in her apron pocket.

▶ Alice walked through the looking/glass into a backward world.

44b Use a hyphen to connect two or more words functioning together as an adjective before a noun.

▶ Mrs. Douglas gave Toshiko a seashell and some newspaper‑

wrapped fish to take home to her mother.

▶ Priscilla Hood is not yet a well‑known candidate.

Newspaper-wrapped and *well-known* are adjectives used before the nouns *fish* and *candidate*.

Generally, do not use a hyphen when such compounds follow the noun.

▶ After our television campaign, Priscilla Hood will be well/known.

Do not use a hyphen to connect *-ly* adverbs to the words they modify.

▶ A slowly/moving truck tied up traffic.

NOTE: In a series, hyphens are suspended.

Do you prefer first-, second-, or third-class tickets?

44c Hyphenate the written form of fractions and of compound numbers from twenty-one to ninety-nine.

▶ One-fourth of my income goes to pay off the national debt.
   ^

44d Use a hyphen with the prefixes *all-, ex-* (meaning "former"), and *self-* and with the suffix *-elect.*

▶ The charity is funneling more money into self-help projects.
   ^

▶ Anne King is our club's president-elect.
   ^

44e A hyphen is used in some words to avoid ambiguity or to separate awkward double or triple letters.

Without the hyphen there would be no way to distinguish between words such as *re-creation* and *recreation.*

Bicycling in the country is my favorite recreation.

The film was praised for its astonishing re-creation of nineteenth-century London.

Hyphens are sometimes used to separate awkward double or triple letters in compound words (*anti-intellectual, cross-stitch*). Always check a dictionary for the standard form of the word.

44f If a word must be divided at the end of a line, divide it correctly.

    1. Divide words between syllables.

▶ When I returned from overseas, I didn't ~~reco~~ *recog-*
~~nize~~
~~gnize~~ *nize* one face on the magazine covers.
         ^

    2. Never divide one-syllable words.

▶ He didn't have the courage or the ~~stren-~~
strength
~~gth~~ to open the door.
 ^

    3. Never divide a word so that a single letter stands alone at the end of a line or fewer than three letters begin a line.

▶ She'll bring her brother with her when she comes ~~a-~~
~~again.~~
~~gain.~~ *again.*
 ^

▶ As audience to *The Mousetrap,* Hamlet is a ~~watch-~~
watcher
~~er~~ watching watchers.
 ^

    4. When dividing a compound word at the end of a line, either make the break between the words that form the compound or put the whole word on the next line.

▶ My niece is determined to become a long-~~dis-~~
distance
~~tance~~ runner when she grows up.
 ^

5. To divide long e-mail and Internet addresses, do not use a hyphen. Break the address after a slash, like this:

> To find a zip code quickly, use the United States Postal Service Web site at < http://www.usps.com/ zip4/ > .

EXERCISE 44–1

Edit the following sentences to correct errors in hyphenation. If a sentence is correct, write "correct" after it. Answers to lettered sentences appear in the back of the book. Example:

> **Zola's first readers were scandalized by his slice‑of‑life**
> ^   ^
>
> **novels.**

a. Gold is the seventy-ninth element in the periodic table.
b. The swiftly-moving tugboat pulled alongside the barge and directed it away from the oil spill in the harbor.
c. The Moche were a pre-Columbian people who established a sophisticated culture in ancient Peru.
d. Your dog is well-known in our neighborhood.
e. Road-blocks were set up along all the major highways leading out of the city.

1. We knew we were driving too fast when our tires skidded on the rain slick surface.
2. The Black Death reduced the population of some medieval villages by two thirds.
3. The flight attendant asked us to fasten our seat belts before liftoff.
4. A well known actress who wishes to remain anonymous has contributed ten thousand dollars toward our scholarship fund.
5. Gail Sheehy writes that at age twenty five many people assume that the choices they make are irrevocable.

ON THE WEB

For an electronic exercise on using hyphens, go to
dianahacker.com/rules

and click on ▶ **Electronic Grammar Exercises**
▶ **Mechanics**
▶ **E-ex 44–1**

45

Capital letters

In addition to the rules in this section, you can use a good dictionary to tell you when to use capital letters.

 GRAMMAR CHECKERS remind you that sentences should begin with capital letters and that some words, such as *Cherokee,* are proper nouns. Many words, however, should be capitalized only in certain contexts, and you must determine when to do so.

45a Capitalize proper nouns and words derived from them; do not capitalize common nouns.

Proper nouns are the names of specific persons, places, and things. All other nouns are common nouns. The following types of words are usually capitalized: names for the deity, religions, religious followers, sacred books; words of family relationship used as names; particular places; nationalities and their languages, races, tribes; educational institutions, departments, degrees, particular courses; government departments, organizations, political parties; historical movements, periods, events, documents; specific electronic sources; and trade names.

PROPER NOUNS	COMMON NOUNS
God (used as a name)	a god
Book of Jeremiah	a book
Uncle Pedro	my uncle
Father (used as a name)	my father
Lake Superior	a picturesque lake
the Capital Center	a center for advanced studies
the South	a southern state
Japan, a Japanese garden	an ornamental garden
University of Wisconsin	a good university
Geology 101	geology
Environmental Protection Agency	a federal agency
Phi Kappa Psi	a fraternity
a Democrat	an independent

PROPER NOUNS	COMMON NOUNS
the Enlightenment	the eighteenth century
the Declaration of Independence	a treaty
the World Wide Web, the Web	a home page
the Internet, the Net	a computer network
Kleenex	a tissue

Months, holidays, and days of the week are treated as proper nouns; the seasons and numbers of the days of the month are not.

> Our academic year begins on a Tuesday in early September, right after Labor Day.

> My mother's birthday is in early summer, on the second of June.

EXCEPTION: Capitalize Fourth of July (or July Fourth) when referring to the holiday.

Names of school subjects are capitalized only if they are names of languages. Names of particular courses are capitalized.

> This semester Austin is taking math, geography, geology, French, and English.

> Professor Anderson offers Modern American Fiction 501 to graduate students.

CAUTION: Do not capitalize common nouns to make them seem important: *Our company is currently hiring computer programmers* (not *Company, Computer Programmers*).

45b Capitalize titles of persons when used as part of a proper name but usually not when used alone.

> Professor Margaret Barnes; Dr. Harold Stevens; John Scott Williams Jr.; Anne Tilton, LL.D.

> District Attorney Marshall was reprimanded for badgering the witness.

> The district attorney was elected for a two-year term.

Usage varies when the title of an important public figure is used alone: *The president* [or *President*] *vetoed the bill.*

45c Capitalize the first, last, and all major words in titles and subtitles of works such as books, articles, songs, and online documents.

In both titles and subtitles, major words such as nouns, pronouns, verbs, adjectives, and adverbs should be capitalized. Minor words such as articles, prepositions, and coordinating conjunctions are not capitalized unless they are the first or last word of a title or subtitle. Capitalize the second part of a hyphenated term in a title if it is a major word but not if it is a minor word.

To see why some of the following titles are italicized and some are put in quotation marks, see 42a and 37d.

> *The Impossible Theater: A Manifesto*
> *The F-Plan Diet*
> "Fire and Ice"
> "I Want to Hold Your Hand"
> *The Canadian Green Page*

Capitalize chapter titles and the titles of other major divisions of a work following the same guidelines used for titles of complete works.

> "Work and Play" in Santayana's *The Nature of Beauty*

45d Capitalize the first word of a sentence.

Obviously the first word of a sentence should be capitalized.

> When lightning struck the house, the chimney collapsed.

When a sentence appears within parentheses, capitalize its first word unless the parentheses appear within another sentence.

> Early detection of breast cancer significantly increases survival rates. (See table 2.)

> Early detection of breast cancer significantly increases survival rates (see table 2).

45e Capitalize the first word of a quoted sentence but not a quoted phrase.

> In *Time* magazine Robert Hughes writes, "There are only about sixty Watteau paintings on whose authenticity all experts agree."

Russell Baker has written that in our country, sports are "the opiate of the masses."

If a quoted sentence is interrupted by explanatory words, do not capitalize the first word after the interruption. (See 37f.)

"If you wanted to go out," he said sharply, "you should have told me."

When quoting poetry, copy the poet's capitalization exactly. Many poets capitalize the first word of every line of poetry; a few contemporary poets dismiss capitalization altogether.

When I consider everything that grows
Holds in perfection but a little moment   — Shakespeare

it was the week   that
i felt the city's narrow breezes rush about
me   — Don L. Lee

45f   **Do not capitalize the first word after a colon unless it begins an independent clause, in which case capitalization is optional.**

Most of the bar's patrons can be divided into two groups: the occasional after-work socializers and the nothing-to-go-home-to regulars.

This we are forced to conclude: The [*or* the] federal government is needed to protect the rights of minorities.

45g   **Capitalize abbreviations for departments and agencies of government, other organizations, and corporations; capitalize the call letters of radio and television stations.**

EPA, FBI, OPEC, IBM, WCRB, KNBC-TV

EXERCISE 45–1

Edit the following sentences to correct errors in capitalization. If a sentence is correct, write "correct" after it. Answers to lettered sentences appear in the back of the book. Example:

On our trip to the West we visited the ~~g~~rand ~~c~~anyon and the
~~g~~reat ~~s~~alt ~~d~~esert.

a. District attorney Johnson was disgusted when the jurors turned in a verdict of not guilty after only one hour of deliberation.
b. Have you seen the Arena Stage production of *A Raisin in the Sun*?
c. Madeline is taking courses in geology, mathematics, french, and english.
d. My Grandfather and Grandmother emigrated from Lithuania in the mid-1960s.
e. I look forward every Spring to walking along the flower-lined paths in Boston's Public Garden.

1. Whenever my brother took us to the movies, he gave us three choices: A brainless beach party flick, a foreign fluff film, or a blood and lust adventure movie.
2. The grunion is an unremarkable fish except for one curious habit: It comes ashore to spawn.
3. In our family, aunt Sandra was notorious for her biting tongue.
4. Historians have described Robert E. Lee as the aristocratic south personified.
5. Because Eileen enjoys working with handicapped children, she is pursuing a degree in Special Education.

ON THE WEB

For an electronic exercise on capitalization, go to
dianahacker.com/rules

and click on ▶ **Electronic Grammar Exercises**
       ▶ **Mechanics**
          ▶ **E-ex 45-1**

Process

Design

Clarity

Grammar

Punctuation

Mechanics

Argument

Research

Basics

Argument

46

Constructing reasonable arguments

In argumentative writing, you take a stand on a debatable issue. The issue being debated might be a matter of public policy:

— Should religious groups be allowed to meet on public school property?
— What is the least dangerous way to dispose of nuclear waste?
— Should the sale of prescription drugs over the Internet be more strictly regulated?

On such questions, reasonable people may disagree.

Reasonable men and women also disagree about many scholarly issues. Psychologists debate the validity of behaviorism; historians interpret causes of the Civil War quite differently; biologists conduct genetic experiments to challenge the conclusions of other researchers.

When you construct a *reasonable* argument, your goal is not simply to win or to have the last word. Your aim is to reveal your current understanding of the truth about a subject or to propose the best solution available for solving a problem — without being needlessly combative. Writing teacher Richard Fulkerson describes such aims well:

> The purpose of argumentation within a free society or within a research field is to reach the best conclusion possible at the time.
>
> — *Teaching the Argument in Writing*

ESL The conventions of argument vary from culture to culture. In the United States, most arguments are direct, not subtle; explicitly organized, not discursive; plainspoken, not poetic. Evidence is usually specific and factual; appeals to intuition or communal wisdom are rare. If you have difficulty writing the kinds of arguments that are valued in the United States, ask your professor for help or visit your school's writing center.

46a   Examine your issue's social and intellectual contexts.

Arguments appear in social and intellectual contexts. Public policy debates obviously arise in social contexts: Grounded in specific times and places, such debates are conducted among groups with competing values and interests. For example, the debate over nuclear power plants has been renewed in the United States in light of energy conerns and the September 11 attacks — with environmentalists, the nuclear industry, consumers, and citizens worried about public safety all weighing in on the argument. Most public policy debates also have intellectual dimensions that address scientific or theoretical concerns. In the case of the nuclear power issue, physicists, biologists, and economists all contribute their expertise.

Scholarly debates clearly play themselves out in intellectual contexts, but they have a social dimension too. Scholars and researchers rarely work in a vacuum: They respond to the contributions of other specialists in the field, often building on others' views and refining them, but at times challenging them. Social bonds develop among scholars who hold similar views, and bad feelings have been known to arise among those belonging to competing schools of thought.

Because many of your readers will be aware of the social and intellectual contexts in which your issue is grounded, you will be at a serious disadvantage if you are not informed. That's why it is a good idea to conduct some research before preparing your argument; consulting even a few sources can help. For example, the student whose paper appears on pages 352–57 became more knowledgeable about his issue — whether to ban recreational snowmobiles from Yellowstone National Park — after consulting a handful of brief sources. This student documented his sources using MLA style (see 54).

46b   View your audience as a panel of jurors.

Do not assume that your audience already agrees with you; instead, envision skeptical readers who, like a panel of jurors, will make up their minds after listening to all sides of the argument. If you are arguing a public policy issue, aim your paper at fellow citizens who represent a variety of opinions. In the case of the debate over nuclear power, for example, imagine a jury representative of those who have a stake in the matter: environmentalists, the nuclear industry, consumers, and citizens worried about public safety.

At times, of course, you can deliberately narrow your audience. If you are working within a word limit, for example, you might not have the space in which to address the concerns of all parties to the nuclear energy debate. Or you might be primarily interested in reaching one segment of a general audience, such as consumers. In such instances, you can still view your audience as a panel of jurors; the jury will simply be a less diverse group.

In the case of scholarly debates, you will be addressing readers who share your interest in an academic discipline such as literature or psychology. Such readers belong to what some have called a *discourse community,* a group with an agreed-upon way of investigating and talking about issues. Though they generally agree about procedures, scholars in an academic discipline often disagree about particular issues. Once you see how they disagree about your issue, it will be easy to imagine a jury that reflects the variety of opinions they hold.

46c In your introduction, establish credibility and state your position.

In argumentative writing, your introduction should ordinarily end with a thesis sentence that states your position on the issue you have chosen to debate (see also 2a). In the sentences leading up to the thesis, establish your credibility with readers by showing that you are knowledgeable and fair-minded. If possible, build common ground with readers who may not be in initial agreement with your views.

In the following introduction, student Kevin Smith presents himself as someone worth listening to. His opening sentence shows that he is familiar with the legal issues surrounding school prayer. His next sentence reveals him to be fair-minded, and it builds common ground by showing that he, like many readers, believes in the value of prayer. Even Smith's thesis builds common ground: "Prayer is too important to be trusted to our public schools."

> Although the Supreme Court has ruled against prayer in public schools on First Amendment grounds, many people still feel that prayers should be allowed. These people, most of whom hold strong religious beliefs, are well intentioned. What they fail to realize is that the Supreme Court decision, although it was made on legal grounds, makes good sense on religious grounds as well. Prayer is too important to be trusted to our public schools.   — Kevin Smith, student

Because Smith takes into consideration the values of those who disagree with him, readers are likely to approach his essay with an open mind.

46d Back up your thesis with persuasive lines of argument.

Arguments of any complexity contain lines of argument that, when taken together, might reasonably persuade readers that the thesis has merit. Here, for example, are the main lines of argument used by a student who opposes regulating use of cell phones while driving:

> Thesis: We should not restrict the use of cell phones in moving vehicles.
>
> — The risks of using a cell phone while driving have not been proved scientifically.
>
> Any risks must be weighed against the benefits of using a phone while driving.
>
> — Instead of restricting use of the phones, we can educate the public on using them responsibly and enforce laws on negligent and reckless driving.

If you sum up your main lines of argument, as in the example just given, you will have a rough outline of your essay. The outline will consist of your central claim — the thesis — and any subordinate claims that back it up. In your paper, you will provide evidence for each of these claims.

46e Support your claims with specific evidence.

You will of course need to support your central claim and any subordinate claims with evidence: facts, statistics, examples and illustrations, expert opinion, and so on. Depending on the issue you have chosen to write about, you may or may not need to do some reading to gather evidence. Some argumentative topics, such as whether your college should continue to support its travel study program, can be developed through personal experience and research tools such as questionnaires and interviews. Most debatable topics, however, require that you consult some written sources.

If any of your evidence is based on reading, you must document your sources. Documentation gives credit to the authors and shows readers how to locate a source in case they want to assess its credibility or explore the issue further (see sections 54 and 59).

Using facts and statistics

A fact is something that is known with certainty because it has been objectively verified: The capital of Wyoming is Cheyenne. Carbon has an atomic weight of 12. John F. Kennedy was assassinated on November 22, 1963. Statistics are collections of numerical facts: Alcohol abuse is a factor in nearly 40 percent of traffic fatalities. Nearly five out of ten U.S. households currently own a DVD player. As of 2002, nearly 28 percent of privately held businesses in the United States were owned by women.

Most arguments are supported at least to some extent by facts and statistics. For example, in the following passage, the writer uses statistics to show that college students are carrying unreasonably high credit card debt.

> A 2001 study by Nellie Mae revealed that while the average credit card debt per college undergraduate is $2,327, more than 20 percent of undergraduates who have at least one credit card maintain a much higher debt level of $3,000 to $7,000 (Barrett).

Writers and politicians often use statistics in selective ways to bolster their partisan views. If you suspect that a writer's handling of statistics is not quite fair, read authors with opposing views, who may give you a fuller understanding of the numbers.

Using examples and illustrations

Examples and illustrations (extended examples, often in story form) rarely prove a point by themselves, but when used in combination with other forms of evidence they flesh out an argument and bring it to life. Because they often have an emotional dimension, they can reach readers in ways that statistics cannot.

In a paper arguing in favor of restricting the use of cell phones while driving, student Angela Daly gives examples of four people who were killed in just one month because drivers were distracted by their phones (see pp. 448–55). Daly supplements this emotionally powerful anecdotal evidence with an analysis of scientific investigations on the dangers of using cell phones while driving.

Citing expert opinion

Although they are no substitute for careful reasoning of your own, the views of an expert can contribute to the force of your argument. For example, in a paragraph describing the dangers of using a cell phone while driving, Angela Daly relies on an expert:

> Frances Bents, an expert on the relation between cell phones and accidents, estimates that 450 to 1,000 crashes a year have some connection to cell phone use (Layton C9).

When you rely on expert opinion, make sure that your source is an expert in the field you are writing about. In some cases you may need to provide credentials showing why your source is worth listening to. When including expert testimony in your paper, you can summarize or paraphrase the expert's opinion or you can quote the expert's exact words. You will of course need to document the source, as in the example just given (see sections 54 and 59).

46f   Anticipate objections; counter opposing arguments.

Readers who already agree with you need no convincing, although a well-argued case for their point of view is always welcome. But indifferent and skeptical readers may resist your arguments because they have minds of their own. To give up a position that seems reasonable, a reader has to see that there is an even more reasonable one. In addition to presenting your own case, therefore, you should review the opposing arguments and attempt to counter them.

There is no best place in an essay to deal with opposing views. Often it is useful to summarize the opposing position early in your essay. After stating your thesis but before developing your own arguments, you might have a paragraph beginning *Critics of this view argue that. . . .* But sometimes a better plan is to anticipate objections as you develop your case paragraph by paragraph. Wherever you decide to deal with opposing arguments, do your best to counter them. Show that those who oppose you are not as persuasive as they claim because their arguments are flawed or because your arguments to the contrary have greater weight.

NOTE: Readers will judge the way you handle opposing views, so do your best to explain the arguments of others accurately and fairly (see 47c).

46g   Build common ground.

As you counter opposing arguments, try to build common ground with readers who do not initially agree with your views. If you can show that you share your readers' values, they may be able to switch to your position without giving up what they feel is important. For example, to persuade people opposed to shooting deer, a state wildlife commission would have to show that it too cares about preserving deer and does not want them to die needlessly. Having established these values in common, the commission might be able to persuade critics that a carefully controlled hunting season is good for the deer population because it prevents starvation caused by overpopulation.

People believe that intelligence and decency support their side of an argument. To change sides, they must continue to feel intelligent and decent. Otherwise they will persist in their opposition.

SAMPLE ARGUMENT PAPER

In the following paper, student Aaron Lund argues that the federal government should ban recreational snowmobiles from

Yellowstone National Park. Notice that Lund is careful to establish common ground with readers who may hold a different view. Notice too that he attempts to counter the arguments of the opposition.

In writing the paper, Lund consulted a handful of sources, two of which he found online. When he quotes from or uses statistics from a source, he cites the source with an MLA (Modern Language Association) in-text citation. Citations in the paper refer readers to the list of works cited at the end of the paper. (See 54).

ON THE WEB

Another student, Rekha Sanghvi, has also written a paper on the topic of snowmobiling in national parks; her paper takes the opposite stand from that taken by Lund. To read Sanghvi's paper, go to **dianahacker.com/rules**

and click on ▶ **Model Papers**
           ▶ **MLA Papers: Sanghvi**

Lund 1

Aaron Lund

Professor Dorn

English 102

15 November 2002

Preserving Yellowstone's Winter Wilderness

Although a few recreational snowmobilers destroy
fragile ecosystems and harass animals as they ride through
the wilderness, most love and respect this country's natural
heritage. That's why they brave the cold to explore what is
left of wild America--including Yellowstone National Park.
Unfortunately, however, even respectful snowmobilers are
unwittingly damaging what they love. Because snowmobiles
create both air and noise pollution and because their use
in the park strains the already lean budget of our park
service, recreational snowmobiles should be banned from
Yellowstone National Park.

In 2002, the Bush administration, under pressure from
the snowmobile industry, proposed to reverse the National
Park Service's 2000 plan that would have phased out recreational snowmobile use in Yellowstone. In addition to
reversing the earlier plan, the new policy would increase
the number of snowmobiles allowed into the park per day.
This policy is a step in the wrong direction.

It may be hard to imagine that 1,100 snowmobiles a
day (the proposed limit) could cause an air pollution problem in a park half the size of Connecticut, but in fact they
can. The air pollution at park entrances has already become

(margin annotations)

Lund builds
common
ground with
readers who
may disagree
with him.

Thesis states
the main
point.

Background
information
puts the thesis
in context.

Lund intro-
duces his
first line of
argument.

Lund 2

so bad in winter, according to environmental reporter Julie
Cart, that fresh air has to be pumped into the kiosks where
snowmobiles line up and park rangers have been forced to
wear respirators. Park visitors, including the snowmobilers
themselves, have no such protection.

Sources are documented with MLA citations.

The Bluewater Network, an environmental group, reports that the most common snowmobiles, those with two-
stroke engines, "discharge up to one-third of their fuel
unburned into the environment and are one of the largest
unchecked sources of hydrocarbon pollution nationwide"
(1). Bluewater Network cites numerous scientific studies
linking carbon monoxide pollutants to snowmobiles. One of
these studies, which was conducted in the mid-1990s after
many rangers complained of dizziness and nausea, found
that carbon monoxide levels at park entrances exceeded
those allowed by the National Ambient Air Quality Standard
(2). Clearly, such a level of pollution is a health risk to
the park's employees and to its visitors.

Lund supports his points with specific evidence.

In addition to polluting the air, snowmobiles are
noisy, disturbing the peace and quiet that park visitors
have a right to expect. One study cited by Bluewater Network reports that twelve snowmobiles traveling together
could be heard as far as two miles away (5). Even a travel-
writer for Yellowstone Journal, a magazine financed to a
great extent by advertising from snowmobile manufacturers
and rental services, advises readers about areas in the park
free from "the constant hum of the other snowmobiles"

Transition prepares readers for the second line of argument.

Argument

(Johnson 7). Whether such noise adversely affects the park's wildlife remains a debated question, but the possibility exists.

Lund counters an opposing argument.

Some who favor keeping the park open to snowmobiles argue that newer, four-stroke machines cause less air and noise pollution than older models. While this is true, the new machines still pollute more than cars, and their decibel level is reduced only slightly ("Snowmobile"). Also, because the newer snowmobiles cost at least $3,000 more than the older ones, it is unlikely that individuals would choose to buy them or that rental companies could afford to upgrade. At present there are no strict guarantees that only the newer models would be allowed into the park.

Lund presents his third line of argument.

Like most federal agencies, the National Park Service faces serious budget constraints. Funds that should be used to preserve Yellowstone National Park and its wildlife have been diverted to deal with the snowmobile issue. A single environmental impact study of the problem cost taxpayers nearly $250,000 in early 2002 (Greater Yellowstone Coalition), and the park service estimates that implementing the new plan would cost one million dollars ("Snowmobile"). Also, park rangers are spending an increasing amount of their valuable time policing snowmobilers. In 2002, park rangers issued 338 citations for illegal snowmobiling activity, twice as many as in 2001, in addition to hundreds of warnings (Greater Yellowstone Coalition). Although most snowmobilers remain law-abiding, a disturbing number of joyriders violate speed limits, stray from marked trails, and

Lund 4

pursue animals for the thrill of the chase. Policing such
activities was not what most park rangers had in mind
when they signed up for jobs as preservers of this country's
treasured natural resources.

Opponents of a ban argue that a central mission of
the park service is to provide access to national parks--
access not only to the physically fit (such as snowshoers
and cross-country skiers) but to ordinary people, including
those who are handicapped. Admittedly, winter access
is important, but ordinary people can enjoy the park
by means other than snowmobiles. Snowcoaches (buses
on skis) already take visitors into the park, and one road
into the park is plowed and open to cars in winter. Also,
the park service's mission is not just to provide access
to the parks; no less important is its mission to
preserve the parks' pristine natural resources for future
generations.

Even with a ban on snowmobiling in the park itself,
the Yellowstone area would still earn the title of Snowmobiling Capital of America. Virtually all of the streets of
West Yellowstone, the area's major town, are open to
snowmobilers, and many trails run out of the town. The
Big Sky Trail extends for 110 miles, and the 360-mile Con-
tinental Divide Snowmobile Trail offers sledders "groomed
trails, spectacular mountain scenery, wide-open spaces, and
lots of opportunities to view wildlife" (Johnson 7). Because the Yellowstone area offers so many winter trails,
there is no need to allow snowmobiles in the park itself.

Lund counters a possible objection to his thesis.

Lund suggests a reasonable alternative for snowmobilers.

Conclusion
echoes the
thesis without
dully repeat-
ing it.

A ban on snowmobiles would give park visitors a quiet, pollution-free experience, and it would allow the park service to devote more of its limited resources to one of its primary missions: the protection of natural resources. Whether on cross-country skis or from the heated comfort of a snowcoach, visitors would still be able to appreciate Yellowstone's beauty--its geysers, its wildlife, and its snow-covered vistas--throughout the park's long winter.

Lund 6

Works Cited

Bluewater Network. <u>Snowmobile Position Paper</u>. Apr. 2002.

    11 pp. 12 Nov. 2002 <www.bluewaternetwork.org/

    reports/rep_pl_snow_snowposition.pdf>.

Cart, Julie. "Plan Backs Snowmobiles at Parks." <u>Los Angeles

    Times</u> 8 Nov. 2002: A12- . <u>National Newspaper Index</u>.

    InfoTrac. Boston Public Lib. 11 Nov. 2002 <http://

    infotrac.galegroup.com>.

Greater Yellowstone Coalition. "Yellowstone Experiences

    Worst Year Ever for Illegal Snowmobile Activity."

    <u>Greater Yellowstone Coalition</u>. 4 Apr. 2002.

    6 Nov. 2002 <http://greateryellowstone.org/

    snowmobiles_violations_ nr.html>.

Johnson, Shelli. "Greater Yellowstone Region Is a Snow-

    mobiling Mecca." <u>Yellowstone Journal</u> Winter 2002-03:

    6-7.

"Snowmobile Plan All Wet." Editorial. <u>Denver Post</u> 9 Nov.

    2002: B25- . <u>Colorado Newsstand</u>. ProQuest. Auraria

    Lib., Denver. 10 Nov. 2002 <http://proquest.umi.com>.

Works cited page uses MLA style.

47

Evaluating arguments

In your reading and in your own writing, evaluate all arguments for logic and fairness. Many arguments can stand up to critical scrutiny. Often, however, a line of argument that at first seems reasonable turns out to be fallacious, unfair, or both.

> **ON THE WEB**
>
> For links to resources that will help you evaluate arguments, go to
> **dianahacker.com/rules**
>
> and click on ▶ **Links Library**
>   ▶ **Critical Thinking**

47a Distinguish between reasonable and fallacious argumentative tactics.

A number of unreasonable argumentative tactics are known as *logical fallacies.* Most of the fallacies — such as hasty generalizations and false analogies — are misguided or dishonest uses of legitimate argumentative strategies. The examples in this section suggest when such strategies are reasonable and when they are not.

Generalizing (inductive reasoning)

Writers and thinkers generalize all the time. We look at a sample of data and conclude that data we have not observed will most likely conform to what we have seen before. From a spoonful of soup, we conclude just how salty the whole bowl will be. After numerous bad experiences with an airline, we decide to book future flights with one of its competitors instead.

When we draw a conclusion from an array of facts, we are engaged in inductive reasoning. Such reasoning deals in probability, not certainty. For a conclusion to be highly probable, it must be based on evidence that is sufficient, representative, and relevant. (See the chart on p. 361.)

The fallacy known as a *hasty generalization* is a conclusion based on insufficient or unrepresentative evidence.

HASTY GENERALIZATION

Deaths from drug overdoses in Metropolis have doubled in the past three years. Therefore, more Americans than ever are dying from drug abuse.

Data from one city do not justify a conclusion about the whole United States.

A *stereotype* is a hasty generalization about a group. Here are a few examples.

STEREOTYPES

Women are bad bosses.

Politicians are corrupt.

Asian students are exceptionally intelligent.

Stereotyping is common because of our human tendency to perceive selectively. We tend to see what we want to see; that is, we notice evidence confirming our already formed opinions and fail to notice evidence to the contrary. For example, if you have concluded that politicians are corrupt, your stereotype will be confirmed by news reports of legislators being indicted — even though every day the media describe conscientious officials serving the public honestly and well.

NOTE: Many hasty generalizations contain words like *all, ever, always,* and *never,* when qualifiers such as *most, many, usually,* and *seldom* would be more accurate.

Drawing analogies

An analogy points out a similarity between two things that are otherwise different. Analogies can be an effective means of arguing a point. In fact, our system of case law, which relies heavily on precedents, makes extensive use of reasoning by analogy. A prosecutor may argue, for example, that X is guilty because his actions resemble those of Y and Z, who were judged guilty in previous rulings. In response, the defense may maintain that the actions of X bear only a superficial resemblance to those of Y and Z and that in legally relevant respects they are in fact quite different.

It is not always easy to draw the line between a reasonable and an unreasonable analogy. At times, however, an analogy is clearly off-base, in which case it is called a *false analogy.*

FALSE ANALOGY

If we can put humans on the moon, we should be able to find a cure for the common cold.

The writer has falsely assumed that because two things are alike in one respect, they must be alike in others. Putting human beings on the moon and finding a cure for the common cold are both scientific challenges, but the technical problems confronting medical researchers are quite different from those solved by space scientists.

Tracing causes and effects

Demonstrating a connection between causes and effects is rarely a simple matter. For example, to explain why a chemistry course has a high failure rate, you would begin by listing possible causes: inadequate preparation of students, poor teaching, large class size, lack of qualified tutors, and so on. Next you would investigate each possible cause. To see whether inadequate preparation contributes to the high failure rate, for instance, you might compare the math and science backgrounds of successful and failing students. To see whether large class size is a contributing factor, you might run a pilot program of small classes and compare grades in the small classes with those in the larger ones. Only after investigating the possible causes would you be able to weigh the relative impact of each cause and suggest appropriate remedies.

Because cause-and-effect reasoning is so complex, it is not surprising that writers frequently oversimplify it. In particular, writers sometimes assume that because one event follows another, the first is the cause of the second. This common fallacy is known as *post hoc,* from the Latin *post hoc, ergo propter hoc,* meaning "after this, therefore because of this."

Testing inductive reasoning

Though inductive reasoning leads to probable and not absolute truth, you can assess a conclusion's likely probability by asking three questions. This chart shows how to apply those questions to a sample conclusion based on a survey.

CONCLUSION   The majority of students on our campus would subscribe to high-speed Internet access if it were available.

EVIDENCE   In a recent survey, 923 of 1,515 students questioned say they would subscribe to high-speed Internet access.

1. Is the evidence sufficient?
That depends. On a small campus (say, 3,000 students), the pool of students surveyed would be sufficient for market research, but on a large campus (say, 30,000), 1,515 students are only 5 percent of the population. If that 5 percent were known to be truly representative of the other 95 percent, however, even such a small sample would be sufficient (see question 2).

2. Is the evidence representative?
The evidence is representative if those responding to the survey reflect the characteristics of the entire student population: age, sex, level of technical expertise, amount of disposable income, and so on. If most of those surveyed are majoring in technical fields, for example, the researchers would be wise to question the survey's conclusion.

3. Is the evidence relevant?
The answer is yes. The survey question is directly linked to the conclusion. A question about the number of hours spent on the Internet, by contrast, would not be relevant, because it would not be about *subscribing to high-speed Internet access.*

POST HOC FALLACY

Since Governor Smith took office, unemployment of minorities in the state has decreased by 7 percent. Governor Smith should be applauded for reducing unemployment among minorities.

The writer must show that Governor Smith's policies are responsible for the decrease in unemployment; it is not enough to show that the decrease followed the governor's taking office.

Weighing options

Especially when reasoning about problems and solutions, writers must weigh options. To be fair, a writer should mention the full range of options, showing why one is superior to the others or might work well in combination with others.

It is unfair to suggest that there are only two alternatives when in fact there are more. Writers who set up a false choice between their preferred option and one that is clearly unsatisfactory are guilty of the *either . . . or* fallacy.

> **EITHER . . . OR FALLACY**
>
> Our current war against drugs has not worked. Either we should legalize drugs or we should turn the drug war over to our armed forces and let them fight it.

Clearly there are other options, such as increased funding for drug prevention and treatment.

Making assumptions

An assumption is a claim that is taken to be true — without the need of proof. Most arguments are based to some extent on assumptions, since writers rarely have the time and space to prove all of the conceivable claims on which the argument is based. For example, someone arguing about the best means of limiting population growth in developing countries might well assume that the goal of limiting population growth is worthwhile. For most audiences, there would be no need to articulate this assumption or to defend it.

There is a danger, however, in failing to spell out and prove a claim that is clearly controversial. Consider the following short argument, in which a key claim is missing.

> **ARGUMENT WITH MISSING CLAIM**
>
> Violent crime is increasing.
> Therefore, we should vigorously enforce the death penalty.

The writer seems to be assuming that the death penalty deters violent criminals — and that most audiences will agree. Obviously, neither is a safe assumption.

When a missing claim is an assertion that few would agree with, we say that a writer is guilty of a *non sequitur* (Latin for "does not follow").

NON SEQUITUR

Mary loves good food; therefore she will be an excellent chef.

Few people would agree with the missing claim — that lovers of good food always make excellent chefs.

Deducing conclusions (deductive reasoning)

When we deduce a conclusion, we — like Sherlock Holmes — put things together. We establish that a general principle is true, that a specific case is an example of that principle, and that therefore a particular conclusion is a certainty. In real life, such absolute reasoning rarely happens. Approximations of it, however, sometimes occur.

Deductive reasoning can often be structured in a three-step argument called a *syllogism*. The three steps are the major premise, the minor premise, and the conclusion.

1. Anything that increases radiation in the environment is dangerous to public health. (Major premise)
2. Nuclear reactors increase radiation in the environment. (Minor premise)
3. Therefore, nuclear reactors are dangerous to public health. (Conclusion)

The major premise is a generalization. The minor premise is a specific case. The conclusion follows from applying the generalization to the specific case.

Deductive arguments break down if one of the premises is not true or if the conclusion does not logically follow from the premises. In the following short argument, the major premise is very likely untrue.

UNTRUE PREMISE

The police do not give speeding tickets to people driving less than five miles per hour over the limit. Sam is driving fifty-nine miles per hour in a fifty-five-mile-per-hour zone. Therefore, the police will not give Sam a speeding ticket.

,e conclusion is true only if the premises are true. If the police sometimes give tickets for less than five-mile-per-hour violations, Sam cannot safely conclude that he will avoid a ticket.

In the following argument, both premises might be true, but the conclusion does not follow logically from them.

CONCLUSION DOES NOT FOLLOW

All members of our club ran in this year's Boston Marathon. Jay ran in this year's Boston Marathon. Therefore, Jay is a member of our club.

The fact that Jay ran the marathon is no guarantee that he is a member of the club. Presumably, many runners are nonmembers.

Assuming that both premises are true, the following argument holds up.

CONCLUSION FOLLOWS

All members of our club ran in this year's Boston Marathon. Jay is a member of our club. Therefore, Jay ran in this year's Boston Marathon.

47b Distinguish between legitimate and unfair emotional appeals.

There is nothing wrong with appealing to readers' emotions. After all, many issues worth arguing about have an emotional as well as a logical dimension. For example, in a newspaper article, writers George McGovern and Robert Dole have a good reason for tugging at readers' emotions: Their subject is hungry schoolchildren. In their introduction, McGovern and Dole appeal to readers' emotions by describing a scene from a documentary.

LEGITIMATE EMOTIONAL APPEAL

The most moving scene was filmed in a school where all students — even those who were too poor to pay for a meal — were required to go to the cafeteria at lunchtime. One 9- or 10-year-old boy was asked how he felt standing at the rear of the room watching his better-off classmates eat. Lowering his head, the boy confessed softly, "I'm ashamed."

As we all know, however, emotional appeals are frequently misused. Many of the arguments we see in the media, for instance, strive to win our sympathy rather than our intelligent agreement. A TV commercial suggesting that you will be thin and sexy if you drink a certain diet beverage is making a pitch to emotions. So is a political speech that recommends electing John D'Eau because he is a devoted husband and father who fought for his country in Desert Storm.

The following passage illustrates several types of unfair emotional appeals.

UNFAIR EMOTIONAL APPEALS

This progressive proposal to build a ski resort in the state park has been carefully researched by Western Trust, the largest bank in the state; furthermore, it is favored by a majority of the local merchants. The only opposition comes from narrow-minded, do-gooder environmentalists who care more about trees than they do about people; one of their leaders was actually arrested for disturbing the peace several years ago.

Words with strong positive or negative connotations, such as *progressive* and *do-gooder,* are examples of *biased language.* Attacking the persons who hold a belief (environmentalists) rather than refuting their argument is called *ad hominem,* a Latin term meaning "to the man." Associating a prestigious name (Western Trust) with the writer's side is called *transfer.* Claiming that an idea should be accepted because a large number of people are in favor (the majority of merchants) is called the *bandwagon appeal.* Bringing in irrelevant issues (the arrest) is a *red herring,* named after a trick used in fox hunts to mislead the dogs by dragging a smelly fish across the trail.

47c Judge how fairly a writer handles opposing views.

The way in which a writer deals with opposing views is telling. Some writers address the arguments of the opposition fairly, conceding points when necessary and countering others, all in a civil spirit. Other writers will do almost anything to win an argument: either ignoring opposing views altogether or misrepresenting such views and attacking their proponents.

Argument

In your own writing, you build credibility by addressing opposing arguments fairly. (See also 46f.) In your reading, you can assess the credibility of your sources by looking at how they deal with views not in agreement with their own.

Describing the views of others

Writers and politicians often deliberately misrepresent the views of others. One way they do this is by setting up a "straw man," a character so weak that he is easily knocked down. The *straw man* fallacy consists of an oversimplification or outright distortion of opposing views. For example, in a California debate over attempts to control the mountain lion population, pro-lion groups characterized their opponents as trophy hunters bent on shooting harmless lions and sticking them on the walls of their dens. In truth, such hunters were only one faction of those who saw a need to control the lion population.

In response to the District of Columbia's request for voting representation, some politicians have set up a straw man, as shown in the following example.

STRAW MAN FALLACY

Washington, DC, residents are lobbying for statehood. Giving a city such as the District of Columbia the status of a state would be unfair.

The straw man wants statehood. In fact, most District citizens are lobbying for voting representation in any form, not necessarily through statehood.

Quoting opposing views

Writers often quote the words of writers who hold opposing views. In general, this is a good idea, for it assures some level of fairness and accuracy. At times, though, both the fairness and accuracy are an illusion.

A source may be misrepresented when it is quoted out of context. All quotations are to some extent taken out of context, but a fair writer will explain that context to readers. To select a provocative sentence from a source and to ignore the more moderate sentences surrounding it is both unfair and misleading. Sometimes a source is deliberately distorted through the device of ellipsis dots. Ellipsis dots tell readers that words have been omitted from the original source. When those words are crucial to an author's meaning, omitting them is obviously unfair. (See also 39d.)

ORIGINAL SOURCE

Johnson's *History of the American West* is riddled with inaccuracies and astonishing in its blatantly racist description of the Indian wars. — B. R., reviewer

MISLEADING QUOTATION

According to B. R., Johnson's *History of the American West* is "astonishing in its . . . description of the Indian wars."

EXERCISE 47–1

Explain what is illogical in the following brief arguments. It may be helpful to identify the logical fallacy or fallacies by name. Answers to lettered sentences appear in the back of the book.

a. All of my blind dates have been embarrassing disasters, so I know this one will be too.
b. If you're old enough to vote, you're old enough to drink. Therefore, the drinking age should be lowered to eighteen.
c. This country has been run too long by old, out-of-date, out-of-touch, entrenched politicians protecting the special interests that got them elected.
d. It was possible to feed a family of four on $100 a week before Governor Leroy took office and drove up food prices.
e. If you're not part of the solution, you're part of the problem.

1. Whenever I wash my car, it rains. I have discovered a way to end all droughts — get all the people to wash their cars.
2. Either learn how to build a Web site or you won't be able to get a decent job after college.
3. College professors tend to be sarcastic. Three of my five professors this semester make sarcastic remarks.
4. Although Ms. Bell's book on Joe DiMaggio was well researched, I doubt that an Australian historian can contribute much to our knowledge of an American baseball player.
5. Self-righteous nonsmoking fanatics have eroded our basic individual freedoms by railroading the passage of oppressive anti-smoking laws that interfere with our natural right to make our own decisions.

6. If professional sports teams didn't pay athletes such high salaries, we wouldn't have so many kids breaking their legs at hockey and basketball camps.

7. Ninety percent of the students oppose a tuition increase; therefore, the board of trustees should not pass the proposed increase.

8. If the president had learned the lesson of Vietnam, he would realize that sending U.S. troops into a foreign country can only end in disaster.

9. A mandatory ten-cent deposit on bottles and cans will eliminate litter because everyone I know will return the containers for the money rather than throw them away.

10. Soliciting money to save whales and baby seals is irresponsible when thousands of human beings can't afford food and shelter.

Process

Design

Clarity

Grammar

Punctuation

Mechanics

Argument

Research

Basics

Research

Most college research assignments ask you to pose a question worth exploring, to read widely in search of possible answers, to interpret what you read, to draw reasoned conclusions, and to support those conclusions with valid and well-documented evidence.

Admittedly, the process takes time: time for researching and time for drafting, revising, and documenting the paper in the style recommended by your instructor, such as MLA (see 54) or APA (see 59). Before beginning a research project, you should set a realistic schedule of deadlines. For example, one student constructed the following schedule for a paper assigned on October 1 and due October 31.

SCHEDULE	FINISHED BY
1. Choose a possible topic.	October 2
2. Talk with a reference librarian and plan a search strategy.	3
3. Locate sources.	5
4. Read and take notes.	10
5. Decide on a tentative thesis and outline.	11
6. Draft the paper.	16
7. Visit the writing center to get help with ideas for revision.	17
8. Do further research if necessary.	20
9. Revise the paper.	25
10. Prepare a list of works cited.	26
11. Type and proofread the final draft.	28

48

Conducting research

Throughout this section, you will encounter examples related to three sample research papers:

— A paper on the issue of whether to limit use of cell phones while driving, written by a student in an English composition class (see pp. 448–55). The student, Angela Daly, uses the MLA (Modern Language Association) style of documentation.

— A paper on a scientific controversy about the ability of apes to acquire language skills, written by a student in a psychology class (see pp. 485–94). The student, Karen Shaw, uses the APA (American Psychological Association) style of documentation.

— A paper on the extent to which Civil War general Nathan Bedford Forrest can be held responsible for the Fort Pillow massacre, written by a student in a history class. The student, Ned Bishop, uses the CMS (*Chicago Manual of Style*) documentation system. Bishop's paper and guidelines for CMS documentation appear on the *Rules for Writers* Web site (dianahacker.com/rules).

48a Pose possible questions worth exploring.

Working within the guidelines of your assignment, pose a few questions that seem worth researching. Here, for example, are some preliminary questions jotted down by students enrolled in a variety of classes in different disciplines.

— Should the FCC broaden its definition of indecent programming to include violent programming?

— Which geological formations are the safest repositories for nuclear waste?

— Will a ban on human cloning threaten important medical research?

— What was Marcus Garvey's contribution to the fight for racial equality?

— How can governments and zoos help preserve China's endangered panda?

— Why was amateur archaeologist Heinrich Schliemann such a controversial figure in his own time?

As you formulate possible questions, make sure that they are appropriate lines of inquiry for a research paper. Choose questions that are narrow (not too broad), challenging (not too bland), and grounded (not too speculative).

Choosing a narrow question

If your initial question is too broad, given the length of the paper you plan to write, look for ways to restrict your focus. Here, for example, is how two students narrowed their initial questions.

TOO BROAD

— What are the hazards of fad diets?

— What causes homelessness?

NARROWER

— What are the hazards of liquid diets?

— How has deinstitutionalization of the mentally ill contributed to the problem of homelessness?

Choosing a challenging question

Your research paper will be more interesting to both you and your audience if you base it on an intellectually challenging line of inquiry. Avoid bland questions that fail to provoke thought or engage readers in a debate.

TOO BLAND

— What is obsessive-compulsive disorder?

— Where is wind energy being used?

CHALLENGING

— What treatments for obsessive-compulsive disorder show the most promise?

— Does investing in wind energy make economic sense?

You may well need to address a bland question in the course of answering a more challenging one. For example, if you were writing about promising treatments for obsessive-compulsive disorder, you would no doubt answer the question "What is obsessive-compulsive disorder?" at some point in your paper. It would be a mistake, however, to use the bland question as the focus for the whole paper.

Choosing a grounded question

Finally, you will want to make sure that your research question is grounded, not too speculative. Although speculative questions — such as those that address philosophical, ethical, or religious issues — are worth asking and may receive some attention in a research paper, they are inappropriate central questions. The central argument of a research paper should be grounded in facts; it should not be based entirely on beliefs.

TOO SPECULATIVE

— Is capital punishment moral?
— What is the difference between a just and an unjust law?

GROUNDED

— Does capital punishment deter crime?
— Should we adjust our laws so that penalties for possession of powdered cocaine and crack cocaine are comparable?

ON THE WEB

For an electronic exercise on choosing an appropriate research question, go to **dianahacker.com/rules**

and click on ▶ **Electronic Research Exercises**
▶ **E-ex 48-1**

48b Map out a search strategy.

A search strategy is a systematic plan for tracking down sources. To create a search strategy appropriate for your research question, consult a reference librarian and perhaps take a look at your library's Web site, which will give you an overview of available resources.

Getting help

Reference librarians are information specialists who can save you time by steering you toward relevant and reliable sources. With the help of an expert, you can make the best use of electronic databases, Web search engines, and other reference tools.

When you ask a reference librarian for help, be prepared to answer a number of questions:

— What is your assignment?
— In which academic discipline are you writing?

— What is your tentative research question?

— How long will the paper be?

— How much time can you spend on the project?

It's a good idea to bring a copy of the assignment with you.

In addition to speaking with a reference librarian, you might log on to your library's Web site, which will typically include links to the library's catalog and to a variety of databases and electronic sources. In addition, you may find links to other Web sites selected by librarians for their quality. The home page for Columbia University's library appears below.

Choosing an appropriate search strategy

There is no single search strategy that works for every topic. For some topics, it may be appropriate to search for information in newspapers, magazines, and Web sites. For others, the best sources might be found in scholarly journals and books

LIBRARY HOME PAGE

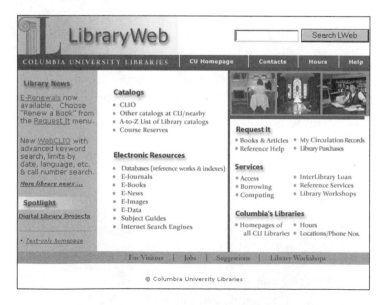

and specialized reference works. Still other topics might be enhanced by field research — interviews, surveys, or direct observation, for example.

With the help of a reference librarian, each of the students mentioned on pages 370–71 constructed a search strategy appropriate for his or her research question.

ANGELA DALY Angela Daly's topic, the dangers of using cell phones while driving, was so current that books were an unlikely source (by the time a book is published, it is already dated). To find up-to-date information on her topic, Daly decided to

- search a general database for articles in magazines, newspapers, and journals
- use Web search engines, such as *Google,* to locate relevant sites, online articles, and government publications

KAREN SHAW Karen Shaw's topic, the extent to which apes have learned language, has been the subject of psychological studies for many years, and it has been featured in the popular press (newspapers and magazines aimed at the general public). Thinking that both popular and scholarly works would be appropriate, Shaw decided to

- locate books through the library's online catalog
- search a general database for popular articles
- search a specialized database, *PsycINFO,* for scholarly articles

NED BISHOP Ned Bishop's topic, the role played by Nathan Bedford Forrest in the Fort Pillow massacre, is an issue that has been investigated and debated by professional historians. Given the nature of his historical topic, Ned Bishop decided to

- locate books through the library's online catalog
- search a specialized database, *America: History and Life,* for scholarly articles
- locate 1864 newspaper articles by using a print index
- search the Web for historical primary sources that have been posted online

48c To locate articles, search a database or consult a print index.

Libraries subscribe to a variety of electronic databases (sometimes called *periodical databases*). Though these are usually accessed through an Internet browser, they provide quality sources that aren't available for free on the Web.

What databases offer

Your library's databases will lead you to articles in newspapers, magazines, and scholarly or technical journals. Many of the databases also list references to additional sources, such as scholarly books, government documents, and dissertations. Though each library is unique, here are some database services you may find available:

> *InfoTrac, EBSCOhost,* or *ProQuest.* Most libraries have one of these database services, which offer access to multidisciplinary periodical databases covering newspaper, magazine, and journal articles.
>
> *FirstSearch.* A collection of specialized databases, including *ArticleFirst* for journal articles and *WorldCat,* a huge catalog of library collections.
>
> *Lexis-Nexis.* A collection of databases particularly strong for current news and business and legal information.

Your library also may have specific databases that focus on a particular subject area, such as the following:

> *ERIC.* An education database.
>
> *MLA Bibliography.* A database of literary criticism.
>
> *MEDLINE.* A database of medical research.
>
> *PsycINFO.* A psychology research database.

Many databases include the full text of at least some articles; others list only citations or citations with short summaries called *abstracts.* When the full text is not available, the citation will give you enough information to track down an article at your library or through interlibrary loan.

Refining searches in databases

Most electronic databases allow you to combine search terms in a variety of ways. The help feature of a database will give you specific advice about search techniques. Some of the most common ways to refine a search are listed here.

— Search for two or more terms:

apes AND language

— Search for a word string by putting it in quotation marks:

"American Sign Language"

— Search for any one of related terms:

"pygmy chimpanzee" OR bonobo OR Kanzi

— Exclude a term from a search:

bonobo NOT Kanzi

— Substitute a "wild card" symbol for letters that might vary:

synta* [to search for *syntax* or *syntactical*]

Many databases also allow you to restrict a search by date of publication (for example, within the last year).

How to search a database

To find articles on your topic in a database, you will most likely start with a keyword search. If the first keyword you try results in no matches, experiment with other terms. If you retrieve too many matches, narrow your search by using one of the strategies listed in the chart on this page.

For her paper on the dangers of using a cell phone while driving, Angela Daly conducted a keyword search in a general periodical database. She typed in *"cell phones" AND driving;* her search brought up thirty-six possible articles, some of which looked promising (see the search results screen on p. 378).

When to use a print index

If you want to search for articles published before the 1980s, you may need to turn to a print index. For example, Ned Bishop

DATABASE SCREEN: RESULTS OF A KEYWORD SEARCH

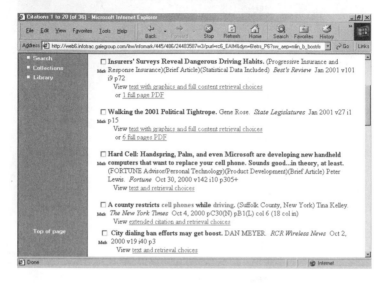

consulted the *New York Times Index* to locate newspaper articles written in April 1864, just after the battle at Fort Pillow. To find older magazine articles, consult the *Readers' Guide to Periodical Literature* or *Poole's Index to Periodical Literature* or ask a librarian for help.

48d To locate books, consult the library's catalog.

The books your library owns are listed in its computer catalog, along with other resources such as videos. You can search the catalog by author, title, or subject. Most of the time you will want to search by subject, using what is called a *keyword search*. A keyword search will not search the full text of books but only the title, subject headings, and sometimes tables of contents.

When a first search yields too few results, try searching by a broader topic. Then, once you find a book that looks on target, read the subject headings listed for it; they may be good search terms to try. When your search retrieves too many results, use the strategies for refining a search listed in the chart on page 377. Some catalogs also allow you to limit a search to books published after a certain date, a technique useful for excluding outdated books.

When Karen Shaw, whose topic was apes and language, entered the keyword search *apes AND language* into the computer catalog, she retrieved a list of twelve books. The complete record for one of those books is shown below. She wrote down the call number — the book's address on the library shelves. As she worked, Shaw noticed that several books on her topic were shelved in the same area.

48e To locate a wide variety of sources, turn to the Web.

For some (but not all) topics, the Web is an excellent resource. For example, government agencies post information on the Web, and the sites of many organizations are filled with information about the issues they cover. Museums and libraries often post digital versions of primary sources, such as historical documents, on the Web. However, secondary sources, such as

COMPUTER CATALOG SCREEN: COMPLETE RECORD FOR A BOOK

Author	Savage-Rumbaugh, E. Sue, 1946-
Title	Apes, language, and the human mind / Sue Savage-Rumbaugh, Stuart G. Shanker, Talbot J. Taylor
Publisher	New York : Oxford University Press, 1998

LOCATION	CALL #	STATUS
Main General	QL737.P96 S254 1998	DUE 06-27-01

Descript.	x, 244 p. : ill. ; 24 cm
Subject	Bonobo -- Psychology
	Kanzi (Bonobo)
	Human-animal communication
	Language acquisition
	Neurolinguistics
Alt author	Shanker, Stuart
	Taylor, Talbot J
Bibliog.	Includes bibliographical references (p. 233-239) and index
ISBN	0195109864 (alk. paper)
LCCN	98014600

many scholarly articles and literary criticism, may be available only in print form. Even online versions of such sources are accessible only to subscribers, such as libraries, that pay a fee.

Although the Web can be a rich source of information, some of which can't be found anywhere else, it lacks quality control. As you probably know, anyone can publish on the Web, so you'll need to evaluate online sources with special care (see 49c).

This section describes the following Web resources: search engines, directories, archives, government and news sites, and online discussions.

ON THE WEB

For live links to the sources listed in this section, go to
dianahacker.com/rules

and click on ▶ **Links Library**
        ▶ **Conducting Research**

Search engines

Search engines take your search terms and seek matches among millions of Web pages. Some search engines go into more depth than others, but none can search the entire Web. Often it is a good idea to try more than one search engine, since each locates sources in its own way.

For current information about search engines, visit *Search Engine Watch* at <http://www.searchenginewatch.com>. This site classifies search engines, evaluates them, and provides updates on new search features. Following are some popular search engines:

    Google <http://www.google.com>

    All the Web <http://www.alltheweb.com>

    AltaVista <http://www.altavista.com>

    HotBot <http://www.hotbot.lycos.com>

When using a search engine, focus your search as narrowly as possible to prevent getting an unmanageable number of

Restricting searches in Web search engines

Although search engines vary, most allow you to restrict a search in several ways. Some of the most common ways to restrict a search are listed here.

- Use combinations of keywords to search for sites containing two or more terms:

  apes language Kanzi

- Use word strings, alone or in combination, to search for sites containing the exact strings:

  "American Sign Language"
  "American Sign Language" "pygmy chimpanzees"

- Exclude words from the search:

  apes language NOT orangutan

- Restrict by date:

  past six months

- Restrict by domain:

  .edu [or .gov or .org]

- Restrict by keyword location:

  in title [or in the URL]

matches (often called *hits*). Some of the most common ways to restrict a search are given in the chart on this page. For her paper on using cell phones while driving, Angela Daly had difficulty restricting the number of hits. When she typed "*cell phones*" and *driving* into a search engine, she got over 40,000 matches. To narrow her search, Daly tried "*cell phones while driving*" and *accidents*. The result was 433 matches, still too many, so she restricted one of her next searches to government-sponsored sites with URLs ending in *.gov*. The resulting list consisted of just 11 items, including promising sites sponsored by the National Highway Traffic Safety Administration (see the search results screen on p. 382).

SEARCH ENGINE SCREEN: RESULTS OF AN ADVANCED SEARCH

Directories

Unlike search engines, which are powered by software known as *bots,* directories have a human touch. Directories are put together by information specialists who arrange sites by topic: education, health, public issues, and so on. Many search engines, such as *Google* and *Lycos,* offer a directory as an optional means of conducting a search.

Some directories are more selective and therefore more useful for scholarly research than the directories that typically accompany a search engine. For example, the directory for the *Scout Report Archives* was created with a research audience in mind; it includes annotations that are both descriptive and evaluative. The following list includes directories especially useful for scholarly research:

Infomine <http://infomine.ucr.edu >

Scout Report Archives <http://scout.wisc.edu/archives >

Librarian's Index to the Internet <http://www.lii.org >

World Wide Web Virtual Library <http://www.vlib.org >

Archives

Archives contain the texts of poems, books, speeches, political cartoons, and historically significant documents such as the Declaration of Independence and the Emancipation Proclamation. The materials in these sites are usually limited to older works because of copyright laws. The following online archives are impressive collections:

American Memory <http://memory.loc.gov>

Avalon Project <http://www.yale.edu/lawweb/avalon/avalon.htm>

Electronic Text Center <http://etext.lib.virginia.edu>

Eurodocs <http://library.byu.edu/~rdh/eurodocs>

Internet History Sourcebooks <http://www.fordham.edu/halsall>

The Making of America <http://moa.umdl.umich.edu>

Government and news sites

For current topics, both government and news sites can prove useful. Many government agencies at every level provide online information. Government-maintained sites include resources such as legal texts, facts and statistics, government reports, and searchable reference databases. Here are just a few government sites (notice that the last one will lead you to others):

Census Bureau <http://www.census.gov>

Fedstats <http://www.fedstats.gov>

Thomas Legislative Information <http://thomas.loc.gov>

United Nations <http://www.un.org>

U.S. Federal Government Agencies Directory <http://www.lib.lsu.edu/gov/fedgov.html>

Many news organizations offer up-to-date information on the Web. However, archived information may be available only for a fee; check with your library to see if it subscribes to a news archive that you can access at no charge. The following are some news sites on the Web:

CNN <http://www.cnn.com>

Kidon Media-Link <http://www.kidon.com/media-link/index.html>

NewsLink <http://newslink.org>

New York Times <http://www.nytimes.com>

Online discussions

The Web offers various ways of communicating with experts and others who share an interest in your topic. Some online discussions resemble voice mail: Messages are posted and retrieved at different times. Others are like talking on the phone: They take place in real time.

Discussions that do not take place in real time, known as *asynchronous communications,* include e-mail discussion lists (sometimes called LISTSERVs), Usenet newsgroups, Web forums (chat pages), and bulletin boards. To find publicly available lists, go to one of these Web sites:

CataList <http://www.lsoft.com/catalist.html>

Directory of Scholarly and Professional E-Conferences <http://www.kovacs.com/directory/>

Topica <http://www.liszt.com>

Tile.Net <http://tile.net/lists/>

Google Groups <http://groups.google.com/>

Real-time discussions, known as *synchronous communications,* include MUDs, MOOs, and chat rooms. Some are ongoing forums; others are set up to allow a group of people to communicate about a particular project or issue at a specific time.

NOTE: Be aware that many of the people you contact will not be experts on your topic. Although you are more likely to find serious and worthwhile commentary in moderated mailing lists and scholarly discussion forums than in more freewheeling newsgroups, it is difficult to guarantee the credibility of anyone you meet online.

48f Consider other research tools.

In addition to articles, books, and Web sources, you may want to consult reference works such as encyclopedias and almanacs. Bibliographies (lists of works written on a topic) and citations in scholarly works are other useful tools.

Reference works

The reference section of your library holds both general and specialized encyclopedias, handbooks, atlases, and biographical references. These sources are good places to find facts, statistics, and overviews of topics. Check with a reference librarian to see which works are most appropriate for your topic. A librarian will also be able to tell you which works are available in electronic format.

GENERAL REFERENCE WORKS Here are a few frequently used general references that you might want to turn to:

Encyclopedia Americana

The New Encyclopaedia Britannica

The Oxford English Dictionary

Statistical Abstract of the United States

National Geographic Atlas of the World

Webster's New Biographical Dictionary

NOTE: Although general encyclopedias are often a good place to find background about your topic, you should rarely use them as sources for your final paper. Most instructors expect you to rely on more specialized sources.

SPECIALIZED REFERENCE WORKS Most specialized reference works contain material written by eminent scholars in the field. Works such as *The New Grove Dictionary of Music and Musicians,* the *McGraw-Hill Encyclopedia of Science and Technology,* and the *Encyclopedia of Bioethics* can provide solid overviews of topics within those subject areas.

ON THE WEB

For lists of specialized reference works, organized by academic discipline, go to **dianahacker.com/rules**

and click on ▶ **Research and Documentation Online**
▶ **Finding Sources**

Bibliographies and scholarly citations

Bibliographies are lists of works written on a particular topic. They include enough information about each work (author's name, title, publication data) so that you can locate the book or article. In some cases bibliographies are annotated: They contain abstracts giving a brief overview of each work's contents.

In addition to stand-alone, book-length bibliographies, scholarly books and articles list the works the author has cited, usually at the end of an article or a book. These lists can be useful shortcuts. For example, most of the scholarly articles Karen Shaw consulted contained citations to related research studies; through these citations, Shaw quickly located additional relevant sources on her topic, apes and language.

48g Consider doing field research.

For a composition class, you might want to visit your local historical society to research a paper on some aspect of your town's early history, such as the role it played in the underground railroad. For a sociology class, you might decide to study campus trends in classroom participation: Which students are most, and least, involved in class discussions, and why? At work you might need to learn how food industry executives are responding to reports that their companies have cut portions of some food products while increasing prices. Projects like these may be enhanced by, and sometimes centered on, your own field research.

49

Evaluating sources

With electronic search tools, you can often locate dozens or even hundreds of potential sources for your topic — far more than you will have time to read. Your challenge will be to zero in on a reasonable number of quality sources, those truly worthy of your time and attention. Later, once you have decided on some sources worth consulting, your challenge will be to read them with an open mind and a critical eye.

49a   Select sources worth your time and attention.

Sections 48c, 48d, and 48e show how to restrict the number of "hits" that come up in databases, in the library's online book catalog, and in search engines. This section shows how to scan through the lists of hits looking for those that seem most promising.

Scanning lists of hits in a database

Most databases, such as those offered by *ProQuest* and *Lexis-Nexis*, list at least the following information, which can help you decide if a source is relevant, current, scholarly enough, and neither too short nor too long for your purposes.

Title and brief description (How relevant?)

Date (How current?)

Name of periodical (How scholarly?)

Length (How extensive in coverage?)

For example, consider just a few of the hits Ned Bishop came up with when he consulted a general database in search of articles on the Fort Pillow massacre, using the search term "*Fort Pillow.*"

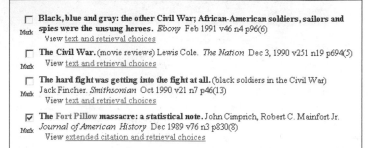

By scanning the titles, Bishop saw that only one contained the term *Fort Pillow*. This title and the name of the periodical — *Journal of American History* — suggested that the source was scholarly. The 1989 publication date was not a problem, since currency is not necessarily a key issue for historical topics. The article's length (eight pages) is given in parentheses at the end of the citation. While the article may seem short, the topic — a statistical note — is narrow enough to ensure adequate depth of coverage. Bishop decided the article was worth consulting.

Bishop chose not to consult the other sources. The first is a brief article in a popular magazine, the second is a movie review, and the third surveys a topic that is far too broad, "black soldiers in the Civil War."

Scanning lists of hits in a book catalog

The library's book catalog will usually give you a fairly short list of hits. A book's title and date of publication will often be your first clues as to whether the book is worth consulting. If a title looks interesting, you can click on it for further information: the book's subject matter and its length, for example.

Scanning lists of hits in a search engine

Anyone can publish on the Web, and unreliable sites often masquerade as legitimate sources of information. As you scan through a list of hits, look for the following clues about the probable relevance, currency, and reliability of a site — but be prepared to be disappointed, as the clues are by no means foolproof.

Title, keywords, and lead-in text (How relevant?)

A date (How current?)

An indication of the site's sponsor or purpose (How reliable?)

The URL, especially the domain name (How relevant? How reliable?)

The visual on this page shows a few of the hits that Karen Shaw retrieved after typing the keywords *apes* and *language* into a search engine; she limited her search to works with these words in the title.

Shaw rejected the first source because it was just a message in an online mailing list, and she skipped the third one because it sounded too promotional. The last source looked promising because of its university affiliation, though in fact it turned out to be a student paper.

Shaw was uncertain about the second hit, which was a commercial site, but she clicked on it. It was an impressive site, nicely designed, well written, and documented with footnotes and a bibliography; the only problem was that its author was nowhere to be found. Reluctantly, she decided not to use the information from the site in her paper.

LINGUIST List 7.144: Systemic-Functional WWW, **Apes** & **Language**
LINGUIST List 7.144. Tue Jan 30 1996. FYI: Systemic-Functional WWW,
Apes & **Language**. ... Message 2: **Apes** & **Language** syllabus. ...
www.linguistlist.org/issues/7/7-144.html - 11k - Cached - Similar pages

Can **Apes** Acquire **Language**?
Can **Apes** Acquire **Language**? Why have people embarked
on these Ape language studies? Some if ...
www.fortunecity.com/greenfield/twyford/73/thoughts.html - 11k - Cached - Similar pages

YORK UNIVERSITY PROFESSOR'S BOOK PROVES **APES** CAPABLE OF ...
... to learn more about **language** in autistic and mentally handicapped children are
among those applauding the findings of **Apes**, **Language**, and the Human Mind. ...
www.yorku.ca/ycom/release/archive/080498.htm - 9k - Cached - Similar pages

Language in **Apes**
... Adams has some perceptive comments about "this business of trying to teach **apes language**"
(Adams & Carwardine 1993: 23). While sitting four feet away from a ...
Description: Introductory overview of ape **language** research, its history and its practice.
Category: Science > Social Sciences > Anthropology > Enculturated Apes
www.math.uwaterloo.ca/~dmswitze/apelang.html - 34k - Cached - Similar pages

49b Read with an open mind and a critical eye.

As you begin reading the sources you have chosen, keep an open mind. Do not let your personal beliefs prevent you from listening to new ideas and opposing viewpoints. Your research question — not a snap judgment about the question — should guide your reading. When you read critically, you are not necessarily judging an author's work harshly; you are simply examining its assumptions, assessing its evidence, and weighing its conclusions.

Distinguishing between primary and secondary sources

As you begin assessing evidence in a text, consider whether you are reading a primary or a secondary source. Primary sources are original documents such as letters, diaries, legislative bills, laboratory studies, field research reports, and eyewitness accounts. Secondary sources are commentaries on primary sources. A primary source for Ned Bishop was Nathan Bedford Forrest's official report on the Battle of Fort Pillow. Bishop also consulted a number of secondary sources, some of which relied heavily on primary sources such as letters.

Although a primary source is not necessarily more reliable than a secondary source, it has the advantage of being a firsthand account. Naturally, you can better evaluate what a secondary source says if you have first read any primary sources it discusses.

Being alert for signs of bias

Both in print and online, some sources are more objective than others. If you were exploring the conspiracy theories surrounding John F. Kennedy's assassination, for example, you wouldn't look to a supermarket tabloid, such as the *National Enquirer,* for answers. Even publications that are considered reputable can be editorially biased. For example, *USA Today, National Review,* and *Ms.* are all credible sources, but they are also likely to interpret events quite differently from one another. If you are uncertain about a periodical's special interests, check *Magazines for Libraries.* To check the reputation of a book, consult *Book Review Digest.* A reference librarian can help you locate these resources.

Like publishers, some authors are more objective than others. No authors are altogether objective, of course, since they are

Evaluating all sources

CHECKING FOR SIGNS OF BIAS

- Does the author or publisher have political leanings or religious views that could affect objectivity?
- Is the author or publisher associated with a special-interest group, such as Greenpeace or the National Rifle Association, that might see only one side of an issue?
- How fairly does the author treat opposing views?
- Does the author's language show signs of bias?

ASSESSING AN ARGUMENT

- What is the author's central claim or thesis?
- How does the author support this claim—with relevant and sufficient evidence or with just a few anecdotes or emotional examples?
- Are statistics accurate? Have they been used fairly? (It is possible to "lie" with statistics by using them selectively or by omitting mathematical details.)
- Are any of the author's assumptions questionable?
- Does the author consider opposing arguments and refute them persuasively? (See 47c.)
- Does the author fall prey to any logical fallacies? (See 47a.)

human beings with their own life experiences, values, and beliefs. But if you have reason to believe that an author is particularly biased, you will want to assess his or her arguments with special care. For a list of questions worth asking, see the chart at the top of this page.

Assessing the author's argument

In nearly all subjects worth writing about, there is some element of argument, so don't be surprised to encounter experts who disagree. When you find areas of disagreement, you will want to read your sources' arguments with special care, testing them with your own critical intelligence. Questions such as those in the chart on this page can help you weigh the strengths and weaknesses of each author's argument.

49c Assess Web sources with special care.

As you have no doubt discovered, Web sources can be deceptive. Sophisticated-looking sites can be full of dubious information, and the identities of those who created a site are often hidden, along with their motives for having created it. Even hate sites may be cleverly disguised to look legitimate. In contrast, sites with reliable information can stand up to careful scrutiny. For a checklist on evaluating Web sources, see below.

Evaluating Web sources

CAUTION: If the authorship and the sponorship of a site are both unclear, be extremely suspicious of the site.

AUTHORSHIP

- Is there an author? You may need to do some clicking and scrolling to find the author's name. Check the home page or an "about this site" link.
- Can you tell whether an author is knowledgeable and credible? Look for a home page, which may provide evidence of the author's expertise.

SPONSORSHIP

- Who, if anyone, sponsors the site? The sponsor of a site is often named and described on the home page.
- What does the domain name tell you? The domain name often specifies the type of group hosting the site: commercial (.com), educational (.edu), nonprofit (.org), governmental (.gov), military (.mil), or network (.net).

PURPOSE AND AUDIENCE

- Why was the site created: To argue a position? To sell a product? To inform readers?
- Who is the site's intended audience?

CURRENCY

- How current is the site? Check for the date of publication or the latest update.
- How current are the site's links? If many of the links no longer work, the site may be too dated for your purposes.

In researching her topic on the dangers of using a cell phone while driving, Angela Daly encountered sites that raised her suspicions. In particular, some sites were sponsored by the wireless communications industry, which has an obvious interest in preventing laws restricting use of their products. Even a site sponsored by the Harvard Center for Risk Analysis seemed somewhat suspect, since the wireless industry funded the center's study concluding that the risk of using a cell phone while driving is low compared with other risks.

EVALUATING A WEB SITE

① The source is within a site sponsored by the National Conference of State Legislatures, an organization of state lawmakers and members of their staffs who track state-level policy issues and activity. The domain .org marks this sponsor as a nonprofit organization.

② Clear dates of publication and update show currency.

③ The author is a credible expert whose credentials can be verified. Contact information is given at the end of the article.

Knowing that the creator of a site could be biased is not sufficient reason, however, to reject the site's information out of hand. For example, the Harvard Center for Risk Analysis offered evidence that was worth considering. Nevertheless, when you know something about the creator of a site and have a sense of a site's purpose, you will be in a good position to evaluate the likely worth of its information. Consider, for example, the authors and the purposes of the two sites pictured on page 393 and below. Not surprisingly, Angela Daly decided that the first Web site was more useful for her project than the second.

EVALUATING A WEB SITE

1 The site is sponsored by a law firm that specializes in personal-injury law.

2 The relative size and placement of the toll-free number suggests the site's intended audience: injured people seeking to file a personal-injury lawsuit (and probably not researchers seeking objective information about relevant legislation or even statistics).

3 The site mentions an article in a reputable journal, but ultimately the purpose of the site is to sell a service.

ON THE WEB

For links to resources that will help you evaluate s(
on the Web, go to **dianahacker.com/rules**

and click on ▶ **Links Library**
▶ **Conducting Research**

396

50

Managing information; avoiding plagiarism

An effective researcher is a good record keeper. Whether you decide to keep records on paper or on your computer — or both — your challenge as a researcher will be to find systematic ways of managing information. More specifically, you will need methods for maintaining a working bibliography (see 50a), keeping track of source materials (see 50b), and taking notes without plagiarizing (stealing from) your sources (see 50c).

50a Maintain a working bibliography.

Keep a record of any sources you decide to consult. You will need this record, called a *working bibliography,* when you compile the list of works cited (or, for APA, your reference list) that will appear at the end of your paper. (The format of this list depends on the documentation style you are using. For MLA style, see 54; for APA style, see 59.) Your working bibliography will probably contain more sources than you will actually use and put in your list of works cited.

Researchers once recorded bibliographic information on 3″ × 5″ note cards. Today, however, most researchers print out this information from the library's computer catalog, periodical databases, and the Web. The printouts usually contain all the information you need to create the list of works cited. That information is given in the chart on page 396.

ᴀ*Research Guide*

Information for a working bibliography

For books

- All authors; any editors or translators
- Title and subtitle
- Edition (if not the first)
- Publication information: city, publisher, and date

For periodical articles

- All authors of the article
- Title and subtitle of the article
- Title of the magazine, journal, or newspaper
- Date and volume, issue, and page numbers, if relevant

For articles from electronic databases

- Publication information for the source
- Name of the database (and item number, if relevant)
- Name of the subscription service and its URL, if available
- Library where you retrieved the source
- Date you retrieved the source

For Web sources

- All authors, editors, or translators of the work
- Editor or compiler of the Web site, if relevant
- Title and subtitle of the source and title of the longer work (if applicable)
- Publication information for a print version of the source, if available
- Title of the site, if available
- Date of publication (or latest update), if available
- Any page or paragraph numbers
- Name of the site's sponsoring organization
- Date you visited the site and the site's URL

NOTE: For the exact bibliographic format to be used in the final paper, see 54b (MLA) or 59b (APA).

CAUTION: For Web sources, some bibliographic information may not be available, but spend time looking for it before assuming that it doesn't exist. Look especially for the author's name, the date of publication (or latest update), and the name of any sponsoring organization. Such information should not be omitted unless it is genuinely unavailable.

50b Keep track of source materials.

The best way to keep track of source materials is to photocopy them or print them out (except, of course, for books). Working with photocopies and printouts — as opposed to relying on memory or hastily written notes — has several benefits. It saves you time spent in the library. It allows you to highlight key passages, perhaps even color-coding passages to reflect topics in your outline. And you can annotate the text in the margins and get a head start on the process of taking notes. Finally, working with hard copy reduces the chances of unintentional plagiarism, since you will be able to compare your use of a source in your paper with the actual source, not just with your notes (see 50c).

NOTE: It's especially important to keep hard copies of Web sources, which may change or even become inaccessible. Make sure that your copy includes the site's URL and the date of access, information needed for your list of works cited.

When much of their material comes from the Web, some researchers prefer to organize their source material online — by downloading relevant material into files. This can be an efficient method of working, but it carries dangers. Although it is easy to patch information from downloaded files into your own paper, do so with caution. Some researchers have unwittingly plagiarized their sources because they lost track of which words came from sources and which were their own. To prevent unintentional plagiarism, put quotation marks around any text that you have patched into your own work. In addition, you might use a different color for text from your source so it stands out unmistakably as someone else's (not your own) writing.

50c   As you take notes, avoid unintentional plagiarism.

You will discover that it is amazingly easy to borrow too much language from a source as you take notes. Do not allow this to happen. You are guilty of the academic offense known as *plagiarism* if you half-copy the author's sentences — either by mixing the author's phrases with your own without using quotation marks or by plugging your synonyms into the author's sentence structure. (For examples of this kind of plagiarism, see 52 and 57.)

To prevent unintentional borrowing, resist the temptation to look at the source as you take notes — except when you are quoting. Keep the source close by so you can check for accuracy, but don't try to put ideas in your own words with the source's sentences in front of you.

There are three kinds of note taking: summarizing, paraphrasing, and quoting. As you take notes, be sure to include exact page references, since you will need the page numbers later if you use the information in your paper.

ESL

If you come from a culture that stresses memorization and recitation of classic texts, you may not see the need to document such sources — or even to use quotation marks to indicate that you are using the exact words of your source. In the United States, however, written texts and any original ideas they contain are viewed as the author's property. When using an author's property, writers must follow certain conventions or risk being charged with the ethical and legal offense known as *plagiarism.*

Summarizing without plagiarizing

A summary condenses information, perhaps reducing a chapter to a short paragraph or a paragraph to a single sentence. A summary should be written in your own words; if you use phrases from the source, put them in quotation marks.

Here is a passage from an original source that John Garcia read when researching a paper on mountain lions. Following the passage is Garcia's summary of the source.

ORIGINAL SOURCE

In some respects, the increasing frequency of mountain lion encounters in California has as much to do with a growing *human* population as it does with rising mountain lion numbers.

The scenic solitude of the western ranges is prime cougar habitat, and it is falling swiftly to the developer's spade. Meanwhile, with their ideal habitat already at its carrying capacity, mountain lions are forcing younger cats into less suitable terrain, including residential areas. Add that cougars have generally grown bolder under a lengthy ban on their being hunted, and an unsettling scenario begins to emerge.

— Rychnovsky, "Clawing into Controversy," p. 40

SUMMARY

Source: Rychnovsky, "Clawing into Controversy" (40)

Encounters between mountain lions and humans are on the rise in California because increasing numbers of lions are competing for a shrinking habitat. As the lions' wild habitat shrinks, older lions force younger lions into residential areas. These lions have lost some of their fear of humans because of a ban on hunting.

Paraphrasing without plagiarizing

Like a summary, a paraphrase is written in your own words; but whereas a summary reports significant information in fewer words than the source, a paraphrase retells the information in roughly the same number of words. If you retain occasional choice phrases from the source, use quotation marks so you will know later which phrases are not your own.

As you read the following paraphrase of the original source on pages 398–99, notice that the language is significantly different from that in the original.

PARAPHRASE

Source: Rychnovsky, "Clawing into Controversy" (40)

Californians are encountering mountain lions more frequently because increasing numbers of humans and a rising population of lions are competing for the same territory. Humans have moved into mountainous regions once dominated by the lions, and the wild habitat that is left cannot sustain the current lion population. Therefore, the older lions are forcing younger lions out of the wilderness and into residential areas. And because of a ban on hunting, these younger lions have become bolder--less fearful of encounters with humans.

Using quotation marks to avoid plagiarizing

A quotation consists of the exact words from a source. In your notes, put all quoted material in quotation marks; do not trust yourself to remember later which words, phrases, and passages you have quoted and which are your own. When you quote, be sure to copy the words of your source exactly, including punctuation and capitalization. In the following example, John Garcia quotes from the original source on pages 398–99.

QUOTATION

> Source: Rychnovsky, "Clawing into Controversy" (40)
>
> Rychnovsky explains that because the mountain lions' natural habitat can no longer sustain the population, older lions "are forcing younger cats into less suitable terrain, including residential areas."

WRITING MLA PAPERS

Most English instructors and some humanities instructors will ask you to document sources with the Modern Language Association (MLA) system of citations described in section 54. When writing an MLA paper that is based on sources, you face three main challenges in addition to documenting your sources: (1) supporting a thesis, (2) avoiding plagiarism, and (3) integrating quotations and other source material.

Examples in this section are drawn from research two students conducted on the use of cell phones while driving. Angela Daly's research paper on this topic appears on pages 448–55. Daly calls for legislation restricting use of cell phones while driving. Paul Levi's paper opposing such legislation appears on the companion Web site for *Rules for Writers* (see p. 447 for the URL).

NOTE: For cross-disciplinary advice on finding and evaluating sources and on managing information, see sections 48–50.

51

Supporting a thesis

Most research assignments ask you to form a thesis, or main idea, and to support that thesis with well-organized evidence.

51a Form a tentative thesis.

Once you have read a variety of sources and considered all sides of your issue, you are ready to form a tentative thesis: a one-sentence (or occasionally a two-sentence) statement of your central idea. In a research paper, your thesis will answer the central research question you posed earlier (see 48a). Here, for example, is Angela Daly's research question and her tentative thesis statement.

DALY'S RESEARCH QUESTION

Should states regulate use of cell phones in moving vehicles?

DALY'S TENTATIVE THESIS

States should regulate use of cell phones on the road because many drivers are using the phones irresponsibly and causing accidents.

Once you have written a rough draft and perhaps done more reading, you may decide to revise your tentative thesis, as Daly did.

DALY'S REVISED THESIS

States must regulate use of cell phones on the road because drivers using phones are seriously impaired and because laws on negligent and reckless driving are not sufficient to punish offenders.

The thesis usually appears at the end of the introductory paragraph. To read Angela Daly's thesis in the context of her introduction, see page 448.

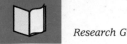

ON THE WEB

For an electronic exercise on thesis statements in MLA research papers, go to **dianahacker.com/rules**

and click on ▶ **Electronic Research Exercises**
▶ **E-ex 54-1**

51b Organize your evidence.

The body of your paper will consist of evidence in support of your thesis. Instead of getting tangled up in a complex, formal outline, sketch an informal plan that organizes your evidence in bold strokes. Angela Daly, for example, used this simple plan to outline the structure of her argument in support of the thesis mentioned earlier:

— Drivers distracted by cellular phones are seriously impaired.

— Current laws on negligent and reckless driving are not adequate.

— In the United States, laws must be passed on the state level.

Once you have written a rough draft, a more formal outline can be a useful way to shape the complexities of your argument. See 1d for an example.

52

Avoiding plagiarism

Your research paper is a collaboration between you and your sources. To be fair and ethical, you must acknowledge your debt to the writers of those sources. If you don't, you are guilty of plagiarism, a serious academic offense.

Three different acts are considered plagiarism: (1) failing to cite quotations and borrowed ideas, (2) failing to enclose borrowed language in quotation marks, and (3) failing to put summaries and paraphrases in your own words.

ON THE WEB

For electronic exercises on avoiding plagiarism in MLA papers, go to **dianahacker.com/rules**

and click on ▶ **Electronic Research Exercises**
            ▶ **E-ex 52-1 through 52-3**

52a Cite quotations and borrowed ideas.

You must of course cite all direct quotations. You must also cite any ideas borrowed from a source: summaries and paraphrases; statistics and other specific facts; and visuals such as cartoons, graphs, or diagrams.

The only exception is common knowledge—general information that your readers may know or could easily locate in any number of reference sources. For example, it is well known that Toni Morrison won the Nobel Prize in literature in 1993 and that Emily Dickinson published only a handful of her many poems during her life. As a rule, when you have seen certain general information repeatedly in your reading, you don't need to cite it. However, when information has appeared in only a few sources, when it is highly specific (as with statistics), or when it is controversial, you should cite it.

The Modern Language Association recommends a system of in-text citations. Here, briefly, is how the MLA citation system usually works:

1. The source is introduced by a signal phrase that names its author.
2. The material being cited is followed by a page number in parentheses.
3. At the end of the paper, a list of works cited (arranged alphabetically according to authors' last names) gives complete publication information about the source.

IN-TEXT CITATION

According to Donald Redelmeier and Robert Tibshirani, "The use of cellular telephones in motor vehicles is associated with a quadrupling of the risk of a collision during the brief period of a call" (453).

ENTRY IN THE LIST OF WORKS CITED

Redelmeier, Donald A., and Robert J. Tibshirani. "Association
between Cellular-Telephone Calls and Motor Vehicle
Collisions." New England Journal of Medicine 336 (1997):
453-58.

Handling an MLA citation is not always this simple. For a
detailed discussion of possible variations, see 54.

52b Enclose borrowed language in quotation marks.

To show readers that you are using a source's exact phrases or
sentences, you must enclose them in quotation marks unless
they have been set off from the text by indenting (see p. 410).
To omit the quotation marks is to claim — falsely — that the
language is your own. Such an omission is plagiarism even if
you have cited the source.

ORIGINAL SOURCE

Future cars will provide drivers with concierge services, web-
based information, online e-mail capabilities, CD-ROM access,
on-screen and audio navigation technology, and a variety of
other information and entertainment services.
— Matt Sundeen, "Cell Phones and Highway Safety:
2000 State Legislative Update," p. 1

PLAGIARISM

Matt Sundeen points out that in cars of the future drivers will
have concierge services, web-based information, online e-mail
capabilities, CD-ROM access, on-screen and audio navigation
technology, and a variety of other information and entertainment services (1).

BORROWED LANGUAGE IN QUOTATION MARKS

Matt Sundeen points out that in cars of the future drivers will
have "concierge services, web-based information, online e-mail
capabilities, CD-ROM access, on-screen and audio navigation
technology, and a variety of other information and entertainment services" (1).

52c Put summaries and paraphrases in your own words.

A summary condenses information from a source; a paraphrase repeats this information in about the same number of words. When you summarize or paraphrase, it is not enough to name the source; you must restate the source's meaning using your own language. (See also 50c.) You are guilty of plagiarism if you half-copy the author's sentences—either by mixing the author's phrases with your own without using quotation marks or by plugging your synonyms into the author's sentence structure.

The first paraphrase of the following source is plagiarized—even though the source is cited—because too much of its language is borrowed from the original. The underlined strings of words have been copied word-for-word (without quotation marks). In addition, the writer has closely echoed the sentence structure of the source, merely plugging in some synonyms (*demonstrated* for *shown, devising* for *designing,* and *car* for *automotive*).

ORIGINAL SOURCE

The automotive industry has not shown good judgment in designing automotive features that distract drivers. A classic example is the use of a touch-sensitive screen to replace all the controls for radios, tape/CD players, and heating/cooling. Although an interesting technology, such devices require that the driver take his eyes off the road.

—Tom Magliozzi and Ray Magliozzi,
Letter to a Massachusetts state senator, p. 3

PLAGIARISM: UNACCEPTABLE BORROWING

Radio show hosts Tom and Ray Magliozzi argue that <u>the automotive industry has not</u> demonstrated <u>good judgment in</u> devising car <u>features that distract drivers</u>. One feature is <u>a touch-sensitive screen</u> that replaces <u>controls for radios, tape/CD players, and heating/cooling</u>. Although the technology is interesting, <u>such devices require that</u> a driver look away from the road (3).

To avoid plagiarizing an author's language, resist the temptation to look at the source while you are summarizing or paraphrasing. Close the book, write from memory, and then open the book to check for accuracy. This technique prevents you from being captivated by the words on the page.

ACCEPTABLE PARAPHRASE

Radio show hosts Tom and Ray Magliozzi claim that motor vehicle manufacturers do not always design features with safety in mind. For example, when designers replaced radio, CD player, and temperature control knobs with touch-sensitive panels, they were forgetting one thing: To use the panels, drivers would need to take their eyes off the road (3).

53

Integrating sources

With practice, you will learn to integrate information from sources — quotations, summaries, paraphrases, and facts — smoothly into your own text.

> **ON THE WEB**
>
> For electronic exercises on integrating quotations in MLA papers, go to **dianahacker.com/rules**
>
> and click on ▶ **Electronic Research Exercises**
> ▶ **E-ex 53-1 and 53-2**

53a Use signal phrases to integrate quotations; limit your use of quotations.

Using signal phrases

Readers need to move from your own words to the words of a source without feeling a jolt. Avoid dropping quotations into the text without warning. Instead, provide clear signal phrases, usually including the author's name, to prepare readers for a quotation.

DROPPED QUOTATION

In 2000, the legislature of Suffolk County passed a law restricting drivers' use of handheld phones. "The bill prohibits the use of a cell phone while driving unless it is equipped with an earpiece or can act like a speakerphone, leaving the driver's hands free" (Kelley 1).

QUOTATION WITH SIGNAL PHRASE

In 2000, the legislature of Suffolk County passed a law restricting drivers' use of handheld phones. According to journalist Tina Kelley, "The bill prohibits the use of a cell phone while driving unless it is equipped with an earpiece or can act like a speakerphone, leaving the driver's hands free" (1).

To avoid monotony, vary both the language and the placement of your signal phrases. The models in the chart on page 408 suggest a range of possibilities.

When your signal phrase includes a verb, choose one that is appropriate in the context. Is your source arguing a point, making an observation, reporting a fact, drawing a conclusion, refuting an argument, or stating a belief? By choosing an appropriate verb, you can make your source's stance clear. See the chart for a list of verbs commonly used in signal phrases.

Limiting your use of quotations

Although it is tempting to insert many long quotations in your paper and to use your own words only for connecting passages, do not quote excessively. It is almost impossible to integrate numerous long quotations smoothly into your own text.

Except for certain legitimate uses of quotations, use your own words to summarize and paraphrase your sources and to explain your own ideas.

Varying signal phrases in MLA papers

MODEL SIGNAL PHRASES

In the words of researchers Redelmeier and Tibshirani, "..."
As Matt Sundeen has noted, "..."
Patti Pena, mother of a child killed by a driver distracted by a cell phone, points out that "..."
"...," writes Christine Haughney, "..."
"...," claims wireless industry spokesperson Annette Jacobs.
Radio hosts Tom and Ray Magliozzi offer a persuasive counter-argument: "..."

VERBS IN SIGNAL PHRASES

acknowledges	comments	endorses	reasons
adds	compares	grants	refutes
admits	confirms	illustrates	rejects
agrees	contends	implies	reports
argues	declares	insists	responds
asserts	denies	notes	suggests
believes	disputes	observes	thinks
claims	emphasizes	points out	writes

WHEN TO USE QUOTATIONS

— When language is especially vivid or expressive
— When exact wording is needed for technical accuracy
— When it is important to let the debaters of an issue explain their positions in their own words
— When the words of an important authority lend weight to an argument
— When language of a source is the topic of your discussion (as in an analysis or interpretation)

It is not always necessary to quote full sentences from a source. To reduce your reliance on the words of others, you can often integrate a phrase from a source into your own sentence structure.

Redelmeier and Tibshirani found that hands-free phones were not any safer in vehicles than other cell phones. They suggest that crashes involving cell phones may "result from a driver's limitations with regard to attention rather than dexterity" (456).

Using the ellipsis mark and brackets

Two useful marks of punctuation, the ellipsis mark and brackets, allow you to keep quoted material to a minimum and to integrate it smoothly into your text.

THE ELLIPSIS MARK   To condense a quoted passage, you can use the ellipsis mark (three spaced periods) to indicate that you have omitted words. What remains must be grammatically complete.

The University of North Carolina Highway Safety Research Center has begun a study assessing a variety of driver distractions. According to Allyson Vaughan, "The research . . . is intended to inject some empirical evidence into the debate over whether talking on wireless phones while driving leads to accidents" (1).

The writer has omitted the words *funded by the AAA Foundation for Traffic Safety,* which appeared in the source.

On the rare occasions when you want to omit one or more full sentences, use a period before the three ellipsis dots.

Redelmeier and Tibshirani acknowledge that their study "indicates an association but not necessarily a causal relation between the use of cellular telephones while driving and a subsequent motor vehicle collision. . . . In addition, our study did not include serious injuries . . ." (457).

Ordinarily, do not use an ellipsis mark at the beginning or at the end of a quotation. Your readers will understand that the quoted material is taken from a longer passage, so such marks are not necessary. The only exception occurs when words at the end of the final quoted sentence have been dropped. In such cases, put three ellipsis dots before the closing quotation mark and parenthetical reference, as in the example just given.

Obviously you should not use an ellipsis mark to distort the meaning of your source.

BRACKETS   Brackets allow you to insert your own words into quoted material. You can insert words in brackets to explain a confusing reference or to keep a sentence grammatical in your context.

> According to economists Robert Hahn and Paul Tetlock, "Some studies say they [hands-free phones] would have no impact on accidents, while others suggest the reductions could be sizable" (2).

To indicate an error in a quotation, insert [sic] right after the error. See also 39c.

Setting off long quotations

When a quoted passage takes up more than four typed lines of prose or more than three lines of poetry in your paper, set off the quotation by indenting it one inch (or ten spaces) from the left margin.

Long quotations should be introduced by an informative sentence, usually followed by a colon. Quotation marks are unnecessary because the indented format tells readers that the words are taken word-for-word from the source.

> Tom and Ray Magliozzi are not impressed by economists who conduct risk-benefit analyses of phone use by drivers:
>
>> Other critics [of regulation of cell phones]--some from prestigious "think tanks"--perform what appear to be erudite cost/benefit analyses. The problem here is that the benefits are always in units of convenience and productivity while the costs are in units of injuries and people's lives! (2)

Notice that at the end of an indented quotation the parenthetical citation goes outside the final mark of punctuation.

53b Use signal phrases to introduce most summaries and paraphrases.

Introduce most summaries and paraphrases with a signal phrase that names the author and places the material in context. Readers will then understand that everything between the signal phrase and the parenthetical citation summarizes or paraphrases the cited source.

Without the signal phrase (underlined) in the following example, readers might think that only the quotation at the end is being cited, when in fact the whole paragraph is based on the source. *phrase*

Alasdair Cain and Mark Burris report that research on traffic accidents and cell phone use has been inconclusive. Many factors play a role: for example, the type of phone (hands-free or not), the extent to which the conversation is distracting, and the demographic profile of the driver. Although research suggests that phoning in a moving vehicle affects driver performance, studies have failed to quantify the degree of driver impairment. Cain and Burris write that drivers using cell phones on the road "were anywhere from 34 percent to 300 percent more likely to have an accident" (1).

There are times, however, when a signal phrase naming the author is not necessary. When the context makes clear where the cited material begins, you may omit the signal phrase and include the authors' last names in the parentheses: (Cain and Burris 1).

53c With statistics and other facts, a signal phrase may not be needed.

When you are citing a statistic or other specific fact, a signal phrase is often not necessary. In most cases, readers will understand that the citation refers to the statistic or fact (not the whole paragraph).

Reviewing an MLA paper: Use of sources

USE OF QUOTATIONS

- Is quoted material enclosed within quotation marks (unless it has been set off from the text)? (See 52b.)
- Is quoted language word-for-word accurate? If not, do brackets or ellipsis marks indicate the changes or omissions? (See pp. 409–10.)
- Does a clear signal phrase (usually naming the author) prepare readers for each quotation? (See 53a.)
- Is each quotation documented with an in-text citation? (See 54a.)

USE OF SUMMARIES AND PARAPHRASES

- Are summaries and paraphrases free of plagiarized wording— not copied or half-copied from the source? (See 52c.)
- Are summaries and paraphrases documented with in-text citations? (See 54a.)
- Do readers know where the material being cited begins? In other words, does a signal phrase mark the beginning of the cited material unless the context makes clear exactly what is being cited? (See 53b.)

USE OF STATISTICS AND OTHER FACTS

- Are statistics and facts (other than common knowledge) documented with in-text citations? (See 52a.)
- If there is no signal phrase, will readers understand exactly which facts are being cited? (See 53c.)

As of 2000, there were about ninety million cell phone users in the United States, with 85% of them using their phones while on the road (Sundeen 1).

There is nothing wrong, however, with using a signal phrase to introduce a statistic or other fact.

Matt Sundeen reports that as of 2000, there were about ninety million cell phone users in the United States, with 85% of them using their phones while on the road (1).

54

Documenting sources

In English and in some humanities classes, you will be asked to use the MLA (Modern Language Association) system for documenting sources, which is set forth in the *MLA Handbook for Writers of Research Papers,* 6th ed. (New York: MLA, 2003). MLA recommends in-text citations that refer readers to a list of works cited.

An in-text citation names the author of the source, often in a signal phrase, and gives the page number in parentheses. At the end of the paper, a list of works cited provides publication information about the source; the list is alphabetized by authors' last names (or by titles for works without authors). There is a direct connection between the in-text citation and the alphabetical listing. In the following example, that link is highlighted in teal.

IN-TEXT CITATION

Matt Sundeen notes that drivers with cell phones place an estimated 98,000 emergency calls each day and that the phones "often reduce emergency response times and actually save lives" (1).

ENTRY IN THE LIST OF WORKS CITED

Sundeen, Matt. "Cell Phones and Highway Safety: 2000 State Legislative Update." National Conference of State Legislatures. Dec. 2000. 9 pp. 27 Feb. 2001 <http://ncsl.org/programs/esnr/cellphone.pdf>.

For a list of works cited that includes this entry, see pages 454–55.

Directory to MLA in-text citation models

54a MLA in-text citations

MLA in-text citations are made with a combination of signal phrases and parenthetical references. A signal phrase indicates that something taken from a source (a quotation, summary, paraphrase, or fact) is about to be used; usually the signal phrase includes the author's name. The parenthetical reference, which comes after the cited material, normally includes at least a page number. In the following models, the elements of the in-text citation are shown in color.

IN-TEXT CITATION

One driver, Peter Cohen, says that after he was rear-ended, the guilty party emerged from his vehicle still talking on the phone (127).

Readers can look up the author's last name in the alphabetized list of works cited, where they will learn the work's title and other publication information. When readers decide to consult the source, the page number will take them straight to the passage that has been cited.

NOTE: If your cited material runs to more than one page, give the range of pages (such as 235–36 or 399–400).

Basic rules for print and electronic sources

The MLA system of in-text citations, which depends heavily on authors' names and page numbers, was created in the early 1980s with print sources in mind. Because some of today's electronic sources have unclear authorship and lack page numbers, they present a challenge. Nevertheless, the basic rules are the same for both print and electronic sources.

The models in this section (items 1–5) show how the MLA system usually works and explain what to do if your source has no author or page numbers.

■ **1. AUTHOR NAMED IN A SIGNAL PHRASE** Ordinarily, introduce the material being cited with a signal phrase that includes the author's name. In addition to preparing readers for the source, the signal phrase allows you to keep the parenthetical citation brief.

> Christine Haughney reports that shortly after Japan made it illegal to use a handheld phone while driving, "accidents caused by using the phones dropped by 75 percent" (A8).

The signal phrase — "Christine Haughney reports that" — names the author; the parenthetical citation gives the page number of the newspaper article in which the quoted words may be found.

Notice that the period follows the parenthetical citation. When a quotation ends with a question mark or an exclamation point, leave the end punctuation inside the quotation mark and add a period after the parentheses: ". . . ?" (8). (See also the note on p. 303.)

■ **2. AUTHOR NAMED IN PARENTHESES** If a signal phrase does not name the author, put the author's last name in parentheses along with the page number.

> Most states do not keep adequate records on the number of
> times cell phones are a factor in accidents; as of December
> 2000, only ten states were trying to keep such records
> (Sundeen 2).

Use no punctuation between the name and the page number.

■ **3. AUTHOR UNKNOWN** Either use the complete title in a signal phrase or use a short form of the title in parentheses. Titles of books are underlined; titles of articles and other short works are put in quotation marks.

> As of 2001, at least three hundred towns and municipalities had
> considered legislation regulating use of cell phones while driving
> ("Lawmakers" 2).

CAUTION: Before assuming that a Web source has no author, do some detective work. Often the author's name is available but is hard to find. For example, it may appear at the end of the source, in tiny print. Or it may appear on another page of the site, such as the home page.

NOTE: If a source has no known author but was prepared by a corporate entity, such as an organization or a government agency, name the corporate entity as the author (see item 9 on p. 418).

■ **4. PAGE NUMBER UNKNOWN** You may omit the page number if a work lacks page numbers, as is the case with many Web sources. Although printouts from Web sites usually show page numbers, printers don't always provide the same page breaks; for this reason, MLA recommends treating such sources as unpaginated.

> The California Highway Patrol opposes restrictions on the use of
> phones while driving, claiming that distracted drivers can
> already be prosecuted (Jacobs).

> According to Jacobs, the California Highway Patrol opposes
> restrictions on the use of phones while driving, claiming that
> distracted drivers can already be prosecuted.

When the pages of a Web source are stable (as in PDF files), however, supply a page number in your in-text citation. (For example, the Web source by Sundeen cited on p. 413 has stable pages, so a page number is included in the citation.)

NOTE: If a Web source numbers its paragraphs or screens, give the abbreviation "par." or "pars." or the word "screen" or "screens" in the parentheses: (Smith, par. 4).

■ **5. ONE-PAGE SOURCE** If the source is one page long, MLA allows (but does not require) you to omit the page number. Many instructors will want you to supply the page number because without it readers may not know where your citation ends or, worse yet, may not realize that you have provided a citation at all.

No page number given

Milo Ippolito reports that the driver who struck and killed a two-year-old while using her cell phone got off with a light sentence even though she left the scene of the accident and failed to call 911 for help. In this and in similar cases, traffic offenders dis tracted by cell phones have not been sufficiently punished under current laws.

Page number given

Milo Ippolito reports that the driver who struck and killed a two-year-old while using her cell phone got off with a light sentence even though she left the scene of the accident and failed to call 911 for help (J1). In this and in similar cases, traffic offenders distracted by cell phones have not been sufficiently punished under current laws.

Variations on the basic rules

This section describes the MLA guidelines for handling a variety of situations not covered by the basic rules just given. Again, these rules on in-text citations are the same for both traditional print sources and electronic sources.

■ **6. TWO OR MORE TITLES BY THE SAME AUTHOR** If your list of works cited includes two or more titles by the same author, mention the title of the work in the signal phrase or include a short version of the title in the parentheses.

On December 6, 2000, reporter Jamie Stockwell wrote that distracted driver Jason Jones had been charged with "two counts of
vehicular manslaughter . . . in the deaths of John and Carole
Hall" ("Phone" B1). The next day Stockwell reported the judge's
ruling: Jones "was convicted of negligent driving and fined
$500, the maximum penalty allowed" ("Man" B4).

Titles of articles and other short works are placed in quotation
marks, as in the example just given. Titles of books are underlined.

In the rare case when both the author's name and a short
title must be given in parentheses, separate them with a comma.

According to police reports, there were no skid marks indicating
that the distracted driver who killed John and Carole Hall had
not even tried to stop (Stockwell, "Man" B4).

■ **7. TWO OR THREE AUTHORS** Name the authors in the signal
phrase, as in the following example, or include their last names
in the parenthetical reference: (Redelmeier and Tibshirani 453).

Redelmeier and Tibshirani found that "the risk of a collision
when using a cellular telephone was four times higher than the
risk when a cellular telephone was not being used" (453).

When three authors are named in the parentheses, separate the
names with commas: (Alton, Davies, and Rice 56).

■ **8. FOUR OR MORE AUTHORS** Name all of the authors or include only the first author's name followed by "et al." (Latin for
"and others"). Make sure that your citation matches the entry
in the list of works cited (see also item 2 on p. 424).

The study was extended for two years, and only after results
were reviewed by an independent panel did the researchers
publish their findings (Blaine et al. 35).

■ **9. CORPORATE AUTHOR** When the author is a corporation, an
organization, or a government agency, name the corporate author either in the signal phrase or in the parentheses.

> Researchers at the Harvard Center for Risk Analysis found that
> the risks of driving while phoning were small compared with
> other driving risks (3-4).

In the list of works cited, the Harvard Center for Risk Analysis
is treated as the author and alphabetized under *H.*

When a government agency is treated as the author, it will be
alphabetized in the list of works cited under the name of the government, such as "United States" (see item 3 on p. 425). For this
reason, you must name the government in your in-text citation.

> The United States Department of Transportation provides nation-
> wide statistics on traffic fatalities.

■ **10. AUTHORS WITH THE SAME LAST NAME** If your list of works
cited includes works by authors with the same last name, include the author's first name in the signal phrase or first initial
in the parentheses.

> Estimates of the number of accidents caused by distracted drivers
> vary because little evidence is being collected (D. Smith 7).

■ **11. INDIRECT SOURCE (SOURCE QUOTED IN ANOTHER SOURCE)**
When a writer's or a speaker's quoted words appear in a source
written by someone else, begin the citation with the abbreviation "qtd. in."

> According to Richard Retting, "As the comforts of home and the
> efficiency of the office creep into the automobile, it is becoming
> increasingly attractive as a work space" (qtd. in Kilgannon A23).

■ **12. ENCYCLOPEDIA OR DICTIONARY** Unless an encyclopedia or
a dictionary has an author, it will be alphabetized in the list of
works cited under the word or entry that you consulted — not
under the title of the reference work itself (see item 13 on
p. 428). Either in your text or in your parenthetical reference,
mention the word or the entry. No page number is required,
since readers can easily look up the word or entry.

> The word <u>crocodile</u> has a surprisingly complex etymology
> ("Crocodile").

■ **13. MULTIVOLUME WORK** If your paper cites more than one volume of a multivolume work, indicate which volume you are referring to, followed by a colon and the page number in the parentheses.

> In his studies of gifted children, Terman describes a pattern of
> accelerated language acquisition (2: 279).

If your paper cites only one volume of a multivolume work, you will include the volume number in the list of works cited and will not need to include it in the parentheses.

■ **14. TWO OR MORE WORKS** To cite more than one source, separate the citations with a semicolon.

> The dangers of mountain lions to humans have been well
> documented (Rychnovsky 40; Seidensticker 114; Williams 30).

■ **15. AN ENTIRE WORK** To cite an entire work, use the author's name in the signal phrase or the parenthetical reference. There is of course no need to use a page number.

> Robinson succinctly describes the status of the mountain lion
> controversy in California.

■ **16. WORK IN AN ANTHOLOGY** Put the name of the author of the work (not the editor of the anthology) in the signal phrase or the parentheses.

> In "A Jury of Her Peers," Mrs. Hale describes both a style of
> quilting and a murder weapon when she utters the last words of
> the story: "We call it--knot it, Mr. Henderson" (Glaspell 302).

In the list of works cited, the work is alphabetized under Glaspell, not under the name of the editor of the anthology.

■ **17. LEGAL SOURCE** For well-known historical documents, such as articles of the United States Constitution, and for laws in the United States Code, provide a parenthetical citation in the text: (US Const., art. 1, sec. 2) or (12 USC 3412, 2000). There is no need to provide a works cited entry.

Legislative acts and court cases are included in the works cited list (see item 50 on p. 442). Your in-text citation should name the act or case either in a signal phrase or in parentheses. In the text of a paper, names of acts are not underlined, but names of cases are.

> The Jones Act of 1917 granted U.S. citizenship to Puerto Ricans.

> In 1857, Chief Justice Roger B. Taney declared in the case of Dred Scott v. Sandford that blacks, whether enslaved or free, could not be citizens of the United States.

Literary works and sacred texts

Literary works and sacred texts are usually available in a variety of editions. Your list of works cited will specify which edition you are using, and your in-text citation will usually consist of a page number from the edition you consulted (see item 18).

However, MLA suggests that when possible you should give enough information — such as book parts, play divisions, or line numbers — that readers can locate the cited passage in any edition of the work (see items 19–21).

NOTE: In the examples in items 18, 19, and 20, the author's name is included in the citations. In your paper, you will include the author's name the first time you cite a work, but there is no need to repeat the name later in your paper — as long as your context makes clear what work you are citing.

■ **18. LITERARY WORKS WITHOUT PARTS OR LINE NUMBERS** Many literary works, such as most short stories and many novels and plays, do not have parts or line numbers that you can refer to. In such cases, simply cite the page number.

> At the end of Kate Chopin's "The Story of an Hour," Mrs. Mallard drops dead upon learning that her husband is alive. In the final irony of the story, doctors report that she has died of a "joy that kills" (25).

■ **19. VERSE PLAYS AND POEMS** For verse plays, MLA recommends giving act, scene, and line numbers that can be located in any edition of the work. Use arabic numerals, and separate the numbers with periods.

In Shakespeare's <u>King Lear</u>, Gloucester, blinded for suspected treason, learns a profound lesson from his tragic experience: "A man may see how this world goes / with no eyes" (4.2.148-49).

For a poem, cite the part (if there are a number of parts) and the line numbers, separated by a period.

When Homer's Odysseus comes to the hall of Circe, he finds his men "mild / in her soft spell, fed on her drug of evil" (10.209-11).

For poems that are not divided into parts, use line numbers. For a first reference, use the word "lines": (lines 5–8). Thereafter use just the numbers: (12–13).

■ **20. NOVELS WITH NUMBERED DIVISIONS** When a novel has numbered divisions, put the page number first, followed by a semicolon, and then indicate the book, part, or chapter in which the passage may be found. Use abbreviations such as "bk." and "ch."

One of Kingsolver's narrators, teenager Rachel, pushes her vocabulary beyond its limits. For example, Rachel complains that being forced to live in the Congo with her missionary family is "a sheer tapestry of justice" because her chances of finding a boyfriend are "dull and void" (117; bk. 2, ch. 10).

■ **21. SACRED TEXTS** When citing a sacred text such as the Bible or the Koran, name the edition you are using in your works cited entry (see p. 428). In your parenthetical citation, give the book, chapter, and verse (or their equivalent), separated by periods. Common abbreviations for books of the Bible are acceptable.

Consider the words of Solomon: "If your enemies are hungry, give them food to eat. If they are thirsty, give them water to drink" (<u>Holy Bible</u>, Prov. 25.21).

ON THE WEB

For electronic exercises on using MLA documentation style, go to
dianahacker.com/rules

and click on ▶ **Electronic Research Exercises**
▶ **E-ex 54-1 through 54-3**

Directory to MLA works cited models

54b   MLA list of works cited

An alphabetized list of works cited, which appears at the end of your research paper, gives publication information for each of the sources you have cited in the paper. (For information about preparing this list, see pp. 446–47; for a sample list of works cited, see pp. 454–55.)

NOTE: Unless your instructor asks for them, omit sources not actually cited in the paper, even if you read them.

General guidelines for listing authors

Alphabetize entries in the list of works cited by authors' last names (if a work has no author, alphabetize it by its title). The author's name is important because citations in the text of the paper refer to it and readers will be looking for it at the beginning of an entry in the alphabetized list.

NAME CITED IN TEXT

According to Matt Sundeen, . . .

BEGINNING OF WORKS CITED ENTRY

Sundeen, Matt.

Items 1–5 show how to begin an entry for a work with a single author, multiple authors, a corporate author, an unknown author, and multiple works by the same author. What comes after this first element of your citation will depend on the kind of source you are citing (see items 6–56).

NOTE: For a book, an entry in the works cited list will sometimes begin with an editor (see item 9 on p. 427).

■ **1. SINGLE AUTHOR**   For a work with one author, begin the entry with the author's last name, followed by a comma; then give the author's first name, followed by a period.

Tannen, Deborah.

■ **2. MULTIPLE AUTHORS**   For works with two or three authors, name the authors in the order in which they are listed in the source. Reverse the name of only the first author.

Walker, Janice R., and Todd Taylor.

Wilmut, Ian, Keith Campbell, and Colin Tudge.

For a work with four or more authors, either name all of the authors or name the first author, followed by "et al." (Latin for "and others").

Sloan, Frank A., Emily M. Stout, Kathryn Whetten-Goldstein, and Lan Liang.

Sloan, Frank A., et al.

■ **3. CORPORATE AUTHOR** When the author of a print document or Web site is a corporation, a government agency, or some other organization, begin your entry with the name of the group.

First Union.

United States. Bureau of the Census.

American Automobile Association.

NOTE: Make sure that your in-text citation also treats the organization as the author (see item 9 on p. 418).

■ **4. UNKNOWN AUTHOR** When the author of a work is unknown, begin with the work's title. Titles of articles and other short works, such as brief documents from Web sites, are put in quotation marks. Titles of books and other long works, such as entire Web sites, are underlined.

Article or other short work

"Media Giants."

Book or other long work

Atlas of the World.

Before concluding that the author of a Web source is unknown, check carefully (see the caution on p. 416). Also remember that an organization may be the author (see item 3 on this page).

■   **5. TWO OR MORE WORKS BY THE SAME AUTHOR**   If your list of works cited includes two or more works by the same author, use the author's name only for the first entry. For other entries use three hyphens followed by a period. The three hyphens must stand for exactly the same name or names as in the first entry. List the titles in alphabetical order.

Atwood, Margaret. <u>Alias Grace: A Novel</u>. New York: Doubleday, 1996.

---. <u>The Robber Bride</u>. New York: Doubleday, 1993.

Books

Items 6–19 apply to print books. For online books, see item 29 on page 434.

■   **6. BASIC FORMAT FOR A BOOK**   For most books, arrange the information into three units, each followed by a period and one space: (1) the author's name; (2) the title and subtitle, underlined; and (3) the place of publication, the publisher, and the date.

```
    ┌──1──┐  ┌──────2──────┐  ┌──────3──────┐
```
Tan, Amy. <u>The Bonesetter's Daughter</u>. New York: Putnam, 2001.

Take the information about the book from its title page and copyright page. Use a short form of the publisher's name; omit terms such as *Press, Inc.,* and *Co.* except when naming university presses (Harvard UP, for example). If the copyright page lists more than one date, use the most recent one.

■   **7. AUTHOR WITH AN EDITOR**   Begin with the author and title, followed by the name of the editor. The abbreviation "Ed." means "Edited by," so it is the same for one or multiple editors.

Kerouac, Jack. <u>Atop an Underwood</u>. Ed. Paul Marion. New York:
      Penguin, 2000.

■   **8. AUTHOR WITH A TRANSLATOR**   Begin with the name of the author. After the title, write "Trans." (for "Translated by") and the name of the translator.

Allende, Isabel. <u>Daughter of Fortune</u>. Trans. Margaret Sayers Peden.
      New York: Harper, 2000.

■ **9. EDITOR** An entry for a work with an editor is similar to that for a work with an author except that the name is followed by a comma and the abbreviation "ed." for "editor" (or "eds." for "editors").

Craig, Patricia, ed. The Oxford Book of Travel Stories. Oxford: Oxford

UP, 1996.

■ **10. WORK IN AN ANTHOLOGY** Begin with (1) the name of the author of the selection, not with the name of the editor of the anthology. Then give (2) the title of the selection; (3) the title of the anthology; (4) the name of the editor (preceded by "Ed." for "Edited by"); (5) publication information; and (6) the pages on which the selection appears.

Desai, Anita. "Scholar and Gypsy." The Oxford Book of Travel Stories.
Ed. Patricia Craig. Oxford: Oxford UP, 1996. 251-73.

If you wish, you may cross-reference two or more works from the same anthology. Provide an entry for the anthology (see item 9 above). Then in separate entries list the author and title of each selection, followed by the last name of the editor of the anthology and the page numbers on which the selection appears.

Desai, Anita. "Scholar and Gypsy." Craig 251-73.

Malouf, David. "The Kyogle Line." Craig 390-96.

Alphabetize the entry for the anthology under the name of its editor (Craig); alphabetize the entries for the selections under the names of the authors (Desai, Malouf).

■ **11. EDITION OTHER THAN THE FIRST** If you are citing an edition other than the first, include the number of the edition after the title (or after the names of any translators or editors that appear after the title): 2nd ed., 3rd ed., and so on.

Auletta, Ken. The Underclass. 2nd ed. Woodstock, NY: Overlook,

2000.

■ **12. MULTIVOLUME WORK** Include the total number of volumes before the city and publisher, using the abbreviation "vols."

Conway, Jill Ker, ed. Written by Herself. 2 vols. New York: Random,
  1996.

If your paper cites only one of the volumes, give the volume number before the city and publisher and give the total number of volumes after the date.

Conway, Jill Ker, ed. Written by Herself. Vol. 2. New York: Random,
  1996. 2 vols.

■ **13. ENCYCLOPEDIA OR DICTIONARY ENTRY** When an encyclopedia or a dictionary is well known, simply list the author of the entry (if there is one), the title of the entry, the title of the reference work, the edition number (if any), and the date of the edition.

Posner, Rebecca. "Romance Languages." The New Encyclopaedia
  Britannica: Macropaedia. 15th ed. 1987.

"Sonata." The American Heritage Dictionary of the English Language.
  4th ed. 2000.

Volume and page numbers are not necessary because the entries in the source are arranged alphabetically and therefore are easy to locate.

If a reference work is not well known, provide full publication information as well.

■ **14. SACRED TEXT** Give the title of the edition of the sacred text (taken from the title page), underlined; the editor's name (if any); and publication information.

Holy Bible: New Living Translation. Wheaton: Tyndale, 1996.

■ **15. FOREWORD, INTRODUCTION, PREFACE, OR AFTERWORD** Begin with the author of the foreword or other book part, followed by the name of that part. Then give the title of the book; the author of the book, preceded by the word "By"; and the editor of the book (if any). After the publication information, give the page numbers for the part of the book being cited.

Morris, Jan. Introduction. Letters from the Field, 1925-1975. By
  Margaret Mead. New York: Perennial-Harper, 2001. xix-xxiii.

If the book part being cited has a title, include it in quotation marks after the author's name and before the name of the book part.

■ **16. BOOK WITH A TITLE IN ITS TITLE** If the book contains a title normally underlined, neither underline the internal title nor place it in quotation marks.

Vanderham, Paul. James Joyce and Censorship: The Trials of Ulysses.

New York: New York UP, 1997.

If the title within the title is normally put in quotation marks, retain the quotation marks and underline the entire title.

Faulkner, Dewey R., ed. Twentieth Century Interpretations of "The

Pardoner's Tale." Englewood Cliffs: Prentice, 1973.

■ **17. BOOK IN A SERIES** Before the publication information, cite the series name as it appears on the title page, followed by the series number, if any.

Malena, Anne. The Dynamics of Identity in Francophone Caribbean

Narrative. Francophone Cultures and Lits. Ser. 24. New York:

Lang, 1998.

■ **18. REPUBLISHED BOOK** After the title of the book, cite the original publication date, followed by the current publication information. If the republished book contains new material, such as an introduction or afterword, include information about the new material after the original date.

Hughes, Langston. Black Misery. 1969. Afterword Robert O'Meally. New

York: Oxford UP, 2000.

■ **19. PUBLISHER'S IMPRINT** If a book was published by an imprint (a division) of a publishing company, link the name of the imprint and the name of the publisher with a hyphen, putting the imprint first.

Truan, Barry. Acoustic Communication. Westport: Ablex-Greenwood,

2000.

Articles in periodicals

This section shows how to prepare works cited entries for articles in magazines, scholarly journals, and newspapers. In addition to consulting the models in this section, you will at times need to turn to other models as well:

— More than one author: see item 2 (p. 424)

— Corporate author: see item 3 (p. 425)

— Unknown author: see item 4 (p. 425)

— Online article: see item 32 (p. 436)

— Article from a subscription service: see item 31 (p. 435)

NOTE: For articles appearing on consecutive pages, provide the range of pages, such as 121–29 or 298–310. When an article does not appear on consecutive pages, give the number of the first page followed by a plus sign: 32 + .

■ **20. ARTICLE IN A MAGAZINE** List, in order, separated by periods, (1) the author's name; (2) the title of the article, in quotation marks; and (3) the title of the magazine, underlined. Then give (4) the date and the page numbers, separated by a colon. Abbreviate the names of the months except May, June, and July.

If the magazine is issued monthly, give just the month and year.

```
      ┌──── 1 ────┐  ┌──────── 2 ────────┐  ┌──── 3 ────┐
Kaplan, Robert D. "History Moving North." Atlantic Monthly
      ┌──── 4 ────┐
Feb. 1997: 21+.
```

If the magazine is issued weekly, give the exact date.

Lord, Lewis. "There's Something about Mary Todd." US News and World
  Report 19 Feb. 2001: 53.

■ **21. ARTICLE IN A JOURNAL PAGINATED BY VOLUME** Many scholarly journals continue page numbers throughout the year instead of beginning each issue with page 1; at the end of the year, the issues are collected in a volume. To find an article, readers need only the volume number, the year, and the page numbers.

Ryan, Katy. "Revolutionary Suicide in Toni Morrison's Fiction." African
  American Review 34 (2000): 389-412.

■ **22. ARTICLE IN A JOURNAL PAGINATED BY ISSUE**   If each issue of the journal begins with page 1, you need to indicate the number of the issue. After the volume number, put a period and the issue number.

Wood, Michael. "Broken Dates: Fiction and the Century." Kenyon

   Review 22.3 (2000): 50-64.

■ **23. ARTICLE IN A DAILY NEWSPAPER**   Begin with the name of the author, if known, followed by the title of the article. Next give the name of the newspaper, the date, and the page number (including the section letter). Use a plus sign (+) after the page number if the article does not appear on consecutive pages.

Murphy, Sean P. "Decisions on Status of Tribes Draw Fire." Boston

   Globe 27 Mar. 2001: A2.

If the section is marked with a number rather than a letter, handle the entry as follows:

Wilford, John Noble. "In a Golden Age of Discovery, Faraway Worlds

   Beckon." New York Times 9 Feb. 1997, late ed., sec. 1: 1+.

When an edition of the newspaper is specified on the masthead, name the edition after the date and before the page reference (eastern ed., late ed., natl. ed., and so on), as in the example just given.

If the city of publication is not obvious, include it in brackets after the name of the newspaper: *City Paper* [Washington, DC].

■ **24. EDITORIAL IN A NEWSPAPER**   Cite an editorial as you would an unsigned article, adding the word "Editorial" after the title.

"All Wet." Editorial. Boston Globe 12 Feb. 2001: A14.

■ **25. LETTER TO THE EDITOR**   Name the writer, followed by the word "Letter" and the publication information for the periodical in which the letter appears.

Shrewsbury, Toni. Letter. Atlanta Journal-Constitution 17 Feb. 2001:

   A13.

■ **26. BOOK OR FILM REVIEW**   Name the reviewer and the title of the review, if any, followed by the words "Rev. of" and the title and author or director of the work reviewed. Add the publication information for the publication in which the review appears.

Gleick, Elizabeth. "The Burdens of Genius." Rev. of The Last Samurai,

by Helen DeWitt. Time 4 Dec. 2000: 171.

Denby, David. "On the Battlefield." Rev. of The Hurricane, dir. Norman

Jewison. New Yorker 10 Jan. 2000: 90-92.

Electronic sources

MLA's guidelines for documenting electronic sources can be found in the *MLA Handbook for Writers of Research Papers* (6th ed., 2003). For more help with citing electronic sources in MLA style, see the list of frequently asked questions in the section "MLA Style" on MLA's Web site, < http://www.mla.org > .

ON THE WEB

For future updates to MLA style, go to MLA's Web site or go to
dianahacker.com/rules

and click on ▶ **Research and Documentation Online**
▶ **Documenting Sources (MLA)**

NOTE: When a Web address in a works cited entry must be divided at the end of a line, MLA recommends that you break it after a slash. Do not insert a hyphen.

■ **27. AN ENTIRE WEB SITE** Begin with (1) the name of the author or corporate author (if known) and (2) the title of the site, underlined. Then give (3) the names of any editors, (4) the date of publication or last update, (5) the name of any sponsoring organization, (6) the date of access, and (7) the URL in angle brackets. Provide as many of these elements as apply and as are available. In the following example, items 3 and 5 do not apply.

With author

```
      ┌──────1──────┐ ┌──────2──────┐ ┌4┐ ┌──6──┐
Peterson, Susan Lynn. The Life of Martin Luther. 1999. 9 Mar. 2001
      ┌────────────7────────────┐
    <http://pweb.netcom.com/~supeters/luther.htm>.
```

With corporate (group) author

United States. Environmental Protection Agency. <u>Values and</u>
<u>Functions of Wetlands</u>. 25 May 1999. 24 Mar. 2001 <http://
www.epa.gov-owow/wetlands/facts/fact2.html>.

Author unknown

<u>Margaret Sanger Papers Project</u>. 18 Oct. 2000. History Dept., New York
U. 3 Apr. 2001 <http://www.nyu.edu/projects/sanger/>.

With editor

<u>Exploring Ancient World Cultures</u>. Ed. Anthony F. Beavers. 1997. U of
Evansville. 12 Mar. 2001 <http://eawc.evansville.edu/index.htm>.

NOTE: If the site has no title, substitute a description, such as
"Home page," for the title. Do not underline the words or put
them in quotation marks.

Block, Marylaine. Home page. 5 Mar. 2001. 12 Apr. 2001 <http://
www.marylaine.com>.

■ **28. SHORT WORK FROM A WEB SITE** Short works are those that
appear in quotation marks in MLA style: articles, poems, and
other documents that are not book length. For a short work
from a Web site, include as many of the following elements as
apply and as are available: (1) author's name; (2) title of the
short work, in quotation marks; (3) title of the site, underlined;
(4) date of publication or last update; (5) sponsor of the site (if
not named as the author or given as the title of the site); (6)
date you accessed the source; and (7) the URL in angle brackets.

Usually at least some of these elements will not apply or
will be unavailable. In the following example, no sponsor or
date of publication was available. (The date given is the date on
which the researcher accessed the source.)

With author

```
  ┌──── 1 ────┐ ┌──────────── 2 ────────────┐ ┌── 3 ──┐
```
Shiva, Vandana. "Bioethics: A Third World Issue." <u>NativeWeb</u>.
```
  ┌──── 6 ────┐ ┌──────────────── 7 ────────────────
```
15 Sept. 2001 <http://www.nativeweb.org/pages/legal/
```
  ────────────┐
```
shiva.html>.

Author unknown

"Media Giants." Frontline: The Merchants of Cool. 2001. PBS Online.

7 Mar. 2001 <http://www.pbs.org/wgbh/pages/frontline/shows/

cool/giants>.

NOTE: When the URL for a short work from a Web site is very long, you may give the URL for the home page and indicate the path by which readers can access the source.

"Obesity Trends among U.S. Adults between 1985 and 2001." Centers

for Disease Control and Prevention. 3 Jan. 2003. 17 Feb. 2003

<http://www.cdc.gov>. Path: Health Topics A-Z: Obesity Trends;

U.S. Obesity Trends 1985 to 2001.

■ **29. ONLINE BOOK** When a book or a book-length work such as a play or a long poem is posted on the Web as its own site, give as much publication information as is available, followed by your date of access and the URL. (See also the models for print books on pp. 426–29.)

Rawlins, Gregory J. E. Moths to the Flame. Cambridge: MIT P, 1996.

3 Apr. 2001 <http://mitpress.mit.edu/e-books/Moths/

contents.html>.

If the book-length work is posted on a scholarly Web site, provide information about that site.

Jacobs, Harriet Ann. Incidents in the Life of a Slave Girl. Boston,

1861. Documenting the American South: The Southern Experience

in Nineteenth-Century America. Ed. Ji-Hae Yoon and Natalia

Smith. 1998. Academic Affairs Lib., U of North Carolina, Chapel

Hill. 14 Mar. 2001 <http://docsouth.unc.edu/jacobs/jacobs.html>.

■ **30. PART OF AN ONLINE BOOK** Place the part title before the book's title. If the part is a short work such as a poem or an essay, put its title in quotation marks. If the part is an introduction or other division of the book, do not use quotation marks.

Adams, Henry. "Diplomacy." The Education of Henry Adams. Boston:

Houghton, 1918. Bartleby.com: Great Books Online. 1999. 17 Feb.

2003 <http://bartleby.com/159/8.html>.

Bryan, William S., and Robert Rose. Preface. A History of the Pioneer

    Families of Missouri. St. Louis: Bryan, 1876. University of

    Missouri Digital Library. 2002. 20 Feb. 2003 <http://

    digital.library.umsystem.edu/cgi-bin/Ebind2h3/umkc3>.

■ **31. WORK FROM A SERVICE SUCH AS *INFOTRAC*** Libraries pay for access to databases through subscription services such as *Info-Trac*. When you retrieve a work from a subscription service, give as much of the following information as is available: (1) publication information for the source (see the models for articles in periodicals on pp. 430–32); (2) the name of the database, underlined; (3) the name of the service; (4) the name and location of the library where you retrieved the article; (5) the date on which you retrieved the article; and (6) the URL of the service.

The following models are for articles retrieved through three popular library subscription services. The *InfoTrac* source is a scholarly article in a journal paginated by volume (see item 21 on p. 430); the *EBSCOhost* source is an article in a bimonthly magazine (see item 20 on p. 430); and the *ProQuest* source is an article in a daily newspaper (see item 23 on p. 431).

InfoTrac

Johnson, Kirk. "The Mountain Lions of Michigan." Endangered Species

    Update 19.2 (2002): 27+. Expanded Academic Index. InfoTrac.

    U of Michigan Lib., Ann Arbor. 26 Nov. 2002 <http://

    infotrac.galegroup.com>.

EBSCOhost

Darnovsky, Marcy. "Embryo Cloning and Beyond." Tikkun July-Aug.

    2002: 29-32. Academic Search Premier. EBSCOhost. Portland

    Community Coll. Lib., Portland, OR. 1 Nov. 2002 <http://

    search.epnet.com>.

ProQuest

Kolata, Gina. "Scientists Debating Future of Hormone Replacement."

    New York Times 23 Oct. 2002: A20. ProQuest. Drew U Lib.,

    Madison, N.J. 26 Nov. 2002 <http://www.proquest.com>.

NOTE: When you access a work through a personal subscription service such as *America Online,* give the information about the source, followed by the name of the service, the date of access, and the keyword used to retrieve the source.

Conniff, Richard. "The House That John Built." Smithsonian Feb. 2001.

America Online. 11 Mar. 2001. Keyword: Smithsonian Magazine.

■ **32. ARTICLE IN AN ONLINE PERIODICAL** When citing online articles, follow the guidelines for printed articles (see items 20–26), giving whatever information is available in the online source. End the citation with your date of access and the URL.

NOTE: In some online articles, paragraphs are numbered. For such articles, include the total number of paragraphs in your citation, as in the next example.

From an online scholarly journal

Belau, Linda. "Trauma and the Material Signifier." Postmodern

Culture 11.2 (2001): 37 pars. 30 Mar. 2001 <http://

jefferson.village.virginia.edu/pmc/current.issue/11.2belau.html>.

From an online magazine

Morgan, Fiona. "Banning the Bullies." Salon.com 15 Mar. 2001. 2 Apr.

2001 <http://www.salon.com/news/feature/2001/03/15/

bullying/index.html>.

From an online newspaper

Whillon, Phil. "Ready or Not." Los Angeles Times 2 Dec. 2001. 3 Dec.

2001 <http://www.latimes.com/news/la-foster-special.special>.

■ **33. CD-ROM** Treat a CD-ROM as you would any other source, but name the medium before the publication information.

"Pimpernel." The American Heritage Dictionary of the English

Language. 4th ed. CD-ROM. Boston: Houghton, 2000.

Wattenberg, Ruth. "Helping Students in the Middle." American

Educator 19.4 (1996): 2-18. ERIC. CD-ROM. SilverPlatter. Sept.

1996.

■ **34. E-MAIL** To cite an e-mail, begin with the writer's name and the subject line. Then write "E-mail to" followed by the name of the recipient. End with the date of the message.

O'Donnell, Patricia. "Re: Interview questions." E-mail to the author.

    15 Mar. 2001.

■ **35. POSTING TO AN ONLINE LIST, FORUM, OR GROUP** Communications through e-mail discussion lists (often called LISTSERVs), Web forums, and Usenet newsgroups do not take place in real time. (For real-time online communications, see item 36.) When possible, cite archived versions of postings, which are more permanent and easier to retrieve. If you cannot locate an archived version, keep a copy of the posting for your records.

Begin the entry with the author's name, followed by the title or subject line; the words "Online posting"; the date of the posting; the name of the list, forum, or newsgroup; and your date of access. Then, for a discussion list, give the URL of the list if it is available; otherwise give the e-mail address of the list moderator. For a Web forum, give the network address. For a Usenet group, use the prefix "news:" followed by the name of the newsgroup.

Discussion list posting

Edwards, David. "Media Lens." Online posting. 20 Dec. 2001. Media

    Lens Archives. 10 Apr. 2002 <http://groups.yahoo.com/group/

    medialens/message/25>.

Web forum posting

Brown, Oliver. "Welcome." Online posting. 8 Oct. 2002. Chester Coll.

    Students Web Forum. 20 Feb. 2003 <http://www.voy.com/

    113243/>.

Newsgroup posting

Reedy, Tom. "Re: Macbeth an Existential Nightmare?" Online posting.

    9 Mar. 2002. 8 Apr. 2002 <news:humanities.lit.authors.shakespe>.

■ **36. POSTING TO A MUD OR A MOO** MUDs and MOOs are forums that allow communication in real time. Include the writer's name (if relevant), a description and date of the event, the title of the forum, the date of access, and the electronic address, beginning with the prefix "telnet://."

Carbone, Nick. Planning for the future. 1 Mar. 2001. TechRhet's

Thursday night MOO. 1 Mar. 2001 <telnet://

connections.moo.mud.org:3333>.

If possible, cite an archived version of the posting.

Multimedia sources (including online versions)

Multimedia sources include visuals (such as works of art), audio works (such as sound recordings), audiovisuals (such as films), and live events (such as the performance of a play).

When citing multimedia sources that you retrieved online, consult the appropriate model in this section and give whatever information is available for the online source; then end the citation with your date of access and the URL. (See items 37, 40, and 44 for examples.)

■ **37. WORK OF ART** Cite the artist's name, followed by the title of the artwork, usually underlined, and the institution and city in which the artwork can be found. If you want to indicate the work's date, include it after the title. For a work of art you viewed online, end your citation with your date of access and the URL.

Constable, John. Dedham Vale. Victoria and Albert Museum, London.

van Gogh, Vincent. The Starry Night. 1889. Museum of Mod. Art,

New York. 3 Feb. 2003 <http://moma.org/collection/depts/

paint_sculpt/blowups/paint_sculpt_003.html>.

■ **38. CARTOON** Begin with the cartoonist's name, followed by the title of the cartoon (if it has one) in quotation marks, the word "Cartoon," and the publication information for the publication in which the cartoon appears.

Rall, Ted. "Search and Destroy." Cartoon. Village Voice 23 Jan. 2001: 6.

■ **39. ADVERTISEMENT** Name the product or company being advertised, followed by the word "Advertisement." Give publication information for the source in which the advertisement appears.

Truth by Calvin Klein. Advertisement. Vogue Dec. 2000: 95-98.

■ **40. MAP OR CHART** Cite a map or chart as you would a book or a short work within a longer work. Add the word "Map" or "Chart" following the title.

Serbia. Map. 2 Feb. 2001. 17 Mar. 2003 <http://www.biega.com/
serbia.html>.

Joseph, Lori, and Bob Laird. "Driving While Phoning Is Dangerous."
Chart. USA Today 16 Feb. 2001: 1A.

■ **41. MUSICAL COMPOSITION** Cite the composer's name, followed by the title of the work. Underline the title of an opera, a ballet, or a composition identified by name, but do not underline or use quotation marks around a composition identified by number or form.

Ellington, Duke. Conga Brava.

Haydn, Franz Joseph. Symphony no. 88 in G.

■ **42. SOUND RECORDING** Begin with the name of the person you want to emphasize: the composer, conductor, or performer. For a long work, give the title, underlined, followed by names of pertinent artists (such as performers, readers, or musicians) and the orchestra and conductor (if relevant). End with the manufacturer and the date.

Bizet, Georges. Carmen. Perf. Jennifer Laramore, Thomas Moser, Angela
Gheorghiu, and Samuel Ramey. Bavarian State Orch. and Chorus.
Cond. Giuseppe Sinopoli. Warner, 1996.

For a song, put the title in quotation marks. If you include the name of the album, underline it.

Chapman, Tracy. "Paper and Ink." Telling Stories. Elektra, 2000.

■ **43. FILM OR VIDEO** Begin with the title, underlined. For a film, cite the director and the lead actors or narrator ("Perf." or "Narr."), followed by the name of the distributor and the year of the film's release. For a videotape or DVD, add "Videocassette" or "DVD" before the name of the distributor.

Chocolat. Dir. Lasse Hallström. Perf. Juliette Binoche, Judi Dench, Alfred Molina, Lena Olin, and Johnny Depp. Miramax, 2001.

High Fidelity. Dir. Stephen Frears. Perf. John Cusack, Iben Hjejle, Jack Black, and Todd Louiso. 2000. Videocassette. Walt Disney Video, 2001.

■ **44. RADIO OR TELEVISION PROGRAM** Begin with the title of the radio segment or television episode (if there is one) in quotation marks, followed by the title of the program, underlined. Next give relevant information about the program's writer ("By"), director ("Dir."), performers ("Perf."), or host ("Host"). Then name the network, the local station (if any), and the date the program was broadcast.

"Monkey Trial." American Experience. PBS. WGBH, Boston. 18 Mar. 2003.

"Live in 4A: Konstantin Soukhovetski." Performance Today. Natl. Public Radio. 2 May 2002. 10 May 2002 <http://www.npr.org/programs/pt/features/4a/soukhovetski.02.html>.

If there is a series title, include it after the title of the program, neither underlined nor in quotation marks.

Mysteries of the Pyramids. On the Inside. Discovery Channel. 7 Feb. 2001.

■ **45. RADIO OR TELEVISION INTERVIEW** Begin with the name of the person who was interviewed, followed by the word "Interview." End with the information about the program as in item 44.

McGovern, George. Interview. Charlie Rose. PBS. WNET, New York. 1 Feb. 2001.

■ **46. LIVE PERFORMANCE** For a live performance of a play, a ballet, an opera, or a concert, begin with the title of the work performed. Then name the author or composer of the work (preceded by the word "By"), followed by as much information about the performance as is available: the director ("Dir."), choreographer ("Chor."), or conductor ("Cond."); the major performers ("Perf."); the theater, ballet, or opera company; the theater and its city; and the date of the performance.

Art. By Yasmina Reza. Dir. Matthew Warchus. Perf. Philip Franks, Leigh

   Lawson, and Simon Shephard. Whitehall Theatre, London. 3 Dec.

   2001.

Cello Concerto No. 2. By Eric Tanguy. Cond. Seiji Ozawa. Perf. Mstislav

   Rostropovich. Boston Symphony Orch. Symphony Hall, Boston.

   5 Apr. 2002.

■ **47. LECTURE OR PUBLIC ADDRESS** Cite the speaker's name, followed by the title of the lecture (if any), the organization sponsoring the lecture, the location, and the date.

Cohran, Kelan. "Slavery and Astronomy." Adler Planetarium, Chicago.

   21 Feb. 2001.

■ **48. PERSONAL INTERVIEW** Begin with the name of the person you interviewed. Then write "Personal interview," followed by the date of the interview.

Shaikh, Michael. Personal interview. 22 Mar. 2001.

Other sources (including online versions)

This section includes a variety of traditional print sources not covered elsewhere. For sources obtained on the Web, consult the appropriate model in this section and give whatever information is available for the online source; then end the citation with the date on which you accessed the source and the URL. (See the second example under item 49.)

■ **49. GOVERNMENT PUBLICATION** Treat the government agency as the author, giving the name of the government followed by the name of the agency.

United States. Natl. Council on Disability. Promises to Keep: A Decade

   of Federal Enforcement of the Americans with Disabilities Act.

   Washington: GPO, 2000.

For government documents published online, give as much publication information as is available and end your citation with the date of access and the URL.

United States. Dept. of Transportation. Natl. Highway Traffic Safety

    Administration. An Investigation of the Safety Implications of

    Wireless Communications in Vehicles. Nov. 1999. 20 May 2001

    <http://www.nhtsa.dot.gov/people/injury/research/wireless>.

■ **50. LEGAL SOURCE** For articles of the United States Constitution and laws in the United States Code, no works cited entry is required; instead, simply give an in-text citation (see item 17 on p. 420).

For a legislative act, begin with the name of the act. Then provide the act's Public Law number, its date of enactment, and its Statutes at Large number.

Electronic Freedom of Information Act Amendments of 1996. Pub. L.

    104-418. 2 Oct. 1996. Stat. 3048.

For a court case, name the first plaintiff and first defendant. Then give the case number, the court name, and the date of the decision. In a works cited entry, the name of the case is not underlined.

Utah v. Evans. No. 01-714. Supreme Ct. of the US. 20 June 2002.

■ **51. PAMPHLET** Cite a pamphlet as you would a book.

Commonwealth of Massachusetts. Dept. of Jury Commissioner. A Few

    Facts about Jury Duty. Boston: Commonwealth of Massachusetts,

    1997.

■ **52. DISSERTATION** Begin with the author's name, followed by the dissertation title in quotation marks, the abbreviation "Diss.," the name of the institution, and the year the dissertation was accepted.

Jackson, Shelley. "Writing Whiteness: Contemporary Southern

    Literature in Black and White." Diss. U of Maryland, 2000.

For dissertations that have been published in book form, underline the title. After the title and before the book's publication information, add the abbreviation "Diss.," the name of the institution, and the year the dissertation was accepted.

Damberg, Cheryl L. Healthcare Reform: Distributional Consequences of an Employer Mandate for Workers in Small Firms. Diss. Rand Graduate School, 1995. Santa Monica: Rand, 1996.

■ **53. ABSTRACT OF A DISSERTATION** Cite an abstract as you would an unpublished dissertation. After the dissertation date, give the abbreviation *DA* or *DAI* (for *Dissertation Abstracts* or *Dissertation Abstracts International*), followed by the volume number, the date of publication, and the page number.

Chen, Shu-Ling. "Mothers and Daughters in Morrison, Tan, Marshall, and Kincaid." Diss. U of Washington, 2000. DAI 61 (2000): 2289.

■ **54. PUBLISHED PROCEEDINGS OF A CONFERENCE** Cite published conference proceedings as you would a book, adding information about the conference after the title.

Kartiganer, Donald M., and Ann J. Abadie. Faulkner at 100: Retrospect and Prospect. Proc. of Faulkner and Yoknapatawpha Conf., 27 July-1 Aug. 1997, U of Mississippi. Jackson: UP of Mississippi, 2000.

■ **55. PUBLISHED INTERVIEW** Name the person interviewed, followed by the title of the interview (if there is one). If the interview does not have a title, include the word "Interview" followed by a period after the interviewee's name. Give publication information for the work in which the interview was published.

Renoir, Jean. "Renoir at Home: Interview with Jean Renoir." Film Quarterly 50.1 (1996): 2-8.

If the name of the interviewer is relevant, include it after the name of the interviewee.

Prince. Interview with Bilge Ebiri. Yahoo! Internet Life 7.6 (2001): 82-85.

■ **56. PERSONAL LETTER** Begin with the writer's name and add the phrase "Letter to the author," followed by the date.

Coggins, Christopher. Letter to the author. 6 May 2001.

54c MLA information notes (optional)

Researchers who use the MLA system of parenthetical documentation (see 54a) may also use information notes for one of two purposes:

1. to provide additional material that might interrupt the flow of the paper yet is important enough to include
2. to refer readers to any sources not discussed in the paper

Information notes may be footnotes or endnotes. Footnotes appear at the foot of the page; endnotes appear on a separate page at the end of the paper, just before the list of works cited. For either style, the notes are numbered consecutively throughout the paper. The text of the paper contains a raised arabic numeral that corresponds to the number of the note.

TEXT

Local governments are more likely than state governments to pass legislation against using a cell phone while driving.[1]

NOTE

[1] For a discussion of local laws banning cell phone use, see Sundeen 8.

55

Manuscript format; sample paper

55a Manuscript format

The following guidelines on formatting a paper and preparing a list of works cited are consistent with advice given in the *MLA Handbook for Writers of Research Papers*, 6th ed. (New York: MLA, 2003). For a sample MLA paper, see 55b.

Formatting the paper

MLA papers should be formatted as follows.

MATERIALS Use good-quality 8½″ × 11″ white paper. Secure the pages with a paper clip. Unless your instructor suggests otherwise, do not staple or bind the pages.

TITLE AND IDENTIFICATION MLA does not require a title page. On the first page of your paper, place your name, your instructor's name, the course title, and the date on separate lines against the left margin. Then center your title. (See p. 448 for a sample first page.)

If your instructor requires a title page, ask for guidelines on formatting it. A format similar to the one on page 485 will most likely be acceptable.

PAGINATION Put the page number preceded by your last name in the upper right corner of each page, one-half inch below the top edge. Use arabic numerals (1, 2, 3, and so on).

MARGINS, LINE SPACING, AND PARAGRAPH INDENTS Leave margins of one inch on all sides of the page. Do not justify (align) the right margin.

Double-space throughout the paper. Do not add extra lines of space above or below the title of the paper or between paragraphs.

Indent the first line of each paragraph one-half inch (or five spaces) from the left margin.

LONG QUOTATIONS When a quoted passage takes up more than four typed lines of prose or three lines of verse in your paper, set it off from the text by indenting the entire quotation one inch (or ten spaces) from the left margin. Double-space the indented quotation, and don't add extra space above or below it.

Quotation marks are not needed when a quotation has been set off from the text by indenting. See page 410 for an example.

WEB ADDRESSES When a Web address mentioned in the text of your paper must be divided at the end of a line, do not insert a hyphen (a hyphen could appear to be part of the address). For MLA rules on dividing Web addresses in your list of works cited, see page 447.

HEADINGS MLA neither encourages nor discourages the use of headings and currently provides no guidelines for their use.

VISUALS MLA classifies visuals as tables and figures (figures include graphs, charts, maps, photographs, and drawings). Label each table with an arabic numeral (Table 1, Table 2, and so on) and provide a clear caption that identifies the subject. The label and caption should appear on separate lines above the table, flush left. Below the table, give its source in a note like this one:

> Source: John M. Violanti, "Cellular Phones and Fatal Traffic
> Collisions," Accident Analysis and Prevention 30 (1998): 521.

For each figure, place a label and a caption below the figure, flush left. They need not appear on separate lines. The word "Figure" may be abbreviated to "Fig." Include source information following the caption.

Visuals should be placed in the text, as close as possible to the sentences that relate to them unless your instructor prefers them in an appendix. See page 450 for an example of a visual in the text of a paper.

Preparing the list of works cited

Begin the list of works cited on a new page at the end of the paper. Center the title Works Cited about one inch from the top of the page. Double-space throughout. See page 454 for a sample list of works cited.

ALPHABETIZING THE LIST Alphabetize the list by the last names of the authors (or editors); if a work has no author or editor, alphabetize it by the first word of the title other than *A, An,* or *The.*

If your list includes two or more works by the same author, use the author's name only for the first entry. For subsequent entries use three hyphens followed by a period. List the titles in alphabetical order. See also item 5 on page 426.

INDENTING Do not indent the first line of each works cited entry, but indent any additional lines one-half inch (or five spaces). This technique highlights the names of the authors, making it easy for readers to scan the alphabetized list.

WEB ADDRESSES Do not insert a hyphen when dividing a Web address at the end of a line. Break the line after a slash. Also, insert angle brackets around the URL.

For advice about how to cite sources with long URLs, see item 28 on page 433.

If your word processing program automatically turns Web addresses into hot links (by underlining them and highlighting them in color), turn off this feature.

ON THE WEB

For advice on using your word processor to format a works cited page, go to **dianahacker.com/rules**

and click on ▶ **Additional Resources**
▶ **Formatting Help**

55b Sample MLA research paper

On the following pages is a research paper on the topic of cell phones and driving, written by Angela Daly, a student in a composition class. Daly's paper is documented with MLA-style in-text citations and a list of works cited. Annotations in the margins of the paper draw your attention to features of special interest.

ON THE WEB

Another student, Paul Levi, has also written a paper on the topic of cell phones and driving; his paper takes the opposite stand from that taken by Angela Daly. To read Levi's paper, go to **dianahacker.com/rules**

and click on ▶ **Model Papers**
▶ **MLA papers: Levi**

Daly 1

Angela Daly

Professor Chavez

English 101

14 March 2001

A Call to Action:

Regulate Use of Cell Phones on the Road

When a cell phone goes off in a classroom or at a concert, we are irritated, but at least our lives are not endangered. When we are on the road, however, irresponsible cell phone users are more than irritating: They are putting our lives at risk. Many of us have witnessed drivers so distracted by dialing and chatting that they resemble drunk drivers, weaving between lanes, for example, or nearly running down pedestrians in crosswalks. A number of bills to regulate use of cell phones on the road have been introduced in state legislatures, and the time has come to push for their passage. Regulation is needed because drivers using phones are seriously impaired and because laws on negligent and reckless driving are not sufficient to punish offenders.

No one can deny that cell phones have caused traffic deaths and injuries. Cell phones were implicated in three fatal accidents in November 1999 alone. Early in November, two-year-old Morgan Pena was killed by a driver distracted by his cell phone. Morgan's mother, Patti Pena, reports that the driver "ran a stop sign at 45 mph, broadsided my vehicle and killed Morgan as she sat in her car seat." A week

Title is centered.

Opening sentences catch readers' attention.

Thesis asserts Angela Daly's main point.

Daly uses a clear topic sentence.

Signal phrase names the author of the quotation; no page number is available.

Daly 2

later, corrections officer Shannon Smith, who was guarding prisoners by the side of the road, was killed by a woman distracted by a phone call (Besthoff). On Thanksgiving weekend that same month, John and Carole Hall were killed when a Naval Academy midshipman crashed into their parked car. The driver said in court that when he looked up from the cell phone he was dialing, he was three feet from the car and had no time to stop (Stockwell B8).

Expert testimony, public opinion, and even cartoons suggest that driving while phoning is dangerous. Frances Bents, an expert on the relation between cell phones and accidents, estimates that between 450 and 1,000 crashes a year have some connection to cell phone use (Layton C9). In a survey published by Farmers Insurance Group, 87% of those polled said that cell phones affect a driver's ability, and 40% reported having close calls with drivers distracted by phones. Many cartoons have depicted the very real dangers of driving while distracted (see Fig. 1).

Scientific research confirms the dangers of using phones while on the road. In 1997 an important study appeared in the New England Journal of Medicine. The authors, Donald Redelmeier and Robert Tibshirani, studied 699 volunteers who made their cell phone bills available in order to confirm the times when they had placed calls. The participants agreed to report any nonfatal collision in which they were involved. By comparing the time of a collision with the phone records, the researchers assessed

Author's name is given in parentheses; no page is available.

Page number is given when available.

Clear topic sentences like this one are used throughout the paper.

Summary and long quotation are introduced with a signal phrase naming the authors.

Daly 3

"YEP... GOT MY CELLPHONE, MY PAGER, MY INTERNET LINK, MY WIRELESS FAX, AND THANKS TO THIS NIFTY SATELLITE NAVIGATING SYSTEM, I KNOW PRECISELY WHERE I AM AT ALL TIMES!"

Fig. 1. Chan Lowe, cartoon, Washington Post 22 July 2000: A21.

Illustration has figure number, label, and source information.

the dangers of driving while phoning. Here are their results:

Long quotation is set off from the text; quotation marks are omitted.

> We found that using a cellular telephone was associated with a risk of having a motor vehicle collision that was about four times as high as that among the same drivers when they were not using their cellular telephones. This relative risk is similar to the hazard associated with driving with a blood alcohol level at the legal limit. (456)

In reports by news media, the latter claim was exaggerated ("similar to" is not "equal to"), but the comparison with drunk driving is startling nonetheless.

A 1998 study focused on Oklahoma, one of the few states to keep records on fatal accidents involving cell phones. Using police records, John M. Violanti of the

Daly 4

Rochester Institute of Technology investigated the relation between traffic fatalities in Oklahoma and the use or presence of a cell phone. He found a ninefold increase in the risk of fatality if a phone was being used and a doubled risk simply when a phone was present in a vehicle (522-23). The latter statistic is interesting, for it suggests that those who carry phones in their cars may tend to be more negligent (or prone to distractions of all kinds) than those who do not.

Summary begins with a signal phrase naming the author (see bottom of previous page) and ends with page numbers in parentheses.

Some groups have argued that state traffic laws make legislation regulating cell phone use unnecessary. Sadly, this is not true. Laws on traffic safety vary from state to state, and drivers distracted by cell phones can get off with light punishment even when they cause fatal accidents. For example, although the midshipman mentioned earlier was charged with vehicular manslaughter for the deaths of John and Carole Hall, the judge was unable to issue a verdict of guilty. Under Maryland law, he could only find the defendant guilty of negligent driving and impose a $500 fine (Layton C1). Such a light sentence is not unusual. The driver who killed Morgan Pena in Pennsylvania received two tickets and a $50 fine--and retained his driving privileges (Pena). In Georgia, a young woman distracted by her phone ran down and killed a two-year-old; her sentence was ninety days in boot camp and five hundred hours of community service (Ippolito J1). The families of the victims are understandably distressed by laws that lead to such light sentences.

Daly counters an opposing argument.

Facts are documented with in-text citations: authors' names and page numbers (if available) in parentheses.

Research Guide

When certain kinds of driver behavior are shown to be especially dangerous, we wisely draft special laws making them illegal and imposing specific punishments. Running red lights, failing to stop for a school bus, and drunk driving are obvious examples; phoning in a moving vehicle should be no exception. Unlike more general laws covering negligent driving, specific laws leave little ambiguity for law officers and for judges and juries imposing punishments. Such laws have another important benefit: They leave no ambiguity for drivers. Currently, drivers can tease themselves into thinking they are using their car phones responsibly because the definition of "negligent driving" is vague.

As of December 2000, twenty countries were restricting use of cell phones in moving vehicles (Sundeen 8). In the United States, it is highly unlikely that legislation could be passed on the national level, since traffic safety is considered a state and local issue. To date, only a few counties and towns have passed traffic laws restricting cell phone use. For example, in Suffolk County, New York, it is illegal for drivers to use a handheld phone for anything but an emergency call while on the road (Haughney A8). The first town to restrict use of handheld phones was Brooklyn, Ohio (Layton C9). Brooklyn, the first community in the country to pass a seat belt law, has once again shown its concern for traffic safety.

Laws passed by counties and towns have had some effect, but it makes more sense to legislate at the state level. Local laws are not likely to have the impact of

Daly uses an analogy to justify passing a special law.

Daly explains why U.S. laws need to be passed on the state level.

Transition helps readers move from one paragraph to the next.

Daly 6

state laws, and keeping track of a wide variety of local
ordinances is confusing for drivers. Even a spokesperson
for Verizon Wireless has said that statewide bans are
preferable to a "crazy patchwork quilt of ordinances" (qtd.
in Haughney A8). Unfortunately, although a number of bills
have been introduced in state legislatures, as of early 2001
no state law seriously restricting use of the phones had
passed--largely because of effective lobbying from the
wireless industry.

> Daly cites an indirect source: words quoted in another source.

Despite the claims of some lobbyists, tough laws regulating phone use can make our roads safer. In Japan, for
example, accidents linked to cell phones fell by 75% just a
month after the country prohibited using a handheld phone
while driving (Haughney A8). Research suggests and
common sense tells us that it is not possible to drive an
automobile at high speeds, dial numbers, and carry on con-
versations without significant risks. When such behavior is
regulated, obviously our roads will be safer.

> Daly counters a claim made by some opponents.

Because of mounting public awareness of the dangers
of drivers distracted by phones, state legislators must begin to take the problem seriously. "It's definitely an issue
that is gaining steam around the country," says Matt
Sundeen of the National Conference of State Legislatures
(qtd. in Layton C9). Lon Anderson of the American Automobile Association agrees: "There is momentum building," he
says, to pass laws (qtd. in Layton C9). The time has come
for states to adopt legislation restricting the use of cell
phones in moving vehicles.

> For variety Daly places a signal phrase after a brief quotation.

> The paper ends with Daly's stand on the issue.

Daly 7

Heading is
centered.

Works Cited

Besthoff, Len. "Cell Phone Use Increases Risk of Accidents,

but Users Willing to Take the Risk." <u>WRAL Online</u>. 11

The URL is
broken after
a slash. No
hyphen is
inserted.

Nov. 1999. 12 Jan. 2001 <http://www.wral-tv.com/

news/wral/1999/1110-talking-driving/>.

Farmers Insurance Group. "New Survey Shows Drivers Have

Had 'Close Calls' with Cell Phone Users." <u>Farmers</u>

<u>Insurance Group</u>. 8 May 2000. 12 Jan. 2001

<http://www.farmersinsurance.com/

news_cellphones.html>.

List is alpha-
betized by
authors' last
names (or by
title when a
work has no
author).

Haughney, Christine. "Taking Phones out of Drivers' Hands."

<u>Washington Post</u> 5 Nov. 2000: A8.

Ippolito, Milo. "Driver's Sentence Not Justice, Mom Says."

<u>Atlanta Journal-Constitution</u> 25 Sept. 1999: J1.

Layton, Lyndsey. "Legislators Aiming to Disconnect

Motorists." <u>Washington Post</u> 10 Dec. 2000: C1+.

First line of
each entry is
at the left mar-
gin; extra lines
are indented
1/2" (or five
spaces).

Lowe, Chan. Cartoon. <u>Washington Post</u> 22 July 2000: A21.

Pena, Patricia N. "Patti Pena's Letter to Car Talk." <u>Cars.com</u>.

Car Talk. 10 Jan. 2001 <http://cartalk.cars.com/About/

Morgan-Pena/letter.html>.

Redelmeier, Donald A., and Robert J. Tibshirani. "Association

between Cellular-Telephone Calls and Motor Vehicle

Collisions." <u>New England Journal of Medicine</u> 336

(1997): 453-58.

Double-spacing
is used
throughout.

Stockwell, Jamie. "Phone Use Faulted in Collision."

<u>Washington Post</u> 6 Dec. 2000: B1+.

Daly 8

Sundeen, Matt. "Cell Phones and Highway Safety: 2000
State Legislative Update." National Conference of State
Legislatures. Dec. 2000. 9 pp. 27 Feb. 2001
<http://ncsl.org/programs/esnr/ccellphone.pdf>.

Violanti, John M. "Cellular Phones and Fatal Traffic
Collisions." Accident Analysis and Prevention 30
(1998): 519-24.

WRITING APA PAPERS

Most writing assignments in the social sciences are either reports of original research or reviews of the literature written about a particular research topic. Often an original research report contains a "review of the literature" section that places the writer's project in the context of previous research.

Social science instructors will often ask you to document sources with the American Psychological Association (APA) system of in-text citations and references described in 59. In addition to documenting your sources, you face three main challenges when writing a social science paper that draws on written sources: (1) supporting a thesis, (2) avoiding plagiarism, and (3) integrating quotations and other source material.

NOTE: For cross-disciplinary advice on finding and evaluating sources and on managing information, see sections 48–50.

56

Supporting a thesis

Most assignments ask you to form a thesis, or main idea, and to support that thesis with well-organized evidence.

56a Form a thesis.

A thesis, which usually appears at the end of the introduction, is a one-sentence (or occasionally a two-sentence) statement of your central idea. In a paper reviewing the literature on a topic, this thesis analyzes the often competing conclusions drawn by a variety of researchers.

Your paper will address a central research question, and your thesis will express a reasonable answer to that question, given the current state of research in the field. Here, for example, is a research question posed by a student in a psychology class, along with that student's thesis.

RESEARCH QUESTION

How and to what extent have the great apes — gorillas, chimpanzees, and orangutans — demonstrated language abilities akin to those of humans?

POSSIBLE THESIS

Researchers agree that apes have acquired fairly large vocabularies in American Sign Language and in artificial languages, but they have drawn quite different conclusions in addressing the following questions: (1) How spontaneously have apes used language? (2) How creatively have apes used language? (3) To what extent can apes create sentences? (4) What are some implications of the ape language studies?

ON THE WEB

For an electronic exercise on thesis statements in APA papers, go to **dianahacker.com/rules**

and click on   ▶ **Electronic Research Exercises**
                   ▶ **E-ex 56–1**

56b   Organize your evidence.

The American Psychological Association encourages the use of headings to help readers follow the organization of a paper. For an original research report, the major headings often follow a standard model: Method, Results, Discussion. For a paper that reviews the literature on a research topic, headings will vary, depending on the topic (see pp. 485–94 for an example).

57

Avoiding plagiarism

Your research paper is a collaboration between you and your sources. To be fair and ethical, you must acknowledge your debt to the writers of those sources. If you don't, you are guilty of plagiarism, a serious academic offense.

Three different acts are considered plagiarism: (1) failing to cite quotations and borrowed ideas, (2) failing to enclose borrowed language in quotation marks, and (3) failing to put summaries and paraphrases in your own words.

ON THE WEB

For electronic exercises on avoiding plagiarism in APA papers, go to **dianahacker.com/rules**

and click on ▶ **Electronic Research Exercises**
▶ **E-ex 57-1 and 57-2**

57a Cite quotations and borrowed ideas.

You must of course cite all direct quotations. You must also cite any ideas borrowed from a source: summaries and paraphrases, statistics and other specific facts, and visuals such as cartoons, graphs, or diagrams.

The only exception is common knowledge — general information that your readers may know or could easily locate in any number of reference sources. For example, the approximate population of the United States is common knowledge among sociologists and economists, and psychologists are familiar with Freud's theory of the unconscious. As a rule, when you have seen certain general information repeatedly in your reading, you don't need to cite it. However, when information has appeared in only a few sources, when it is highly specific (as with statistics), or when it is controversial, you should cite it.

The American Psychological Association recommends an author-date style of citations. Here, very briefly, is how the author-date system often works. See 59 for a detailed discussion of variations.

1. The source is introduced by a signal phrase that includes the last names of the authors followed by the date of publication in parentheses.
2. The material being cited is followed by a page number in parentheses.
3. At the end of the paper, an alphabetized list of references gives publication information about the source.

IN-TEXT CITATION

Noting that apes' brains resemble those of our human ancestors, Leakey and Lewin (1992) argued that in ape brains "the cognitive foundations on which human language could be built are already present" (p. 244).

ENTRY IN THE LIST OF REFERENCES

Leakey, R., & Lewin, R. (1992). *Origins reconsidered: In search of what makes us human.* New York: Doubleday.

57b Enclose borrowed language in quotation marks.

To show readers that you are using a source's exact phrases or sentences, you must enclose them in quotation marks. To omit the quotation marks is to claim — falsely — that the language is your own. Such an omission is plagiarism even if you have cited the source.

ORIGINAL SOURCE

No animal has done more to renew interest in animal intelligence than a beguiling, bilingual bonobo named Kanzi, who has the grammatical abilities of a 2-1/2-year-old child and a taste for movies about cavemen.   — Linden, "Animals," 1986, p. 57

PLAGIARISM

According to Linden (1986), no animal has done more to renew interest in animal intelligence than a beguiling, bilingual bonobo named Kanzi, who has the grammatical abilities of a 2-1/2-year-old child and a taste for movies about cavemen (p. 57).

BORROWED LANGUAGE IN QUOTATION MARKS

According to Linden (1986), "No animal has done more to renew interest in animal intelligence than a beguiling, bilingual bonobo named Kanzi, who has the grammatical abilities of a 2-1/2-year-old child and a taste for movies about cavemen" (p. 57).

NOTE: When long quotations are set off from the text by indenting, quotation marks are not needed (see p. 464).

57C Put summaries and paraphrases in your own words.

A summary condenses information; a paraphrase reports information in about the same number of words. When you summarize or paraphrase, you must restate the source's meaning using your own language. You are guilty of plagiarism if you half-copy the author's sentences — either by mixing the author's well-chosen phrases without using quotation marks or by plugging your own synonyms into the author's sentence structure. The following paraphrases are plagiarized — even though the source is cited — because their language is too close to that of the source.

ORIGINAL SOURCE

If the existence of a signing ape was unsettling for linguists, it was also startling news for animal behaviorists.

— Davis, *Eloquent Animals,* 1976, p. 26

UNACCEPTABLE BORROWING OF PHRASES

Davis (1976) observed that the existence of a signing ape unsettled linguists and startled animal behaviorists (p. 26).

UNACCEPTABLE BORROWING OF STRUCTURE

Davis (1976) observed that if the presence of a sign-language-using chimp was disturbing for scientists studying language, it was also surprising to scientists studying animal behavior (p. 26).

To avoid plagiarizing an author's language, set the source aside, write from memory, and consult the source later to check for accuracy. This strategy prevents you from being captivated by the words on the page.

ACCEPTABLE PARAPHRASE

Davis (1976) observed that both linguists and animal behaviorists were taken by surprise upon learning of an ape's ability to use sign language (p. 26).

58

Integrating sources

By carefully integrating quotations and other source material into your own text, you help readers understand whose views they are hearing—yours or those of your sources. In addition, you show readers where cited material begins and where it ends.

NOTE: APA recommends using the past tense or the present perfect tense in phrases that introduce most sources: *Davis noted that* or *Davis has noted that* (not *Davis notes that*). Use the present tense, however, for discussing the results of an experiment (*the results show*) or explaining conclusions that are not in dispute (*researchers agree*).

It is generally acceptable in the social sciences to call authors by their last name only, even on a first mention. If your paper refers to two authors with the same last name, use initials as well.

ON THE WEB

For electronic exercises on integrating quotations in APA papers, go to **dianahacker.com/rules**

and click on ▶ **Electronic Research Exercises**
▶ **E-ex 58-1 and 58-2**

58a Integrate quotations as smoothly as possible.

Readers need to move from your own words to the words of a source without feeling a jolt.

Using signal phrases

Avoid dropping quotations into the text without warning. Instead, provide clear signal phrases, usually including the author's name and the date of publication, to prepare readers for the quotation.

DROPPED QUOTATION

Even more significant is the pattern of combining symbols that Kanzi developed on his own. "When he gave an order combining two symbols for action--such as 'chase' and 'hide'--it was important for him that the first action--'chase'--be done first" (Gibbons, 1991, p. 1561).

QUOTATION WITH SIGNAL PHRASE

Even more significant is the pattern of combining symbols that Kanzi developed on his own. According to Gibbons (1991), "When he gave an order combining two symbols for action--such as 'chase' and 'hide'--it was important for him that the first action--'chase'--be done first" (p. 1561).

To avoid monotony, try to vary the language and placement of your signal phrases. The models in the chart on the next page suggest a range of possibilities.

When the signal phrase includes a verb, choose one that suits the context. Is your source arguing a point, making an observation, reporting a fact, refuting an argument, or suggesting a theory? By choosing an appropriate verb, you can make your source's stance clear. See the chart on the next page for a list of verbs commonly used in signal phrases in APA papers.

Using the ellipsis mark

To condense a quoted passage, use the ellipsis mark (three spaced periods) to indicate that you have omitted words. What remains must be grammatically complete.

Eckholm (1985) reported that "a 4-year-old pygmy chimpanzee . . . has demonstrated what scientists say are the most humanlike linguistic skills ever documented in another animal" (p. A1).

The writer has omitted the words *at a research center near Atlanta,* which appeared in the original.

To omit a full sentence or more, use a period before the ellipsis dots.

According to Wade (1980), the horse Clever Hans "could apparently count by tapping out numbers with his hoof. . . . Clever

Varying signal phrases in APA papers

MODEL SIGNAL PHRASES

In the words of Terrace, "..."

As Davis has noted, "..."

The Gardners, Washoe's trainers, pointed out that "..."

"...," claimed linguist Noam Chomsky.

"...," wrote Eckholm, "..."

Psychologist H. S. Terrace has offered an odd argument for this view: "..."

Terrace answered these objections with the following analysis: "..."

VERBS IN SIGNAL PHRASES

admitted	contended	reasoned
agreed	declared	refuted
argued	denied	rejected
asserted	emphasized	reported
believed	insisted	responded
claimed	noted	suggested
compared	observed	thought
confirmed	pointed out	wrote

Hans owes his celebrity to his master's innocence. Von Osten sincerely believed he had taught Hans to solve arithmetical problems" (p. 1349).

Ordinarily, do not use an ellipsis mark at the beginning or at the end of a quotation. Readers will understand that the quoted material is taken from a longer passage.

Using brackets

Brackets (square parentheses) allow you to insert words of your own into quoted material, perhaps to explain a confusing reference or to keep a sentence grammatical in your context.

Seyfarth (1982) has written that "Premack [a scientist at the University of Pennsylvania] taught a seven-year-old chimpanzee,

Sarah, that the word for 'apple' was a small, plastic triangle" (p. 13).

To indicate an error in a quotation, insert [*sic*] — italicized and in brackets — after the error.

Setting off long quotations

When you quote forty or more words, set off the quotation by indenting it one-half inch (or five spaces) from the left margin.

Long quotations should be introduced by an informative sentence, usually followed by a colon. Quotation marks are unnecessary because the indented format tells readers that the words are taken word-for-word from the source.

> Hart (1996) has described the kinds of linguistic signs and symbols used in the early ape language experiments:
>
> > Researchers attempted to teach individual signs derived from American Sign Language (ASL) to Washoe, a chimpanzee; Koko, a gorilla; and Chantek, an orangutan. Sarah, a chimpanzee, learned to manipulate arbitrary plastic symbols standing for words, and another chimpanzee, named Lana, used an early computer keyboard, with arbitrary symbols the researchers called lexigrams. (p. 108)

Notice that at the end of an indented quotation the parenthetical citation goes outside the final mark of punctuation.

58b Integrate summaries and paraphrases.

Summaries and paraphrases are written in your own words. As with quotations, you should introduce most summaries and paraphrases of a source with a signal phrase that mentions the author and the date of publication and places the material in context. Readers will then understand where the summary or paraphrase begins.

Without the signal phrase (underlined) in the following example, readers might think that only the last sentence is being cited, when in fact the whole paragraph is based on the source.

> Studies at the Yerkes Primate Center in Atlanta broke new ground. <u>Researchers Greenfield and Savage-Rumbaugh (1990)</u>

reported that the pygmy chimp Kanzi seemed to understand simple grammatical rules about lexigram order. For instance, Kanzi learned that in two-word utterances action precedes object, an ordering also used by human children at the two-word stage. What is impressive, noted Greenfield and Savage-Rumbaugh, is that in addition to being semantically related, most of Kanzi's lexigram combinations are original (p. 556).

There are times, however, when a signal phrase naming the author is not necessary. When the context makes clear where the cited material begins, you may omit the signal phrase and include the authors' names in the parentheses: (Greenfield & Savage-Rumbaugh, 1990, p. 556).

58c Integrate statistics and other facts.

When you are citing a statistic or other specific fact, a signal phrase is often not necessary. In most cases, readers will understand that the citation refers to the statistic or fact (not the whole paragraph).

By the age of ten, Kanzi had learned to communicate about 200 symbols on his computerized board (Lewin, 1991).

There is nothing wrong, however, with using a signal phrase.

Lewin (1991) reported that by the age of ten, Kanzi had learned to communicate about 200 symbols on his computerized board.

59

Documenting sources

In most social science classes, you will be asked to use the APA system for documenting sources, which is set forth in the *Publication Manual of the American Psychological Association,* 5th ed. (Washington: APA, 2001). APA recommends in-text citations that refer readers to a list of references.

An in-text citation names the author of the source (often in a signal phrase), gives the date of publication, and at times includes a page number in parentheses. At the end of the paper, a list of references provides publication information about the source; the list is alphabetized by authors' last names (or by titles for works without authors). There is a direct link between the in-text citation and the alphabetical listing. In the following example, that link is highlighted in teal.

IN-TEXT CITATION

Rumbaugh (1995) reported that "Kanzi's comprehension of over 600 novel sentences of request was very comparable to Alia's; both complied with requests without assistance on approximately 70% of the sentences" (p. 722).

ENTRY IN THE LIST OF REFERENCES

Rumbaugh, D. (1995). Primate language and cognition: Common ground. *Social Research, 62,* 711-730.

Directory to APA in-text citation models

1. Basic format for a quotation, 467
2. Basic format for a summary or a paraphrase, 467
3. A work with two authors, 467
4. A work with three to five authors, 468
5. A work with six or more authors, 468
6. Unknown author, 468
7. Organization as author, 468
8. Two or more works in the same parentheses, 469
9. Authors with the same last name, 469
10. Personal communication, 469
11. An electronic document, 469
12. Indirect source, 471
13. Two or more works by the same author in the same year, 471

59a APA in-text citations

The APA's in-text citations provide at least the author's last name and the date of publication. For direct quotations and some paraphrases, a page number is given as well. In the following models, the elements of the in-text citation are shown in teal.

NOTE: APA style requires the use of the past tense or the present perfect tense in signal phrases introducing cited material: *Smith (2003) reported, Smith (2003) has argued.*

■ **1. BASIC FORMAT FOR A QUOTATION** Ordinarily, introduce the quotation with a signal phrase that includes the author's last name followed by the date of publication in parentheses. Put the page number (preceded by "p.") in parentheses after the quotation.

> Hart (1996) wrote that some primatologists "wondered if apes had learned Language, with a capital *L*" (p. 109).

If the author is not named in a signal phrase, place the author's last name, the year, and the page number in parentheses after the quotation: (Hart, 1996, p. 109).

■ **2. BASIC FORMAT FOR A SUMMARY OR A PARAPHRASE** Include the author's last name and the date either in a signal phrase introducing the material or in parentheses following it. A page number is not required for a summary or a paraphrase, but include one if it would help readers find the passage in a long work (as in item 3).

> According to Hart (1996), researchers took Terrace's conclusions seriously, and funding for language experiments soon declined.

> Researchers took Terrace's conclusions seriously, and funding for language experiments soon declined (Hart, 1996).

■ **3. A WORK WITH TWO AUTHORS** Name both authors in the signal phrase or parentheses each time you cite the work. In the parentheses, use "&" between the authors' names; in the signal phrase, use "and."

> Greenfield and Savage-Rumbaugh (1990) have acknowledged that Kanzi's linguistic development was slower than that of a human child (p. 567).

> Kanzi's linguistic development was slower than that of a human child (Greenfield & Savage-Rumbaugh, 1990, p. 567).

■ **4. A WORK WITH THREE TO FIVE AUTHORS** Identify all authors in the signal phrase or parentheses the first time you cite the source.

> The chimpanzee Nim was raised by researchers who trained him in American Sign Language by molding and guiding his hands (Terrace, Petitto, Sanders, & Bever, 1979).

In subsequent citations, use the first author's name followed by "et al." in either the signal phrase or the parentheses.

> Nim was able to string together as many as 16 signs, but their order appeared quite random (Terrace et al., 1979).

■ **5. A WORK WITH SIX OR MORE AUTHORS** Use the first author's name followed by "et al." in the signal phrase or parentheses.

> The ape language studies have shed light on the language development of children with linguistic handicaps (Savage-Rumbaugh et al., 1993).

■ **6. UNKNOWN AUTHOR** If the author is unknown, mention the work's title in the signal phrase or give the first word or two of the title in the parenthetical citation. Titles of articles and chapters are put in quotation marks; titles of books and reports are italicized.

> Chimpanzees in separate areas of Africa differ in a range of behaviors: in their methods of cracking nuts, for example, or in their grooming rituals. A team of researchers has concluded that many of these behaviors are cultural, not just responses to environmental factors ("Chimps," 1999).

NOTE: In the rare case when "Anonymous" is specified as the author, treat it as if it were a real name: (Anonymous, 2001). In the list of references, also use the name Anonymous as author.

■ **7. ORGANIZATION AS AUTHOR** If the author is a government agency or other organization, name the organization in the signal phrase or in the parenthetical citation the first time you cite the source.

According to the Language Research Center (2000), linguistic research with apes has led to new methods of treating humans with learning disabilities such as autism and dyslexia.

If the organization has a familiar abbreviation, you may include it in brackets the first time you cite the source and use the abbreviation alone in later citations.

FIRST CITATION   (National Institute of Mental Health [NIMH], 2001)

LATER CITATIONS   (NIMH, 2001)

■ **8. TWO OR MORE WORKS IN THE SAME PARENTHESES** When your parenthetical citation names two or more works, put them in the same order that they appear in the reference list, separated by semicolons.

Researchers argued that the apes in the early language experiments were merely responding to cues (Sebeok & Umiker-Sebeok, 1979; Terrace, 1979).

■ **9. AUTHORS WITH THE SAME LAST NAME** To avoid confusion, use initials with the last names if your reference list includes two or more authors with the same last name.

Research by E. Smith (1989) revealed that . . .

■ **10. PERSONAL COMMUNICATION** Interviews, letters, e-mail, and other person-to-person communications should be cited as follows:

One of Patterson's former aides, who worked with the gorilla Michael, believes that he was capable of joking and lying in sign language (E. Robbins, personal communication, January 4, 2001).

Do not include personal communications in your reference list.

■ **11. AN ELECTRONIC DOCUMENT** When possible, cite an electronic document as you would any other document (using the author-date style).

R. Fouts and D. Fouts (1999) have explained one benefit of ape language research: It has shown us how to teach children with linguistic disabilities.

Electronic sources may lack authors' names or dates. In addition, they may lack page numbers (required in some citations). Here are APA's guidelines for handling sources without authors' names, dates, or page numbers.

Unknown author

If no author is named, mention the title of the document in a signal phrase or give the first word or two of the title in parentheses (see also item 6 on p. 468). (If an organization serves as the author, see item 7 on p. 468.)

According to a BBC article, chimpanzees at sites in West Africa, Tanzania, and Uganda exhibit culture-specific patterns of behavior when grooming one another ("Chimps," 1999).

Unknown date

When the date is unknown, APA recommends using the abbreviation "n.d." (for "no date").

Attempts to return sign-language-using apes to the wild have had mixed results (Smith, n.d.).

No page numbers

APA ordinarily requires page numbers for quotations, and it recommends them for summaries or paraphrases from long sources. When an electronic source lacks stable numbered pages, your citation should include — if possible — information that will help readers locate the particular passage being cited.

When an electronic document has numbered paragraphs, use the paragraph number preceded by the symbol ¶ or by the abbreviation "para.": (Hall, 2001, ¶ 5) *or* (Hall, 2001, para. 5). If neither a page nor a paragraph number is given and the document contains headings, cite the appropriate heading and indicate which paragraph under that heading you are referring to.

According to Kirby (1999), some critics have accused activists in the Great Ape Project of "exaggerating the supposed similarities of the apes [to humans] to stop their use in experiments" (Shared Path section, para. 6).

NOTE: Electronic files using portable document format (PDF) often have stable page numbers. For such sources, give the page number in the parenthetical citation.

■ **12. INDIRECT SOURCE** If you use a source that was cited in another source (a secondary source), name the original source in your signal phrase. List the secondary source in your reference list and include it in your parenthetical citation, preceded by the words "as cited in." In the following example, Booth is the secondary source.

Linguist Noam Chomsky has dismissed the studies on Kanzi with a flippant analogy: "To maintain that Kanzi has language ability is like saying a man can fly because he can jump in the air" (as cited in Booth, 1990, p. A3).

■ **13. TWO OR MORE WORKS BY THE SAME AUTHOR IN THE SAME YEAR** When your list of references includes more than one work by the same author in the same year, use lowercase letters ("a," "b," and so on) with the year to order the entries in the reference list. (See item 6 on p. 474.) Use those same letters with the year in the in-text citation.

Research by Kennedy (2000b) has yielded new findings about the role of gender in the functioning of small groups.

ON THE WEB

For electronic exercises on using APA documentation style, go to
dianahacker.com/rules

and click on ▶ **Electronic Research Exercises**
▶ **E-ex 59–1 through 59–3**

Directory to APA reference list models

GENERAL GUIDELINES FOR LISTING AUTHORS

1. Single author, 472
2. Multiple authors, 473
3. Organization as author, 473
4. Unknown author, 474
5. Two or more works by the same author, 474
6. Two or more works by the same author in the same year, 474

ARTICLES IN PERIODICALS

7. Article in a journal paginated by volume, 474
8. Article in a journal paginated by issue, 475
9. Article in a magazine, 475
10. Article in a newspaper, 475
11. Letter to the editor, 475
12. Review, 475

BOOKS

13. Basic format for a book, 476
14. Editors, 476
15. Translation, 476

16. Edition other than the first, 476
17. Article or chapter in an edited book, 477
18. Multivolume work, 477

ELECTRONIC SOURCES

19. Article from an online periodical, 477
20. Article from a database, 478
21. Nonperiodical Web document, 478
22. Chapter or section in a Web document, 479
23. E-mail, 479
24. Online posting, 479
25. Computer program, 480

OTHER SOURCES

26. Dissertation abstract, 480
27. Government document, 480
28. Report from a private organization, 480
29. Conference proceedings, 480
30. Motion picture, 480
31. Television program, 481

59b   APA references

In APA style, the alphabetical list of works cited, which appears at the end of the paper, is titled "References." Following are models illustrating APA style for entries in the list of references. Observe all details: capitalization, punctuation, use of italics, and so on. For advice on preparing the list, see pages 483–84. For a sample reference list, see pages 493–94.

General guidelines for listing authors

Alphabetize entries in the list of references by authors' last names; if a work has no author, alphabetize it by its title. The first element of each entry is important because citations in the text of the paper refer to it and readers will be looking for it in the alphabetized list. The date of publication appears immediately after the first element of the entry.

NAME AND DATE CITED IN TEXT

Duncan (2003) has reported that . . .

BEGINNING OF ENTRY IN THE LIST OF REFERENCES

Duncan, B. (2003).

Items 1–4 show how to begin an entry for a work with a single author, multiple authors, an organization as author, and an unknown author. Items 5 and 6 show how to begin an entry when your list includes two or more works by the same author or two or more works by the same author in the same year.

What comes after the first element of your citation will depend on the kind of source you are citing (see items 7–31).

■ **1. SINGLE AUTHOR** Begin the entry with the author's last name, followed by a comma and the author's initial(s). Then give the date in parentheses.

Conran, G. (2003).

■ **2. MULTIPLE AUTHORS** List up to six authors by last names, followed by initials. Use an ampersand (&) instead of the word "and."

Walker, J. R., & Taylor, T. (1998).

Sloan, F. A., Stout, E. M., Whetten-Goldstein, K., & Liang, L. (2000).

If there are more than six authors, list the first six and "et al." (meaning "and others") to indicate that there are others.

■ **3. ORGANIZATION AS AUTHOR** When the author is an organization, begin with the name of the organization.

American Psychiatric Association. (2003).

NOTE: If the organization is also the publisher, see item 28.

■ **4. UNKNOWN AUTHOR** Begin with the work's title. Titles of books are italicized. Titles of articles are neither italicized nor put in quotation marks. (For APA's rules on capitalization of titles, see p. 484.)

Oxford essential world atlas. (1996).

EMFs on the brain. (1995, January 21).

■ **5. TWO OR MORE WORKS BY THE SAME AUTHOR** Use the author's name for all entries. List the entries by year, the earliest first.

Schlechty, P. C. (1997).

Schlechty, P. C. (2001).

■ **6. TWO OR MORE WORKS BY THE SAME AUTHOR IN THE SAME YEAR** List the works alphabetically by title. In the parentheses, following the year, add "a," "b," and so on. Use these same letters when giving the year in the in-text citation.

Kennedy, C. (2000a). Group dynamics.

Kennedy, C. (2000b). Share-taking in small groups.

Articles in periodicals

This section shows how to prepare an entry for an article in a journal, a magazine, or a newspaper. In addition to consulting the models in this section, you may need to refer to items 1–6 (general guidelines for listing authors).

NOTE: For articles on consecutive pages, provide the range of pages at the end of the citation (see item 7 for an example). When an article does not appear on consecutive pages, give all page numbers (see item 10 for an example).

■ **7. ARTICLE IN A JOURNAL PAGINATED BY VOLUME** Many professional journals continue page numbers throughout the year instead of beginning each issue with page 1; at the end of the year, the issues are collected in a volume. After the italicized title of the journal, give the volume number (also italicized), followed by the page numbers.

Morawski, J. (2000). Social psychology a century ago. *American Psychologist, 55,* 427-431.

■ **8. ARTICLE IN A JOURNAL PAGINATED BY ISSUE** When each issue of a journal begins with page 1, include the issue number in parentheses after the volume number. Italicize the volume number but not the issue number.

Scruton, R. (1996). The eclipse of listening. *The New Criterion, 15*(3), 5-13.

■ **9. ARTICLE IN A MAGAZINE** In addition to the year of publication, list the month and, for weekly magazines, the day. If there is a volume number, include it (italicized) after the title.

Raloff, J. (2001, May 12). Lead therapy won't help most kids. *Science News, 159,* 292.

■ **10. ARTICLE IN A NEWSPAPER** Begin with the name of the author, followed by the exact date of publication. (If the author is unknown, see also item 4.) Page numbers are introduced with "p." (or "pp.").

Haney, D. Q. (1998, February 20). Finding eats at mystery of appetite. *The Oregonian,* pp. A1, A17.

■ **11. LETTER TO THE EDITOR** Letters to the editor appear in journals, magazines, and newspapers. Follow the appropriate model and insert the words "Letter to the editor" in brackets before the name of the periodical.

Carter, R. (2000, July). Shot in the dark? [Letter to the editor]. *Scientific American, 283*(1), 8.

■ **12. REVIEW** Reviews of books and other media appear in a variety of periodicals. Follow the appropriate model for the periodical. For a review of a book, give the title of the review (if there is one), followed by the words "Review of the book" and the title of the book in brackets.

Gleick, E. (2000, December 14). The burdens of genius [Review of the
book *The Last Samurai*]. *Time, 156,* 171.

For a film review, write "Review of the motion picture," and for
a TV review, write "Review of the television program." Treat
other media in a similar way.

Books

In addition to consulting the items in this section, you may need
to refer to items 1–6 (general guidelines for listing authors).

■ **13. BASIC FORMAT FOR A BOOK** Begin with the author's name,
followed by the date and the book's title. End with the place of
publication and the name of the publisher.

Highmore, B. (2001). *Everyday life and cultural theory.* New York:
Routledge.

■ **14. EDITORS** For a book with an editor but no author, begin
with the name of the editor (or editors) followed by the abbreviation "Ed." (or "Eds.") in parentheses.

Duncan, G. J., & Brooks-Gunn, J. (Eds.). (1997). *Consequences of
growing up poor.* New York: Russell Sage Foundation.

For a book with an author and an editor, begin with the author's
name. Give the editor's name in parentheses after the title of
the book, followed by the abbreviation "Ed." (or "Eds.").

Plath, S. (2000). *The unabridged journals* (K. V. Kukil, Ed.). New York:
Anchor.

■ **15. TRANSLATION** After the title, name the translator, followed by the abbreviation "Trans.," in parentheses. Add the
original date of the work's publication in parentheses at the end
of the entry.

Singer, I. B. (1998). *Shadows on the Hudson* (J. Sherman, Trans.). New
York: Farrar, Straus and Giroux. (Original work published 1957)

■ **16. EDITION OTHER THAN THE FIRST** Include the number of the
edition in parentheses after the title.

Helfer, M. E., Keme, R. S., & Drugman, R. D. (1997). *The battered child*

(5th ed.). Chicago: University of Chicago Press.

■ **17. ARTICLE OR CHAPTER IN AN EDITED BOOK** Begin with the author, year of publication, and title of the article or chapter. Then write "In" and give the editor's name, followed by "Ed." in parentheses; the title of the book; and the page numbers of the article or chapter in parentheses. End with the book's publication information.

Meskell, L. (2001). Archaeologies of identity. In I. Hodder (Ed.),

Archaeological theory today (pp. 187-213). Cambridge, England:

Polity Press.

■ **18. MULTIVOLUME WORK** Give the number of volumes after the title.

Wiener, P. (Ed.). (1973). *Dictionary of the history of ideas* (Vols. 1-4).

New York: Scribner's.

Electronic sources

The following guidelines for electronic sources are based on the fifth edition of the *Publication Manual of the American Psychological Association* (2001). Any updates will be posted on the APA Web site, <http://www.apastyle.org>.

ON THE WEB

For future updates in APA style, go to the APA's Web site or to
dianahacker.com/rules

and click on ▶ **Research and Documentation Online**
▶ **Documenting Sources (APA)**

■ **19. ARTICLE FROM AN ONLINE PERIODICAL** When citing online articles, follow the guidelines for printed articles (see items 7–12), giving whatever information is available in the online source. If the article also appears in a printed journal, a URL is not required; instead, include "Electronic version" in brackets after the title of the article.

Whitmeyer, J. M. (2000). Power through appointment [Electronic
    version]. *Social Science Research 29*(4), 535-555.

If there is no print version, include the date you accessed the
source and the article's URL.

Ashe, D. D., & McCutcheon, L. E. (2001). Shyness, loneliness, and
    attitude toward celebrities. *Current Research in Social Psychology,
    6*(9). Retrieved July 3, 2001, from http://www.uiowa.edu/
    ~grpproc/crisp/crisp.6.9.htm

NOTE: When you have retrieved an article from a newspaper's
searchable Web site, give the URL for the site, not for the exact
source.

Cary, B. (2001, June 18). Mentors of the mind. *Los Angeles Times*.
    Retrieved July 5, 2001, from http://www.latimes.com

■   **20. ARTICLE FROM A DATABASE**   Libraries pay for access to
electronic databases such as *PsycINFO* and *JSTOR*, which are
not otherwise available to the public. To cite an article from an
electronic database, include the publication information from
the source (see items 7–12). End the citation with your date of
access, the name of the database, and the document number (if
applicable).

Holliday, R. E., & Hayes, B. K. (2001). Dissociating automatic and
    intentional processes in children's eyewitness memory. *Journal of
    Experimental Child Psychology, 75*(1), 1-5. Retrieved February 21,
    2001, from Expanded Academic ASAP database (A59317972).

■   **21. NONPERIODICAL WEB DOCUMENT**   To cite a nonperiodical
Web document, such as a report, list as many of the following
elements as are available.

   Author's name
   Date of publication (if there is no date, use "n.d.")
   Title of document (in italics)
   Date you accessed the source
   A URL that will take readers directly to the source

In the first of the following models, the source has both an author and a date; in the second, the source lacks a date.

Cain, A., & Burris, M. (1999, April). *Investigation of the use of mobile phones while driving*. Retrieved January 15, 2000, from http://www.cutr.eng.usf.edu/its/mobile_phone_text.htm

Archer, Z. (n.d.). *Exploring nonverbal communication*. Retrieved July 18, 2001, from http://zzyx.ucsc.edu/~archer

If a source has no author, begin with the title and follow it with the date in parentheses.

NOTE: If you retrieved the source from a university program's Web site, name the program in your retrieval statement.

Cosmides, L., & Tooby, J. (1997). *Evolutionary psychology: A primer*. Retrieved July 5, 2001, from the University of California, Santa Barbara, Center for Evolutionary Psychology Web site: http://www.psych.ucsb.edu/research/cep/primer.html

■ **22. CHAPTER OR SECTION IN A WEB DOCUMENT** Begin with the author, the year of publication, and the title of the chapter or section. Then write "In" and give the title of the document, followed by any identifying information in parentheses. End with your date of access and the URL for the chapter or section.

Heuer, R. J., Jr. (1999). Keeping an open mind. In *Psychology of intelligence analysis* (chap. 6). Retrieved July 7, 2001, from http://www.cia.gov/csi/books/19104/art9.html

■ **23. E-MAIL** E-mail messages and other personal communications are not included in the list of references.

■ **24. ONLINE POSTING** If an online posting cannot be retrieved (because the newsgroup or forum does not maintain archives), cite it as a personal communication in the text of your paper and do not include it in the list of references. If the posting can be retrieved from an archive, treat it as follows, giving as much information as is available.

Eaton, S. (2001, June 12). Online transactions [Msg 2]. Message
    posted to news://sci.psychology.psychotherapy.moderated

■   **25. COMPUTER PROGRAM** Add the words "Computer software" in brackets after the title of the program.

Kaufmann, W. J., III, & Comins, N. F. (1998). Discovering the universe
    (Version 4.1) [Computer software]. New York: Freeman.

Other sources

■   **26. DISSERTATION ABSTRACT**

Yoshida, Y. (2001). Essays in urban transportation (Doctoral
    dissertation, Boston College, 2001). *Dissertation Abstracts
    International, 62,* 7741A.

■   **27. GOVERNMENT DOCUMENT**

U.S. Census Bureau. (2000). *Statistical abstract of the United States.*
    Washington, DC: U.S. Government Printing Office.

■   **28. REPORT FROM A PRIVATE ORGANIZATION** If the publisher is
the author, give the word "Author" as the publisher. If the report
has an author, begin with the author's name, and name the publisher at the end.

American Psychiatric Association. (2000). *Practice guidelines for the
    treatment of patients with eating disorders* (2nd ed.). Washington,
    DC: Author.

■   **29. CONFERENCE PROCEEDINGS**

Schnase, J. L., & Cunnius, E. L. (Eds.). (1995). *Proceedings of CSCL
    '95: The First International Conference on Computer Support for
    Collaborative Learning.* Mahwah, NJ: Erlbaum.

■   **30. MOTION PICTURE** To cite a motion picture (film, video, or
DVD), list the director and the year of the picture's release. Give
the title, followed by "Motion picture" in brackets, the country
where it was made, and the name of the studio.

Soderbergh, S. (Director). (2000). *Traffic* [Motion picture]. United States: Gramercy Pictures.

■ **31. TELEVISION PROGRAM** To cite a television program, list the producer and the date it was aired. Give the title, followed by "Television broadcast" in brackets, the city, and the television network or service.

Pratt, C. (Executive Producer). (2001, December 2). *Face the nation* [Television broadcast]. Washington, DC: CBS News.

For a television series, use the year in which the series was produced, and follow the title with "Television series" in brackets. For an episode in a series, list the writer and director and the year. After the episode title put "Television series episode" in brackets. Follow with information about the series.

Janows, J. (Executive Producer). (2000). *Culture shock* [Television series]. Boston: WGBH.

Loeterman, B. (Writer), & Gale, B. (Director). (2000). Real justice [Television series episode]. In M. Sullivan (Executive Producer), *Frontline*. Boston: WGBH.

60

Manuscript format; sample paper

60a Manuscript format

The American Psychological Association makes a number of recommendations for formatting a paper and preparing a list of references.

Formatting the paper

APA guidelines for formatting a paper are endorsed by many instructors in the social sciences.

MATERIALS AND TYPEFACE Use good-quality 8½″ × 11″ white paper. Avoid a typeface that is unusual or hard to read.

TITLE PAGE The APA does not provide guidelines for preparing the title page of a college paper, but instructors may want you to include one. See page 485 for an example.

PAGE NUMBERS AND RUNNING HEAD In the upper right-hand corner of each page, type a short version of your title, followed by five spaces and the page number. Number all pages, including the title page.

MARGINS AND LINE SPACING Use margins of one inch on all sides of the page. Do not justify (align) the right margin. Double-space throughout the paper.

LONG QUOTATIONS See page 464 for APA's guidelines for setting long quotations off from the text.

ABSTRACT If your instructor requires one, include an abstract on its own page after the title page. Center the word Abstract one inch from the top of the page.

An abstract is a 75-to-100-word paragraph that provides readers with a quick overview of your essay. It should express your main idea and your key points; it might also briefly suggest any implications or applications of the research you discuss in the paper.

HEADINGS Although headings are not always necessary, their use is encouraged in the social sciences. For undergraduate papers, one level of heading will usually be sufficient.

In APA style, major headings are centered. Capitalize the first word of the heading, along with all words except articles, short prepositions, and coordinating conjunctions.

VISUALS The APA classifies visuals as tables and figures (figures include graphs, charts, drawings, and photographs). Keep visuals as simple as possible. Label each table with an arabic numeral (Table 1, Table 2, and so on) and provide a clear title. The label and title should appear on separate lines above the table, flush left. Below the table, give its source in a note:

Note. From "Innovation Roles: From Souls of Fire to Devil's Advocates," by M. Meyer, 2000, *The Journal of Business Communication, 37,* p. 338.

For each figure, place a label and a caption below the figure, flush left. They need not appear on separate lines. In the text of your paper, discuss the most significant features of each visual. Place the visual as close as possible to the sentences that relate to them unless your instructor prefers them in an appendix.

Preparing the list of references

Begin your list of references on a new page at the end of the paper. Center the title References about one inch from the top of the page. Double-space throughout. For a sample reference list, see pages 493–94.

INDENTING ENTRIES APA recommends using a hanging indent: Type the first line of an entry flush left and indent any additional lines one-half inch (or five spaces), as shown in the list on pages 493–94.

ALPHABETIZING THE LIST Alphabetize the reference list by the last names of the authors (or editors); when a work has no author or editor, alphabetize by the first word of the title other than *A, An,* or *The.*

If your list includes two or more works by the same author, arrange the entries by year, the earliest first. If your list includes two or more works by the same author in the same year, arrange them alphabetically by title. Add the letters "a," "b," and so on within the parentheses after the year. Use only the year for articles in journals: (2002a). Use the full date for articles in magazines and newspapers in the reference list: (2001a, July 7). Use only the year in the in-text citation.

AUTHORS' NAMES Invert all authors' names and use initials instead of first names. With two or more authors, use an ampersand (&) before the last author's name. Separate the names with commas. Include names for the first six authors; if there are additional authors, end the list with "et al." (Latin for "and others").

TITLES OF BOOKS AND ARTICLES Italicize the titles and subtitles of books; capitalize only the first word of the title and subtitle (and all proper nouns). Capitalize names of periodicals as you would capitalize them normally (see 45c).

ABBREVIATIONS FOR PAGE NUMBERS Abbreviations for "page" and "pages" ("p." and "pp.") are used before page numbers of newspaper articles and articles in edited books (see item 10 on p. 475 and item 17 on p. 477) but not before page numbers of articles in magazines and journals (see items 7–9 on pp. 474–75).

BREAKING A URL When a URL must be divided, break it after a slash or before a period. Do not insert a hyphen.

NOTE: The sample reference list (see pp. 493–94) shows how to type your list of references.

For information about the exact format of each entry in your list, consult the models on pages 472–81.

ON THE WEB

For advice on using your word processor to format a reference list page, go to **dianahacker.com/rules**

and click on ▶ **Additional Resources**
                    ▶ **Formatting Help**

60b Sample APA paper

Following is a research paper written by Karen Shaw, a student in a psychology class. Shaw's assignment was to write a "review of the literature" paper documented with APA-style citations and references.

In preparing her final manuscript, Shaw followed the APA guidelines. She did not include an abstract because her instructor did not require one.

ON THE WEB

For a downloadable version of Karen Shaw's paper, with marginal annotations, go to **dianahacker.com/rules**

and click on ▶ **Model Papers**
                    ▶ **APA paper: Shaw**

Apes and Language   1 Short title and page number for student papers.

Apes and Language:

A Review of the Literature

Full title, writer's name, name and section number of course, instructor's name, and date (all centered).

Karen Shaw

Psychology 110, Section 2

Professor Verdi

March 2, 2001

486 Research Guide

Apes and Language   2

Full title,
centered.

The writer sets
up her organi-
zation in her
thesis.

Headings,
centered,
help readers
follow the
organization.

A signal phrase
names all four
authors and
gives date in
parentheses.

Apes and Language:

A Review of the Literature

Over the past 30 years, researchers have demonstrated that the great apes (chimpanzees, gorillas, and orangutans) resemble humans in language abilities more than had been thought possible. Just how far that resemblance extends, however, has been a matter of some controversy.

Researchers agree that the apes have acquired fairly large vocabularies in American Sign Language and in artificial languages, but they have drawn quite different conclusions in addressing the following questions:

1. How spontaneously have apes used language?

2. How creatively have apes used language?

3. Can apes create sentences?

4. What are the implications of the ape language studies?

This review of the literature on apes and language focuses on these four questions.

How Spontaneously Have

Apes Used Language?

In an influential article, Terrace, Petitto, Sanders, and Bever (1979) argued that the apes in language experiments were not using language spontaneously but were merely imitating their trainers, responding to conscious or unconscious cues. Terrace and his colleagues at Columbia University had trained a chimpanzee, Nim, in American Sign Language, so their skepticism about the apes' abilities received much attention. In fact, funding for ape language research was sharply reduced following publication of their 1979 article "Can an Ape Create a Sentence?"

In retrospect, the conclusions of Terrace et al. seem to have been premature. Although some early ape language studies had not been rigorously controlled to eliminate cuing, even as early as the 1970s R. A. Gardner and B. T. Gardner were conducting double-blind experiments that prevented any possibility of cuing (Fouts, 1997, p. 99). Since 1979, researchers have diligently guarded against cuing.

Perhaps the best evidence that apes are not merely responding to cues is that they have signed to one another spontaneously, without trainers present. Like many of the apes studied, gorillas Koko and Michael have been observed signing to one another (Patterson & Linden, 1981). At Central Washington University the baby chimpanzee Loulis, placed in the care of the signing chimpanzee Washoe, mastered nearly fifty signs in American Sign Language without help from humans. "Interestingly," wrote researcher Fouts (1997), "Loulis did *not* pick up any of the seven signs that we [humans] used around him. He learned only from Washoe and [another chimp] Ally" (p. 244).

The extent to which chimpanzees spontaneously use language may depend on their training. Terrace trained Nim using the behaviorist technique of operant conditioning, so it is not surprising that many of Nim's signs were cued. Many other researchers have used a conversational approach that parallels the process by which human children acquire language. In an experimental study, O'Sullivan and

Because the author (Fouts) is not named in the signal phrase, his name and the year appear in parentheses, along with the page number.

An ampersand links the names of two authors in parentheses.

Brackets indicate words not in original source.

A page number is required for a quotation.

The word "and" links the names of two authors in the signal phrase.

Apes and Language   4

Yeager (1989) contrasted the two techniques, using Terrace's Nim as their subject. They found that Nim's use of language was significantly more spontaneous under conversational conditions.

How Creatively Have
Apes Used Language?

There is considerable evidence that apes have invented creative names. One of the earliest and most controversial examples involved the Gardners' chimpanzee Washoe. Washoe, who knew signs for "water" and "bird," once signed "water bird" when in the presence of a swan. Terrace et al. (1979) suggested that there was "no basis for concluding that Washoe was characterizing the swan as a 'bird that inhabits water.' " Washoe may simply have been "identifying correctly a body of water and a bird, in that order" (p. 895).

Other examples are not so easily explained away. The bonobo Kanzi has requested particular films by combining symbols on a computer in a creative way. For instance, to ask for *Quest for Fire*, a film about early primates discovering fire, Kanzi began to use symbols for "campfire" and "TV" (Eckholm, 1985). The gorilla Koko, who learned American Sign Language, has a long list of creative names to her credit: "elephant baby" to describe a Pinocchio doll, "finger bracelet" to describe a ring, "bottle match" to describe a cigarette lighter, and so on (Patterson & Linden, 1981, p. 146). If Terrace's analysis of the "water bird" example is applied to the examples just mentioned, it does not hold.

When this article was first cited, all four authors were named. In subsequent citations of a work with three to five authors, "et al." is used after the first author's name.

The writer interprets the evidence; she doesn't just report it.

Surely Koko did not first see an elephant and then a baby before signing "elephant baby"--or a bottle and a match before signing "bottle match."

Can Apes Create Sentences?

The early ape language studies offered little proof that apes could combine symbols into grammatically ordered sentences. Apes strung together various signs, but the sequences were often random and repetitious. Nim's series of sixteen signs is a case in point: "give orange me give eat orange me eat orange give me eat orange give me you" (Terrace et al., 1979, p. 895).

More recent studies with bonobos at the Language Research Center in Atlanta have broken new ground. Kanzi, a bonobo trained by Savage-Rumbaugh, seems to understand simple grammatical rules about word order. For instance, Kanzi learned that in two-word utterances action precedes object, an ordering also used by human children at the two-word stage. In a major article reporting on their research, Greenfield and Savage-Rumbaugh (1990) wrote that Kanzi rarely "repeated himself or formed combinations that were semantically unrelated" (p. 556).

More important, Kanzi began on his own to create certain patterns that may not exist in English but can be found among deaf children and in other human languages. For example, Kanzi used his own rules when combining action symbols. Symbols that involved an invitation to play, such as "chase," would appear first; symbols that indicated what was to be done during play ("hide") would appear

The writer draws attention to an important article.

Research Guide

second. Kanzi also created his own rules when combining gestures and symbols. He would use the symbol first and then gesture, a practice often followed by young deaf children (Greenfield & Savage-Rumbaugh, 1990, p. 560).

The writer gives a page number for this summary because the article is long.

In a later study, Kanzi's abilities to understand spoken language were shown to be similar to those of a 2-1/2-year-old human, Alia. Rumbaugh (1995) reported that "Kanzi's comprehension of over 600 novel sentences of request was very comparable to Alia's; both complied with the requests without assistance on approximately 70% of the sentences" (p. 722). A recent monograph provided examples of the kinds of sentences both Kanzi and Alia were able to understand:

A quotation longer than 40 words is set off from the text. Quotation marks are not used.

> For example, the word *ball* occurred in 76 different sentences, including such different requests as "Put the leaves in your ball," "Show me the ball that's on TV," "Vacuum your ball," and "Go do ball slapping with Liz." Overall, 144 different content words, many of which were presented in ways that required syntactic parsing for a proper response (such as "Knife your ball" vs. "Put the knife in the hat"), were utilized in the study. (Savage-Rumbaugh et al., 2000, pp. 101-102)

The researchers concluded that neither Kanzi nor Alia could have demonstrated understanding of such requests without comprehending syntactical relationships among the words in a sentence.

What Are the Implications of the

Ape Language Studies?

Kanzi's linguistic abilities are so impressive that they may help us understand how humans came to acquire language. Pointing out that 99% of our genetic material is held in common with the chimpanzees, Greenfield and Savage-Rumbaugh (1990) have suggested that something of the "evolutionary root of human language" can be found in the "linguistic abilities of the great apes" (p. 540). Noting that apes' brains are similar to those of our human ancestors, Leakey and Lewin (1992) argued that in ape brains "the cognitive foundations on which human language could be built are already present" (p. 244).

The suggestion that there is a continuity in the linguistic abilities of apes and humans has created much controversy. Linguist Noam Chomsky has strongly asserted that language is a unique human characteristic (Booth, 1990). Terrace has continued to be skeptical of the claims made for the apes, as have Petitto and Bever, coauthors of the 1979 article that caused such skepticism earlier (Gibbons, 1991).

The writer presents a balanced view of the philosophical controversy.

Recently, neurobiologists have made discoveries that may cause even the skeptics to take notice. Ongoing studies at the Yerkes Primate Research Center have revealed remarkable similarities in the brains of chimpanzees and humans. Through brain scans of live chimpanzees, researchers have found that, as with humans, "the language-controlling PT [*planum temporale*] is larger on the left side

Research Guide

of the chimps' brain than on the right. But it is not later-
alized in monkeys, which are less closely related to humans
than apes are" (Begley, 1998, p. 57).

The tone of
the conclusion
is objective.

Although the ape language studies continue to

generate controversy, researchers have shown over the

past 30 years that the gap between the linguistic abilities

of apes and humans is far less dramatic than was once

believed.

Apes and Language   9

References

List of references begins on a new page. Heading is centered.

Begley, S. (1998, January 19). Aping language. *Newsweek, 131,* 56-58.

Booth, W. (1990, October 29). Monkeying with language: Is chimp using words or merely aping handlers? *The Washington Post,* p. A3.

Eckholm, E. (1985, June 25). Kanzi the chimp: A life in science. *The New York Times,* pp. C1, C3.

List is alphabetized by authors' last names.

Fouts, R. (1997). *Next of kin: What chimpanzees have taught me about who we are.* New York: William Morrow.

Gibbons, A. (1991). Déjà vu all over again: Chimp-language wars. *Science, 251,* 1561-1562.

The first line of an entry is at the left margin; subsequent lines indent ½" (or five spaces).

Greenfield, P. M., & Savage-Rumbaugh, E. S. (1990). Grammatical combination in *Pan paniscus:* Processes of learning and invention in the evolution and development of language. In S. T. Parker & K. R. Gibson (Eds.), *"Language" and intelligence in monkeys and apes: Comparative developmental perspectives* (pp. 540-578). Cambridge: Cambridge University Press.

Leakey, R., & Lewin, R. (1992). *Origins reconsidered: In search of what makes us human.* New York: Doubleday.

Double-spacing is used throughout.

O'Sullivan, C., & Yeager, C. P. (1989). Communicative context and linguistic competence: The effect of social setting on a chimpanzee's conversational skill. In R. A. Gardner, B. T. Gardner, & T. E. Van Cantfort (Eds.), *Teaching sign language to chimpanzees* (pp. 269-279). Albany: SUNY Press.

Patterson, F., & Linden, E. (1981). *The education of Koko.*
New York: Holt, Rinehart & Winston.

Rumbaugh, D. (1995). Primate language and cognition:
Common ground. *Social Research, 62,* 711-730.

Savage-Rumbaugh, E. S., Murphy, J. S., Sevcik, R. A.,
Brakke, K. E., Williams, S. L., Rumbaugh, D. M., et al.
(2000). *Language comprehension in ape and child:
Monograph.* Atlanta, GA: Language Research Center.
Retrieved January 6, 2000, from the Language Research
Center Web site: http://www.gsu.edu/~wwwlrc/
monograph.html

Terrace, H. S., Petitto, L. A., Sanders, R. J., & Bever, T. G.
(1979). Can an ape create a sentence? *Science, 206,*
891-902.

(see 45a). If the problem is one of word choice, we may speak of *concrete* versus *abstract nouns* (see 18b). The distinction between *count* nouns and *noncount nouns* is useful primarily for nonnative speakers of English (see 30a and 30b). The term *collective noun* refers to a set of nouns that may cause problems with subject-verb or pronoun-antecedent agreement (see 21f and 22b).

EXERCISE 61–1

Underline the nouns (and noun/adjectives) in the following sentences. Answers to lettered sentences appear in the back of the book. Example:

Idle hands are the devil's workshop.

a. The sun will set without your assistance.   — Hebrew proverb
b. Pride is at the bottom of all great mistakes.   — John Ruskin
c. Success breeds confidence.   — Beryl Markham
d. The ultimate censorship is the flick of the dial.
                                                             — Tom Smothers
e. Our national flower is the concrete cloverleaf.
                                                             — Lewis Mumford
1. Truthfulness so often goes with ruthlessness.   — Dodie Smith
2. Luck is a matter of preparation meeting opportunity.
                                                             — Oprah Winfrey
3. Problems are only opportunities in work clothes.
                                                             — Henry Kaiser
4. A woman must have money and a room of her own.
                                                             — Virginia Woolf
5. Language helps form the limits of our reality.   — Dale Spender

61b Pronouns

A pronoun is a word used in place of a noun. Usually the pronoun substitutes for a specific noun, known as its *antecedent*.

When the *wheel* squeaks, *it* is greased.

Although most pronouns function as substitutes for nouns, some can function as adjectives modifying nouns.

This hanging will surely be a lesson to me.

Because they have the form of a pronoun and the function of an adjective, such pronouns may be called *pronoun/adjectives*.

Pronouns are classified as personal, possessive, intensive and reflexive, relative, interrogative, demonstrative, indefinite, and reciprocal.

PERSONAL PRONOUNS   Personal pronouns refer to specific persons or things. They always function as noun equivalents.

Singular: I, me, you, she, her, he, him, it

Plural: we, us, you, they, them

POSSESSIVE PRONOUNS   Possessive pronouns indicate ownership.

Singular: my, mine, your, yours, her, hers, his, its

Plural: our, ours, your, yours, their, theirs

Some of these possessive pronouns function as adjectives modifying nouns: *my, your, his, her, its, our, their.*

INTENSIVE AND REFLEXIVE PRONOUNS   Intensive pronouns emphasize a noun or another pronoun (The senator *herself* met us at the door). Reflexive pronouns, which have the same form as intensive pronouns, name a receiver of an action identical with the doer of the action (Paula cut *herself*).

Singular: myself, yourself, himself, herself, itself

Plural: ourselves, yourselves, themselves

RELATIVE PRONOUNS   Relative pronouns introduce subordinate clauses functioning as adjectives (The man *who robbed us* was never caught). In addition to introducing the clause, the relative pronoun, in this case *who,* points back to a noun or pronoun that the clause modifies (*man*). (See 63b.)

who, whom, whose, which, that

Some textbooks also treat *whoever, whomever, what,* and *whatever* as relative pronouns. These words introduce noun clauses; they do not point back to a noun or pronoun. (See 63b.)

INTERROGATIVE PRONOUNS   Interrogative pronouns introduce questions (*Who* is expected to win the election?).

who, whom, whose, which, what

DEMONSTRATIVE PRONOUNS Demonstrative pronouns identify or point to nouns. Frequently they function as adjectives (*This* chair is my favorite), but they may also function as noun equivalents (*This* is my favorite chair).

this, that, these, those

INDEFINITE PRONOUNS Indefinite pronouns refer to nonspecific persons or things. Most are always singular (*everyone, each*); some are always plural (*both, many*); a few may be singular or plural (see 21e). Most indefinite pronouns function as noun equivalents (*Something* is burning), but some can also function as adjectives (*All* campers must check in at the lodge).

all	anything	everyone	nobody	several
another	both	everything	none	some
any	each	few	no one	somebody
anybody	either	many	nothing	someone
anyone	everybody	neither	one	something

RECIPROCAL PRONOUNS Reciprocal pronouns refer to individual parts of a plural antecedent (By turns, we helped *each other* through college).

each other, one another

NOTE: Pronouns cause a variety of problems for writers. See pronoun-antecedent agreement (22), pronoun reference (23), distinguishing between pronouns such as *I* and *me* (24), and distinguishing between *who* and *whom* (25).

EXERCISE 61-2

Underline the pronouns (and pronoun/adjectives) in the following sentences. Answers to lettered sentences appear in the back of the book. Example:

Beware of persons <u>who</u> are praised by <u>everyone</u>.

a. He has every attribute of a dog except loyalty. — Thomas Gore
b. A fall does not hurt those who fly low. — Chinese proverb
c. I have written some poetry that I myself don't understand.
— Carl Sandburg

d. I am firm. You are obstinate. He is a pig-headed fool.
                                           —Katherine Whitehorn
    e. If you haven't anything nice to say about anyone, come and sit by me.
                                         —Alice Roosevelt Longworth

1. Men are taught to apologize for their weaknesses, women for their strengths.   —Lois Wyse
2. Nothing is interesting if you are not interested.
                                         —Helen MacInness
3. We will never have friends if we expect to find them without fault.
                                         —Thomas Fuller
4. The gods help those who help themselves.   —Aesop
5. I awoke one morning and found myself famous.   —Lord Byron

61c Verbs

The verb of a sentence usually expresses action (*jump, think*) or being (*is, become*). It is composed of a main verb possibly preceded by one or more helping verbs:

              MV
The best fish swim near the bottom.

        HV   **MV**
A marriage is not built in a day.

        HV **HV**   **MV**
Even God has been defended with nonsense.

Notice that words can intervene between the helping and the main verb (is *not* built).

Helping verbs

There are a limited number of helping verbs in English: forms of *have, do,* and *be,* which may also function as main verbs; and nine modals, which function only as helping verbs. The verbs *have, do,* and *be* change form to indicate tense; the modals do not.

    FORMS OF *HAVE, DO,* AND *BE*
    have, has, had

do, does, did

be, am, is, are, was, were, being, been

MODALS

can, could, may, might, must, shall, should, will, would, ought to

Main verbs

The main verb of a sentence is always the kind of word that would change form if put into these test sentences:

BASE FORM	Usually I (*walk, ride*).
PAST TENSE	Yesterday I (*walked, rode*).
PAST PARTICIPLE	I have (*walked, ridden*) many times before.
PRESENT PARTICIPLE	I am (*walking, riding*) right now.
-S FORM	Usually he/she/it (*walks, rides*).

If a word doesn't change form when slipped into these test sentences, you can be certain that it is not a main verb. For example, the noun *revolution*, though it may seem to suggest an action, can never function as a main verb. Just try to make it behave like one (*Today I revolution . . . Yesterday I revolutioned . . .*) and you'll see why.

When both the past-tense and the past-participle forms of a verb end in *-ed*, the verb is regular (*walked, walked*). Otherwise, the verb is irregular (*rode, ridden*). (See 27a.)

The verb *be* is highly irregular, having eight forms instead of the usual five: the base form *be;* the present-tense forms *am, is,* and *are;* the past-tense forms *was* and *were;* the present participle *being;* and the past participle *been.*

NOTE: Some verbs are followed by words that look like prepositions but are so closely associated with the verb that they are a part of its meaning. These words are known as *particles.* Common verb-particle combinations include *bring up, call off, drop off, give in, look up, run into,* and *take off.*

A lot of parents *pack up* their troubles and *send* them *off* to camp.　　　　　　　　　　　　　　　　　— Raymond Duncan

NOTE: Verbs cause many problems for writers. See active verbs (8), subject-verb agreement (21), standard English verb forms (27), verb tense and mood (28), and ESL problems with verbs (29).

EXERCISE 61-3

Underline the verbs in the following sentences, including helping verbs and particles. If a verb is part of a contraction (such as *is* in *isn't* or *would* in *I'd*), underline only the letters that represent the verb. Answers to lettered sentences appear in the back of the book. Example:

A full cup <u>must</u> <u>be</u> <u>carried</u> steadily.

a. I can pardon everyone's mistakes except my own. — Cato
b. There are no atheists on turbulent airplanes. — Erica Jong
c. One arrow does not bring down two birds. — Turkish proverb
d. Keep your talent in the dark, and you'll never be insulted.
   — Elsa Maxwell
e. Throw a lucky man into the sea, and he will emerge with a fish in his mouth. — Arab proverb

1. Do not scald your tongue in other people's broth.
   — English proverb
2. Wrong must not win by technicalities. — Aeschylus
3. Love your neighbor, but don't pull down the hedge.
   — Swiss proverb
4. I'd rather have roses on my table than diamonds around my neck.
   — Emma Goldman
5. He is a fine friend. He stabs you in the front.
   — Leonard Louis Levinson

61d Adjectives and articles

An adjective is a word used to modify, or describe, a noun or pronoun. An adjective usually answers one of these questions: Which one? What kind of? How many?

> ADJ
> the lame elephant [Which elephant?]

> ADJ   ADJ
> valuable old stamps [What kind of stamps?]

> ADJ
> sixteen candles [How many candles?]

Adjectives usually precede the words they modify. However, they may also follow linking verbs, in which case they describe the subject (see 62b).

ADJ   ADJ
Good medicine always tastes bitter.

Articles, sometimes classified as adjectives, are used to mark nouns. There are only three: the definite article *the* and the indefinite articles *a* and *an*.

ART   ART
A country can be judged by the quality of its proverbs.

NOTE: Writers sometimes misuse adjectives (see 26b). Nonnative speakers of English often encounter problems with the articles *a, an,* and *the* and occasionally have trouble placing adjectives correctly (see 30 and 31d).

61e Adverbs

An adverb is a word used to modify, or qualify, a verb (or verbal), an adjective, or another adverb. It usually answers one of these questions: When? Where? How? Why? Under what conditions? To what degree?

ADV
Pull gently at a weak rope. [Pull how?]

ADV
Read the best books first. [Read when?]

Adverbs modifying adjectives or other adverbs usually intensify or limit the intensity of the word they modify.

ADV   ADV
Be extremely good, and you will be very lonesome.

The negators *not* and *never* are classified as adverbs. A word such as *cannot* contains the helping verb *can* and the adverb *not*. A contraction such as *can't* contains the helping verb *can* and a contracted form of the adverb *not*.

NOTE: Writers sometimes misuse adverbs (see 26a). Multilingual speakers may have trouble placing adverbs correctly (see 31d).

EXERCISE 61–4

Underline the adjectives and circle the adverbs in the following sentences. If a word is a pronoun in form but an adjective in function, treat it as an adjective. Also treat the articles *a, an,* and *the* as adjectives. Answers to lettered sentences are in the back of the book. Example:

A wild goose (never) laid a tame egg.

   a. General notions are generally wrong.
        — Lady Mary Wortley Montagu
   b. The American public is wonderfully tolerant.   — Anonymous
   c. Wildflowers sometimes grow in an uncultivated field, but they never bloom in an uncultivated mind.   — Anonymous
   d. I'd rather be strongly wrong than weakly right.
        — Tallulah Bankhead
   e. Sleep faster. We need the pillows.   — Yiddish proverb

   1. Success is a public affair; failure is a private funeral.
        — Rosalind Russell
   2. Their civil discussions were not interesting, and their interesting discussions were not civil.   — Lisa Alther
   3. Money will buy a pretty good dog, but it will not buy the wag of its tail.   — Josh Billings
   4. We cannot be too careful in the choice of our enemies.
        — Oscar Wilde
   5. Feelings are untidy.   — Esther Hautzig

61f Prepositions

A preposition is a word placed before a noun or pronoun to form a phrase modifying another word in the sentence. The prepositional phrase nearly always functions as an adjective or as an adverb.

          P   P
The road *to hell* is usually paved *with good intentions.*

To hell functions as an adjective, modifying the noun *road; with good intentions* functions as an adverb, modifying the verb *is paved.* (For more about prepositional phrases, see 63a.)
    There are a limited number of prepositions in English. The most common ones are included in the following list.

about	besides	inside	plus	unto
above	between	into	regarding	up
across	beyond	like	respecting	upon
after	but	near	since	with
against	by	next	than	within
along	concerning	of	through	without
among	considering	off	throughout	
around	despite	on	till	
as	down	onto	to	
at	during	opposite	toward	
before	except	out	under	
behind	for	outside	underneath	
below	from	over	unlike	
beside	in	past	until	

Some prepositions are more than one word long. *Along with, as well as, in addition to,* and *next to* are common examples.

NOTE: Except for certain idiomatic uses (see 18d), prepositions cause few problems for native speakers of English. For nonnative speakers, however, prepositions can cause considerable difficulty (see 29d and 31f).

61g Conjunctions

Conjunctions join words, phrases, or clauses, and they indicate the relation between the elements joined.

COORDINATING CONJUNCTIONS A coordinating conjunction is used to connect grammatically equal elements. The coordinating conjunctions are *and, but, or, nor, for, so,* and *yet*.

Poverty is the parent of revolution *and* crime.

Admire a little ship, *but* put your cargo in a big one.

In the first sentence, *and* connects two nouns; in the second, *but* connects two independent clauses.

CORRELATIVE CONJUNCTIONS Correlative conjunctions come in pairs: *either . . . or; neither . . . nor; not only . . . but also; whether . . . or; both . . . and.* Like coordinating conjunctions, they connect grammatically equal elements.

Either Jack Sprat *or* his wife could eat no fat.

Parts of speech

A **noun** names a person, place, or thing (or an idea).

> N   N   N
> Repetition does not transform a lie into truth.

A **pronoun** substitutes for a noun.

>   PN PN   PN
> When the gods wish to punish us, they heed our prayers.

A **helping verb** comes before a main verb.

> *Modals:* can, could, may, might, must, shall, should, will, would (*also* ought to)
>
> *Forms of* be: be, am, is, are, was, were, being, been
>
> *Forms of* have: have, has, had
>
> *Forms of* do: do, does, did
>
> (The forms of *be, have,* and *do* may also function as main verbs.)

A **main verb** asserts action, being, or state of being.

>   MV   HV   MV
> Charity begins at home but should not end there.

A main verb will always change form when put into these positions in sentences:

> Usually I _____ .   (*walk, ride*)
> Yesterday I _____ .   (*walked, rode*)
> I have _____ many times before. (*walked, ridden*)
> I am _____ right now.   (*walking, riding*)
> Usually he _____ .   (*walks, rides*)

There are eight forms of the highly irregular verb *be: be, am, is, are, was, were, being, been.*

An **adjective** modifies a noun or pronoun, usually answering one of these questions: Which one? What kind of? How many? The articles *a, an,* and *the* are also adjectives.

Parts of speech (*continued*)

ADJ   ADJ
Useless laws weaken necessary ones.

An **ADVERB** modifies a verb, adjective, or adverb, usually answering one of these questions: When? Where? Why? How? Under what conditions? To what degree?

ADV   ADV
People think too historically.

A **PREPOSITION** indicates the relationship between the noun or pronoun that follows it and another word in the sentence.

P   P
A journey of a thousand miles begins with a single step.

Common prepositions: about, across, after, against, along, among, around, as, at, before, behind, below, beside, besides, between, beyond, but, by, concerning, considering, despite, down, during, except, for, from, in, inside, into, like, near, next, of, off, on, onto, opposite, out, outside, over, past, plus, regarding, respecting, since, than, through, throughout, till, to, toward, under, underneath, unlike, until, unto, up, upon, with, within, without

A **CONJUNCTION** connects words or word groups.

Coordinating conjunctions: and, but, or, nor, for, so, yet

Subordinating conjunctions: after, although, as, as if, because, before, even though, how, if, in order that, once, rather than, since, so that, than, that, though, unless, until, when, where, whether, while, why

Correlative conjunctions: either...or, neither . . . nor, not only . . . but also, both . . . and, whether . . . or

Conjunctive adverbs: accordingly, also, anyway, besides, certainly, consequently, conversely, finally, furthermore, hence, however, incidentally, indeed, instead, likewise, meanwhile, moreover, nevertheless, next, nonetheless, otherwise, similarly, specifically, still, subsequently, then, therefore, thus

An **INTERJECTION** expresses surprise or emotion. (Oh! Wow! Hey! Hooray!)

SUBORDINATING CONJUNCTIONS A subordinating conjunction introduces a subordinate clause and indicates its relation to the rest of the sentence. (See 63b.) The most common subordinating conjunctions are *after, although, as, as if, because, before, even though, how, if, in order that, once, rather than, since, so that, than, that, though, unless, until, when, where, whether, while,* and *why.*

> *If* you want service, serve yourself.

CONJUNCTIVE ADVERBS A conjunctive adverb may be used with a semicolon to connect independent clauses; it usually serves as a transition between the clauses. The most common conjunctive adverbs are *consequently, finally, furthermore, however, moreover, nevertheless, similarly, then, therefore,* and *thus.* (See p. 507 for a more complete list.)

> When we want to murder a tiger, we call it sport; *however,* when the tiger wants to murder us, we call it ferocity.

NOTE: The ability to distinguish between conjunctive adverbs and coordinating conjunctions will help you avoid run-on sentences and make punctuation decisions (see 20, 32a, and 34b). The ability to recognize subordinating conjunctions will help you avoid sentence fragments (see 19).

61h Interjections

An interjection is a word used to express surprise or emotion (*Oh! Hey! Wow!*).

62

Sentence patterns

Most English sentences flow from subject to verb to any objects or complements. The vast majority of sentences conform to one of these five patterns:

subject / verb / subject complement

subject / verb / direct object

subject / verb / indirect object / direct object

subject / verb / direct object / object complement

subject / verb

Adverbial modifiers (single words, phrases, or clauses) may be added to any of these patterns, and they may appear nearly anywhere — at the beginning, the middle, or the end.

Predicate is the grammatical term given to the verb plus its objects, complements, and adverbial modifiers.

For a quick-reference chart of sentence patterns, see page 514.

ON THE WEB

For electronic exercises on parts of sentences (subjects, objects, and complements), go to **dianahacker.com/rules**

and click on ▶ **Electronic Grammar Exercises**
                    ▶ **The Basics**
                         ▶ **E-ex 62–1 through 62–5**

62a Subjects

The subject of a sentence names who or what the sentence is about. The *complete subject* is usually composed of a *simple subject,* always a noun or pronoun, and all of its modifiers.

The complete subject

To find the complete subject, ask Who? or What?, insert the verb, and finish the question. The answer is the complete subject.

┌── COMPLETE SUBJECT ──┐
The purity of a revolution usually lasts about two weeks.

Who or what lasts about two weeks? *The purity of a revolution.*

┌─────── COMPLETE SUBJECT ───────┐
Historical books that contain no lies are extremely tedious.

Who or what are extremely tedious? *Historical books that contain no lies.*

COMPLETE SUBJECT
┌──────────────┐
In every country the sun rises in the morning.

Who or what rises in the morning? *The sun.* Notice that *In every country the sun* is not a sensible answer to the question. *In every country* is a prepositional phrase modifying the verb *rises.*

The simple subject

To find the simple subject, strip away all modifiers in the complete subject. This includes single-word modifiers such as *the* and *historical,* phrases such as *of a revolution,* and subordinate clauses such as *that contain no lies.*

┌─ SS ─┐
The purity *of a revolution* usually lasts about two weeks.

┌─ SS ─┐
Historical books that contain no lies are extremely tedious.

┌SS┐
In every country *the sun* rises in the morning.

A sentence may have a compound subject containing two or more simple subjects joined with a coordinating conjunction such as *and, but,* or *or.*

┌── SS ──┐   ┌── SS ──┐
Much industry and little conscience make us rich.

Understood subjects

In imperative sentences, which give advice or issue commands, the verb's subject is understood but not actually present in the sentence. The subject of an imperative sentence is understood to be *you,* as in the following example.

[*You*] Hitch your wagon to a star.

Subject after the verb

Although the subject ordinarily comes before the verb, occasionally it does not. When a sentence begins with *There is* or *There are* (or *There was* or *There were*), the subject follows the verb. The word *There* is an expletive in such constructions, an empty word serving merely to get the sentence started.

```
         ┌── ss ──┐
```
There is *no substitute for victory.*

Occasionally a writer will invert a sentence for effect.

```
      ┌ ss ┐
```
Happy is *the nation that has no history.*

Happy is an adjective, so it cannot be the subject. Turn this sentence around and its structure becomes obvious: *The nation that has no history is happy.*

In questions, the subject frequently appears in an unusual position, sandwiched between parts of the verb.

```
   ┌ss┐
```
Do *married men* make the best husbands?

Turn the question into a statement, and the words will appear in their usual order: *Married men do make the best husbands.* (*Do make* is the verb.)

For more about unusual sentence patterns, see 62c.

NOTE: The ability to recognize the subject of a sentence will help you edit for a variety of problems such as sentence fragments (19), subject-verb agreement (21), and choice of pronouns such as *I* and *me* (24). If English is not your native language, see also 31a and 31b.

EXERCISE 62–1

In the following sentences, underline the complete subject and write *ss* above the simple subject(s). If the subject is an understood *you,* insert it in parentheses. Answers to lettered sentences appear in the back of the book. Example:

ss   ss
Fools and their money are soon parted.

a. Sticks and stones may break my bones, and words can sting like anything. — Anonymous
b. In war, all delays are dangerous. — John Dryden
c. Speak softly and carry a big stick. — Theodore Roosevelt
d. There is nothing permanent except change. — Heraclitus
e. Most of the disputes in the world arise from words.
— Lord Mansfield

1. The structure of every sentence is a lesson in logic.
— J. S. Mill
2. Don't be humble. You're not that great. — Golda Meir
3. In the eyes of its mother, every beetle is a gazelle.
— Moorish proverb
4. The burden of proof lies on the plaintiff. — Legal maxim
5. There are no signposts in the sea. — Vita Sackville-West

62b Verbs, objects, and complements

Section 61c explains how to find the verb of a sentence, which consists of a main verb possibly preceded by one or more helping verbs. A sentence's verb is classified as linking, transitive, or intransitive, depending on the kinds of objects or complements the verb can (or cannot) take.

Linking verbs and subject complements

Linking verbs link the subject to a subject complement, a word or word group that completes the meaning of the subject by renaming or describing it. If the subject complement renames the subject, it is a noun or noun equivalent (sometimes called a *predicate noun*).

```
┌──────────── s ────────────┐ ┌─ v ─┐ ┌─ sc ─┐
The handwriting on the wall may be  a forgery.
```

If the subject complement describes the subject, it is an adjective or adjective equivalent (sometimes called a *predicate adjective*).

```
  s   v   sc
Love is blind.
```

Whenever they appear as main verbs (rather than helping verbs), the forms of be — *be, am, is, are, was, were, being, been* — usually function as linking verbs. In the preceding examples, for instance, the main verbs are *be* and *is*.

Verbs such as *appear, become, feel, grow, look, make, seem, smell, sound,* and *taste* are sometimes linking, depending on the sense of the sentence.

         S   V   ⌐SC⌐
At the touch of love, everyone becomes a poet.

   ⌐——S——⌐   V   SC
At first sight, original art often looks ugly.

When you suspect that a verb such as *becomes* or *looks* is linking, check to see if the word or words following it rename or describe the subject. In the same sentences, *a poet* renames *everyone,* and *ugly* describes *art.*

Transitive verbs and direct objects

A transitive verb takes a direct object, a word or word group that names a receiver of the action.

   ⌐——S—— | V ⌐————DO————⌐
The little snake studies the ways of the big serpent.

The simple direct object is always a noun, such as *ways,* or a pronoun.

Transitive verbs usually appear in the active voice, with the subject doing the action and a direct object receiving the action. Active-voice sentences can be transformed into the passive voice, with the subject receiving the action instead. (See 62c.)

Transitive verbs, indirect objects, and direct objects

The direct object of a transitive verb is sometimes preceded by an indirect object, a noun or pronoun telling to whom or for whom the action of the sentence is done.

   S   V   IO ⌐DO⌐   S⌐—V—⌐ IO ⌐—DO—⌐
You show me a hero, and I will write you a tragedy.

Sentence patterns

Subject / linking verb / subject complement

```
  ┌── S ──┐ V ┌── SC ──┐
```
Advertising is legalized lying. [*Legalized lying* renames *Advertising*.]

```
  ┌── S ──┐  V    SC
```
Great intellects are skeptical. [*Skeptical* describes *Great intellects*.]

Subject / transitive verb / direct object

```
  ┌── S ──┐ ┌── V ──┐ ┌DO┐
```
A stumble may prevent a fall.

Subject / transitive verb / indirect object / direct object

```
   S    V   IO ┌── DO ──┐
```
Fate gives us our relatives.

Subject / transitive verb / direct object / object complement

```
  ┌── S ──┐ ┌── V ──┐DO   OC
```
Our fears do make us traitors. [*Traitors* renames *us*.]

```
  ┌── S ──┐  V  ┌── DO ──┐  OC
```
The pot calls the kettle black. [*Black* describes *the kettle*.]

Subject / intransitive verb

```
   S    V
```
Time flies.

The simple indirect object is always a noun or pronoun. To test for an indirect object, insert the word *to* or *for* before the word or word group in question. If the sentence makes sense, the word or word group is an indirect object.

You show [to] me a hero, and I will write [for] you a tragedy.

An indirect object may be turned into a prepositional phrase using *to* or *for: You show a hero to me, and I will write a tragedy for you.*

Transitive verbs, direct objects, and object complements

The direct object of a transitive verb is sometimes followed by an object complement, a word or word group that completes the direct object's meaning by renaming or describing it.

```
    S       V  ┌─DO─┐ ┌──────── OC ────────┐
People now call a spade an agricultural implement.
```

```
    S    V    ┌──── DO ────┐  OC
Love makes all hard hearts gentle.
```

When the object complement renames the direct object, it is a noun or pronoun (such as *implement*). When it describes the direct object, it is an adjective (such as *gentle*).

Intransitive verbs

Intransitive verbs take no objects or complements. Their pattern is subject/verb.

```
    S    V
Money talks.
```

```
     S         V
Revolutions never go backward.
```

Nothing receives the actions of talking and going in these sentences, so the verbs are intransitive. Notice that such verbs may or may not be followed by adverbial modifiers. In the second sentence, *backward* is an adverb modifying *go*.

NOTE: The dictionary will tell you whether a verb is transitive or intransitive. Some verbs have both transitive and intransitive functions.

TRANSITIVE   Sandra flew her Cessna over the canyon.

INTRANSITIVE   A bald eagle flew overhead.

In the first example, *flew* has a direct object that receives the action: *her Cessna*. In the second example, the verb is followed by an adverb (*overhead*), not by a direct object.

EXERCISE 62-2

Label the subject complements and direct objects in the following sentences, using these labels: *sc, do*. If a subject complement or direct object consists of more than one word, bracket and label all of it. Example:

┌──────── DO ────────┐
You can fool most of the people most of the time.

a. Talk is cheap.   — English proverb
b. An elephant never forgets an injury.   — American proverb
c. A runaway monk never praises his convent.   — Italian proverb
d. Religion is the opium of the people.   — Karl Marx
e. Good medicine always tastes bitter.   — Japanese proverb

1. You can say the nastiest things about yourself without offending anyone.   — Phyllis Diller
2. The quarrels of friends are the opportunities of foes.   — Aesop
3. Art is the signature of civilization.   — Beverly Sills
4. You can tell the ideals of a nation by its advertising.
                                                     — Norman Douglas
5. You can never be too rich or too thin. — Wallis Warfield Simpson

EXERCISE 62-3

Each of the following sentences has either an indirect object followed by a direct object or a direct object followed by an object complement. Label the objects and complements, using these labels: *io, do, oc*. If an object or complement consists of more than one word, bracket and label all of it. Example:

┌──── DO ────┐   OC
Every man thinks his own geese swans.

a. Sorrow makes us wise.   — Alfred Lord Tennyson
b. Too many people make money their primary pursuit.
                                                     — Anonymous
c. Make us happy and you make us good.   — Robert Browning
d. Ask me no questions, and I will tell you no lies. — Anonymous
e. Show me a good loser, and I will show you a failure.
                                                     — Paul Newman

1. Give the devil his due.   — English proverb
2. God gives every bird its proper food, but all must fly for it.
                                                     — Dutch proverb
3. A wide screen makes a bad film worse.   — Samuel Goldwyn

4. Trees and fields tell me nothing.   — Socrates
5. Necessity can make us surprisingly brave.   — Latin proverb

62c   Pattern variations

Although most sentences follow one of the five patterns in the chart on page 514, variations of these patterns commonly occur in questions, commands, sentences with delayed subjects, and passive transformations.

Questions and commands

Questions are sometimes patterned in normal word order, with the subject preceding the verb.

> S   ┌── V ──┐
> Who will take the first step?

Just as frequently, however, the pattern of a question is inverted, with the subject appearing between the helping and main verbs or after the verb.

> HV   S   MV
> Will you take the first step?

> V ┌─── S ───┐
> Why is the first step so difficult?

In commands, the subject of the sentence is an understood *you.*

> [You] Keep your mouth shut and your eyes open.

Sentences with delayed subjects

Writers sometimes choose to delay the subject of a sentence to achieve a special effect such as suspense or humor.

> V ┌─── S ───┐
> Behind the phony tinsel of Hollywood lies the real tinsel.

The subject of the sentence is also delayed in sentences opening with the explctive *There* or *It.* When used as expletives, the words *There* and *It* have no strict grammatical function; they serve merely to get the sentence started.

```
      V ┌─────────── S ───────────┐
```
There is no penalty for overachievement.

```
      V          ┌──────── S ───────┐
```
It is not good to wake a sleeping lion.

The subject in the second example is an infinitive phrase. (See 63c.)

Passive transformations

Transitive verbs, those that can take direct objects, usually appear in the active voice. In the active voice, the subject does the action and a direct object receives the action.

```
              ┌──── S ────┐      V   ┌──── DO ────┐
```
ACTIVE   The early bird sometimes catches the early worm.

Sentences in the active voice may be transformed into the passive voice, with the subject receiving the action instead.

```
              ┌──── S ────┐HV          MV
```
PASSIVE   The early worm is sometimes caught by the early bird.

What was once the direct object (*the early worm*) has become the subject in the passive-voice transformation, and the original subject appears in a prepositional phrase beginning with *by.* The *by* phrase is frequently omitted in passive-voice constructions.

PASSIVE   The early worm is sometimes caught.

Verbs in the passive voice can be identified by their form alone. The main verb is always a past participle, such as *caught* (see 61c), preceded by a form of *be* (*be, am, is, are, was, were, being, been*): *is caught.* Sometimes adverbs intervene (*is sometimes caught*).

NOTE: Writers sometimes use the passive voice when the active voice would be more appropriate (see 8a).

63

Subordinate word groups

Subordinate word groups cannot stand alone. They function only within sentences, usually as adjectives, adverbs, or nouns.

ON THE WEB

For electronic exercises on subordinate word groups (prepositional phrases, verbal phrases, and subordinate clauses), go to
dianahacker.com/rules

and click on ▶ **Electronic Grammar Exercises**
▶ **The Basics**
▶ **E-ex 63-1 through 63-9**

63a Prepositional phrases

A prepositional phrase begins with a preposition such as *at, by, for, from, in, of, on, to,* or *with* (see 61f) and ends with a noun or noun equivalent called its *object.*

Prepositional phrases function as adjectives or adverbs. When functioning as an adjective, a prepositional phrase usually appears right after the noun or pronoun it modifies.

Variety is the spice *of life.*

Adjective phrases answer one or both of the questions Which one? and What kind of? If we ask Which spice? or What kind of spice? we get a sensible answer: *the spice of life.*

Adverbial prepositional phrases modifying the verb can appear nearly anywhere in a sentence.

Do not *judge* a tree *by its bark.*

Tyranny will *in time lead* to revolution.

To the ant, a few drops of rain *are* a flood.

Adverb phrases usually answer one of these questions: When? Where? How? Why? Under what conditions? To what degree?

Do not judge a tree *how? By its bark.*

Tyranny will lead to revolution *when? In time.*

A few drops of rain are a flood *under what conditions? To the ant.*

EXERCISE 63–1

Underline the prepositional phrases in the following sentences. Be prepared to explain the function of each phrase. Answers to lettered sentences appear in the back of the book. Example:

Communism is fascism <u>with a human face</u>. *(Adjective phrase modifying fascism)*

a. On their side, the workers had only the Constitution. The other side had bayonets. — Mother Jones

b. Any mother could perform the job of several air traffic controllers with ease. — Lisa Alther

c. To my embarrassment, I was born in bed with a lady.
— Wilson Mizner

d. Language is the road map of a culture. — Rita Mae Brown

e. In France, cooking is a serious art form and a national sport.
— Julia Child

1. We know that the road to freedom has always been stalked by death. — Angela Davis

2. A society of sheep produces a government of wolves.
— Bertrand de Jouvenal

3. Some people feel with their heads and think with their hearts.
— G. C. Lichtenberg

4. By a small sample, we may know the whole piece.
— Cervantes

5. You and I come by road or rail, but economists travel on infrastructure. — Margaret Thatcher

63b Subordinate clauses

Subordinate clauses are patterned like sentences, having subjects and verbs and sometimes objects or complements. But they function within sentences as adjectives, adverbs, or nouns. They cannot stand alone as complete sentences.

Adjective clauses

Adjective clauses modify nouns or pronouns, usually answering the question Which one? or What kind of? They begin with a relative pronoun (*who, whom, whose, which,* or *that*) or a relative adverb (*when* or *where*).

The arrow *that has left the bow* never returns.

In addition to introducing the clause, the relative pronoun points back to the noun that the clause modifies.

The fur *that warms a monarch* once warmed a bear.

Relative pronouns are sometimes "understood."

The things [*that*] *we know best* are the things [*that*] *we haven't been taught.*

Occasionally an adjective clause is introduced by a relative adverb, usually *when, where,* or *why.*

Home is the place *where you slip in the tub and break your neck.*

The parts of an adjective clause are often arranged as in sentences (subject/verb/object or complement).

                                        s   v   do
We often forgive the people *who bore us.*

Frequently, however, the object or complement appears first, violating the normal order of subject/verb/object.

                                        do   s   v
We rarely forgive those *whom we bore.*

522   *Basics*

NOTE: For punctuation of adjective clauses, see 32e and 33e. If English is not your native language, see 31c for a common problem with adjective clauses.

Adverb clauses

Adverb clauses modify verbs, adjectives, or other adverbs, usually answering one of these questions: When? Where? Why? How? Under what conditions? To what degree? They begin with a subordinating conjunction (*after, although, as, as if, because, before, even though, if, in order that, rather than, since, so that, than, that, though, unless, until, when, where, whether, while*).

When the well is dry, we know the worth of water.

Venice would be a fine city *if it were only drained.*

Adverb clauses are sometimes elliptical, with some of their words being "understood."

When [it is] painted, the room will look larger.

Noun clauses

Noun clauses function as subjects, objects, or complements. They usually begin with one of the following words: *how, that, which, who, whoever, whom, whomever, what, whatever, when, where, whether, whose, why.*

———— S ————
Whoever gossips to you will gossip of you.

———— DO ————
We never forget *that we buried the hatchet.*

The word introducing the clause may or may not play a significant role in the clause. In the preceding example sentences, *whoever* is the subject of its clause, but *that* does not perform a function in its clause.

As with adjective clauses, the parts of a noun clause may appear out of their normal order (subject/verb/object).

DO   S   V
Talent is *what you possess.*

The parts of a noun clause may also appear in their normal order.

                S   V   DO
Genius is *what possesses you.*

EXERCISE 63-2

Underline the subordinate clauses in the following sentences. Be prepared to explain the function of each clause. Answers to lettered sentences appear in the back of the book. Example:

> **Dig a well <u>before you are thirsty</u>.**   *(Adverb clause modifying Dig)*

  a. It is hard to fight an enemy who has outposts in your head.
                                                       — Sally Kempton
  b. A rattlesnake that doesn't bite teaches you nothing.
                                                      — Jessamyn West
  c. If love is the answer, could you please rephrase the question?
                                                        — Lily Tomlin
  d. Dreams say what they mean, but they don't say it in daytime language.
                                                      — Gail Godwin
  e. I generally avoid temptation unless I cannot resist it.
                                                        — Mae West

  1. What history teaches us is that we have never learned anything from it.   — Georg Wilhelm Hegel
  2. When the insects take over the world, we hope that they will remember our picnics with gratitude.   — Anonymous
  3. A woman who will tell her age will tell anything.
                                                      — Rita Mae Brown
  4. If triangles had a god, it would have three sides.
                                                — C. L. de Montesquieu
  5. He gave her a look that you could have poured on a waffle.
                                                       — Ring Lardner

63c   Verbal phrases

A verbal is a verb form that does not function as the verb of a clause. Verbals include infinitives (the word *to* plus the base form of the verb), present participles (the *-ing* form of the verb), and past participles (the verb form usually ending in *-d, -ed, -n, -en,* or *-t*). (See 27a and 61c.)

Verbals can take objects, complements, and modifiers to form verbal phrases. These phrases are classified as participial, gerund, and infinitive.

Participial phrases

Participial phrases always function as adjectives. Their verbals are either present participles, always ending in *-ing*, or past participles, frequently ending in *-d, -ed, -n, -en,* or *-t* (see 27a).

Participial phrases frequently appear immediately following the noun or pronoun they modify.

Truth *kept in the dark* will never save the world.

They can also precede the word they modify or appear at some distance from the word they modify.

Being weak, foxes are distinguished by superior tact.

History is something that never happened, *written by someone who wasn't there.*

Gerund phrases

Gerund phrases are built around present participles (verb forms ending in *-ing*), and they always function as nouns: usually as subjects, subject complements, direct objects, or objects of a preposition.

             S
Justifying a fault doubles it.

                   SC
The secret of education is *respecting the student.*

              DO
Kleptomaniacs can't help *helping themselves.*

             OBJ OF PREP
The hen is an egg's way of *producing another egg.*

Infinitive phrases

Infinitive phrases, usually constructed around *to* plus the base form of the verb (*to call, to drink*), can function as nouns, as adjectives, or as adverbs.

When functioning as a noun, an infinitive phrase may appear in almost any noun slot in a sentence, usually as a subject, subject complement, or direct object.

```
    ┌──────── S ────────┐
```
To side with truth is noble.

```
    ┌──────────── DO ─────────────┐
```
Never try *to leap a chasm in two jumps.*

Infinitive phrases functioning as adjectives usually appear immediately following the noun or pronoun they modify.

We do not have the right *to abandon the poor.*

The infinitive phrase modifies the noun *right.* Which right? *The right to abandon the poor.*

Adverbial infinitive phrases usually qualify the meaning of the verb, telling when, where, how, why, under what conditions, or to what degree an action occurred.

He cut off his nose *to spite his face.*

Why did he cut off his nose? *To spite his face.*

NOTE: In some constructions, the infinitive is unmarked; in other words, the *to* does not appear: *No one can make you* [*to*] *feel inferior without your consent.* (See 29c.)

EXERCISE 63–3

Underline the verbal phrases in the following sentences. Be prepared to explain the function of each phrase. Answers to lettered sentences appear in the back of the book. Example:

> Do you want <u>to be a writer</u>? Then write. *(Infinitive phrase*
>
> *used as direct object of Do want)*

a. Concealing a disease is no way to cure it.   — Ethiopian proverb
b. The trouble with being punctual is that nobody is there to appreciate it.   — Franklin P. Jones
c. Fate tried to conceal him by naming him Smith.
                                        — Oliver Wendell Holmes Jr.
d. Being weak, children quickly learn to beguile us with charm.
                                                        — Anonymous
e. Wrestling with words gave me my moments of greatest meaning.
                                                      — Richard Wright

1. The thing generally raised on city land is taxes.   — C. D. Warner
2. Do not use a hatchet to remove a fly from your friend's forehead.
                                                     — Chinese proverb
3. He has the gall of a shoplifter returning an item for a refund.
                                                        — W. I. E. Gates
4. Tact is the ability to describe others as they see themselves.
                                                  — Mary Pettibone Poole
5. He could never see a belt without hitting below it.
                                                      — Harriet Braiker

63d Appositive phrases

Though strictly speaking they are not subordinate word groups, appositive phrases function somewhat as adjectives do, to describe nouns or pronouns. Instead of modifying nouns or pronouns, however, appositive phrases rename them. In form they are nouns or noun equivalents.

Appositives are said to be "in apposition" to the nouns or pronouns they rename.

> Politicians, *acrobats at heart,* can sit on a fence and yet keep both ears to the ground.

Acrobats at heart is in apposition to the noun *politicians.*

63e Absolute phrases

An absolute phrase modifies a whole clause or sentence, not just one word, and it may appear nearly anywhere in the sentence. It consists of a noun or noun equivalent usually followed by a participial phrase.

His words dipped in honey, the senator mesmerized the crowd.

The senator mesmerized the crowd, *his words dipped in honey.*

64

Sentence types

Sentences are classified in two ways: according to their structure (simple, compound, complex, and compound-complex) and according to their purpose (declarative, imperative, interrogative, and exclamatory).

64a Sentence structures

Depending on the number and types of clauses they contain, sentences are classified as simple, compound, complex, or compound-complex.

Clauses come in two varieties: independent and subordinate. An independent clause is a full sentence pattern that does not function within another sentence pattern: It contains a subject and its modifiers plus a verb and any objects, complements, and modifiers of that verb, and it either stands alone or could stand alone. A subordinate clause is a full sentence pattern that functions within a sentence as an adjective, an adverb, or a noun but that cannot stand alone as a complete sentence. (See 63b.)

Simple sentences

A simple sentence is one independent clause with no subordinate clauses.

```
┌──────── INDEPENDENT CLAUSE ────────┐
Without music, life would be a mistake.
```

This sentence contains a subject (*life*), a verb (*would be*), a complement (*a mistake*), and an adverbial modifier (*Without music*).

A simple sentence may contain compound elements—a compound subject, verb, or object, for example—but it does not contain more than one full sentence pattern. The following sentence is simple because its two verbs (*enters* and *spreads*) share a subject (*Evil*).

┌─────────── INDEPENDENT CLAUSE ───────────┐
Evil enters like a needle and spreads like an oak.

Compound sentences

A compound sentence is composed of two or more independent clauses with no subordinate clauses. The independent clauses are usually joined with a comma and a coordinating conjunction (*and, but, or, nor, for, so, yet*) or with a semicolon. (See 14a.)

┌─ INDEPENDENT CLAUSE ─┐   ┌─── INDEPENDENT CLAUSE ───┐
One arrow is easily broken, but you can't break a bundle of ten.

┌──────── INDEPENDENT CLAUSE ────────┐ ┌─INDEPENDENT –
We are born brave, trusting, and greedy; most of us have
CLAUSE ────────┐
remained greedy.

Complex sentences

A complex sentence is composed of one independent clause with one or more subordinate clauses. (See 63b.)

SUBORDINATE
┌─── CLAUSE ───┐
ADJECTIVE They that sow in tears shall reap in joy.

SUBORDINATE
┌─── CLAUSE ───┐
ADVERB If you scatter thorns, don't go barefoot.

┌────────── SUBORDINATE CLAUSE ──────────┐
NOUN What the scientists have in their briefcases is terrifying.

Compound-complex sentences

A compound-complex sentence contains at least two independent clauses and at least one subordinate clause. The following sentence contains two full sentence patterns that can stand alone.

┌INDEPENDENT CLAUSE┐   ┌── INDEPENDENT CLAUSE ──┐
Tell me what you eat, and I will tell you what you are.

And each independent clause contains a subordinate clause, making the sentence both compound and complex.

┌─── IND CL ───┐   ┌────── IND CL ──────┐
    ┌─SUB CL─┐   ┌─ SUB CL─┐
Tell me what you eat, and I will tell you what you are.

64b Sentence purposes

Writers use declarative sentences to make statements, imperative sentences to issue requests or commands, interrogative sentences to ask questions, and exclamatory sentences to make exclamations.

DECLARATIVE   The echo always has the last word.

IMPERATIVE   Love your neighbor.

INTERROGATIVE   Are second thoughts always wisest?

EXCLAMATORY   I want to wash the flag, not burn it!

EXERCISE 64–1

Identify the following sentences as simple, compound, complex, or compound-complex. Be prepared to identify the subordinate clauses and classify them according to their function: adjective, adverb, or noun. (See 63b.) Answers to lettered sentences appear in the back of the book. Example:

The frog in the well knows nothing of the ocean. *(Simple)*

a. People who sleep like a baby usually don't have one.
                                            — Leo Burke
b. My folks didn't come over on the *Mayflower;* they were there to meet the boat.   — Will Rogers
c. The impersonal hand of the government can never replace the helping hand of a neighbor.   — Hubert Humphrey

d. If you don't go to other people's funerals, they won't go to yours.
—Clarence Day

   e. Tell us your phobias, and we will tell you what you are afraid of.
—Robert Benchley

1. The tragedy of life is that people don't change.
—Agatha Christie

2. Those who cannot remember the past are condemned to repeat it.
—George Santayana

3. The best mind-altering drug is truth.   —Lily Tomlin

4. Morality cannot be legislated, but behavior can be regulated.
—Martin Luther King Jr.

5. Science commits suicide when it adopts a creed. —T. H. Huxley

---

ON THE WEB

For an electronic exercise on identifying sentence types, go to
dianahacker.com/rules

and click on ▶ **Electronic Grammar Exercises**
               ▶ **The Basics**
                    ▶ **E-ex 64-1**

Glossary of Usage

This glossary includes words commonly confused (such as *accept* and *except*), words commonly misused (such as *aggravate*), and words that are nonstandard (such as *hisself*). It also lists colloquialisms and jargon. Colloquialisms are expressions that may be appropriate in informal speech but are inappropriate in formal writing. Jargon is needlessly technical or pretentious language that is inappropriate in most contexts. If an item is not listed here, consult the index. For irregular verbs (such as *sing, sang, sung*), see 27a. For idiomatic use of prepositions, see 18d.

ON THE WEB

Some matters of usage included in this glossary have sparked debates. If you are interested in learning why, go to
dianahacker.com/rules

and click on ▶ **Language Debates**
  bad versus *badly*
  however at the beginning of a sentence
  lie versus *lay*
  myself
  that versus *which*
  Absolute concepts such as *unique*
  who versus *which* or *that*
  who versus *whom*
  you

a, an   Use *an* before a vowel sound, *a* before a consonant sound: *an apple, a peach.* Problems sometimes arise with words beginning with *h.* If the *h* is silent, the word begins with a vowel sound, so use *an: an hour, an heir, an honest senator, an honorable deed.* If the *h* is pronounced, the word begins with a consonant sound, so use *a: a hospital, a hymn, a historian, a hotel.* When an abbreviation or acronym begins with a vowel sound, use *an: an EKG, an MRI, an AIDS* patient.

accept, except   *Accept* is a verb meaning "to receive." *Except* is usually a preposition meaning "excluding." *I will accept all the packages except that one. Except* is also a verb meaning "to exclude." *Please except that item from the list.*

adapt, adopt   *Adapt* means "to adjust or become accustomed"; it is usually followed by *to. Adopt* means "to take as one's own." *Our family adopted a Vietnamese orphan, who quickly adapted to his new surroundings.*

adverse, averse   *Adverse* means "unfavorable." *Averse* means "opposed" or "reluctant"; it is usually followed by *to. I am averse to your proposal because it could have an adverse impact on the economy.*

advice, advise   *Advice* is a noun, *advise* a verb. *We advise you to follow John's advice.*

affect, effect   *Affect* is usually a verb meaning "to influence." *Effect* is usually a noun meaning "result." *The drug did not affect the disease, and it had adverse side effects. Effect* can also be a verb meaning "to bring about." *Only the president can effect such a change.*

aggravate   *Aggravate* means "to make worse or more troublesome." *Overgrazing aggravated the soil erosion.* In formal writing, avoid the colloquial use of *aggravate* meaning "to annoy or irritate." *Her babbling annoyed* (not *aggravated*) *me.*

ain't   *Ain't* is nonstandard. Use *am not, are not* (*aren't*), or *is not* (*isn't*). *I am not* (not *ain't*) *going home for spring break.*

all ready, already   *All ready* means "completely prepared." *Already* means "previously." *Susan was all ready for the concert, but her friends had already left.*

all right   *All right* is written as two words. *Alright* is nonstandard.

all together, altogether   *All together* means "everyone gathered." *Altogether* means "entirely." *We were not altogether certain that we could bring the family all together for the reunion.*

allude   To *allude* to something is to make an indirect reference to it. Do not use *allude* to mean "to refer directly." *In his lecture the professor referred* (not *alluded*) *to several pre-Socratic philosophers.*

allusion, illusion   An *allusion* is an indirect reference. An *illusion* is a misconception or false impression. *Did you catch my allusion to Shakespeare? Mirrors give the room an illusion of depth.*

a lot   *A lot* is two words. Do not write *alot. We have had a lot of rain this spring.* See also *lots, lots of.*

among, between   See *between, among.*

amongst   In American English, *among* is preferred.

amoral, immoral   *Amoral* means "neither moral nor immoral"; it also means "not caring about moral judgments." *Immoral* means "morally wrong." *Until recently, most business courses were taught from an amoral perspective. Murder is immoral.*

amount, number   Use *amount* with quantities that cannot be counted; use *number* with those that can. *This recipe calls for a large amount of sugar. We have a large number of toads in our garden.*

an   See *a, an.*

and etc.   *Et cetera* (*etc.*) means "and so forth"; therefore, *and etc.* is redundant. See also *etc.*

and/or   Avoid the awkward construction *and/or* except in technical or legal documents.

ante-, anti-   The prefix *ante-* means "earlier" or "in front of"; the prefix *anti-* means "against" or "opposed to." *William Lloyd Garrison was a leader of the antislavery movement during the antebellum period.* Anti- should be used with a hyphen when it is followed by a capital letter or a word beginning with *i*.

anybody, anyone   *Anybody* and *anyone* are singular. (See 21e and 22a.)

anymore   Reserve the adverb *anymore* for negative contexts, where it means "any longer." *Moviegoers are rarely shocked anymore by profanity.* Do not use *anymore* in positive contexts. Use *now* or *nowadays* instead. *Interest rates are so low now* (not *anymore*) *that more people can afford to buy homes.*

anyone   See *anybody, anyone.*

anyone, any one   *Anyone,* an indefinite pronoun, means "any person at all." *Any one,* the pronoun *one* preceded by the adjective *any,* refers to a particular person or thing in a group. *Anyone from Chicago may choose any one of the games on display.*

anyplace   *Anyplace* is informal for *anywhere.* Avoid *anyplace* in formal writing.

anyways, anywheres   *Anyways* and *anywheres* are nonstandard. Use *anyway* and *anywhere.*

as   *As* is sometimes used to mean "because." But do not use it if there is any chance of ambiguity. *We canceled the picnic because* (not *as*) *it began raining. As* here could mean "because" or "when."

as, like   See *like, as.*

as to   *As to* is jargon for *about. He inquired about* (not *as to*) *the job.*

averse   See *adverse, averse.*

awful   The adjective *awful* and the adverb *awfully* are too colloquial for formal writing.

awhile, a while   *Awhile* is an adverb; it can modify a verb, but it cannot be the object of a preposition such as *for.* The two-word form *a while* is a noun preceded by an article and therefore can be the object of a preposition. *Stay awhile. Stay for a while.*

back up, backup   *Back up* is a verb phrase. *Back up the car carefully. Be sure to back up your hard drive.* *Backup* is a noun meaning "a duplicate of electronically stored data." *Keep your backup in a safe place. Backup* can also be used as an adjective. *I regularly create backup disks.*

bad, badly   *Bad* is an adjective, *badly* an adverb. (See 26a and 26b.) *They felt bad about being early and ruining the surprise. Her arm hurt badly after she slid headfirst into second base.*

being as, being that   *Being as* and *being that* are nonstandard expressions. Write *because* instead. *Because* (not *Being as*) *I slept late, I had to skip breakfast.*

beside, besides   *Beside* is a preposition meaning "at the side of" or "next to." *Annie Oakley slept with her gun beside her bed. Besides* is a preposition meaning "except" or "in addition to." *No one besides Terrie can have that ice cream. Besides* is also an adverb meaning "in addition." *I'm not hungry; besides, I don't like ice cream.*

between, among   Ordinarily, use *among* with three or more entities, *between* with two. *The prize was divided among several contestants. You have a choice between carrots and beans.*

bring, take   Use *bring* when an object is being transported toward you, *take* when it is being moved away. *Please bring me a glass of water. Please take these flowers to Mr. Scott.*

burst, bursted; bust, busted   *Burst* is an irregular verb meaning "to come open or fly apart suddenly or violently." Its principal parts are *burst, burst, burst. Bursted, bust,* and *busted* are nonstandard.

can, may   The distinction between *can* and *may* is fading, but some writers still observe it in formal writing. *Can* is traditionally reserved for ability, *may* for permission. *Can you ski down the advanced slope without falling? May I help you?*

capital, capitol   *Capital* refers to a city, *capitol* to a building where lawmakers meet. *Capital* also refers to wealth or resources. *The capitol has undergone extensive renovations. The residents of the state capital protested the development plans.*

censor, censure   *Censor* means "to remove or suppress material considered objectionable." *Censure* means "to criticize severely." *The library's new policy of censoring controversial books has been censured by the media.*

cite, site   *Cite* means "to quote as an authority or example." *Site* is usually a noun meaning "a particular place." *He cited the zoning law in his argument against the proposed site of the gas station.* Locations on the Internet are usually referred to as *sites.*

climactic, climatic   *Climactic* is derived from *climax,* the point of greatest intensity in a series or progression of events. *Climatic* is derived from *climate* and refers to meteorological conditions. *The climactic period in the dinosaurs' reign was reached just before severe climatic conditions brought on an ice age.*

coarse, course   *Coarse* means "crude" or "rough in texture." *The coarse weave of the wall hanging gave it a three-dimensional quality. Course* usually refers to a path, a playing field, or a unit of study; the expression *of course* means "certainly." *I plan to take a course in car repair this summer. Of course, you are welcome to join me.*

compare to, compare with   *Compare to* means "to represent as similar." *She compared him to a wild stallion. Compare with* means "to examine the ways in which two things are similar." *The study compared the language ability of apes with that of dolphins.*

complement, compliment   *Complement* is a verb meaning "to go with or complete" or a noun meaning "something that completes." *Compliment* as a verb means "to flatter"; as a noun it means "flattering remark." *Her skill at rushing the net complements his skill at volleying. Mother's flower arrangements receive many compliments.*

conscience, conscious   *Conscience* is a noun meaning "moral principles." *Conscious* is an adjective meaning "aware or alert." *Let your conscience be your guide. Were you conscious of his love for you?*

continual, continuous   *Continual* means "repeated regularly and frequently." *She grew weary of the continual telephone calls. Continuous* means "extended or prolonged without interruption." *The broken siren made a continuous wail.*

could care less   *Could care less* is a nonstandard expression. Write *couldn't care less* instead. *He couldn't (not couldn't) care less about his psychology final.*

could of   *Could of* is nonstandard for *could have. We could have (not could of) had steak for dinner if we had been hungry.*

council, counsel   A *council* is a deliberative body, and a *councilor* is a member of such a body. *Counsel* usually means "advice" and can also mean "lawyer"; *counselor* is one who gives advice or guidance. *The councilors met to draft the council's position paper. The pastor offered wise counsel to the troubled teenager.*

criteria   *Criteria* is the plural of *criterion,* which means "a standard or rule or test on which a judgment or decision can be based." *The only criterion for the scholarship is ability.*

data   *Data* is a plural noun technically meaning "facts or propositions." But *data* is increasingly being accepted as a singular noun. *The new data suggest* (or *suggests*) *that our theory is correct.* (The singular *datum* is rarely used.)

different from, different than   Ordinarily, write *different from. Your sense of style is different from Jim's.* However, *different than* is acceptable to avoid an awkward construction. *Please let me know if your plans are different than* (to avoid *from what*) *they were six weeks ago.*

differ from, differ with   *Differ from* means "to be unlike"; *differ with* means "to disagree." *She differed with me about the wording of the agreement. My approach to the problem differed from hers.*

disinterested, uninterested   *Disinterested* means "impartial, objective"; *uninterested* means "not interested." *We sought the advice of a disinterested counselor to help us solve our problem. He was uninterested in anyone's opinion but his own.*

due to   *Due to* is an adjective phrase and should not be used as a preposition meaning "because of." *The trip was canceled because of* (not *due to*) *lack of interest. Due to* is acceptable as a subject complement and usually follows a form of the verb *be. His success was due to hard work.*

each   *Each* is singular. (See 21e and 22a.)

effect   See *affect, effect.*

either   *Either* is singular. (See 21e and 22a.) (For *either . . . or* constructions, see 21d and 22d.)

elicit, illicit   *Elicit* is a verb meaning "to bring out" or "to evoke." *Illicit* is an adjective meaning "unlawful." *The reporter was unable to elicit any information from the police about illicit drug traffic.*

emigrate from, immigrate to   *Emigrate* means "to leave one country or region to settle in another." *In 1900, my grandfather emigrated from Russia to escape the religious pogroms. Immigrate* means "to enter another country and reside there." *Many Mexicans immigrate to the United States to find work.*

eminent, imminent   *Eminent* means "outstanding" or "distinguished." *We met an eminent professor of Greek history. Imminent* means "about to happen." *The announcement is imminent.*

enthused   Many people object to the use of *enthused* as an adjective. Use *enthusiastic* instead. *The children were enthusiastic* (not *enthused*) *about going to the circus.*

etc.   Avoid ending a list with *etc.* It is more emphatic to end with an example, and in most contexts readers will understand that the list is not exhaustive. When you don't wish to end with an example, *and so on* is more graceful than *etc.* See also *and etc.*

eventually, ultimately   Often used interchangeably, *eventually* is the better choice to mean "at an unspecified time in the future" and *ultimately* is better to mean "the furthest possible extent or greatest extreme." *He knew that eventually he would complete his degree. The existentialist considered suicide the ultimately rational act.*

everybody, everyone   *Everybody* and *everyone* are singular. (See 21e and 22a.)

everyone, every one   *Everyone* is an indefinite pronoun. *Every one,* the pronoun *one* preceded by the adjective *every,* means "each individual or thing in a particular group." *Every one* is usually followed by *of. Everyone wanted to go. Every one of the missing books was found.*

except   See *accept, except.*

expect   Avoid the colloquial use of *expect* meaning "to believe, think, or suppose." *I think* (not *expect*) *it will rain tonight.*

explicit, implicit   *Explicit* means "expressed directly" or "clearly defined"; *implicit* means "implied, unstated." *I gave him explicit instructions not to go swimming. My mother's silence indicated her implicit approval.*

farther, further   *Farther* usually describes distances. *Further* usually suggests quantity or degree. *Chicago is farther from Miami than I thought. You extended the curfew further than you should have.*

fewer, less   *Fewer* refers to items that can be counted; *less* refers to general amounts. *Fewer people are living in the city. Please put less sugar in my tea.*

finalize   *Finalize* is jargon meaning "to make final or complete." Use ordinary English instead. *The architect prepared final drawings* (not *finalized the drawings*).

firstly   *Firstly* sounds pretentious, and it leads to the ungainly series *firstly, secondly, thirdly, fourthly,* and so on. Write *first, second, third* instead.

further   See *farther, further.*

get   *Get* has many colloquial uses. In writing, avoid using *get* to mean the following: "to evoke an emotional response" (*That music always gets to me*); "to annoy" (*After a while his sulking got to me*).

good, well   *Good* is an adjective, *well* an adverb. (See 26.) *He hasn't felt good about his game since he sprained his wrist last season. She performed well on the uneven parallel bars.*

graduate   Both of the following uses of *graduate* are standard: *My sister was graduated from UCLA last year. My sister graduated from UCLA last year.* It is nonstandard, however, to drop the word *from: My sister graduated UCLA last year.* Though this usage is common in informal English, many readers object to it.

grow   Phrases such as *to grow the economy* or *to grow a business* are jargon. Usually the verb *grow* is intransitive (it does not take a direct object). *Our business has grown very quickly.* When *grow* is used in a transitive sense, with a direct object, it means "to cultivate" or "to allow to grow." *We plan to grow tomatoes this year. John is growing a beard.*

hanged, hung   *Hanged* is the past-tense and past-participle form of the verb *hang,* meaning "to execute." *The prisoner was hanged at dawn. Hung* is the past-tense and past-participle form of the verb *hang* meaning "to fasten or suspend." *The stockings were hung by the chimney with care.*

has got, have got   *Got* is unnecessary and awkward in such constructions. It should be dropped. *We have* (not *have got*) *three days to prepare for the opening.*

he   At one time *he* was commonly used to mean "he or she." Today such usage is inappropriate. (See 17f and 22a.)

he/she, his/her   In formal writing, use *he or she* or *his or her.* For alternatives to these wordy constructions, see 17f and 22a.

hisself   *Hisself* is nonstandard. Use *himself.*

hopefully   *Hopefully* means "in a hopeful manner." *We looked hopefully to the future.* Some usage experts object to the use of *hopefully* as a sentence adverb, apparently on grounds of clarity. To be safe, avoid using *hopefully* in sentences such as the following: *Hopefully, your son will recover soon.* At least some educated readers will want you to indicate who is doing the hoping: *I hope that your son will recover soon.*

however   In the past, some writers objected to *however* at the beginning of a sentence, but current experts advise you to place the word according to your meaning and desired emphasis. Any of the following sentences is correct, depending on the intended contrast. *Pam decided, however, to attend Harvard. However, Pam decided to attend Harvard.* (She had been considering other schools.) *Pam, however, decided to attend Harvard.* (Unlike someone else, Pam opted for Harvard.)

hung   See *hanged, hung.*

if, whether   Use *if* to express a condition and *whether* to express alternatives. *If you go on a trip, whether it be to Nebraska or New Jersey, remember to bring traveler's checks.*

illusion   See *allusion, illusion.*

immigrate, emigrate   See *emigrate from, immigrate to.*

imminent   See *eminent, imminent.*

immoral   See *amoral, immoral.*

implement   *Implement* is a pretentious way of saying "do," "carry out," or "accomplish." Use ordinary language instead. *We carried out* (not *implemented*) *the director's orders with some reluctance.*

imply, infer   *Imply* means "to suggest or state indirectly"; *infer* means "to draw a conclusion." *John implied that he knew all about computers, but the interviewer inferred that John was inexperienced.*

ingenious, ingenuous   *Ingenious* means "clever." *Sarah's solution to the problem was ingenious. Ingenuous* means "naive" or "frank." *For a successful manager, Ed is surprisingly ingenuous.*

in, into   *In* indicates location or condition; *into* indicates movement or a change in condition. *They found the lost letters in a box after moving into the house.*

in regards to   *In regards to* confuses two different phrases: *in regard to* and *as regards*. Use one or the other. *In regard to* (or *As regards*) *the contract, ignore the first clause.*

irregardless   *Irregardless* is nonstandard. Use *regardless.*

is when, is where   These mixed constructions are often incorrectly used in definitions. *A run-off election is a second election held to break a tie* (not *is when a second election breaks a tie*). (See 11c.)

it is   *It is* is nonstandard when used to mean "there is." *There is* (not *It is*) *a fly in my soup*

its, it's   *Its* is a possessive pronoun; *it's* is a contraction for *it is*. (See 36c and 36e.) *The dog licked its wound whenever its owner walked into the room. It's a perfect day to walk the twenty-mile trail.*

kind(s)   *Kind* is singular and should be treated as such. Don't write *These kind of chairs are rare.* Write instead *This kind of chair is rare. Kinds* is plural and should be used only when you mean more than one kind. *These kinds of chairs are rare.*

kind of, sort of   Avoid using *kind of* or *sort of* to mean "somewhat." *The movie was somewhat* (not *kind of*) *boring*. Do not put *a* after either phrase. *That kind of* (not *kind of a*) *salesclerk annoys me.*

lay, lie   See *lie, lay.*

lead, led   *Lead* is a noun referring to a metal. *Led* is the past tense of the verb *lead. He led me to the treasure.*

learn, teach   *Learn* means "to gain knowledge"; *teach* means "to impart knowledge." *I must teach* (not *learn*) *my sister to read.*

leave, let   *Leave* means "to exit." *Let* means "to permit." *Let* (not *Leave*) *me help you with the dishes.*

less   See *fewer, less.*

let, leave   See *leave, let.*

liable   *Liable* means "obligated" or "responsible." Do not use it to mean "likely." *You're likely* (not *liable*) *to trip if you don't tie your shoelaces.*

lie, lay   *Lie* is an intransitive verb meaning "to recline or rest on a surface." Its principal parts are *lie, lay, lain. Lay* is a transitive verb meaning "to put or place." Its principal parts are *lay, laid, laid.* (See 27b.)

like, as *Like* is a preposition, not a subordinating conjunction. It can be followed only by a noun or a noun phrase. *As* is a subordinating conjunction that introduces a subordinate clause. In casual speech you may say *She looks like she hasn't slept* or *You don't know her like I do.* But in formal writing, use *as. She looks as if she hasn't slept. You don't know her as I do.* (See prepositions and subordinating conjunctions, 61f and 61g.)

loose, lose *Loose* is an adjective meaning "not securely fastened." *Lose* is a verb meaning "to misplace" or "to not win." *Did you lose your only loose pair of work pants?*

lots, lots of *Lots* and *lots of* are colloquial substitutes for *many, much,* or *a lot.* Avoid using them in formal writing.

mankind Avoid *mankind* whenever possible. It offends many readers because it excludes women. Use *humanity, humans, the human race,* or *humankind* instead.

may See *can, may.*

maybe, may be *Maybe* is an adverb meaning "possibly." *May be* is a verb phrase. *Maybe the sun will shine tomorrow. Tomorrow may be a brighter day.*

may of, might of *May of* and *might of* are nonstandard for *may have* and *might have. We may have* (not *may of*) *had too many cookies.*

media, medium *Media* is the plural of *medium. Of all the media that cover the Olympics, television is the medium that best captures the spectacle of the events.*

most *Most* is colloquial when used to mean "almost" and should be avoided. *Almost* (not *Most*) *everyone went to the parade.*

must of See *may of.*

myself *Myself* is a reflexive or intensive pronoun. Reflexive: *I cut myself.* Intensive: *I will drive you myself.* Do not use *myself* in place of *I* or *me. He gave the flowers to Melinda and me* (not *myself*). (See also 24.)

neither *Neither* is singular. (See 21e and 22a.) For *neither . . . nor* constructions, see 21d and 22d.

none *None* may be singular or plural. (See 21e.)

nowheres *Nowheres* is nonstandard for *nowhere.*

number See *amount, number.*

of Use the verb *have,* not the preposition *of,* after the verbs *could, should, would, may, might,* and *must. They must have* (not *of*) *left early.*

off of *Off* is sufficient. Omit *of. The ball rolled off* (not *off of*) *the table.*

OK, O.K., okay All three spellings are acceptable, but in formal speech and writing avoid these colloquial expressions for consent or approval.

parameters *Parameter* is a mathematical term that has become jargon for "fixed limit," "boundary," or "guideline." Use ordinary English instead. *The task force was asked to work within certain guidelines* (not *parameters*).

passed, past *Passed* is the past tense of the verb *pass*. *Mother passed me another slice of cake. Past* usually means "belonging to a former time" or "beyond a time or place." *Our past president spoke until past midnight. The hotel is just past the next intersection.*

percent, per cent, percentage *Percent* (also spelled *per cent*) is always used with a specific number. *Percentage* is used with a descriptive term such as *large* or *small*, not with a specific number. *The candidate won 80 percent of the primary vote. Only a small percentage of registered voters turned out for the election.*

phenomena *Phenomena* is the plural of *phenomenon*, which means "an observable occurrence or fact." *Strange phenomena occur at all hours of the night in that house, but last night's phenomenon was the strangest of all.*

plus *Plus* should not be used to join independent clauses. *This raincoat is dirty; moreover* (not *plus*), *it has a hole in it.*

precede, proceed *Precede* means "to come before." *Proceed* means "to go forward." *As we proceeded up the mountain path, we noticed fresh tracks in the mud, evidence that a group of hikers had preceded us.*

principal, principle *Principal* is a noun meaning "the head of a school or organization" or "a sum of money." It is also an adjective meaning "most important." *Principle* is a noun meaning "a basic truth or law." *The principal expelled her for three principal reasons. We believe in the principle of equal justice for all.*

proceed, precede See *precede, proceed.*

quote, quotation *Quote* is a verb; *quotation* is a noun. Avoid using *quote* as a shortened form of *quotation*. *Her quotations* (not *quotes*) *from Shakespeare intrigued us.*

raise, rise *Raise* is a transitive verb meaning "to move or cause to move upward." It takes a direct object. *I raised the shades. Rise* is an intransitive verb meaning "to go up." It does not take a direct object. *Heat rises.*

real, really *Real* is an adjective; *really* is an adverb. *Real* is sometimes used informally as an adverb, but avoid this use in formal writing. *She was really* (not *real*) *angry.* (See 26a.)

reason is because Use *that* instead of *because. The reason I'm late is that* (not *because*) *my car broke down.* (See 11c.)

reason why The expression *reason why* is redundant. *The reason* (not *The reason why*) *Jones lost the election is clear.*

relation, relationship *Relation* describes a connection between things. *Relationship* describes a connection between people. *There is a* *relation between poverty and infant mortality. Our business relationship has cooled over the years.*

respectfully, respectively *Respectfully* means "showing or marked by respect." *Respectively* means "each in the order given." *He respectfully submitted his opinion to the judge. John, Tom, and Larry were a butcher, a baker, and a lawyer, respectively.*

sensual, sensuous *Sensual* means "gratifying the physical senses," especially those associated with sexual pleasure. *Sensuous* means "pleasing to the senses," especially those involved in the experience of art, music, and nature. *The sensuous music and balmy air led the dancers to more sensual movements.*

set, sit *Set* is a transitive verb meaning "to put" or "to place." Its principal parts are *set, set, set. Sit* is an intransitive verb meaning "to be seated." Its principal parts are *sit, sat, sat. She set the dough in a warm corner of the kitchen. The cat sat in the warmest part of the room.*

shall, will *Shall* was once used as the helping verb with *I* or *we: I shall, we shall, you will, he/she/it will, they will.* Today, however, *will* is generally accepted even when the subject is *I* or *we.* The word *shall* occurs primarily in polite questions (*Shall I find you a pillow?*) and in legalistic sentences suggesting duty or obligation (*The applicant shall file form 1080 by December 31*).

should of *Should of* is nonstandard for *should have. They should have* (not *should of*) *been home an hour ago.*

since Do not use *since* to mean "because" if there is any chance of ambiguity. *Since we won the game, we have been celebrating with a pitcher of beer. Since* here could mean "because" or "from the time that."

sit See *set, sit.*

site, cite See *cite, site.*

somebody, someone *Somebody* and *someone* are singular. (See 21e and 22a.)

something *Something* is singular. (See 21e.)

sometime, some time, sometimes *Sometime* is an adverb meaning "at an indefinite or unstated time." *Some time* is the adjective *some* modifying the noun *time* and is spelled as two words to mean "a period of time." *Sometimes* is an adverb meaning "at times, now and then." *I'll see you sometime soon. I haven't lived there for some time. Sometimes I run into him at the library.*

suppose to Write *supposed to.*

sure and *Sure and* is nonstandard for *sure to. We were all taught to be sure to* (not *and*) *look both ways before crossing a street.*

take See *bring, take.*

than, then   *Than* is a conjunction used in comparisons; *then* is an adverb denoting time. *That pizza is more than I can eat. Tom laughed, and then we recognized him.*

that   See *who, which, that.*

that, which   Many writers reserve *that* for restrictive clauses, *which* for nonrestrictive clauses. (See 32e.)

theirselves   *Theirselves* is nonstandard for *themselves. The two people were able to push the Volkswagen out of the way themselves* (not *theirselves*).

them   The use of *them* in place of *those* is nonstandard. *Please send those* (not *them*) *flowers to the patient in room 220.*

there, their, they're   *There* is an adverb specifying place; it is also an expletive. Adverb: *Sylvia is lying there unconscious.* Expletive: *There are two plums left. Their* is a possessive pronoun. *Fred and Jane finally washed their car. They're* is a contraction of *they are. They're later than usual today.*

they   The use of *they* to indicate possession is nonstandard. Use *their* instead. *Cindy and Sam decided to sell their* (not *they*) *1975 Corvette.*

this kind   See *kind(s).*

to, too, two   *To* is a preposition; *too* is an adverb; *two* is a number. *Too many of your shots slice to the left, but the last two were right on the mark.*

toward, towards   *Toward* and *towards* are generally interchangeable, although *toward* is preferred in American English.

try and   *Try and* is nonstandard for *try to. The teacher asked us all to try to* (not *and*) *write an original haiku.*

ultimately, eventually   See *eventually, ultimately.*

unique   Avoid expressions such as *most unique, more straight, less perfect, very round.* Something either is unique or it isn't. It is illogical to suggest degrees of uniqueness. (See 26c.)

usage   The noun *usage* should not be substituted for *use* when the meaning intended is "employment of." *The use* (not *usage*) *of computers dramatically increased the company's profits.*

use to   Write *used to.*

utilize   *Utilize* means "to make use of." It often sounds pretentious; in most cases, *use* is sufficient. *I used* (not *utilized*) *the best workers to get the job done fast.*

wait for, wait on   *Wait for* means "to be in readiness for" or "await." *Wait on* means "to serve." *We're only waiting for* (not *waiting on*) *Ruth to take us to the game.*

ways   *Ways* is colloquial when used to mean "distance." *The city is a long way* (not *ways*) *from here.*

weather, whether   The noun *weather* refers to the state of the atmosphere. *Whether* is a conjunction referring to a choice between alternatives. *We wondered whether the weather would clear up in time for our picnic.*

well, good   See *good, well.*

where   Do not use *where* in place of *that. I heard that* (not *where*) *the crime rate is increasing.*

which   See *that, which* and *who, which, that.*

while   Avoid using *while* to mean "although" or "whereas" if there is any chance of ambiguity. *Although* (not *While*) *Gloria lost money in the slot machine, Tom won it at roulette.* Here *While* could mean either "although" or "at the same time that."

who, which, that   Do not use *which* to refer to persons. Use *who* instead. *That,* though generally used to refer to things, may be used to refer to a group or class of people. *Fans wondered how an old man who* (not *that* or *which*) *walked with a limp could play football. The team that scores the most points in this game will win the tournament.* (See 23e.)

who, whom   *Who* is used for subjects and subject complements; *whom* is used for objects. (See 25.)

who's, whose   *Who's* is a contraction of *who is; whose* is a possessive pronoun. *Who's ready for more popcorn? Whose coat is this?* (See 36c and 36e.)

will   See *shall, will.*

would of   *Would of* is nonstandard for *would have. She would have* (not *would of*) *had a chance to play if she had arrived on time.*

you   In formal writing, avoid *you* in an indefinite sense meaning "anyone." (See 23d.) *Any spectator* (not *You*) *could tell by the way John caught the ball that his throw would be too late.*

your, you're   *Your* is a possessive pronoun; *you're* is a contraction of *you are. Is that your new motorcycle? You're on the list of finalists.* (See 36c and 36e.)

Answers to Tutorials and Lettered Exercises

Answers to Tutorial 1, page xx

1. A verb has to agree with its subject. (21)
2. Each pronoun should agree with its antecedent. (22)
3. You should avoid sentence fragments. (19)
4. It's important to use apostrophes correctly. (36)
5. Check for -ed verb endings that have been dropped. (27d)
6. Discriminate carefully between adjectives and adverbs. (26)
7. If your sentence begins with a long introductory word group, use a comma to separate the word group from the rest of the sentence. (32b)
8. Don't write a run-on sentence; you must connect independent clauses with a comma and a coordinating conjunction or with a semicolon. (20)
9. For clarity, a writer must be careful not to shift his or her [not *their*] point of view. *Or* For clarity, writers should be careful not to shift their point of view. (13a)
10. Watch out for dangling modifiers. (12e)

Answers to Tutorial 2, page xxi

1. The index entry "*each*" mentions that the word is singular, so you might not need to look further to realize that the verb should be *has,* not *have.* The first page reference takes you to section 21, which explains in more detail why *has* is correct. The index entry "*has* vs. *have*" also leads you to section 21.
2. The index entry "*lying* vs. *laying*" takes you to section 27b, where you will learn that *lying* (meaning "reclining or resting on a surface") is correct.
3. Look up "*only*" and you will be directed to section 12a, which explains that limiting modifiers such as *only* should be placed before the words they modify. The sentence should read *We looked at only two houses before buying the house of our dreams.*
4. Looking up "*you,* inappropriate use of" leads you to section 23d and the Glossary of Usage, which explain that *you* should not be used to mean "anyone in general." You can revise the sentence by using *a person* or *one* instead of *you,* or you can restructure the sentence completely: *In Saudi Arabia, accepting a gift is considered ill mannered.*
5. The index entries "*I* vs. *me*" and "*me* vs. *I*" take you to section 24, which explains why *me* is correct.

Answers to Tutorial 3, page xxi

1. Section 32c states that, although usage varies, most experts advise using a comma between all items in a series—to prevent possible misreadings or ambiguities. To find this section, Ray Farley would probably use the menu system.
2. Maria Sanchez and Mike Lee would consult section 30, on articles. This section is easy to locate in the menu system.
3. Section 24 explains why "Jane and me" is correct. To find section 24, John Pell could use the menu system if he knew to look under "Problems with pronouns." Otherwise, he could look up "*I* vs. *me*" in the index. Pell could also look up "*myself*" in the index or he could consult the Glossary of Usage, where a cross-reference would direct him to section 24.
4. Selena Young's employees could turn to sections 21 and 27c for help. Young could use the menu system to find these sections if she knew to look under "Subject-verb agreement" or "Standard English verb forms." If she wasn't sure about the grammatical terminology, she could look up "*-s,* as verb ending" or "Verbs, *-s* form of" in the index.
5. Section 26b explains why "I felt bad about her death" is correct. To find section 26b, Joe Thompson could use the menu system if he knew that *bad* versus *badly* is a choice between an adjective and an adverb. Otherwise he could look up "*bad, badly*" in the index or the Glossary of Usage.

Answers to Tutorial 4, page xxii

1. Changing attitudes toward alcohol have *affected* the beer industry.
2. It is *human* nature to think wisely and act foolishly.
3. Correct
4. Our goal this year is to *increase* our profits by 9 percent.
5. Most sleds are pulled by no *fewer* than two dogs and no more than ten.

Answers to Tutorial 5, page xxiii

Benedict, Jeff. Without Reservation: The Making of America's Most Powerful Indian Tribe and the World's Largest Casino. New York: Harper, 2000.

Codoga, Helen. "Casinos on Reservations in the Northeast." E-mail to the author. 10 Apr. 2001.

"Indian Gaming." All Things Considered. Host Robert Siegel. Natl. Public Radio. WDUQ, Pittsburgh. 5 Mar. 2001.

Johnson, Susan. "From Wounded Knee to Capitol Hill." State Legislatures 24.9 (1998). Expanded Academic ASAP. InfoTrac. U of Pittsburgh Lib. 6 Apr. 2001.

National Indian Gaming Association. "Tribal Gaming Myths and Facts." National Indian Gaming Association. 2000. 4 Apr. 2001 <http://www.indiangaming.org/info/pr/myths.shtml>.

Useem, Jerry. "The Big Game: Have American Indians Found Their New Buffalo?" Fortune 2 Oct. 2000: 22+.

EXERCISE 8–1, page 87

Possible revisions:

a. The Prussians defeated the Saxons in 1745.
b. Ahmed, the producer, manages the entire operation.
c. All the referees threw down yellow flags.
d. Emphatic and active; no change
e. Protesters were shouting on the courthouse steps.

EXERCISE 9-1, page 91

Possible revisions:

a. Police dogs are used for finding lost children, tracking criminals, and detecting bombs and illegal drugs.
b. Roger explained to the immigration officer that his visa had expired and that he was applying to have it renewed.
c. It is more difficult to sustain an exercise program than to start one.
d. During basic training, I was told not only what to do but also what to think.
e. Jan wanted to drive to the wine country or at least to Sausalito.

EXERCISE 10-1, page 96

Possible revisions:

a. A good source of vitamin C is a grapefruit or an orange.
b. The women entering VMI can expect haircuts as short as those of the male cadets.
c. The driver went to investigate, only to find that one of the supposedly new tires had blown.
d. Most of the spectators were unhappy with and angered by the decision.
e. Reefs are home to more species than any other ecosystem in the sea.

EXERCISE 11-1, page 100

Possible revisions.

a. Using surgical gloves is a precaution now taken by dentists to prevent contact with patients' blood and saliva.
b. A career in medicine, which my brother is pursuing, requires at least ten years of challenging work.
c. The pharaohs had bad teeth because tiny particles of sand found their way into Egyptian bread.
d. The quality of service has worsened each year.
e. This box contains the key to your future.

EXERCISE 12-1, page 105

Possible revisions:

a. Our English professor asked us to reread the sonnet very carefully, looking for subtleties we had missed on a first reading.
b. The monarch arrived at the gate in a gold carriage pulled by four white horses.
c. By afternoon, Sam had painted almost the entire dining room.
d. After being appointed leader of the expeditionary force by the Spanish viceroy, Coronado spent his time recruiting volunteers for the adventure.
e. Not all fresh vegetables are salt free.

EXERCISE 12-2, page 109

Possible revisions:

a. When I was ten, my parents took me on my first balloon ride.
b. To show our appreciation for your patience, we have enclosed a coupon that you may redeem for the book of your choice.
c. As I nestled in the cockpit, the pounding of the engine was muffled only slightly by my helmet.
d. In choosing her bridesmaids' dresses, she considered cost a major factor.
e. When I was a young man, my mother enrolled me in tap dance classes, hoping I would become the next Gregory Hines.

EXERCISE 13-3, page 114

Possible revisions:

a. Courtroom lawyers have more than a touch of theater in their blood.
b. The interviewer asked if we had brought our proof of birth and citizenship and our passports.
c. Single parents often have only their ingenuity to rely on.
d. When the director travels, you will make the hotel and airline reservations, arrange for a rental car, and prepare a detailed itinerary.
e. Madame Defarge is a sinister figure in Dickens's *A Tale of Two Cities*. On a symbolic level, she represents fate; like the Greek Fates, she knits the fabric of individual destiny.

EXERCISE 14-1, page 121

Possible revisions:

a. The lift chairs were going around so fast that they were bumping the skiers into their seats.
b. Our waitress, costumed in a kimono, had painted her face white and arranged her hair in an upswept lacquered beehive.
c. Student volunteers from Baltimore City Community College help the younger children with their weakest subjects, reading and math.
d. Shore houses were flooded up to the first floor, beaches were washed away, and Brant's Lighthouse was swallowed by the sea.
e. Although Mary will graduate from high school in June, she has not yet decided on a college.

EXERCISE 14-2, page 123

Possible revisions:

a. These particles, known as "stealth liposomes," can hide in the body for a long time without detection.
b. Cocaine, an addictive drug, can seriously harm you both physically and mentally, if death doesn't get you first.
c. Because students, textile workers, and labor unions have loudly protested sweatshop abuses, apparel makers have been forced to examine their labor practices.
d. Developed in a European university, IRC (Internet Relay Chat) was created as a way for a group of graduate students to talk about projects from their dorm rooms.
e. The cafeteria's new menu, which has an international flavor, includes everything from enchiladas and pizza to pad thai and sauerbraten.

EXERCISE 14-3, page 124

Possible revisions:

a. Working as an aide for the relief agency, Gina distributed food and medical supplies.
b. During her three years as an attorney at Pepco, Ms. Brooks has done an excellent job.
c. When the visiting period was nearly over, the prison guard tapped me on the shoulder.
d. My grandfather, who was born eighty years ago in Puerto Rico, raised his daughters the old-fashioned way.
e. By reversing the depressive effect of the drug, the Narcan saved the patient's life.

EXERCISE 16-1, page 134

Possible revisions:

a. Martin Luther King Jr. set a high standard for future leaders.
b. Coach Becker loves to work with young people.
c. Bloom's race for the governorship is futile.
d. A casualty call officer assists the bereaved family in many ways.
e. You will deliver mail to all employees.

EXERCISE 17-1, page 138

Possible revisions:

a. In my youth, my family was poor.
b. This conference will help me serve my clients better.
c. Have you ever been accused of beating a dead horse?
d. Health educators help people change their lifestyles.
e. Passengers should try to complete the customs declaration form before leaving the plane.

EXERCISE 17-2, page 145

Possible revisions:

a. Dr. Geralyn Farmer is the chief surgeon at University Hospital. Dr. Paul Green is her assistant.
b. All applicants want to know how much they will make.
c. Elementary school teachers should understand the concept of nurturing if they intend to be a success.
d. The vice president for community affairs asked Elizabeth and Joseph to serve as cochairs for the Red Cross blood drive.
e. If we do not stop polluting our environment, we will perish.

EXERCISE 18-1, page 149

Possible revisions:

a. We regret this delay; thank you for your patience.
b. Ada's plan is to acquire education and experience to prepare herself for a position as property manager.
c. Tiger Woods, the ultimate competitor, has earned millions of dollars just in endorsements.
d. When Robert Frost died at age eighty-eight, he left a legacy of poems that will make him immortal.
e. I would not advise anyone to pass up a chance to study geology.

EXERCISE 18-2, page 151

Possible revisions:

a. Queen Anne was so angry with Sarah Churchill that she refused to see her again.
b. Correct
c. The parade moved off the street and onto the beach.
d. For the frightened refugees, the dangerous trek across the mountains was preferable to life in a war zone.
e. What type of wedding are you planning?

EXERCISE 18-3, page 153

Possible revisions:

a. John stormed into the room like a hurricane.
b. The president thought that the scientists were using science as a grindstone to sharpen their political axes.
c. The Cubs easily beat the Mets, who were in trouble early in the game today at Wrigley Field.
d. We ironed out the wrinkles in our relationship.
e. Sasha told us that he wasn't willing to put his neck in a financial noose. [*or* . . . willing to go out on a limb — especially a rotten one.]

EXERCISE 19-1, page 162

Possible revisions:

a. The shock of bereavement is often followed by a succession of emotions: denial, sorrow, anger, despair, guilt, remorse, and longing.
b. Cortés and his soldiers were astonished when they looked down from the mountains and saw Tenochtitlán, the magnificent capital of the Aztecs.
c. Although my spoken Spanish is not very good, I can read the language with ease.
d. There are several reasons for not eating meat. One reason is that dangerous chemicals are used throughout the various stages of meat production.
e. To give my family a comfortable, secure home life is my most important goal.

EXERCISE 20-1, page 171

Possible revisions:

a. The city had one public swimming pool that stayed packed with children all summer long.
b. The building is being renovated, so at times we have no heat, water, or electricity.
c. The neighborhood was ruled by gangs. What kind of environment was this for my ten-year-old son?
d. Suddenly there was a loud silence; the shelling had stopped.
e. The car was hardly worth trading because the frame was twisted and the block was warped.

EXERCISE 20-2, page 171

Possible revisions:

a. Wind power for the home is a supplementary source of energy that can be combined with electricity, gas, or solar energy.
b. Correct
c. In the Middle Ages, when the streets of London were dangerous places, it was safer to travel by boat along the Thames.
d. "He's not drunk," I said. "He's in a state of diabetic shock."
e. Are you able to endure boredom, isolation, and potential violence? Then the army may well be the adventure for you.

EXERCISE 21-1, page 183

a. Subject: friendship and support; verb: have. b. Subject: Shelters; verb: offer. c. Subject: source; verb: is. d. Subject: chances; verb: are. e. Subject: cartoon and rhymes; verb: were.

EXERCISE 21-2, page 184

a. One of the main reasons for elephant poaching is the profits received from selling the ivory tusks.
b. Correct
c. Of those who die in single-car wrecks, a majority are drunk.
d. Crystal chandeliers, polished floors, and a new oil painting have transformed Sandra's apartment.
e. Correct

EXERCISE 22-1, page 189

Possible revisions:

a. Every presidential candidate must appeal to a wide variety of ethnic and social groups to win the election.
b. David lent his motorcycle to someone who allowed a friend to use it.
c. The instructor has asked all students to bring their tools to carpentry class.
d. Correct
e. Applicants should be bilingual if they want to qualify for this position.

EXERCISE 23-1, page 195

Possible revisions:

a. Some critics say that the *Challenger* disaster set the space program back five years.
b. Because she had decorated her living room with posters from chamber music festivals, her date thought she was interested in classical music, but actually she preferred rock.
c. In Ethiopia, a person doesn't need much property to be considered well-off.
d. Marianne told Jenny, "I am worried about your mother's illness." [*or* ". . . about my mother's illness."]
e. Though Lewis cried for several minutes after scraping his knee, eventually the pain subsided.

EXERCISE 24-1, page 202

a. Correct [But the writer could change the end of the sentence: . . . *than he is.*]
b. Correct [But the writer could change the end of the sentence: . . . *that he was the murderer.*]
c. She appreciated his telling the truth in such a difficult situation.
d. The director has asked you and me to draft a proposal for a new recycling plan.
e. Five close friends and I rented a station wagon, packed it with food, and drove to Mardi Gras on a three-day weekend.

EXERCISE 24-2, page 202

We, her, he, she, them, their

EXERCISE 25-1, page 207

a. The roundtable featured several scholars whom I had never heard of. [*or* . . . scholars I had never heard of.]
b. Correct
c. Correct
d. Daniel always gives a holiday donation to whoever needs it most.
e. So many of the candidates were overqualified that it was difficult to decide whom to choose.

EXERCISE 26–1, page 213

Possible revisions:

a. Did you do well on last week's chemistry exam?
b. With the budget deadline approaching, our office has hardly had time to handle routine correspondence.
c. Correct
d. The customer complained that he hadn't been treated nicely.
e. Of all my relatives, Uncle Roberto is the cleverest.

EXERCISE 27–1, page 219

a. When I get the urge to exercise, I lie down until it passes.
b. Grandmother had driven our new jeep to the sunrise church service on Savage Mountain, so we were left with the station wagon.
c. A pile of dirty rags was lying at the bottom of the stairs.
d. How did the detective know that the suspect had gone to the office on the night of the murder?
e. Lincoln took good care of his legal clients; the contracts he drew for the Illinois Central Railroad could never be broken.

EXERCISE 27–2, page 226

a. The cops were after my hot rod Lincoln. We were passing cars like they were standing still.
b. The museum visitors were not supposed to touch the exhibits.
c. Our church has all the latest technology, even a closed-circuit television.
d. Christos didn't know about Marlo's promotion because he never listens. He is always talking.
e. Correct

EXERCISE 28–1, page 234

Possible revisions:

a. Correct
b. Watson and Crick discovered the mechanism that controls inheritance in all life: the workings of the DNA molecule.
c. When Hitler decided to kill the Jews in 1941, did he know that Himmler and his SS had had mass murder in mind since 1938?
d. Correct
e. Correct

EXERCISE 29–1, page 239

a. We will make this a better country.
b. There is nothing in the world that TV has not touched on.
c. Did the landlord tell you that he's going to raise the rent?
d. If we can afford to, we will spend our vacation in Canada next summer.
e. The child's innocent world has been taken away from him.

EXERCISE 29–2, page 242

Possible revisions:

a. He would have won the election if he had gone to the inner city to campaign.
b. If Verena wins a scholarship, she will go to graduate school.
c. Whenever there is a fire in our neighborhood, everybody comes out to watch.
d. We will lose our most valuable client unless we update our computer system.
e. If I lived in California, I wouldn't need to buy a winter coat.

EXERCISE 29-3, page 245

Possible answers:

a. I enjoy riding my motorcycle.
b. Will you help Samantha study for the test?
c. The team hopes to work hard and win the championship.
d. Ricardo and his brothers miss surfing during the winter.
e. The babysitter let Roger stay up until midnight.

EXERCISE 31-1, page 256

a. There are some cartons of ice cream in the freezer.
b. I don't use the subway because I am afraid.
c. The prime minister is the most popular leader in my country.
d. We tried to get in touch with the same manager whom we spoke to earlier.
e. Recently there have been a number of earthquakes in Turkey.

EXERCISE 31-2, page 260

a. an attractive young Vietnamese woman
b. a dedicated Catholic priest
c. her old blue wool sweater
d. Joe's delicious Scandinavian bread
e. many beautiful antique bird cages

EXERCISE 31-3, page 261

a. Listening to everyone's complaints all day was irritating.
b. During the long lecture, many students appeared bored.
c. Correct
d. After a great deal of research, the scientist made a fascinating discovery.
e. That blackout was one of the most frightening experiences I've ever had.

EXERCISE 31-4, page 263

a. Whenever we eat at the Centerville Diner, we sit at a small table in the corner of the room.
b. Correct
c. On Wednesdays he leaves work early so he can lift weights at his health club.
d. Our rabbi moved to the Northwest in 1994 and has been with our temple in Seattle since 1996.

EXERCISE 32-1, page 268

a. Alisa brought the injured bird home and fashioned a splint out of Popsicle sticks for its wing.
b. Considered the first Western philosopher, Thales believed that water was the elemental principle underlying all things.
c. If you complete the enclosed card and return it within two weeks, you will receive a free breakfast during your stay.
d. Correct
e. Uncle Swen's dulcimers disappeared as soon as he put them up for sale, but he always kept one for himself.

EXERCISE 32-2, page 270

a. The cold, impersonal atmosphere of the university was unbearable.
b. An ambulance threaded its way through police cars, fire trucks, and irate citizens.
c. Correct

   d. After two broken arms, three cracked ribs, and one concussion, Ken quit the varsity football team.
   e. Correct

EXERCISE 32–3, page 274

   a. Choreographer Alvin Ailey's best-known work, *Revelations,* is more than just a crowd pleaser.
   b. Correct
   c. Correct
   d. A member of an organization that provides housing for AIDS patients was also appointed to the commission.
   e. A 1911 fire at the Triangle Shirtwaist Company, which killed 146 sweatshop workers, led to reforms in working conditions.

EXERCISE 32–4, page 279

   a. Cricket, which originated in England, is also popular in Australia, South Africa, and India.
   b. At the sound of a starting pistol, the horses surged forward toward the first obstacle, a sharp incline three feet high.
   c. After the passage of the Civil Rights Act of 1964, the Ku Klux Klan went underground for a few years, but the group's racist views did not change.
   d. Jan's costume was completed with bright red snakeskin sandals.
   e. Computers must be manufactured in clean, climate-controlled rooms.

EXERCISE 32–5, page 280

   a. On January 15, 1996, our office moved to 29 Commonwealth Avenue, Mechanicsville, Virginia 19607.
   b. Correct
   c. Ms. Carlson, you are a valued customer whose satisfaction is very important to us.
   d. Mr. Mundy was born on July 22, 1939, in Arkansas, where his family had lived for four generations.
   e. Correct

EXERCISE 33–1, page 286

   a. Correct
   b. He wore a thick black wool coat over army fatigues.
   c. Often public figures (Greta Garbo was a good example) go to great lengths to guard their private lives.
   d. She loved early spring flowers such as crocuses, daffodils, forsythia, and irises.
   e. On Pam's wrist was a tattoo of a dragon chasing a tiger.

EXERCISE 34–1, page 291

   a. Do not ask me to be kind; just ask me to act as though I were.
   b. When men talk about defense, they always claim to be protecting women and children, but they never ask the women and children what they think.
   c. When I get a little money, I buy books; if any is left, I buy food and clothes.
   d. Correct
   e. Wit has truth in it; wisecracking is simply calisthenics with words.

EXERCISE 34–2, page 292

   a. Strong black coffee will not sober you up; the truth is that time is the only way to get alcohol out of your system.

b. It is not surprising that our society is increasingly violent; after all, television desensitizes us to brutality at a very early age.
c. There is often a fine line between right and wrong, good and bad, truth and deception.
d. Correct
e. Severe, unremitting pain is a ravaging force, especially when the patient tries to hide it from others.

EXERCISE 35–1, page 295

a. Correct
b. If we have come to fight, we are far too few; if we have come to die, we are far too many.
c. The travel package includes a round-trip ticket to Athens, a cruise through the Cyclades, and all hotel accommodations.
d. The media like to portray my generation as lazy, although polls show that we work as hard as the twentysomethings before us.
e. Fran Lebowitz has this advice for parents: "Never allow your child to call you by your first name. He hasn't known you long enough."

EXERCISE 36–1, page 299

a. Correct
b. The deed must be transferred to the purchaser's name.
c. Each day's menu features a different European country's dish.
d. Sue worked overtime to increase her family's earnings.
e. Ms. Jacobs is unwilling to listen to students' complaints about computer failures and damaged disks.

EXERCISE 37–1, page 306

a. As for the advertisement "Sailors have more fun," if you consider chipping paint and swabbing decks fun, then you will have plenty of it.
b. Correct
c. After winning the lottery, Juanita said that she would give half the money to charity.
d. After the movie Vicki said, "The reviewer called this flick 'trash of the first order.' I guess you can't believe everything you read."
e. Correct

EXERCISE 39–1, page 313

a. A client has left his or her cell phone in our conference room.
b. The thousand dollars that we invested in the stock market just ten years ago has tripled in value.
c. Correct
d. Correct
e. Of the three basic schools of detective fiction — the tea-and-crumpet, the hardboiled detective, and the police procedural — I find the quaint, civilized quality of the tea-and-crumpet school the most appealing.

EXERCISE 40–1, page 318

a. Correct
b. A number of government officials have been reviewing the records of some small brokerage firms in the area.
c. Correct
d. How many pounds have you lost since you began running four miles a day?
e. Denzil spent all night studying for his psychology exam.

EXERCISE 41–1, page 321

a. We have ordered four azaleas, three rhododendrons, and two mountain laurels for the back area of the garden.
b. Correct
c. Correct
d. Eight students in the class had been labeled "learning disabled."
e. The Vietnam Veterans Memorial in Washington, DC, had 58,132 names inscribed on it when it was dedicated in 1982.

EXERCISE 42–1, page 325

a. Howard Hughes commissioned the *Spruce Goose,* a beautifully built but thoroughly impractical wooden aircraft.
b. The old man screamed his anger, shouting to all of us, "I will not leave my money to you worthless layabouts!"
c. I learned the Latin term *ad infinitum* from an old nursery rhyme about fleas: "Great fleas have little fleas upon their back to bite 'em, / Little fleas have lesser fleas and so on *ad infinitum.*"
d. Correct
e. *The City and the Pillar* is an early novel by Gore Vidal.

EXERCISE 44–1, page 337

a. Correct
b. The swiftly moving tugboat pulled alongside the barge and directed it away from the oil spill in the harbor.
c. Correct
d. Your dog is well known in our neighborhood.
e. Roadblocks were set up along all the major highways leading out of the city.

EXERCISE 45–1, page 341

a. District Attorney Johnson was disgusted when the jurors turned in a verdict of not guilty after only one hour of deliberation.
b. Correct
c. Madeline is taking courses in geology, mathematics, French, and English.
d. My grandfather and grandmother emigrated from Lithuania in the mid-1960s.
e. I look forward every spring to walking along the flower-lined paths in Boston's Public Garden.

EXERCISE 47–1, page 367

a. hasty generalization; b. false analogy; c. biased language; d. faulty cause-and-effect reasoning; e. *either . . . or* fallacy

EXERCISE 61–1, page 497

a. sun, assistance; b. Pride, bottom, mistakes; c. Success, confidence; d. censorship, flick, dial; e. flower, concrete (noun/adjective), cloverleaf

EXERCISE 61–2, page 497

a. He, every (pronoun/adjective); b. those, who; c. I, some (pronoun/adjective), that, I, myself; d. I, You, He; e. you, anything, anyone, me

EXERCISE 61–3, page 502

a. can pardon; b. are; c. does bring down; d. Keep, 'll [will] be insulted; e. Throw, will emerge

EXERCISE 61–4, page 504

a. Adjectives: General, wrong; adverb: generally; b. Adjectives: The (article), American, tolerant; adverb: wonderfully; c. Adjectives: an (article), uncultivated, an (article) uncultivated; adverbs: sometimes, never; d. Adjectives: wrong, right; adverbs: rather, strongly, weakly; e. Adjective: the (article); adverb: faster

EXERCISE 62–1, page 511

a. Complete subjects: Sticks and stones, words; simple subjects: Sticks, stones, words; b. Complete subject: all delays; simple subject: delays; c. Complete subject: (You); d. Complete subject: nothing except change; simple subject: nothing; e. Complete subject: Most of the disputes in the world; simple subject: Most

EXERCISE 62–2, page 516

a. Subject complement: cheap; b. Direct object: an injury; c. Direct object: his convent; d. Subject complement: the opium of the people; e. Subject complement: bitter

EXERCISE 62–3, page 516

a. Direct object: us; object complement: wise; b. Direct object: money; object complement: their primary pursuit; c. Direct objects: us, us; object complements: happy, good; d. Indirect objects: me, you; direct objects: no questions, no lies; e. Indirect objects: me, you; direct objects: a good loser, a failure

EXERCISE 63–1, page 520

a. On their side (adverb phrase modifying *had*); b. of several air traffic controllers (adjective phrase modifying *job*), with ease (adverb phrase modifying *could perform*); c. To my embarrassment (adverb phrase modifying *was born*), in bed (adverb phrase modifying *was born*), with a lady (adverb phrase modifying *was born*); d. of a culture (adjective phrase modifying *map*); e. In France (adverb phrase modifying *is*)

EXERCISE 63–2, page 523

a. who has outposts in your head (adjective clause modifying *enemy*); b. that doesn't bite (adjective clause modifying *rattlesnake*); c. If love is the answer (adverb clause modifying *could rephrase*); d. what they mean (noun clause used as direct object of *say*); e. unless I cannot resist it (adverb clause modifying *avoid*)

EXERCISE 63–3, page 525

a. Concealing a disease (gerund phrase used as subject), to cure it (infinitive phrase modifying *way*); b. being punctual (gerund phrase used as object of the preposition *with*), to appreciate it (infinitive phrase modifying *is*); c. to conceal him (infinitive phrase used as direct object), naming him Smith (gerund phrase used as the object of the preposition *by*); d. Being weak (participial phrase modifying *children*), to beguile us with charm (infinitive phrase used as direct object); e. Wrestling with words (gerund phrase used as subject)

EXERCISE 64–1, page 529

a. Complex; who sleep like a baby (adjective clause); b. Compound; c. Simple; d. Complex; If you don't go to other people's funerals (adverb clause); e. Compound-complex; what you are afraid of (noun clause)

(continued from page iv)

Eugene Boe. Excerpt from "Pioneers to Eternity: Norwegians on the Prairie" in *The Immigrant Experience,* edited by Thomas C. Wheeler. Copyright © 1971 by Thomas C. Wheeler. Reprinted by permission of Doubleday, a division of Random House, Inc.

Jane Brody. Excerpt from *Jane Brody's Nutrition Book.* Copyright © 1981 by Jane E. Brody. Reprinted by permission of W. W. Norton & Company, Inc. and Wendy Weil Agency, Inc.

Carlton College Library screen shot. Reprinted by permission.

Bruce Catton. Excerpt from "Grant and Lee: A Study in Contrasts." From *The American Story,* edited by Earl Schenck Miers. Copyright © 1956 U.S. Capitol Historical Society. All rights reserved.

Columbia University Libraries screen shot. © Columbia University Libraries. Reprinted by permission.

Earl Conrad. Excerpt from *Harriet Tubman* by Earl Conrad. Copyright © 1945 by Earl Conrad. Reprinted by permission of Paul S. Eriksson, Publisher.

Emily Dickinson. Opening stanza from "The Snake." From *The Poems of Emily Dickinson,* by Thomas H. Johnson, ed. Copyright © 1951, 1955, 1979 by the President and Fellows of Harvard College. Reprinted by permission of the publishers and the Trustees of Amherst College, Cambridge, Mass.: The Belknap Press of Harvard University Press.

Jane Goodall. Excerpt from *In the Shadow of Man.* Copyright © 1971 by Hugo and Jane van Lawick-Goodall. Published by Houghton Mifflin. Reprinted by permission.

Google screen shot. © 2002 Google, Inc. Reprinted by permission.

Stephen Jay Gould. Excerpt from "Were Dinosaurs Dumb?" in *The Panda's Thumb:More Reflections on Natural History.* Copyright © 1978 by Stephen Jay Gould. Reprinted by permission of W. W. Norton & Company, Inc.

Dan Gutman. Excerpt from *The Way Baseball Works* by Daniel Gutman. Copyright © 1996 by Byron Preiss/Richard Ballantine, Inc. Reprinted with the permission of Simon & Schuster.

Olivia Vlahos. Excerpt from *Human Beginnings.* Reprinted by permission of the author.

Yahoo! screen shots. © 2002 Yahoo! All Rights Reserved. Reprinted by permission.

Voiceoftheinjured.com screen shot. All contents copyright © 2002 Perenich, Carroll, Perenich, Avril & Caulfield, P.A.

Index

G

H

I

N

List of Style Manuals

Rules for Writers describes two commonly used systems of documentation: MLA, used in English and the Humanities (see 54), and APA, used in psychology and the social sciences (see 59). Following is a list of style manuals used in a variety of disciplines.

BIOLOGY (See dianahacker.com/resdoc for more information.)

Council of Biology Editors, *Scientific Style and Format: The CBE Manual for Authors, Editors, and Publishers*. 6th ed. New York: Cambridge UP, 1994.

BUSINESS

American Management Association. *The AMA Style Guide for Business Writing*. New York: AMACOM, 1996.

CHEMISTRY

Dodd, Janet S., ed. *The ACS Style Guide: A Manual for Authors and Editors*. 2nd ed. Washington: Amer. Chemical Soc., 1997.

ENGLISH AND THE HUMANITIES (See 51.)

Gibaldi, Joseph. *MLA Handbook for Writers of Research Papers*. 6th ed. New York: MLA. 2003.

GEOLOGY

Bates, Robert L., Rex Buchanan, and Marla Adkins-Heljeson, eds. *Geowriting: A Guide to Writing, Editing, and Printing in Earth Science*. 5th ed. Alexandria: Amer. Geological Inst., 1995.

GOVERNMENT DOCUMENTS

Garner, Diane L. *The Complete Guide to Citing Government Information Resources: A Manual for Writers and Librarians*. Rev. ed. Bethesda: Congressional Information Service, 1993.

United States Government Printing Office. *Style Manual*. Washington: GPO, 2000.

HISTORY (See dianahacker.com/resdoc for more information.)

The Chicago Manual of Style. 14th ed. Chicago: U of Chicago P, 1993.

JOURNALISM

Goldstein, Norm, ed. *Associated Press Stylebook and Briefing on Media Law*. 35th ed. New York: Associated Press, 2000.

LAW

Harvard Law Review et al. *The Bluebook: A Uniform System of Citation*. 17th ed. Cambridge: Harvard Law Rev. Assn., 2000.

List of Style Manuals

LINGUISTICS

Linguistic Society of America. "LSA Style Sheet." Published annually in the December issue of the *LSA Bulletin*.

MATHEMATICS

American Mathematical Society. *The AMS Author Handbook: General Instructions for Preparing Manuscripts*. Rev. ed. Providence: AMS. 1996.

MEDICINE

Iverson, Cheryl, et al. *American Medical Association Manual of Style: A Guide for Authors and Editors*. 9th ed. Baltimore: Williams, 1998.

MUSIC

Holoman, D. Kern, ed. *Writing about Music: A Style Sheet from the Editors of* 19th-Century Music. Berkeley: U of California P, 1988.

PHYSICS

American Institute of Physics, *Style Manual: Instructions to Authors and Volume Editors for the Preparation of AIP Book Manuscripts*. 5th ed. New York: AIP, 1995.

POLITICAL SCIENCE

American Political Science Association. *Style Manual for Political Science*. Rev. ed. Washington: APSA, 1993.

PSYCHOLOGY AND THE SOCIAL SCIENCES (See 59.)

American Psychological Association, *Publication Manual of the American Psychological Association*. 5th ed. Washington: APA, 2001.

SCIENCE AND TECHNICAL WRITING

American National Standard for the Preparation of Scientific Papers for Written or Oral Presentation. New York: Amer. Natl. Standards Inst., 1979.

Microsoft Corporation. *Microsoft Manual of Style for Technical Publications*. 2nd ed. Redmond: Microsoft, 1998.

Rubens, Philip, ed. *Science and Technical Writing: A Manual of Style*. 2nd ed. New York: Routledge, 2001.

SOCIAL WORK

National Association of Social Workers. *Writing for the NASW Press: Information for Authors*. Rev. ed. Washington: Natl. Assn. of Social Workers Press, 1995.

ESL Menu

Revision Symbols

abbr	faulty abbreviation 40	
ad	adverb or adjective 26	
add	Add needed word 10	
agr	agreement 21, 22	
appr	inappropriate language 17	
art	article 30	
awk	awkward	
cap	capital letter 45	
case	case 24, 25	
cliché	cliché 18e	
coh	coherence 4e	
coord	coordination 14a, 14c	
cs	comma splice 20	
dev	inadequate development 4b	
dm	dangling modifier 12e	
-ed	-ed ending 27d	
emph	emphasis 14	
ESL	English as a second language 29–31	
exact	inexact language 18	
frag	sentence fragment 19	
fs	fused sentence 20	
gl/us	see Glossary of Usage	
hyph	hyphen 44	
idiom	idiom 18d	
inc	incomplete construction 10	
irreg	irregular verb 27a	
ital	italics (underlining) 42	
jarg	jargon 17a	
lc	use lowercase letter 45	
mix	mixed construction 11	
mm	misplaced modifier 12a–d	
mood	mood 28b	
nonst	nonstandard usage 17d, 27	
num	numbers 41	
om	omitted word 10, 30, 31a	

p	punctuation	
⌃,	comma 32	
no ,	no comma 33	
;	semicolon 34	
:	colon 35	
⌃?	apostrophe 36	
" "	quotation marks 37	
. ? !	period, question mark, exclamation point 38	
— ( )	dash, parentheses,	
[ ] ...	brackets, ellipsis mark,	
/	slash 39	
¶	paragraph 4	
pass	ineffective passive 8a	
pn agr	pronoun agreement 22	
proof	proofreading problem 3c	
ref	pronoun reference 23	
run-on	run-on sentence 20	
-s	-s ending on verb 21, 27c	
sexist	sexist language 17f, 22a	
shift	distracting shift 13	
sl	slang 17d	
sp	misspelled word 43	
sub	subordination 14a, 14d	
sv agr	subject-verb agreement 21, 27c	
t	error in verb tense 28a	
trans	transition needed 4e	
usage	see Glossary of Usage	
var	sentence variety 8, 15	
vb	problem with verb 27–29	
w	wordy 16	
//	faulty parallelism	
⌃	insert	
x	obvious error	
#	insert space	
⌣	close up space	